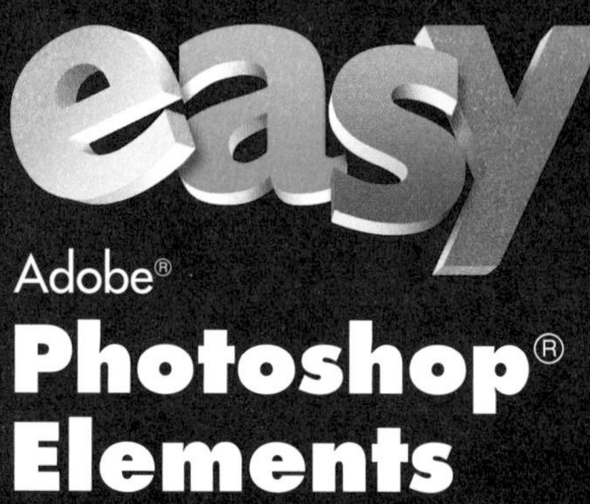

Adobe® Photoshop® Elements

Contents

Copyright © 2004 by Que Publishing

All rights reserved. No part of this book shall be reproduced, stored in a retrieval system, or transmitted by any means, electronic, mechanical, photocopying, recording, or otherwise, without written permission from the publisher. No patent liability is assumed with respect to the use of the information contained herein. Although every precaution has been taken in the preparation of this book, the publisher and author assume no responsibility for errors or omissions. Nor is any liability assumed for damages resulting from the use of the information contained herein.

International Standard Book Number: 0-7897-3112-6

Library of Congress Catalog Card Number: 2004100879

Printed in the United States of America

First Printing: April 2004

07 06 05 04 4 3 2

Trademarks

All terms mentioned in this book that are known to be trademarks or service marks have been appropriately capitalized. Que Publishing cannot attest to the accuracy of this information. Use of a term in this book should not be regarded as affecting the validity of any trademark or service mark.

Adobe and Photoshop are registered trademarks of Adobe Systems, Inc.

Warning and Disclaimer

Every effort has been made to make this book as complete and as accurate as possible, but no warranty or fitness is implied. The information provided is on an "as is" basis. The author and the publisher shall have neither liability nor responsibility to any person or entity with respect to any loss or damages arising from the information contained in this book.

Bulk Sales

Que Publishing offers excellent discounts on this book when ordered in quantity for bulk purchases or special sales. For more information, please contact

U.S. Corporate and Government Sales

1-800-382-3419

corpsales@pearsontechgroup.com

For sales outside of the U.S., please contact

International Sales

1-317-428-3341

international@pearsontechgroup.com

Publisher
Paul Boger

Associate Publisher
Greg Wiegand

Acquisitions Editor
Michelle Newcomb

Development Editor
Laura Norman

Managing Editor
Charlotte Clapp

Project Editor
Tricia Liebig

Production Editor
Seth Kerney

Copy Editor
Geneil Breeze

Indexer
Larry Sweazy

Proofreader
Tonya Simpson

Technical Editor
Kate Binder

Publishing Coordinator
Sharry Lee Gregory

Interior Designer
Anne Jones

Cover Designer
Anne Jones

Page Layout
Michelle Mitchell

About the Author

Gerald Everett Jones is the author of more than 20 technical and business books, including *Real World Digital Video, Excel for Windows Quick&Easy*, and *How to Lie with Charts*. Besides writing technical books for nontechnical readers, he's had experience developing computer graphics software, as well as writing and producing film and video projects. He lives in Santa Monica, California.

Gerald's Web site is **http://www.lapuerta.tv**.

Dedication

To Georja, Marcello, and Zukie

Acknowledgments

My heartfelt appreciation to friends and family who kindly consented to let us reproduce photos of them (in order of appearance): Georja Umano Jones, Eddie Ed O'Brien, Lance A. Schmidt, Ray Weber, Robert Puryear, Jason Teahan, Terry Warren, Billy Campbell, Ren Knerr, Paul Candice, Elizabeth Tsarng-Juen Wu, Donald E. and Kathleen M. Jones, David Illions, James W. Jones, Jessica Jones, Linda Jones, Jason Moment, Zachary E. Jones, Julie-Lynn M. Fries, and Dennis E. and Kathryn M. Fries.

Besides the author's own snaps (of which there may be far too many), contributing photographers were Georja Jones, Lance Schmidt (**www.v-marketing.com**), and Eileen Wu. And special thanks to James W. Jones for his coverage of the Chicago Marathon and Kenneth H. Goldman (**www.walruscarpenter.com**) for travel pictures, aeronautical photos, and original wood carvings.

In case you're wondering, the Devil Dogs are Marcello Mastroianni Jones and Zucchero (Zukie) Jones (**www.comedydogma.com**). And, yes, they will work for low-fat, organic treats.

It takes a team to make a book. Congratulations for an exceptional job to development editor Laura Norman, project editor Tricia Liebig, technical editor Kate Binder, copy editor Geneil Breeze, and the other fine people at Que. Sincere personal thanks to my wife and marvelously versatile model Georja Umano Jones, my agent Matt Wagner, and acquisitions editor Michelle Newcomb.

—Gerald Everett Jones

We Want to Hear from You!

As the reader of this book, *you* are our most important critic and commentator. We value your opinion and want to know what we're doing right, what we could do better, what areas you'd like to see us publish in, and any other words of wisdom you're willing to pass our way.

As an associate publisher for Que Publishing, I welcome your comments. You can email or write me directly to let me know what you did or didn't like about this book—as well as what we can do to make our books better.

Please note that I cannot help you with technical problems related to the topic of this book. We do have a User Services group, however, where I will forward specific technical questions related to the book.

When you write, please be sure to include this book's title and author as well as your name, email address, and phone number. I will carefully review your comments and share them with the author and editors who worked on the book.

Email: **feedback@quepublishing.com**

Mail: Greg Wiegand, Associate Publisher
Que Publishing
800 East 96th Street
Indianapolis, IN 46240 USA

For more information about this book or another Que Publishing title, visit our Web site at **www.quepublishing.com**. Type the ISBN (excluding hyphens) or the title of a book in the Search field to find the page you're looking for.

1 Each step is fully illustrated to show you how it looks onscreen.

It's as Easy as 1-2-3

Each part of this book is made up of a series of short, instructional lessons, designed to help you understand basic information that you need to get the most out of your computer hardware and software.

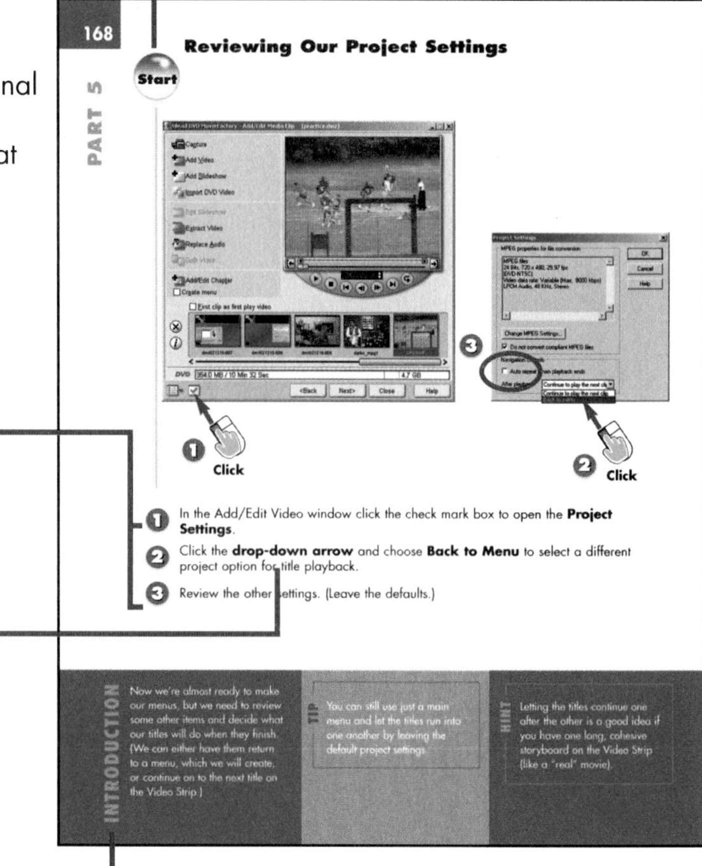

2 Each task includes a series of quick, easy steps designed to guide you through the procedure.

3 Items that you select or click in menus, dialog boxes, tabs, and windows are shown in **bold**.

Introductions explain what you will learn in each task, and **Tips and Hints** give you a heads-up for any extra information you may need while working through the task.

drag

drop

How to Drag: Point to the starting place or object. Hold down the mouse button (right or left per instructions), move the mouse to the new location, then release the button.

See next page: If you see this symbol, it means the task you're working on continues on the next page.

End Task: Task is complete.

Selection: Highlights the area onscreen discussed in the step or task.

Click: Click the left mouse button once.

Right-click: Click the right mouse button once.

Click & Type: Click once where indicated and begin typing to enter your text or data.

Double-click: Click the left mouse button twice in rapid succession.

Pointer Arrow: Highlights an item on the screen you need to point to or focus on in the step or task.

Introduction

This is a book for people who dislike computer books—even for people who might not be particularly fond of computers or adept at using them.

You may simply love your digital camera or just love the ease of sharing photos electronically with a few special people on the planet who really care about what's going on in your life.

And certainly you've got to love the ability to store thousands of pictures on your computer's hard drive, perhaps thousands more on CDs you burn. Gone are the shoeboxes full of curling, faded prints that are still waiting for the happy day when you will have so much time on your hands you'll finally get around to sorting them, labeling them, and pasting them neatly into leather-covered albums.

What's that you say? The shoeboxes are still there?

Don't you own a scanner? Now those prints of yesteryear simply await the happy day when you'll finally get around to sorting them, scanning them....

Let's face it; one thing you don't have is a lot of time.

And if you did find some time, you'd pick up a *real book* by Anne Tyler or John Le Carré, kick back, and enjoy yourself.

Who wants to *read* about computers?

Although I've written quite a few computer books, some of them highly technical, I'm a lot like you.

I love my digital camera. I look forward to sharing my pictures, but don't want to spend hours "playing" with them. I spend enough time sitting at a computer when I'm working. And most of my work doesn't involve photography.

When the Que folks told me they wanted a book titled *Easy Adobe Photoshop Elements 2*, I admit I was less than enthusiastic. After all, I'm not a Photoshop expert. I'm not even a very skilled photographer. (Mostly, I leave my camera on Auto, and I point, shoot, and hope for the best.)

I wondered what I could bring to this project that would make a book you or anyone would want to buy.

Don't get me wrong—I *like* the program a lot. I'd already used the first version for about a year and found it worked as advertised. It's truly a quick and easy set of tools for getting good results. Perhaps like you, I chose Photoshop Elements because it came with my camera (an Olympus Camedia C-700). And, I needed to convert all the photos I took for my book *Real World Digital Video* from color to black and white, enhance their contrast, resize them, and save them in the format the publisher required.

At the same time, I'd heard so much about "Big Photoshop," the product Adobe now calls Photoshop CS (version 8), which for years has been a standard tool of professional photographers and graphic artists. I also knew the application is complicated and technical enough that the local community college offers semester-long courses in its use.

Not for me, I thought.

I assumed, wrongly it turned out, that Photoshop Elements 2 would be a "lite" version of Big Photoshop—a training-wheels program you toyed with until you were ready for an inevitable, expensive graduation to a big-kids' bike. (You probably couldn't do anything serious with it, I figured.)

But I didn't say no to my friends at Que right away. I made a trip to the local book emporium. And I found a whole bookcase full of impressively thick books on Big Photoshop. No surprise there. (You could make a career learning it, much less writing about it, I thought.)

But my heart sank when I found five—would you believe it?—*five* basic picture-driven books like the one Que was asking me to do.

And I found out later—there are quite a few *more*! Some of them are no doubt still on the shelf, next to this one.

So, you may be wondering, as I did, *does the world really need another book on Photoshop Elements?*

Now I can answer confidently, "It sure does!"

Because the next thing I did, I took all those books home. And I bought (yes, shelled out dough for) an official shrink-wrapped package of Photoshop Elements 2, installed it, and dug out the manual.

And I set about teaching myself this "lite" program, using these other supposedly easy books, Adobe's own manual, and the built-in Help system, to guide me.

To my delight, I discovered two key things:

- Photoshop Elements is a fully functional, professional-quality, incredibly powerful program. I now realize that Adobe, in its corporate wisdom, decided to take Big Photoshop to the next logical step—*blissful ease of use*! And they priced it inexpensively—not because it's so much less sophisticated but so that Photoshop Elements can become the tool absolutely everyone, professional or consumer, thinks of first when it comes to digital photography.

- None of the books I bought captured the essence of Photoshop Elements' supreme accomplishment—*invisible technology*. Many of the authors seemed more concerned with looking like experts to other professional photographers. And some others were obviously terribly worried about covering absolutely every wrinkle and option in the application—even if the average person might never need them.

I knew then and there that I could—and I vowed I *would*—write the...

most basic

simplest

easiest

plainest

clearest

handiest

quickest

how-to book on Photoshop Elements humanly possible.

You hold it in your hands...

...the result of teaching Photoshop Elements 2 to myself, from scratch, step-by-step.

My sincere hope is that this easy, picture-driven book contains not one more task, not one more step, not one more tip or hint than you need to get the job done and get on with life.

If I'd found it in the store that day, I'd have just bought it, saved my money on the others, told Que to give it up, and wouldn't have to be explaining to my family and friends why I needed all those snapshots.

May you enjoy this book, thrill as I did at the tricks you can do with Photoshop Elements, and not spend a minute more than you need to with either of them.

PART 1

Learning the Ropes

Back when ships needed favorable winds to get anywhere, new recruits had to learn which ropes to pull to carry out the captain's orders and set sail. This first part of the book is for novice sailors—people who feel more comfortable if they can begin at the beginning—while their ship is still safely docked. Just turn the page to sign on for a brief orientation session: You'll quickly learn the commands, controls, and features of the Photoshop Elements *work area*. For example, you'll find out what a *tool* is and how to select one from the *toolbox*. After you've got your bearings, we can shorthand the steps in later parts and just say, "Click the Crop tool," and move on.

If you're feeling adventurous, don't worry about sailing ahead to another part of the book. You can do most of the tasks in any order, and you can always come back to this part if somehow you get turned around.

Welcome aboard, and fear not: You have nothing to lose but your old film cameras and the tiresome wait for your prints to come back from the lab.

The Photoshop Elements Work Area

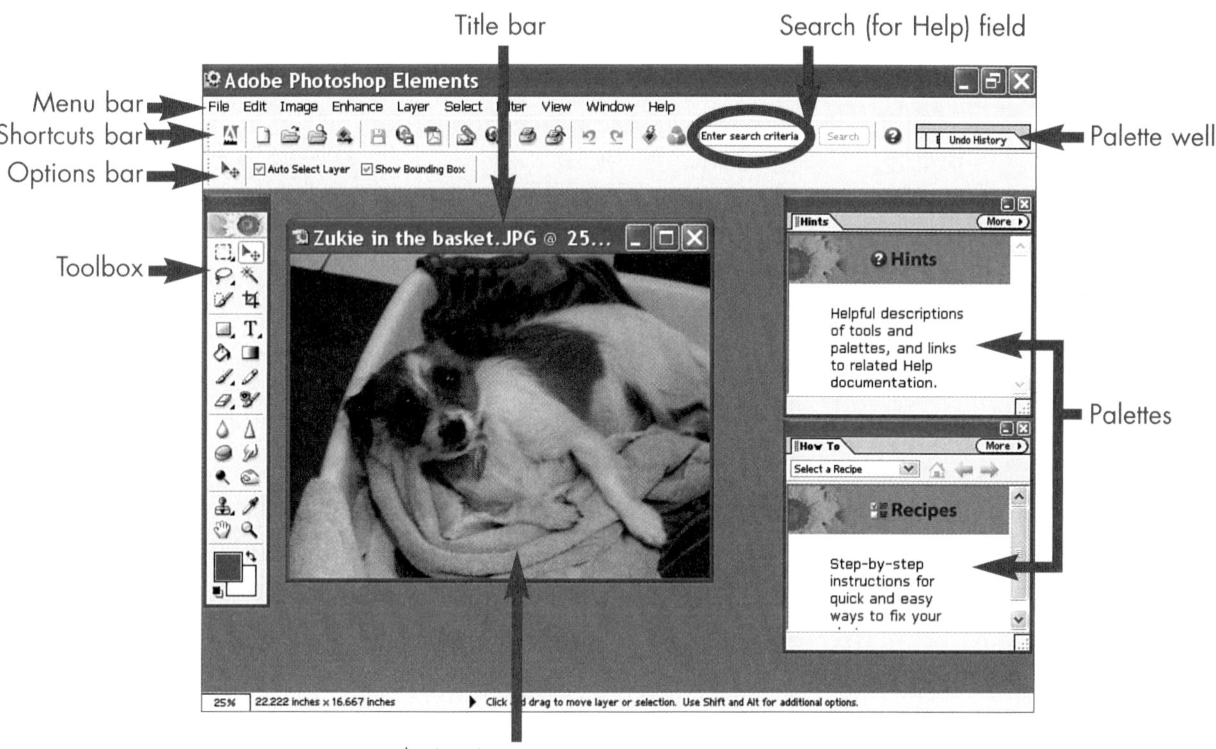

Starting Photoshop Elements and Opening a Picture

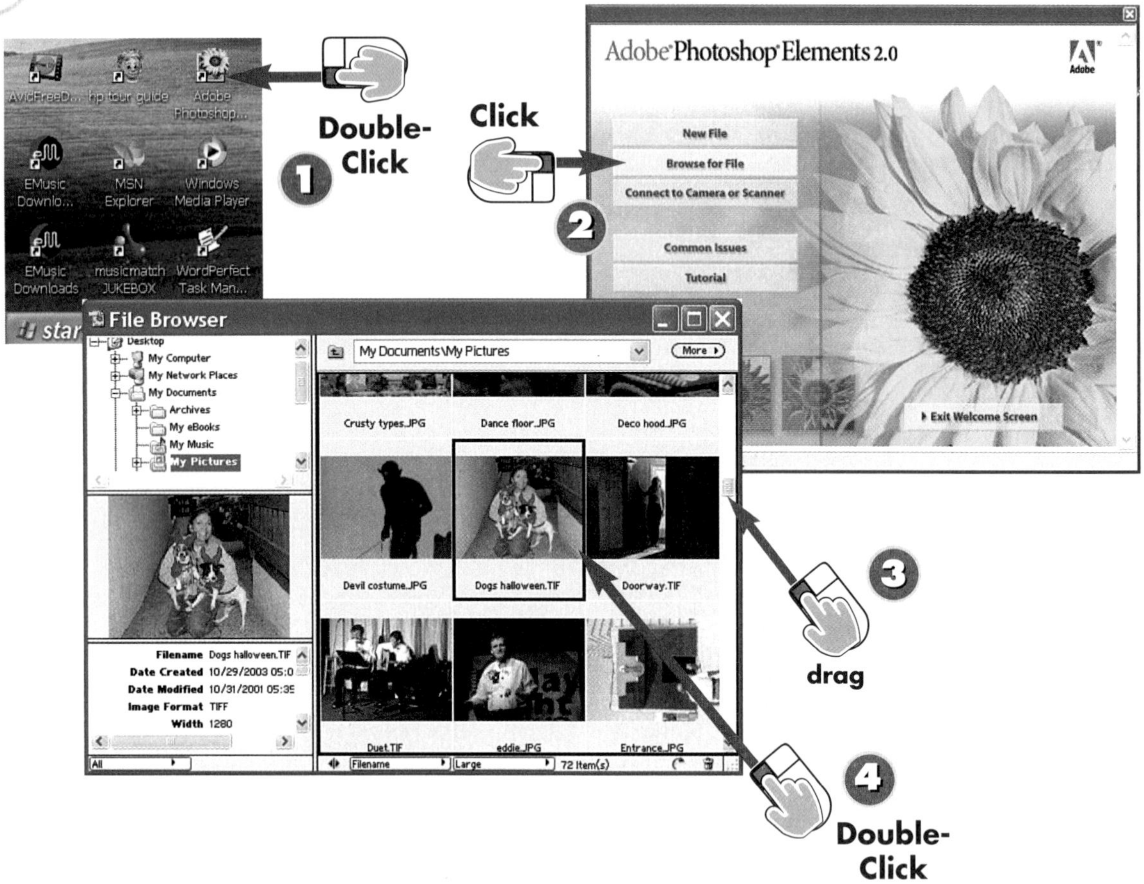

Start

Double-Click

Click

drag

Double-Click

1. Double-click the **Adobe Photoshop Elements 2.0** icon on the Windows Desktop to start the program.
2. Click the **Browse for File** button.
3. Drag the scrollbar until you see the *thumbnail* (small picture) of the picture you want to edit.
4. Double-click the thumbnail. The picture will open in the *active image area*.

End

INTRODUCTION

None of this needs to be complicated. In fact, most kinds of touch-ups are *sooooo* easy, they take just a click or two. Photoshop Elements has lots of built-in smarts, and you rarely need to know much more than a few simple steps to get great-looking results.

TIP

Welcome Back

Click to clear the **Show this screen at startup** check box in the lower-left corner, then select **Exit Welcome Screen**, and you won't see it again. If you ever want it back, select **Window**, **Welcome** from the menu bar.

HINT

Hide and Seek

Don't see your shots? You either didn't load them from your camera or scanner yet, or you stored them in a different folder. You might need to *navigate* the filesystem on your hard drive or CD to find the images you want.

Start

Viewing and Adjusting the Active Image Area

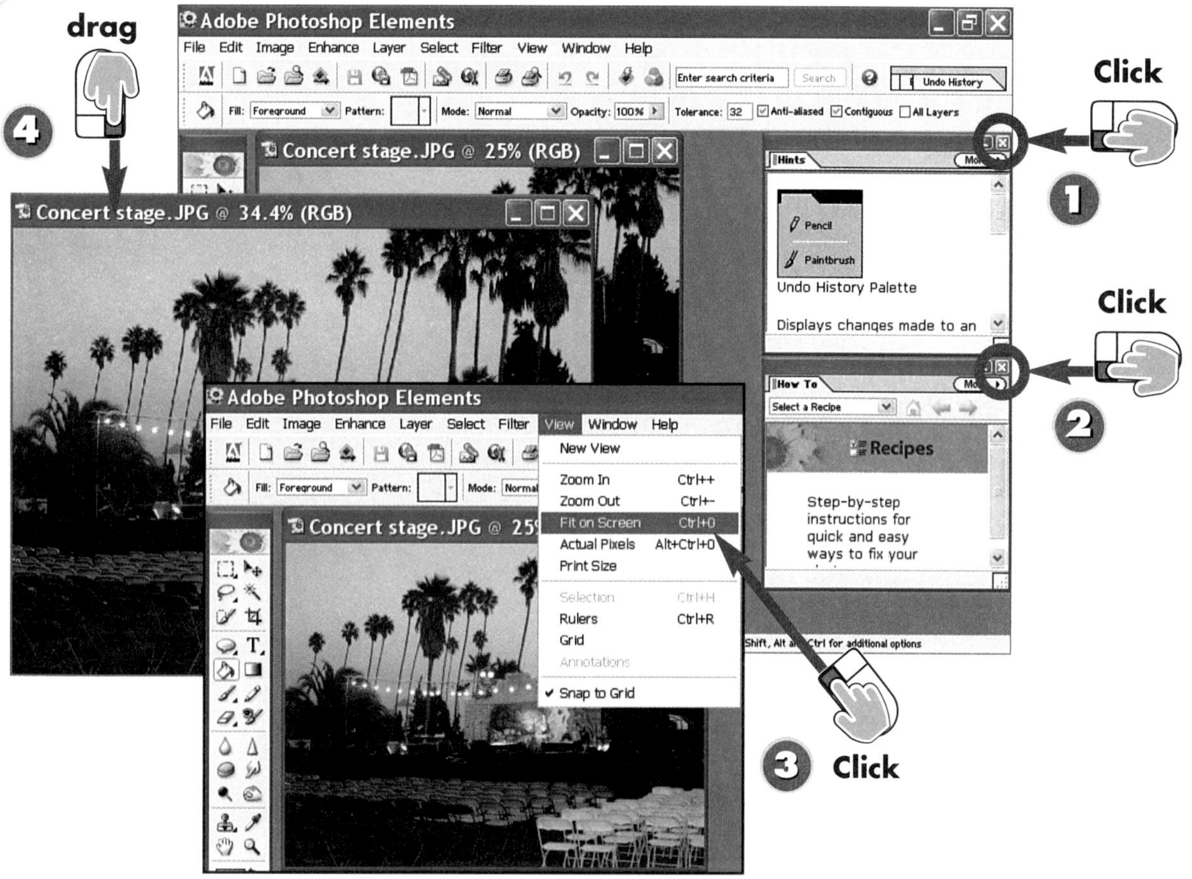

1. To clear the work area, click the ***close box*** (×) of an open *palette*.

2. Close any other open palette.

3. From the menu bar, select **View**, **Fit on Screen** or press **Ctrl+0** (zero). The view of the active image area enlarges to fill the work area.

4. You can move the active image area around by dragging its *title bar*.

INTRODUCTION

When you have a picture file open for editing, you'll usually want to make it as large as possible on the screen. This will give you the clearest overall view, regardless of the actual image size. Then, you can use the Zoom tool (or the View, Zoom In command) to magnify small areas if you need to work in even finer detail.

TIP

Open Windows

You can have several pictures open at the same time. Select one of them for editing (make it active) by clicking its title bar. (If you can't see all the title bars, select **Window**, **Images**, **Cascade** to see them all.)

Using the Shortcuts Bar and Browsing for a File

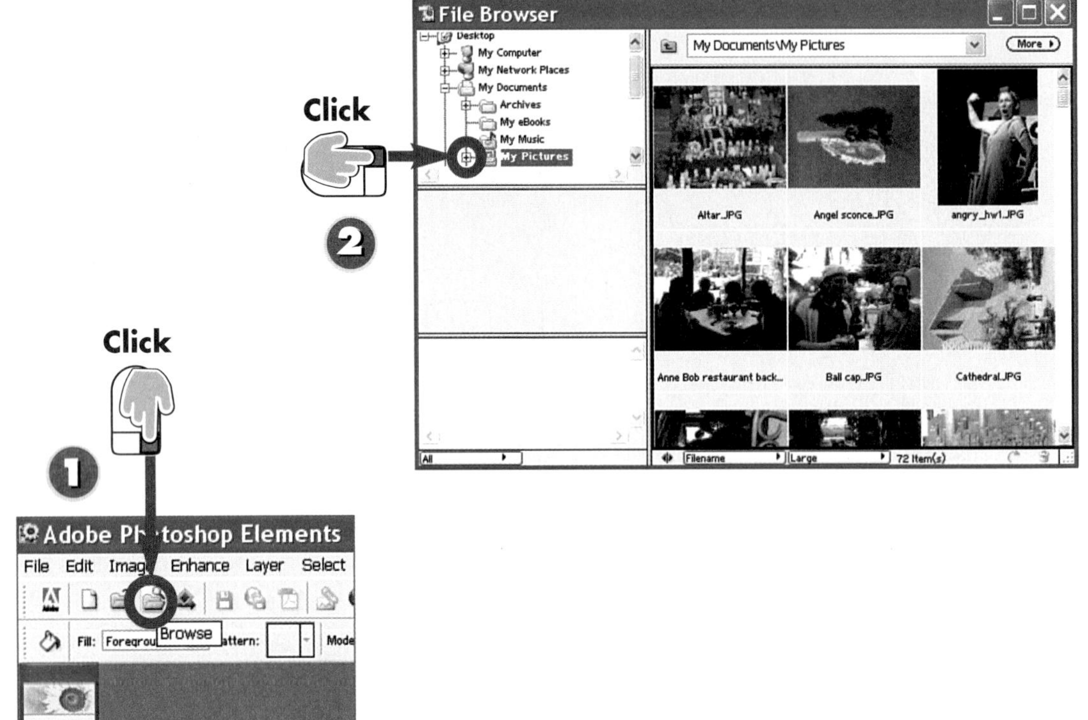

1. To look for a file in folders on the disk, click the **Browse** shortcut.

2. In the directory of folders, click the **Maximize** button (the **+** sign to the left of the folder name) to see the folders inside.

INTRODUCTION

The shortcuts bar is a row of buttons just beneath the menu bar. These buttons represent the most commonly used commands. For example, you can click the Browse shortcut to look through the folders on a disk for the file you want.

TIP

When you hover and pause the pointer over a button in the shortcuts bar, a *ToolTip* appears indicating what it does.

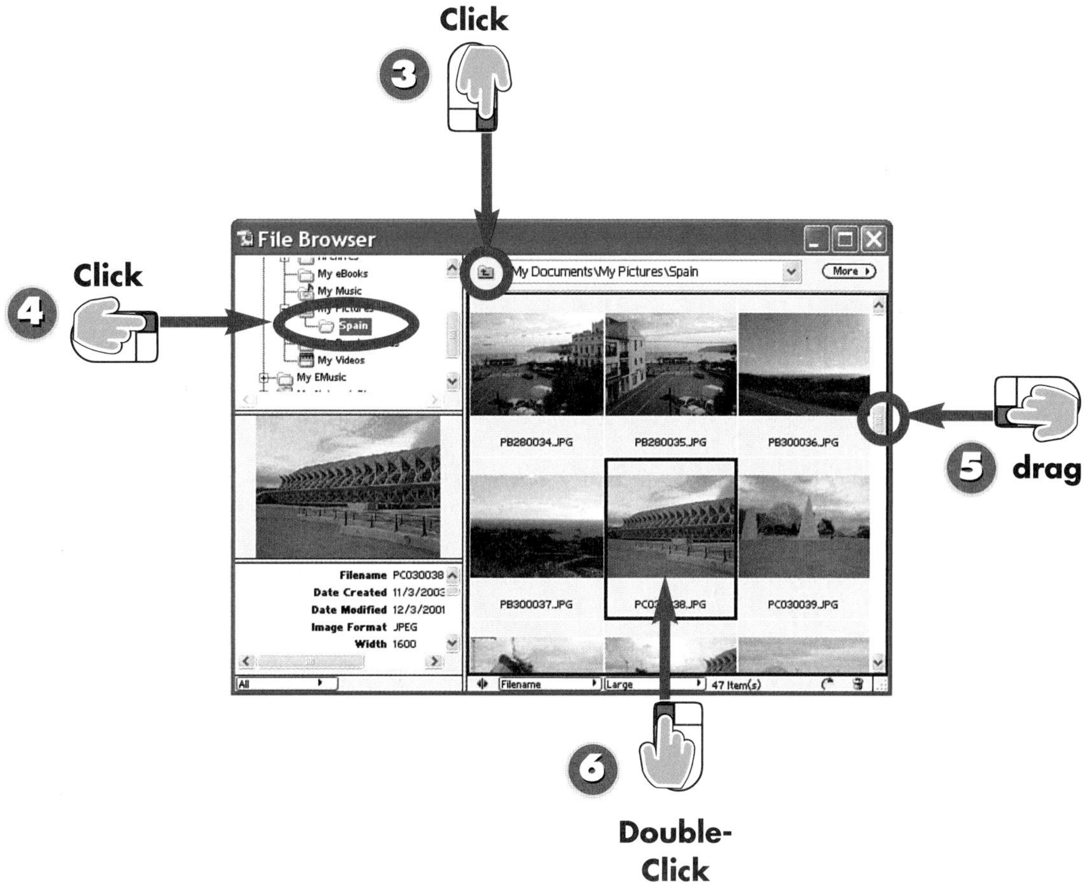

3 Click

4 Click

5 drag

6 Double-Click

3. To *navigate* upward through the directory of folders, click the **Up** button.

4. Click the folder name that contains the picture files you want.

5. Drag the **scrollbar** to browse the picture files in the folder.

6. Double-click the **thumbnail** view of the file you want. It will open in the active image area, ready for editing.

HINT

Exploring Files

The directory of file folders in the top-left corner of the File Browser window works just like Windows Explorer.

Selecting Tools from the Toolbox

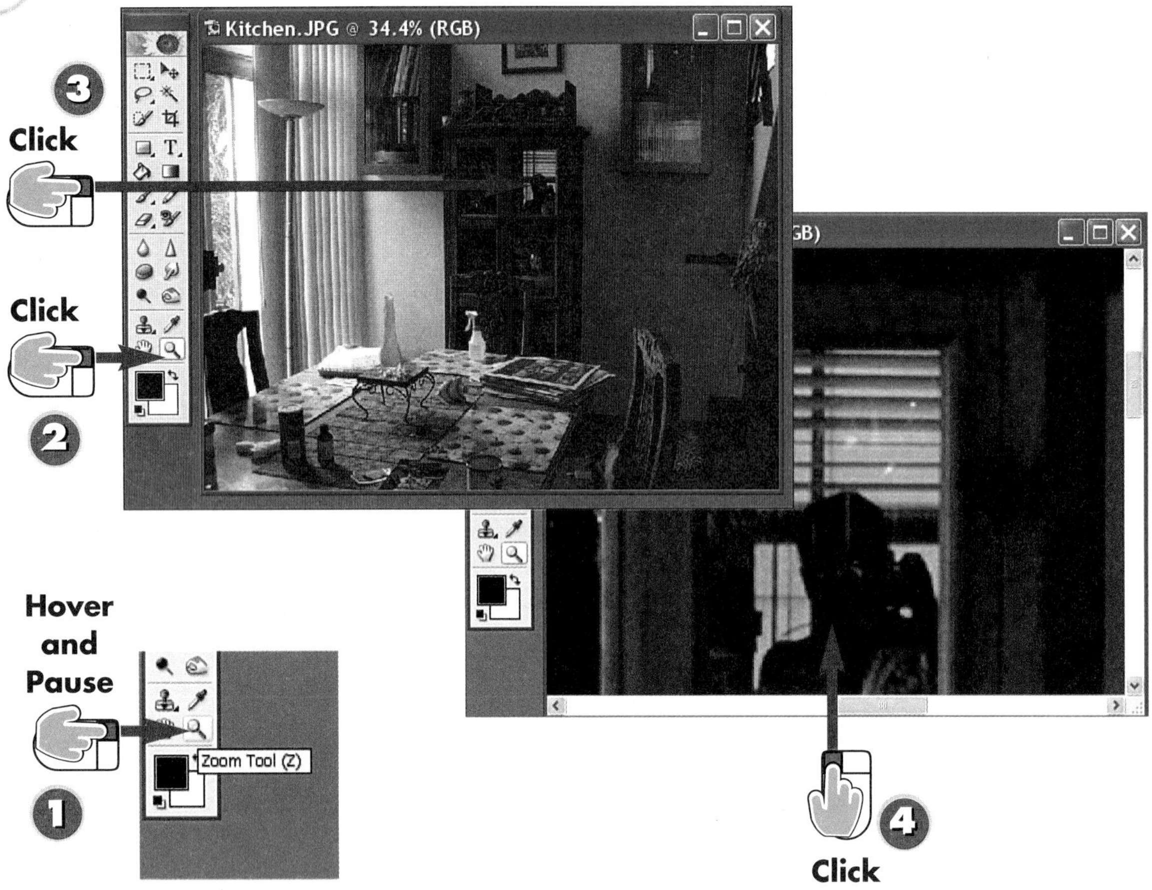

1. Hover and pause the pointer over the **Zoom** tool. Its name will appear in a ToolTip, along with the letter of its *shortcut key*.
2. Click the **Zoom** tool or press **Z**. The pointer changes to a magnifying-glass symbol, and settings that affect the tool appear in the *options bar*.
3. Move the pointer to the center of the area you want enlarged, and click. A magnified view appears in the active image area.
4. Click again and again to enlarge the view in progressive steps. The magnification percentage will appear in the title bar.

INTRODUCTION

Tools in the toolbox help you work on portions of a picture in a variety of ways. An example is the Zoom tool, which enlarges your view of a picture. You can select the Zoom tool by clicking it in the toolbox or by pressing **Z** on the keyboard.

HINT

Zoom In
Zooming doesn't make any changes to the picture itself, just to your view of it in Photoshop Elements so you can work on fine details.

TIP

Shortcut
When using the Zoom tool, right-click anywhere within the active image area and select **Fit on Screen** to quickly view the entire image.

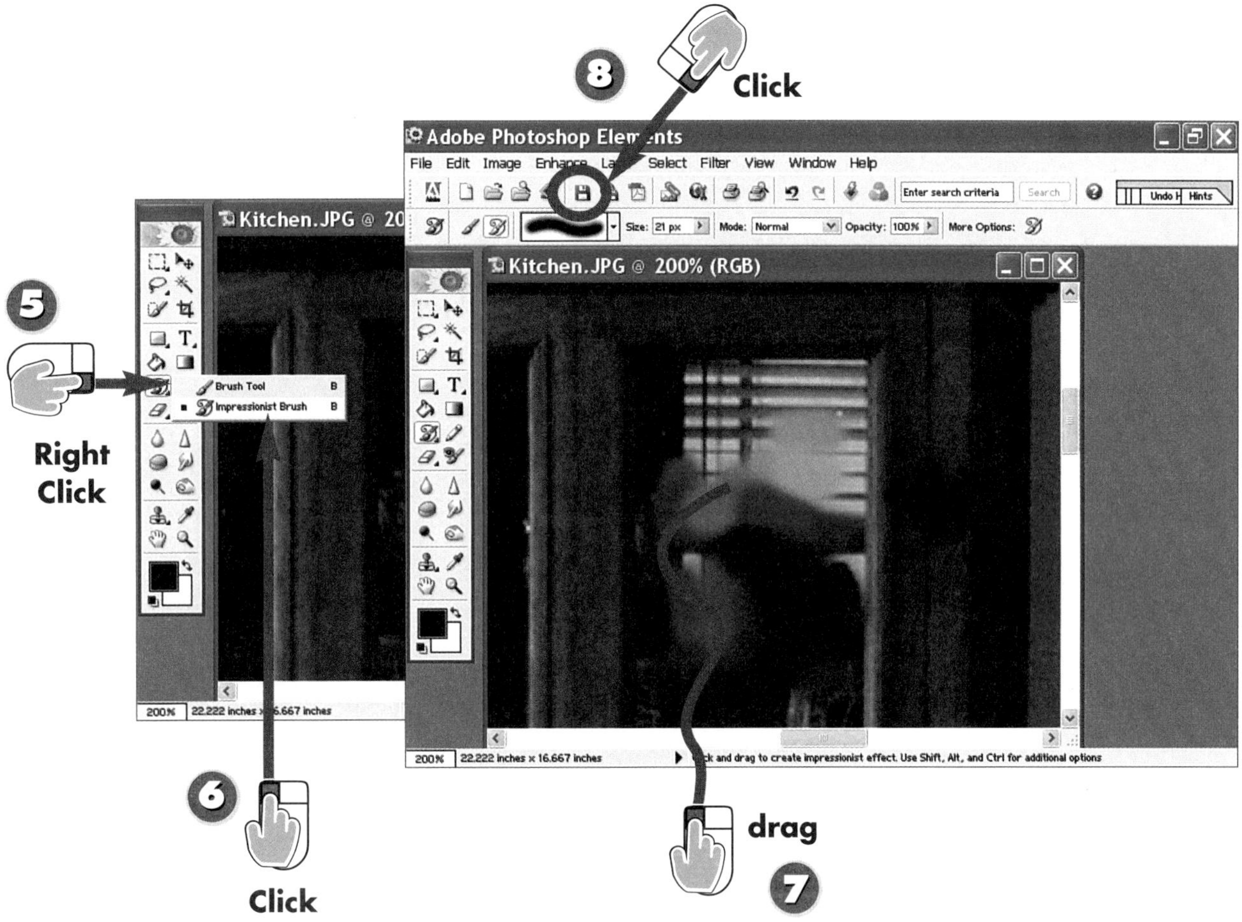

5 Right-click the **Brush Tool**.

6 Click the **Impressionist Brush** tool. The pointer changes to the *brush tip*, and settings for the tool appear in the options bar.

7 Move the pointer to the area of the picture where you want to use the brush; click and drag it around, as if painting, to apply the effect.

8 Because you made a change to the picture, click the **Save** shortcut in the shortcuts bar to save your work.

TIP

Best-Quality Image

After you've made changes to a JPEG file, for best quality, use the **File**, **Save As** command to convert it to TIFF (.TIF) format, or save as a Photoshop (.PSD) file.

HINT

It's All a Blur

For other ways to get softened or blurred effects, try the Smudge or Blur tools, or one of various Blur commands from the Filter menu.

TIP

First Impressions

You can vary the effect of the Impressionist Brush by changing settings in the options bar—Brush Size, Blending Mode, and Opacity—to name a few. To admire the overall result of your brushwork select **View**, **Fit on Screen**.

Controlling How Tools Behave with the Options Bar

Start

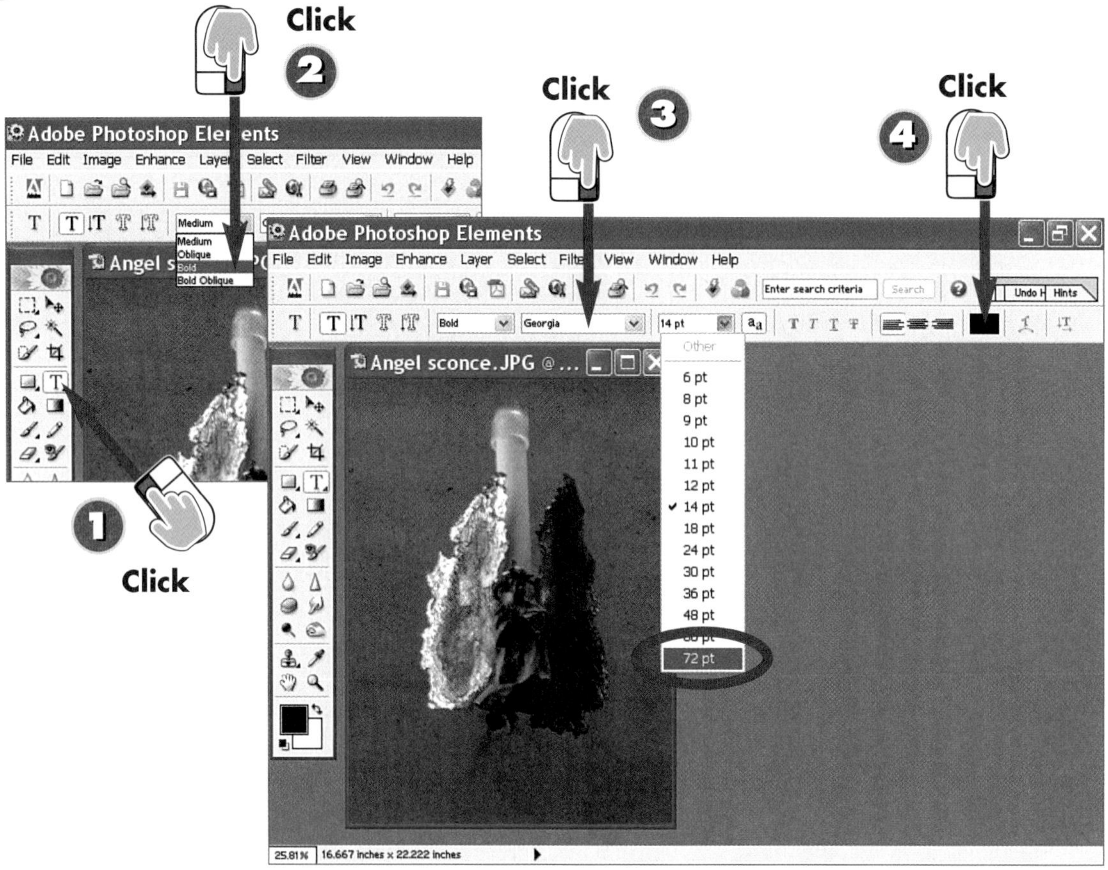

Click 2 — Click 3 — Click 4 — Click 1

1. In the toolbox, click the **Horizontal Type** tool or press **T**. Settings for the tool appear in the options bar.
2. Use the **Font Style** drop-down menu in the options bar to apply a style such as **Bold** to your text.
3. Use the **Font** drop-down menu to select a new font for your text, such as **Georgia**.
4. Using the **Font Size** drop-down menu, make the text larger or smaller, say, **72 pt**. Click the **Text Color** box. The Color Picker window opens.

INTRODUCTION

After you select a tool from the toolbox, you can change settings in the options bar that control its effect. Try it with the Horizontal Type tool.

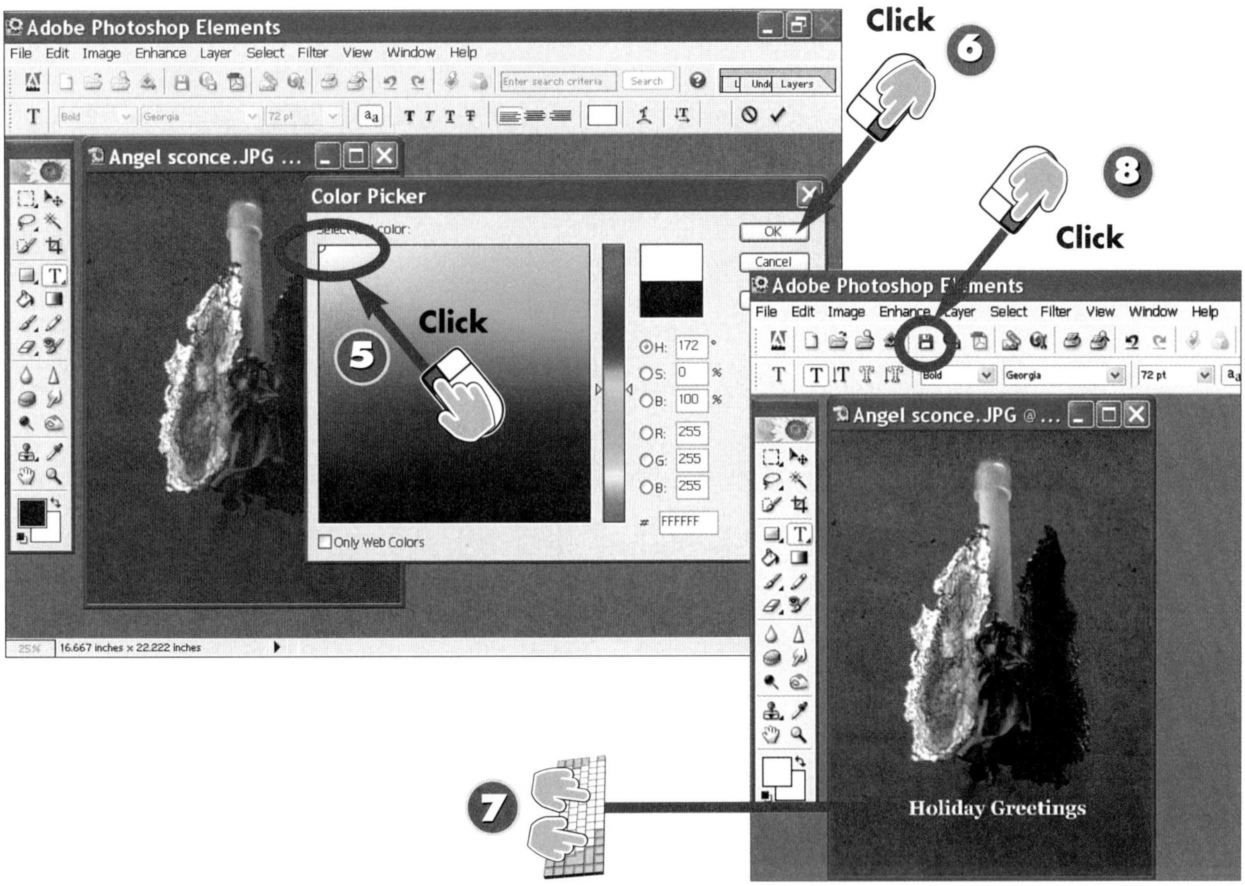

5. In the Color Picker dialog box, click the top-left corner of the *color space* to select **white**.

6. Click **OK**.

7. Type some text, such as **Holiday Greetings**.

8. Click the **Save** shortcut to save your work.

HINT

Settings Retained

Settings you make in the options bar will remain in effect for a particular tool until you change them again, even if you quit and then restart the program.

Using Palettes

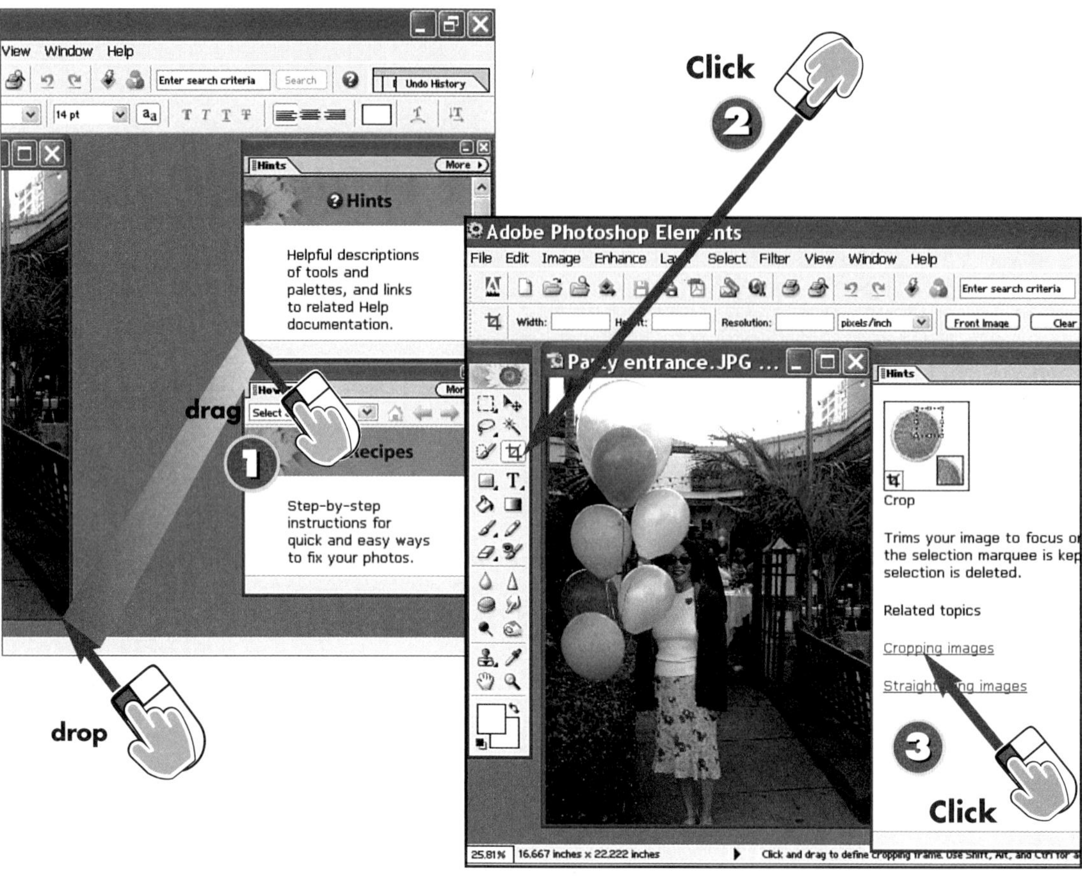

1. Click and drag the bottom-left corner of the Hints palette to make it larger.

2. Click the tool icon or palette tab with which you need help, such as the **Crop** tool. *Related topics* for that feature appear in the Hints palette.

3. Click the topic you want to explore. A separate Help window opens.

INTRODUCTION

Palettes, floating windows that contain commands and help grouped by category, are a truly handy feature. For example, the Hints palette explains how other program features work.

TIP

Get the Hint
If the Hints palette isn't already open, select **Window**, **Reset Palette Locations** from the menu bar.

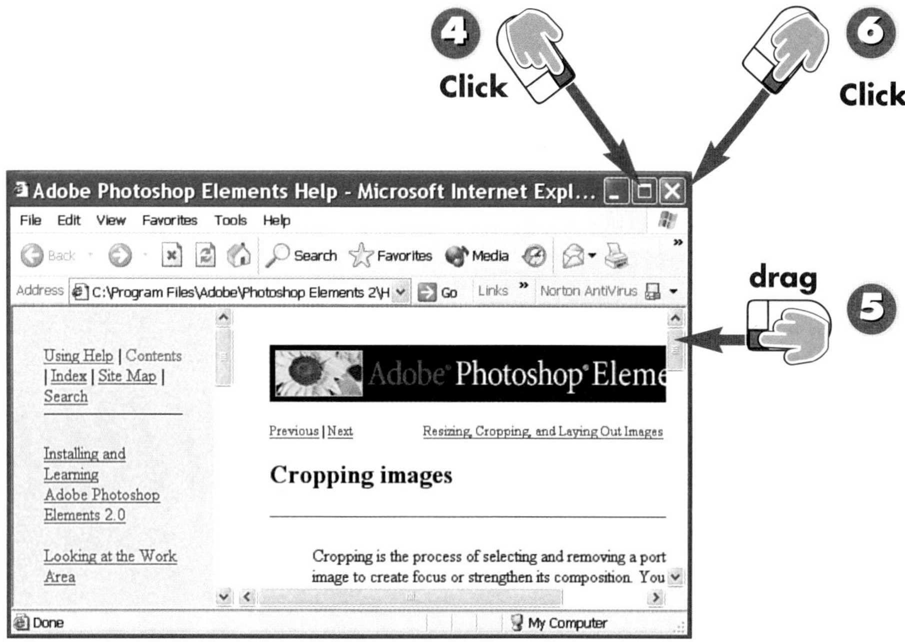

4. Click the **Maximize** button in the Help window to view it full-screen.

5. Drag the scrollbar as you read down the page.

6. When you have the information you need, close the Help window.

TIP

More Hints

After step 1, if you *hover* the pointer over any tool in the toolbar or *palette tab* in the palette well, information about the tool appears in the Hints window.

HINT

Viewing Palettes

To use the palette well effectively, set your Windows screen resolution to at least 1024×768. If you work at 640×480 or 800×600, the tabs are small, in which case it might be easier to select palettes individually from the Windows menu.

Arranging and Controlling Palettes

Start

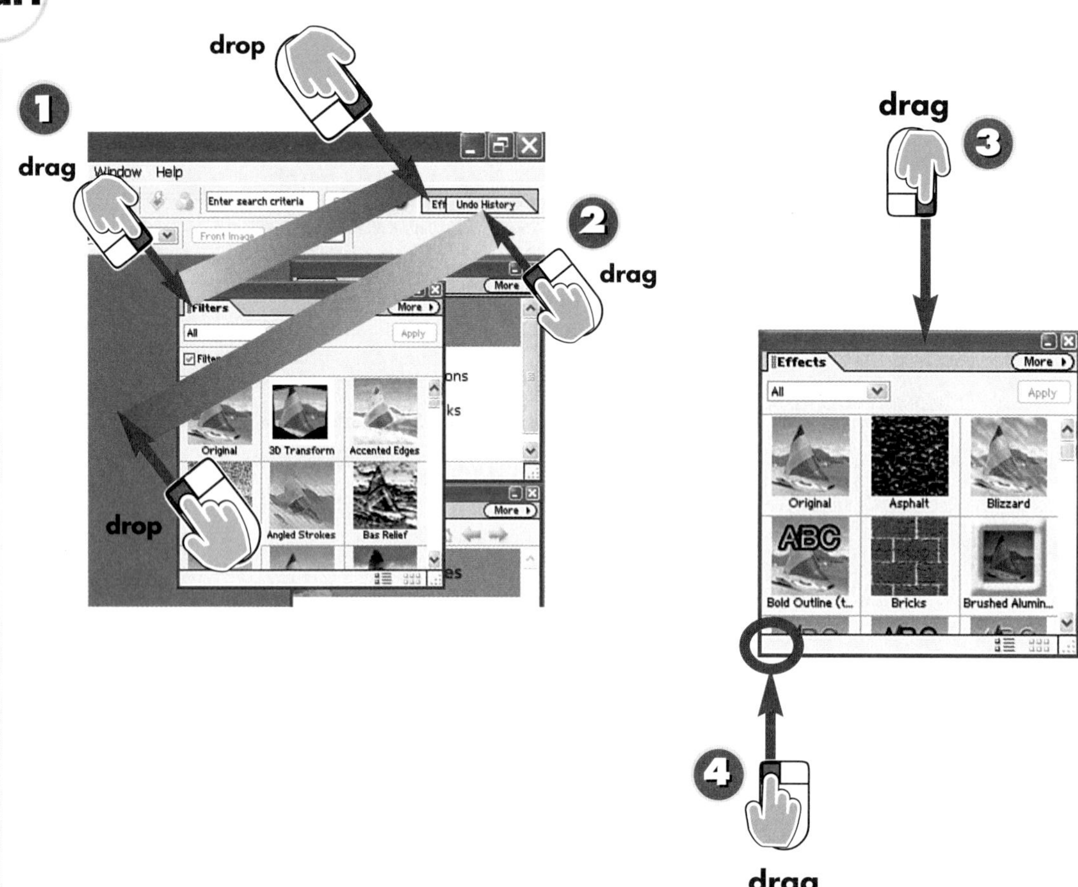

1. *Dock* any open palette (remove it from the work area) by dragging its tab and dropping it into the palette well.
2. *Undock* a palette from the well (open it) by dragging its tab and dropping it back into the work area.
3. Move a palette around in the work area by dragging its title bar.
4. Resize a palette by dragging its size box (or the bottom-left corner or one of its sides).

INTRODUCTION

Having too many palettes open at the same time can clutter your work area. Here's how to tidy up your screen but still have the palettes handy.

TIP

Hidden Tabs

If other palette tabs are covering the one you want, hover the pointer inside the well as you drag from side to side, and the different tabs will pop up. You can right-click to change their order in the stack.

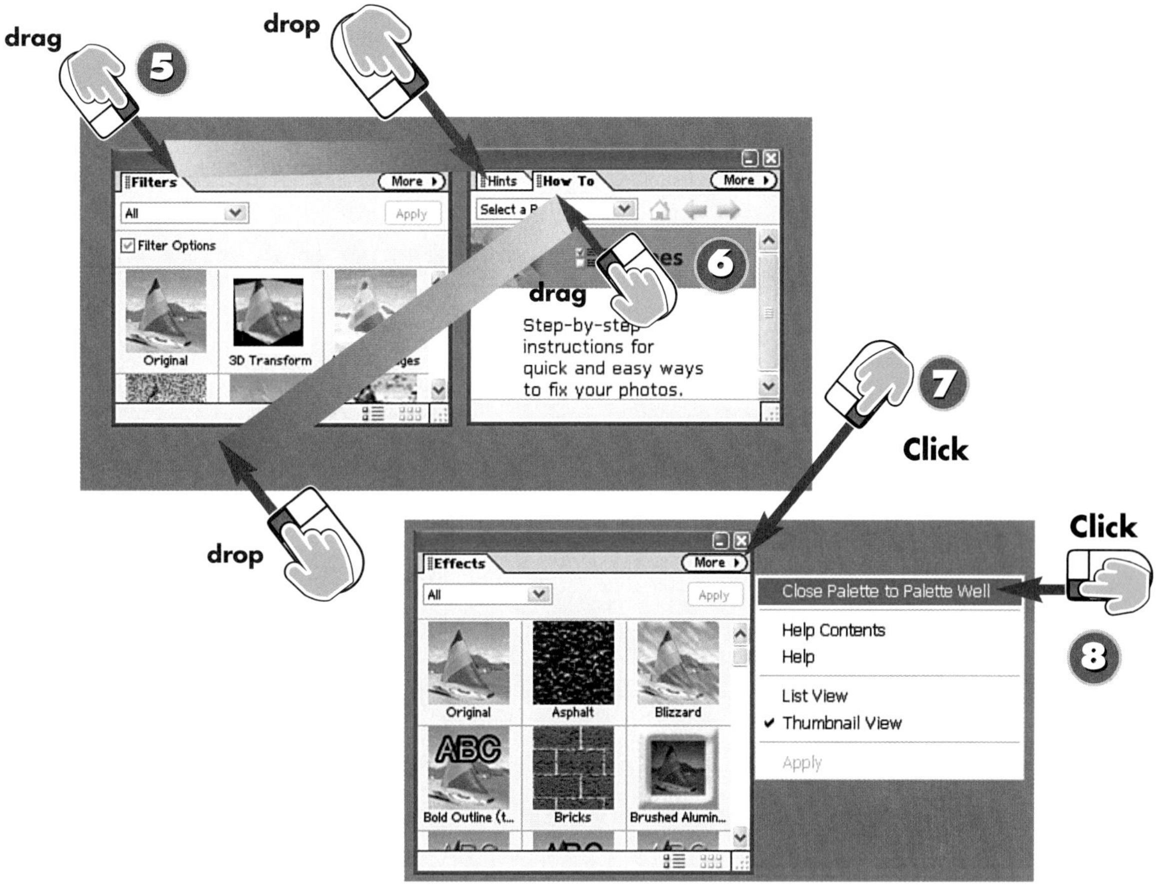

5 *Group* palettes into a single window by dragging the tab of one onto the tab of another.

6 *Ungroup* a palette by dragging its tab away from the grouped window.

7 To select options available for an open palette, click its **More** button.

8 To keep an open palette from being stored in the palette well the next time you close it, uncheck **Close Palette to Palette Well**.

HINT

Getting More

The selections in the More menu are different for each palette. When you click the More button in step 7, a menu will pop up.

TIP

Layer Info

Especially as you begin to combine images or create artwork from them, get in the habit of leaving the Layers palette open. As you add text, graphics, painting, or images, you'll quickly see why keeping track of layers is important.

Using the Search Box and Following a Recipe

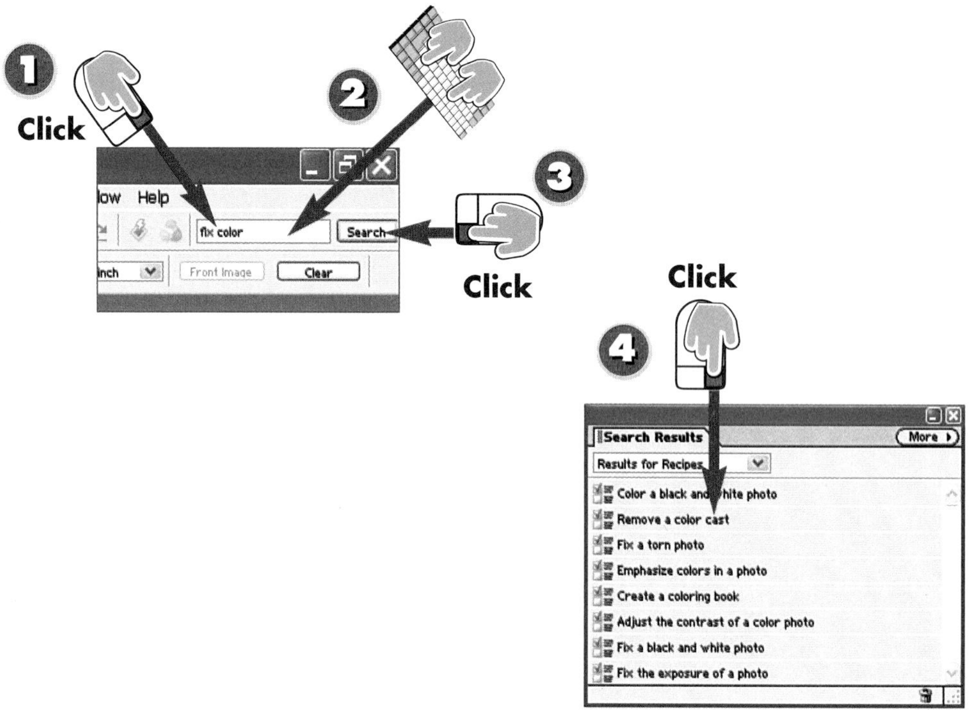

1. Click inside the search box.
2. Type a phrase that describes what you want to do, such as **fix color**.
3. Click the **Search** button, or press **Enter**. If the program finds a match, a list of recipes opens.
4. Click the topic that best fits your request. The How To palette opens, showing step-by-step instructions.

INTRODUCTION

Photoshop Elements has lots of ways to give you suggestions when you can't remember the steps you need to take—or even where to begin. Here's one of the easiest: Just type your request and pick a precooked solution.

HINT

Follow the Recipe
Before you can follow the recipe's steps, you must have a picture open in the active image area. Otherwise, you'll know what to do, but lose the benefit of being able to apply the advice immediately.

TIP

Automation
When the How To palette opens after step 4, for some tasks you can simply click **Do This Step for Me** and Photoshop Elements will do the rest.

Taking a Tutorial

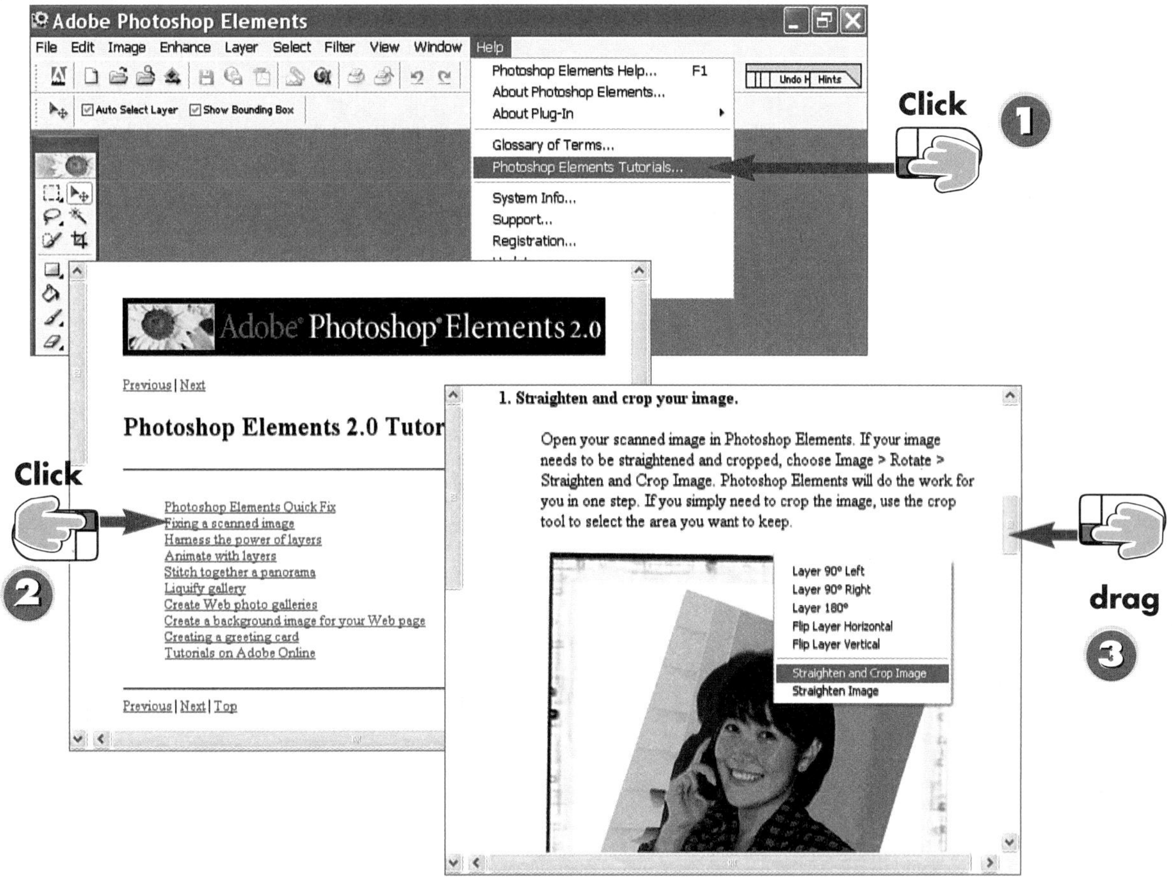

1. From the menu bar, select **Help**, **Photoshop Elements Tutorials**.
2. In the Help window, click the title of the lesson you want.
3. Drag the scrollbar to read through the lesson.

INTRODUCTION

Photoshop Elements has online lessons for popular tasks that take more than a few steps. Try this built-in advice on using the Quick Fix shortcut, fixing scanned imagery, using layers effectively, animating with layers, creating a panorama, making a greeting card, and more.

TIP

Choose from the Index
If you don't see a lesson on the topic you want, look in the recipes in the How To palette, or select **Help**, **Photoshop Elements Help**. Then, click **Index** and select a topic from the alphabetized list.

Setting Your Own Preferences

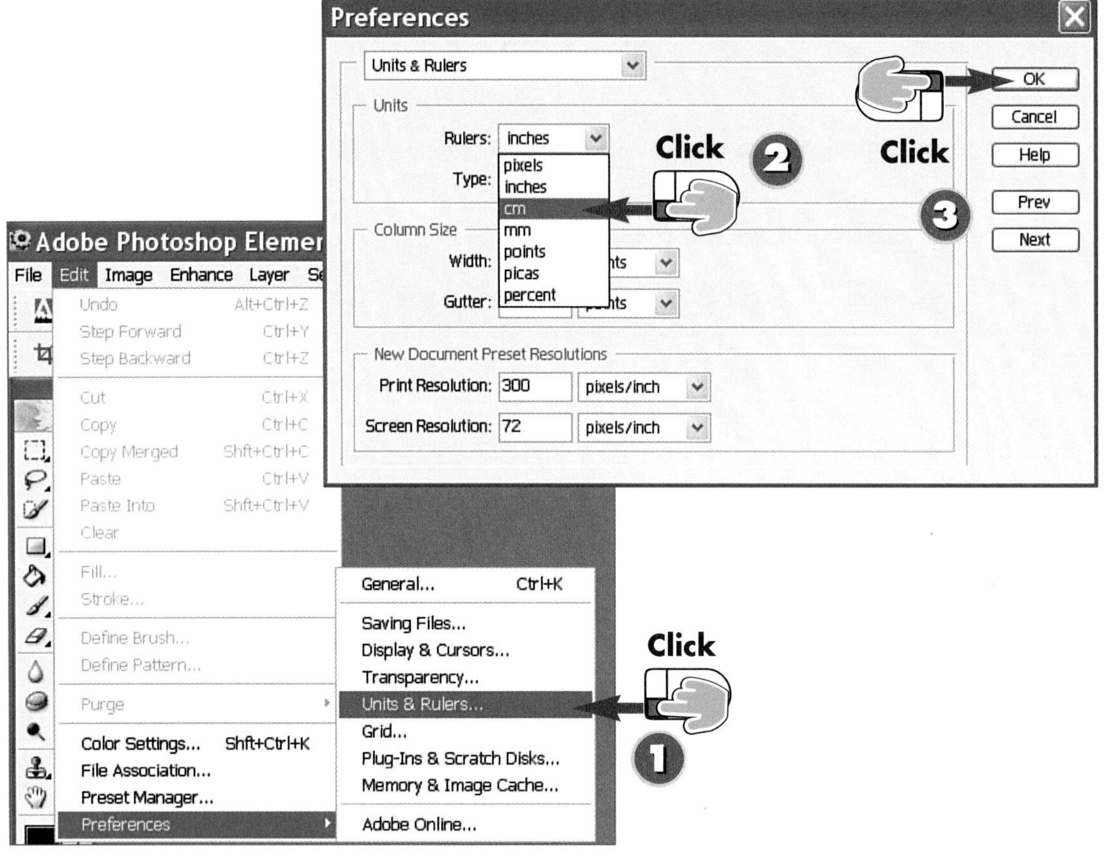

1. From the menu bar, select **Edit**, **Preferences**, and choose one of the commands from the submenu.
2. Set the options you want to change. For example, select **cm** in the **Rulers** drop-down menu to change the unit of measure from inches to centimeters
3. Click **OK**.

INTRODUCTION

Follow these steps if you want to customize how Photoshop Elements shows things to you in the work area, how it saves files, and other options. As just one of many options, these steps explain how to change the unit of measure in the work area from inches to centimeters.

HINT

Default Settings
Experiment with the settings as you get more comfortable with the software. You might find you can improve your efficiency by changing a preference if you are always having to change a setting manually.

TIP

Restore Defaults
To restore default settings, restart the program and when it's finished loading, press **Alt+Ctrl+Shift** and select **Yes**. Defaults will be restored the next time you start the program.

Saving Your Work

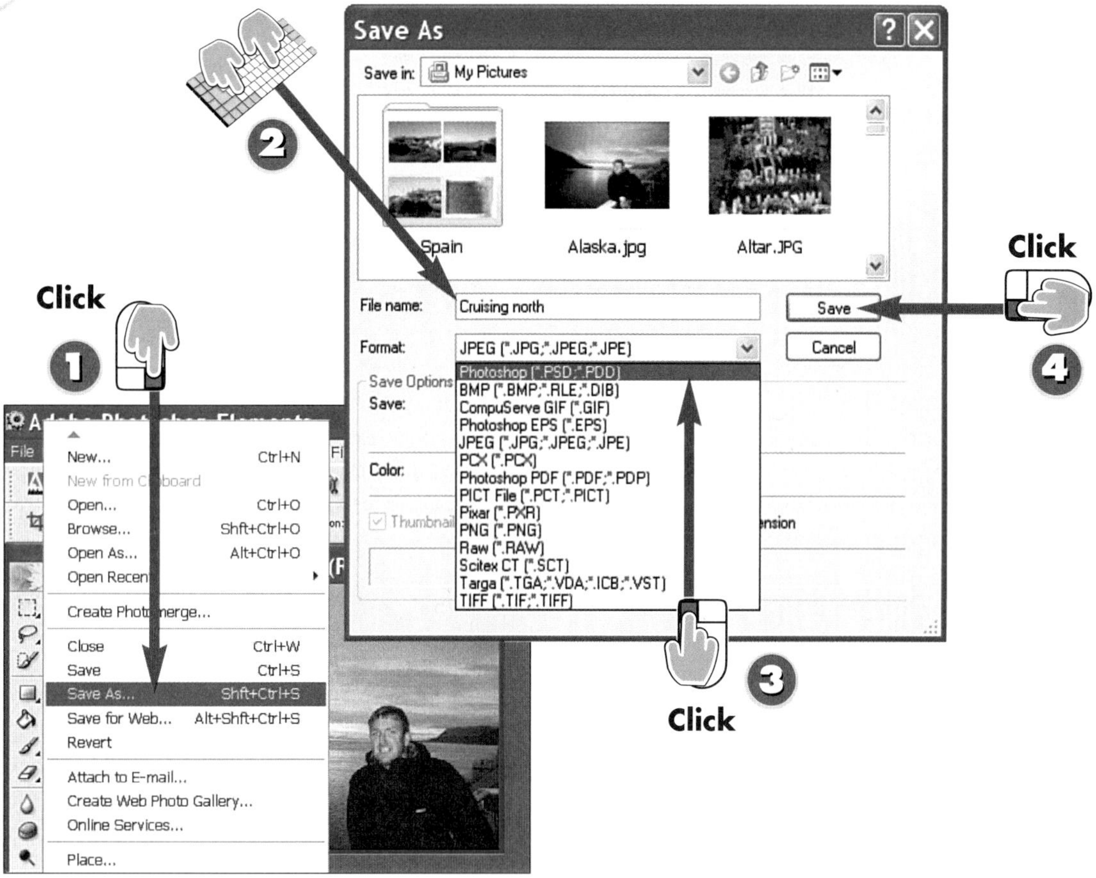

1. To save a file to a different drive or folder or with a different name, select **File**, **Save As** from the menu bar, or press **Shift+Ctrl+S**.
2. Type a name for the new file, such as **Cruising north**. (No need to type the extension, such as .JPG.)
3. Optionally, make a selection from the **Format** drop-down menu to change the file type.
4. Use the **Save In** drop-down menu to store the file in a different folder or on a different drive. Click **Save**.

INTRODUCTION

All the work you do on a picture in Photoshop Elements will be lost unless you save the file to disk. Usually, if you are saving a file for the first time, you can simply click the Save button on the shortcuts bar or press Ctrl+S on the keyboard. If you need to save a file to another location or under a new name, these steps show you how.

TIP

File Types

You can keep digital snapshots in the format the camera makes, usually JPEG (.JPG) files. But if you want more flexibility in editing them later, and best image quality, it's better to save them as Photoshop (.PSD) files.

HINT

Digital Negatives

If your computer can burn CDs, save your unedited camera originals to discs. These are your digital "negatives." That way, if you make changes to the images on your hard drive, you still have a copy of the untouched original.

PART 2

Getting It All Together

In this part, you'll learn how to bring pictures into your computer so you can work with them in Photoshop Elements.

First off, you can't do much of anything with your pictures until they exist as digital files on your computer's hard drive. Photos you take with your digital camera, DV camcorder, or camera phone are already stored as files, but you'll need to transfer them from the camera's internal storage to a disk in the computer.

You can also work with film shots—prints, negatives, and slides—but you'll have to *digitize* them first. That's what a scanner does. It scans a print with a beam of light, breaking the image into a collection of individual colored dots, or *pixels* (picture elements). All digital images are composed of pixels, and the main thing Photoshop Elements does is help you change the colors of thousands or even millions of pixels at once, in interesting and useful ways.

You can also grab pictures from other computer documents and from Web pages on the Internet.

Whether you use the other tasks in this book to work with your shots a little or a lot, you'll also learn how to create finished images as prints, contact sheets, and digital photo archives.

The Ins and Outs of Digital Photography

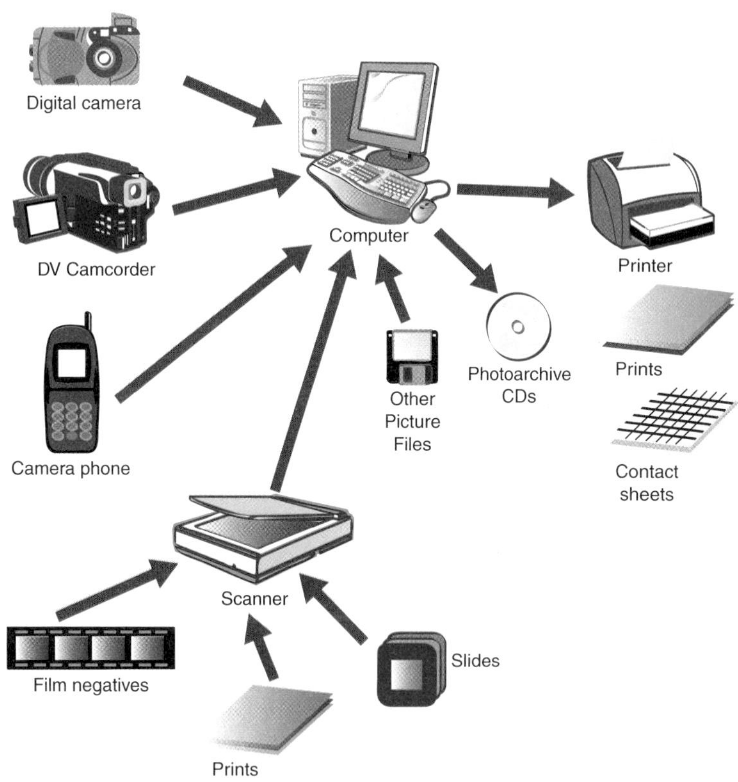

Getting Photos into Your Computer

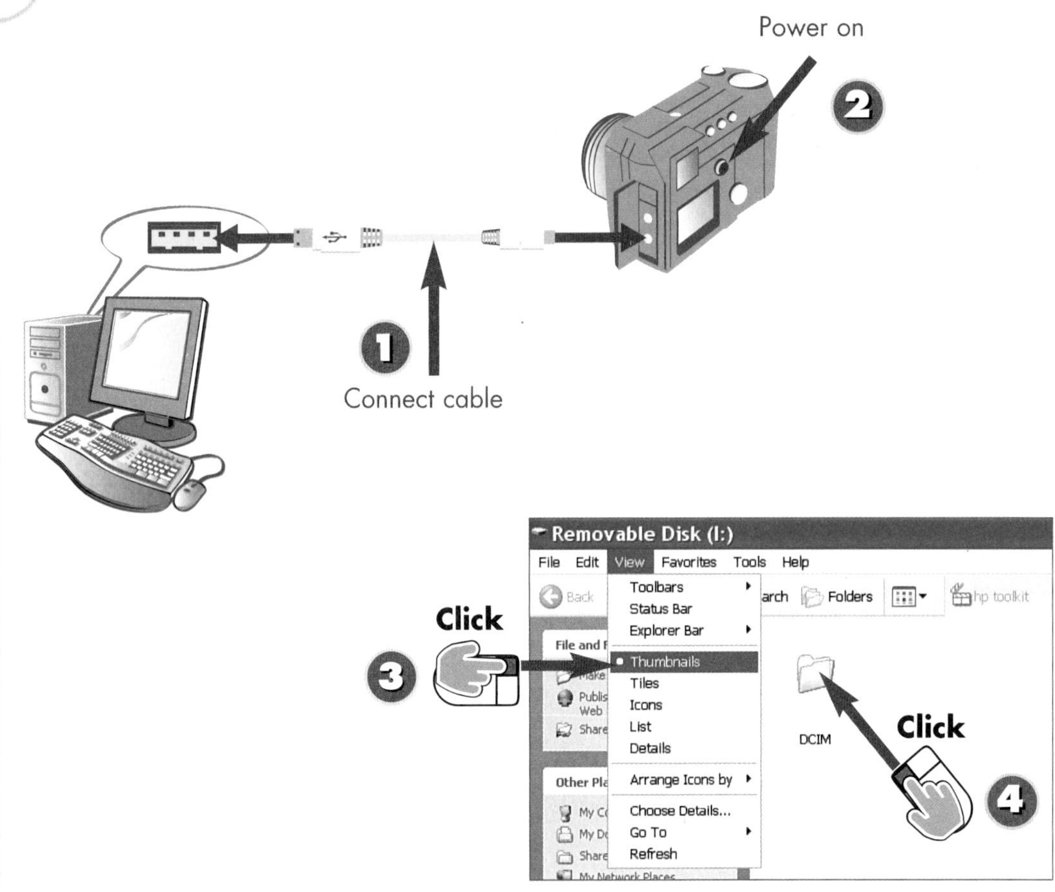

1. Connect the smaller end of the data cable to the camera, and the larger end to the USB port of your PC.
2. Turn the camera power on. Windows should detect the camera, and an Explorer window opens showing its contents.
3. From the Explorer menu bar, select **View**, **Thumbnails**.
4. Navigate by double-clicking the folder (and possibly other folders within it) to find the camera's image files.

INTRODUCTION

Most digital cameras and camera phones come with their own software for browsing image files and *uploading* them to your computer. However, you can use the steps described here to transfer files from most digital picture devices using the built-in functions of Windows.

TIP

Rename a File

To rename files before you copy them, click the filename in Explorer, type a new name, and click outside the filename-entry box. Don't change the extension, though.

HINT

Show Extensions

File extensions might be hidden in Windows. To fix this, in My Computer, select **Tools**, **Folder Options**. Click the **View** tab, and then clear the **Hide File Extensions for Known File Types** check box.

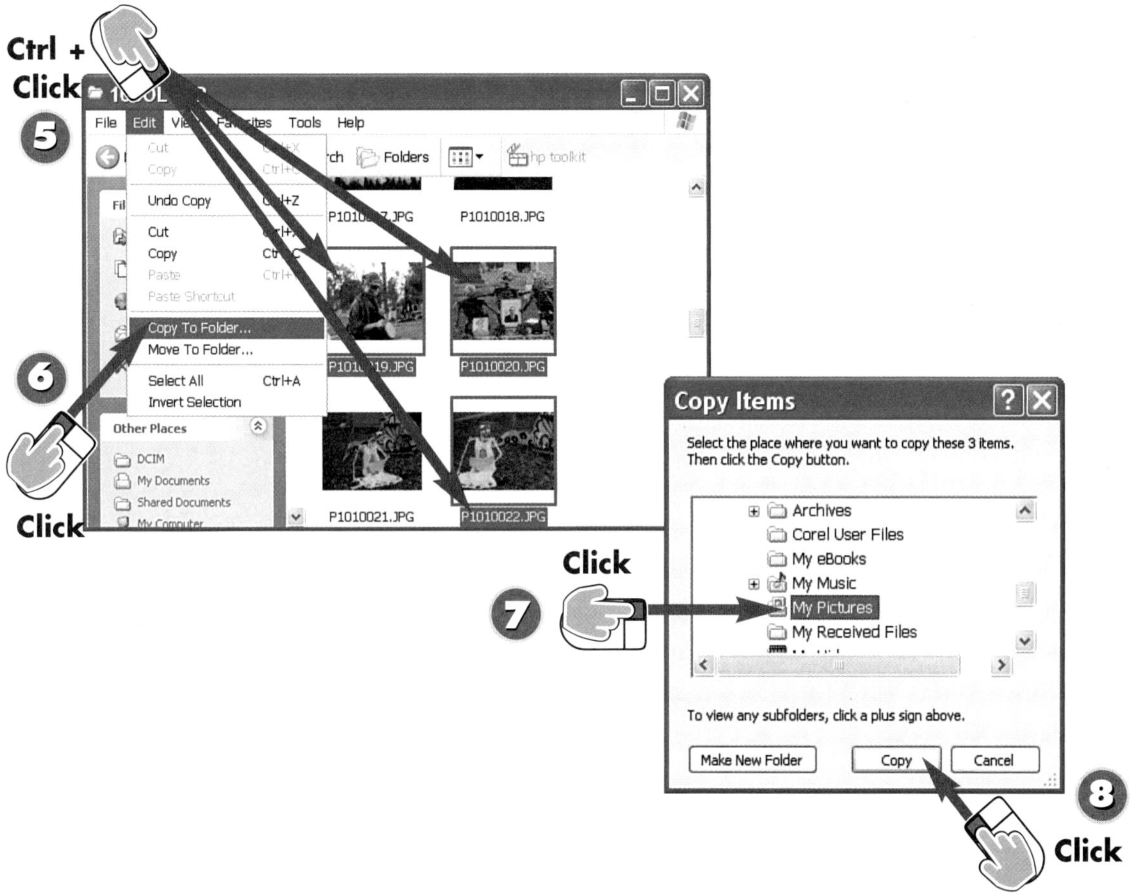

5. Hold down the **Ctrl** key as you click on each file you want.

6. From the menu bar, select **Edit**, **Copy to Folder**. The Copy Items dialog box opens.

7. Navigate the filesystem to select the drive and folder where you want to store the files, such as **My Pictures**.

8. Click **Copy**.

TIP

Multiple Choice
In step 5, if necessary, click and drag the scrollbar to browse through the other images as you select each with **Ctrl+click**. To get all the files, select **Edit**, **Select All** (or press **Ctrl+A**).

TIP

Reorient Yourself
You can quickly change the orientation of shots from *landscape* to *portrait* before you select them in step 5: Right-click the thumbnail and select **Rotate Clockwise** or **Rotate Counter Clockwise**.

Scanning Images

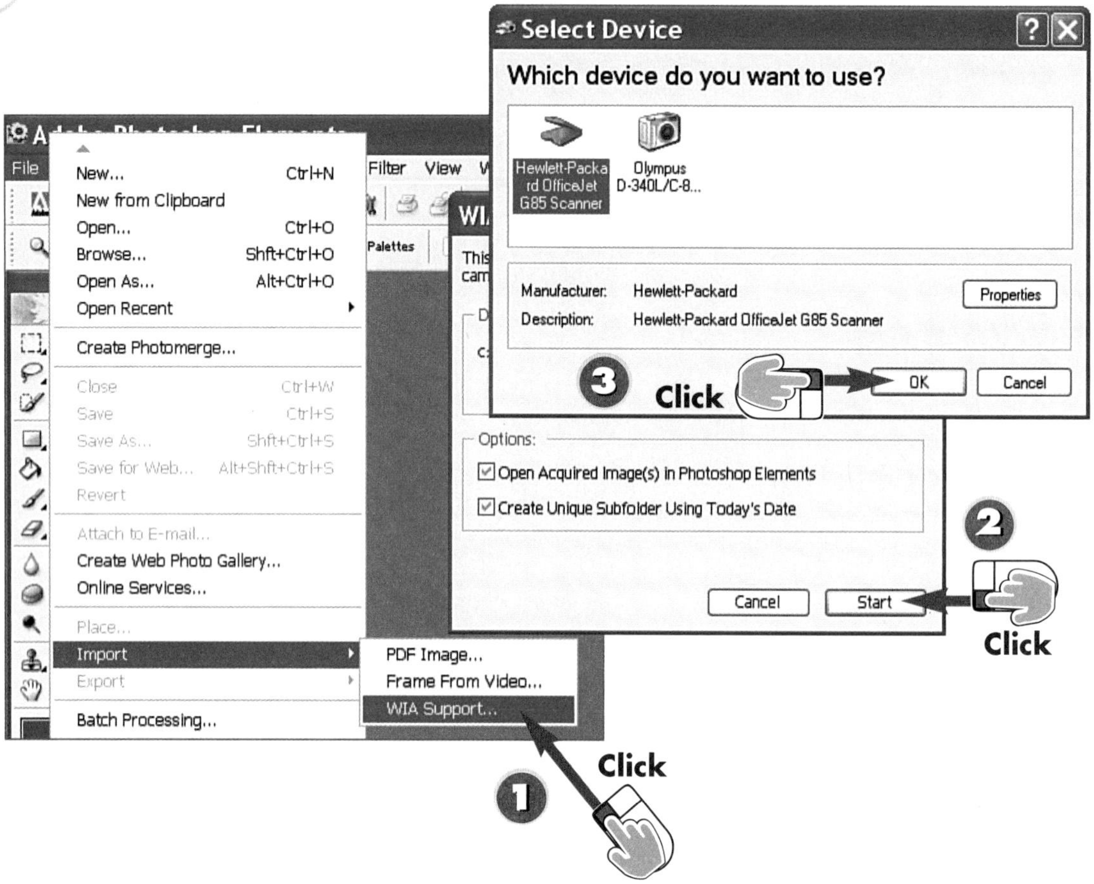

1. With the item to be scanned on the scanner glass and the lid closed, open Photoshop Elements and choose **File**, **Import**, **WIA Support**.
2. Click **Start**.
3. If you have more than one camera or scanner attached to your computer, click the scanning device you want to use, and click **OK**.

INTRODUCTION

Scanning and storing your old snapshots in your computer is not only a wonderful way to reduce clutter and organize those shoeboxes full of prints—but also Photoshop Elements has lots of ways to bring back faded color, touch up complexions, and even erase uninvited guests.

HINT

Final Destination

These steps create a file automatically. Specify the disk location in the Destination Folder field of the WIA Support dialog box. Be sure to resave the file if you edit the image.

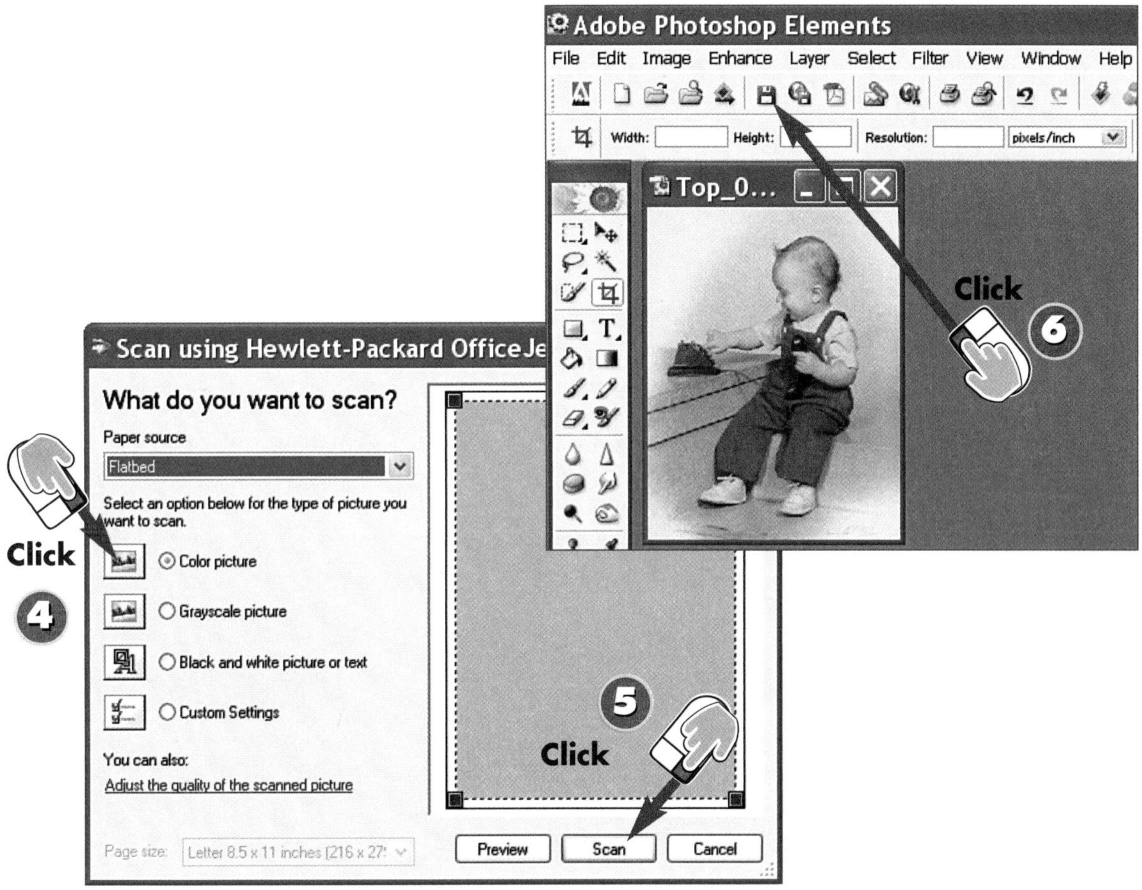

4. Select the type of picture, such as **Color picture**.

5. Click **Scan**. The scanned print appears in the active image area, ready for editing.

6. If you edit the picture, click the **Save** button to save your work.

TIP

Not My Type

The *WIA (Windows Image Acquisition)* Support feature scans a photo as a Windows bitmap (.bmp extension) by default. To change the file type, select **File**, **Save As** and change the **Format** after the image has been imported.

HINT

Scanning Secrets

The dialog box in step 5 might look different, depending on your scanner model. When adjusting quality, you can select Grayscale instead of Black and white to capture shading. Use Color instead of Grayscale if a monochrome picture is *sepia*. For photos you might want to print later, set the resolution to 300 dpi.

Grabbing a Video Frame

Start

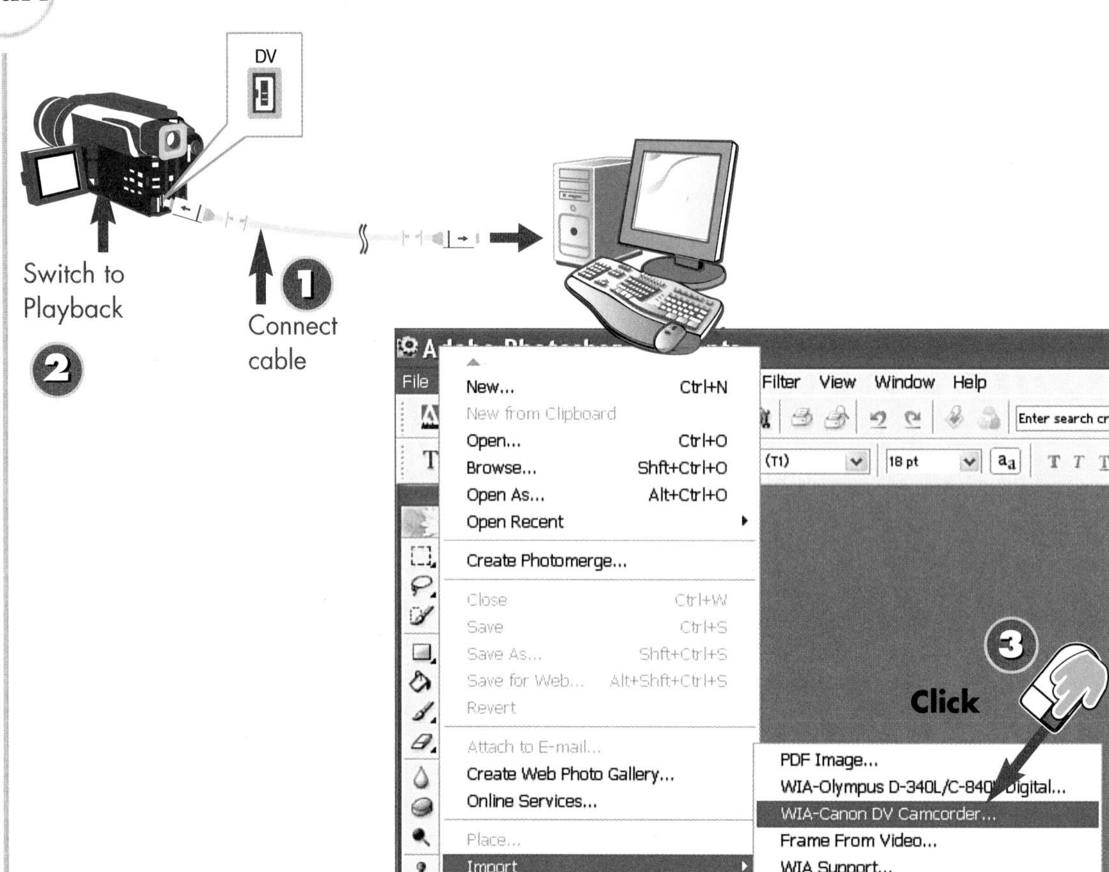

1. Connect the smaller end of the data cable to the camcorder, and the larger end to the FireWire port of your PC.

2. Switch the camcorder to **Playback** (or VCR) mode.

3. From the Photoshop Elements menu bar, select **File**, **Import**, **WIA *<camera name>***. Press **Play** on the camcorder to roll the tape.

INTRODUCTION

Photoshop Elements can't capture still photos from uploaded DV files (.mov extension), but you can follow these steps to capture one or more stills as the camcorder plays back a tape, which achieves the same result.

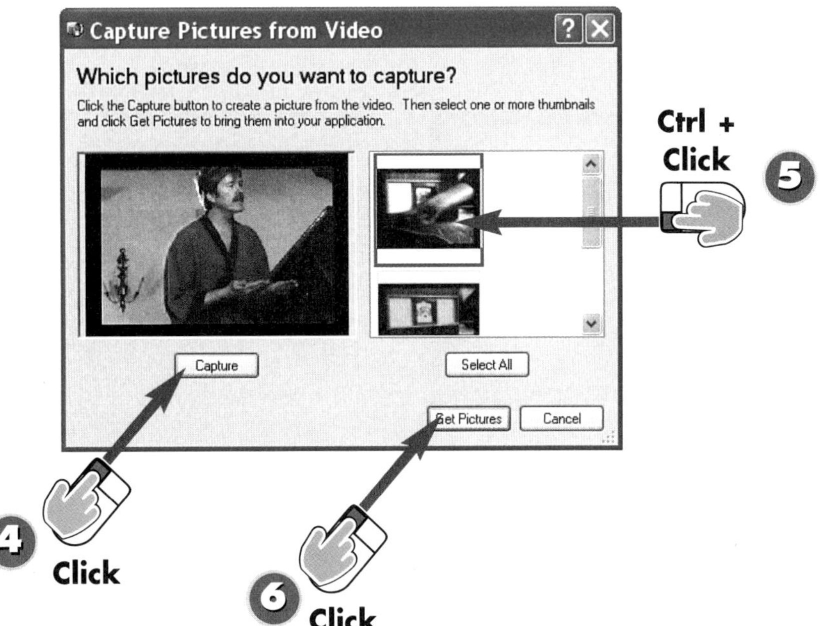

4 Video plays in the screen on the left. When you see the frame you want, click **Capture**. (Repeat if you want multiple frames.)

5 Press **Ctrl** while you click each thumbnail you want (or click **Select All** to get all of them).

6 Click **Get Pictures**. The video stills open for editing in separate windows in the work area.

HINT

Video Capture

To capture video files you already have on disk that are in a format other than .mov, turn the page and follow the steps in "Capturing a Frame from a Video File."

TIP

Other Options

For these steps to work with your camcorder, it must be a WIA device. If you have an older DV camcorder, upload the clips as .mov files, use a video editor such as Pinnacle Studio to save as a Windows movie (.wmv), and then select the **File**, **Import**, **Frame from Video** command instead.

Capturing a Frame from a Video File

Start

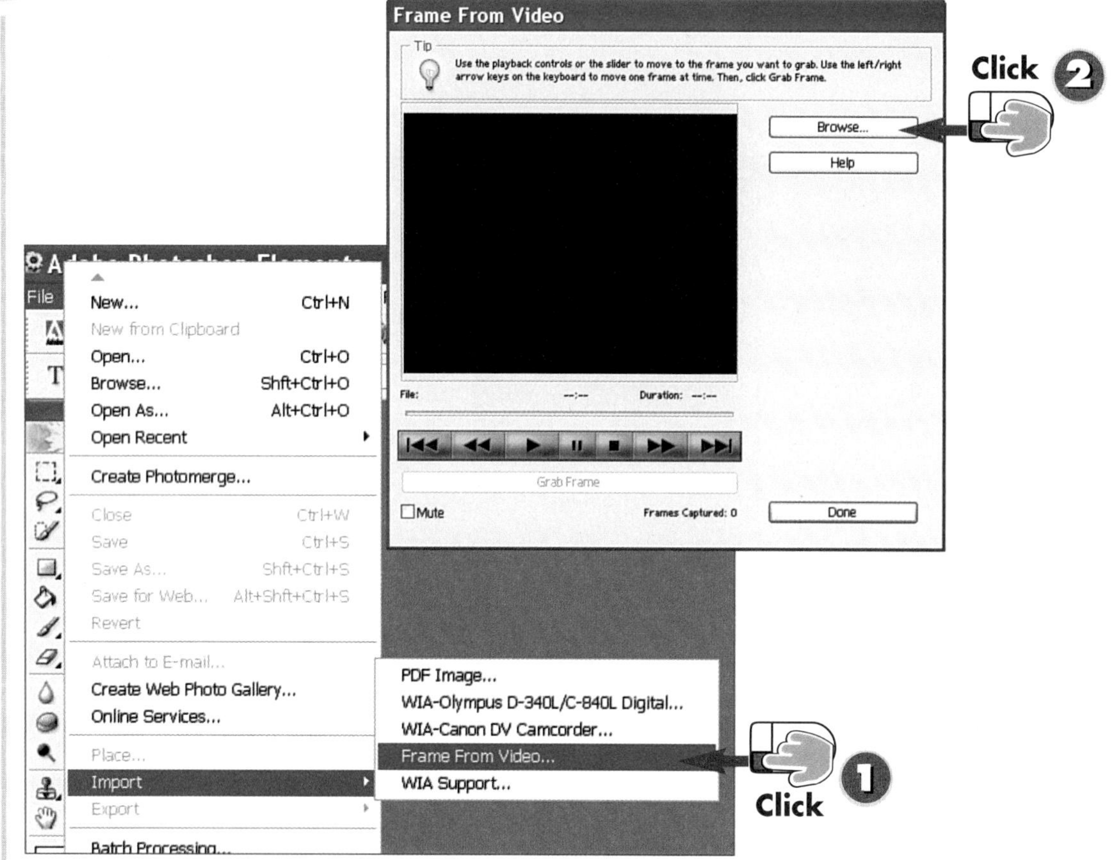

1. From the menu bar, select **File**, **Import**, **Frame From Video**.

2. Click **Browse** to locate the video file to use.

INTRODUCTION

Follow these steps to capture still frames from multimedia files stored on disk as .avi, .mpg, or .mpeg types. To grab video frames from a DV tape (which become .mov files when uploaded), refer to the preceding task, "Grabbing a Video Frame."

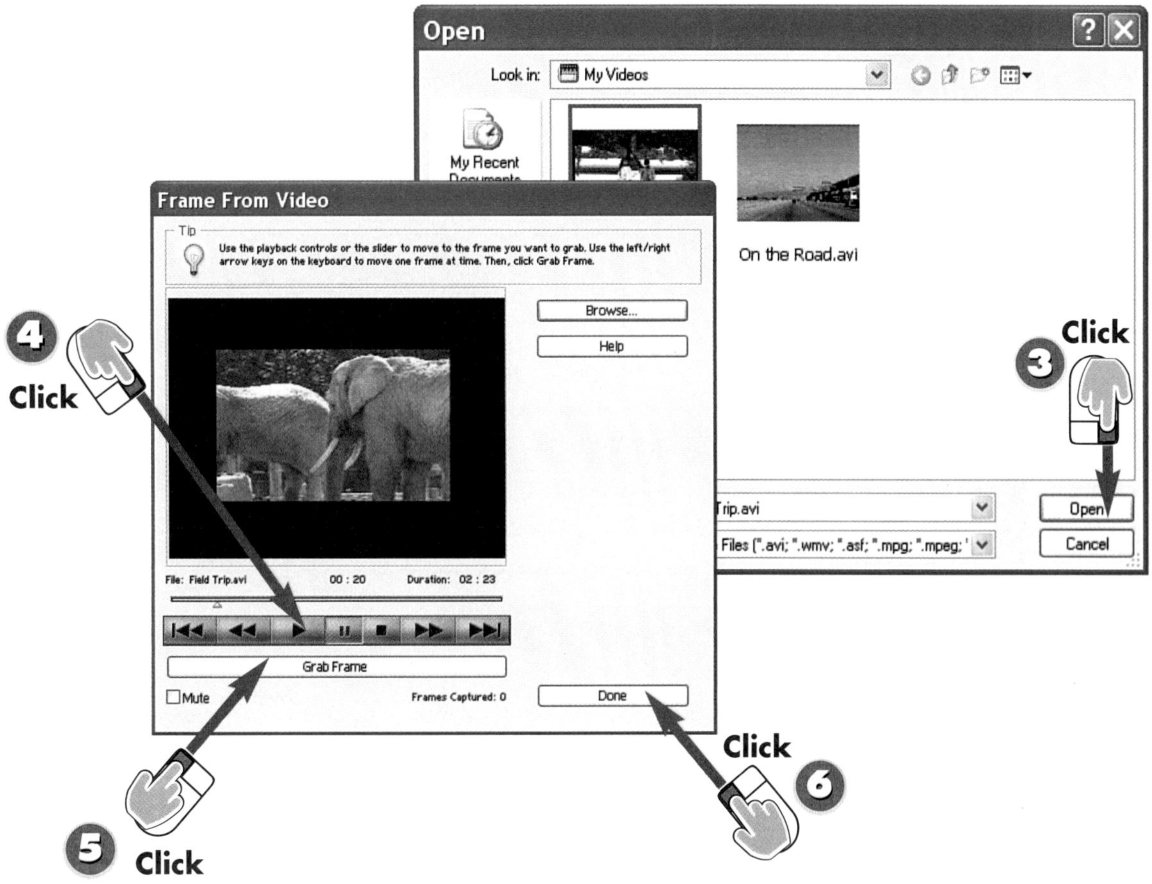

3. Select the File and click **Open**.

4. The video clip opens in the preview pane. Click the **Play** button to start it playing.

5. When you see the frame you want, click **Grab Frame** or press the **Spacebar**. (Repeat if you want multiple frames.)

6. Click **Done**. The frames you selected will open in the work area for editing.

Grab It

For more accuracy in grabbing the exact frame you want in step 6, click the **Pause** button to freeze playback. You can press the **Right** and **Left Arrow** keys to move forward or backward a frame at a time.

HINT

Unwind a Little

If the Rewind and Fast Forward buttons are grayed out, the type of clip you've selected doesn't support rewinding or fast-forwarding.

Taking an Image from the Clipboard

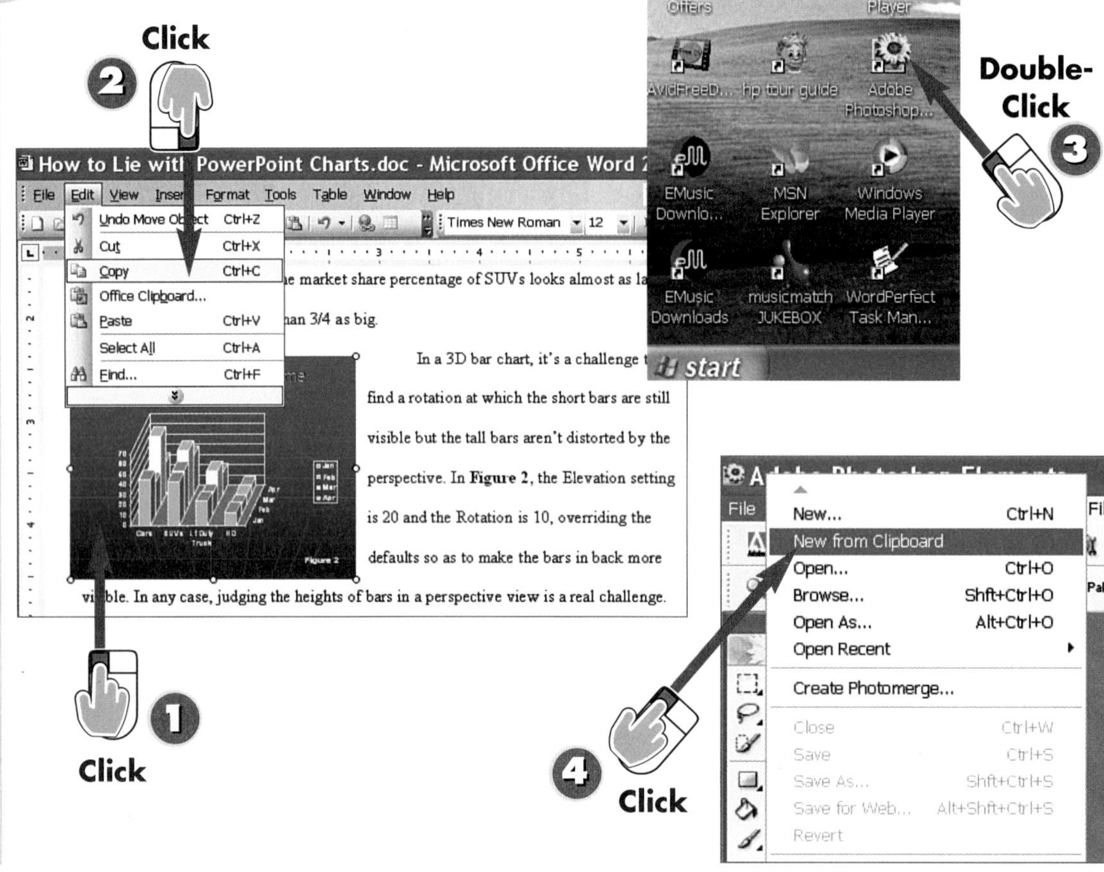

1. In another Windows application, such as Microsoft Word, click the image you want.
2. From the application's menu bar, select **Edit**, **Copy** or press **Ctrl+C**.
3. Start Photoshop Elements (or click its button on the Windows taskbar if it's already open).
4. From the Photoshop Elements menu bar, select **File**, **New from Clipboard**. A copy of the picture opens in the active image window for editing.

INTRODUCTION

The Windows *Clipboard* is a reserved area of your computer's memory designed specifically for exchanging data—such as photos, drawings, or text—among applications. For example, you can open a document in Microsoft Word, select one of the pictures in it, and copy the image into Photoshop Elements.

HINT

Native Files

The copied image comes into Photoshop Elements in whatever format it was in the original document, but if you edit it and then try to save, the program will prompt you to save it as a native Photoshop (.psd) file. Saving a copy of your image as a .psd file is a good idea, as it enables you to continue making edits to the file. If you save as another format, such as .jpg or .gif, the changes you make are incorporated into the file, and you can no longer undo them.

Copying a Picture from a Web Page

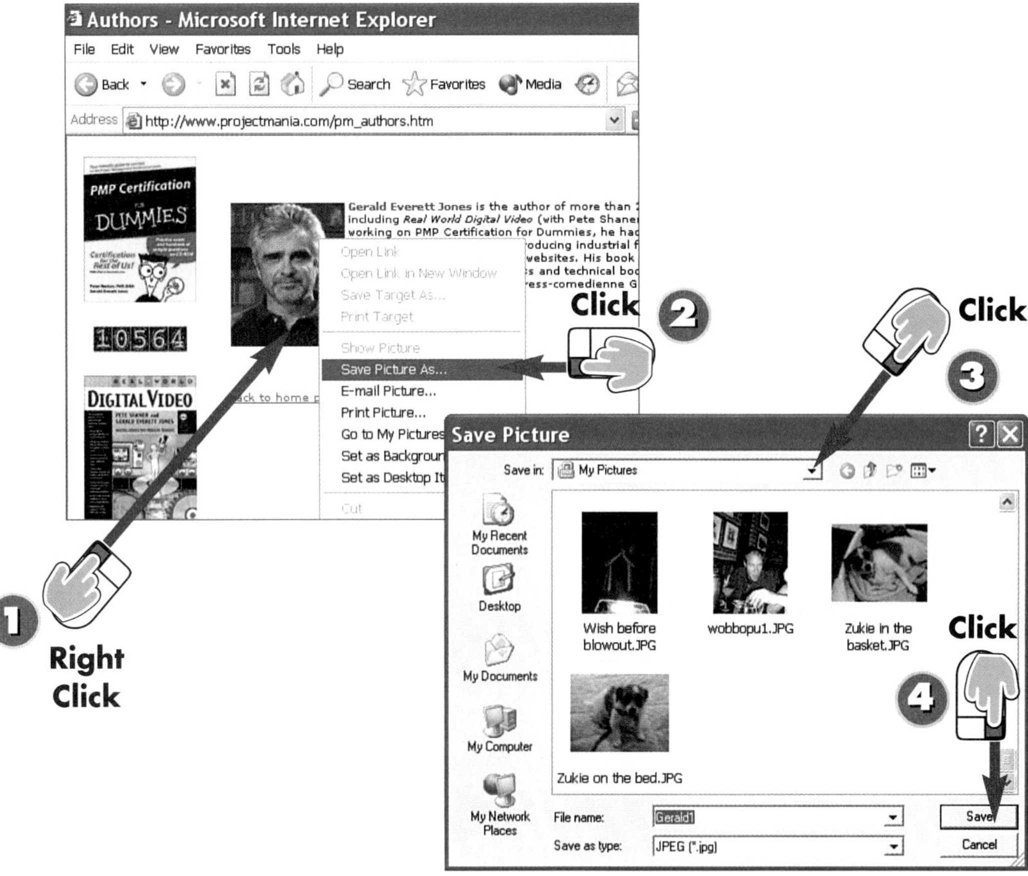

1. While viewing a Web page in Internet Explorer (or other browser), right-click the picture you want.
2. From the pop-up menu, select **Save Picture As** (or the equivalent command in your browser).
3. If necessary, navigate to the folder where you want to store the file.
4. Click **Save**. You're ready to open the file in Photoshop Elements for editing.

INTRODUCTION

Think of the Internet as a global photo library at your fingertips. For example, if you need a photo of the Brooklyn Bridge to illustrate a report, surf to **www.google.com**, click the **Images** tab, and you're sure to find several choices. Then use the steps here to load the image into Photoshop Elements.

HINT

Know Your Rights
Photos and artwork on the Web are subject to copyright. Obtain permission from the rights holder before incorporating them in your Web sites, slide shows, or newsletters.

TIP

A New Name
You can type a new name for the file in the **File Name** box before you select **Save**. Don't type the extension part or try to change it.

Scanning a Slide

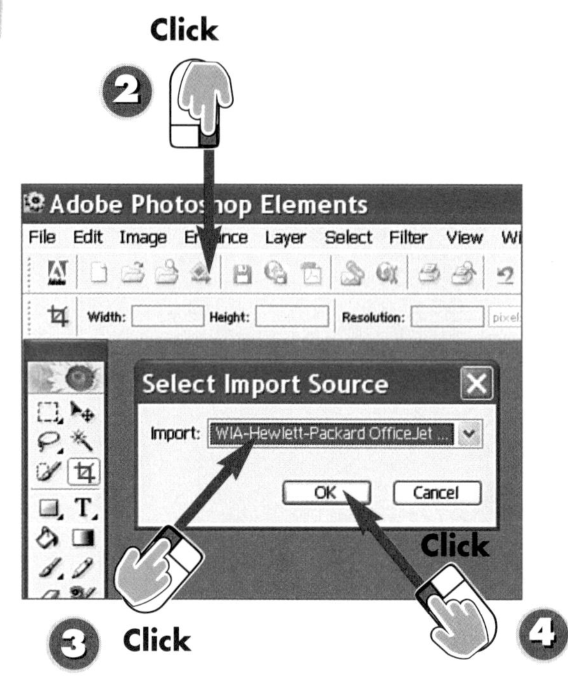

1. Insert the slide in the scanner, emulsion (dull) side up. (If your scanner has a backlit transparency attachment, use it.)
2. From the Shortcuts bar, select the **Import** icon.
3. Select the name of your scanner from the drop-down menu.
4. Click **OK**.

INTRODUCTION

You can scan your old slides much as you do prints. Many scanners have special transparency adapters you can buy, which provide backlight for a brighter, sharper picture. However, you can get good results with these steps, even if you don't have one of these attachments.

HINT

Clean Glass
Start by cleaning the scanner glass. Take color slides out of their paper or plastic mounts so they lie flat. For tips on scanning negatives, look at the next task, "Making a Positive from a Negative."

TIP

Another Route
You can also do the steps described here with the menu commands **File**, **Import**, **WIA Support** or **File**, **Import**, **WIA-<*scanner name*>**.

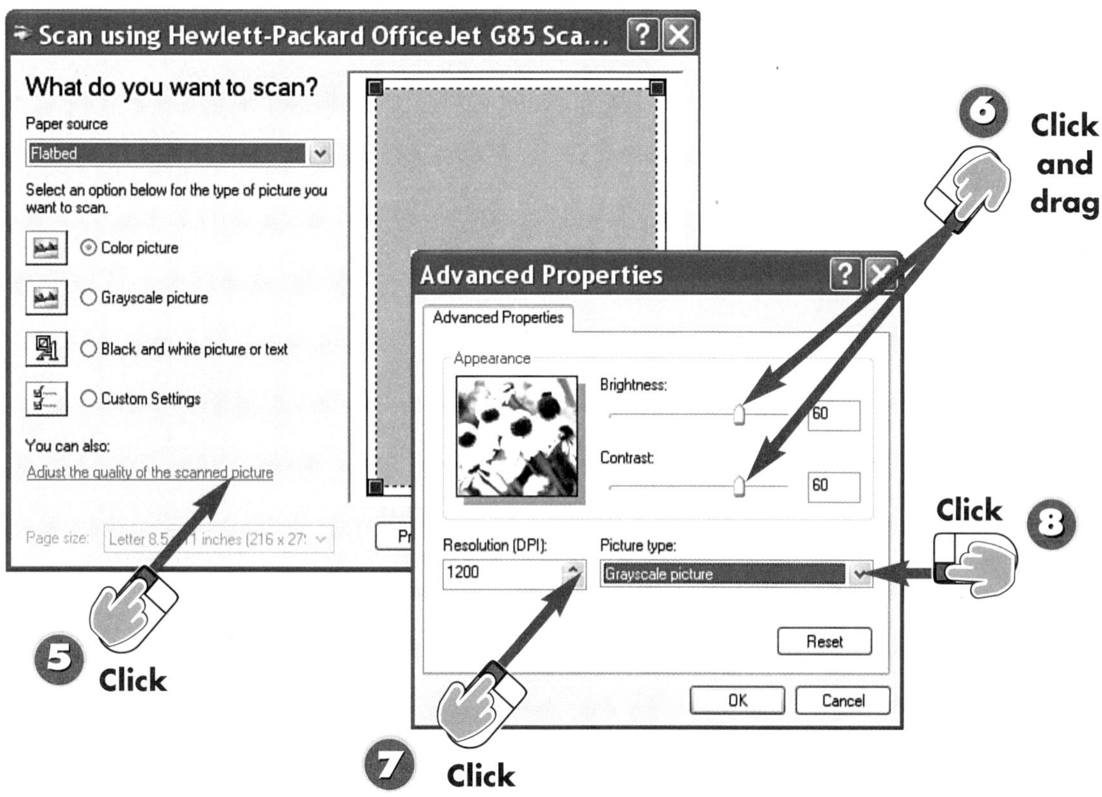

5 Click **Adjust the quality of the scanned picture** (or its equivalent; the dialog window for your scanner might look different).

6 Increase the values of **Brightness** and **Contrast**, especially if you don't have a transparency attachment.

7 Increase the **Resolution** to at least **300 dpi** or more.

8 In the **Picture type** drop-down menu, select **Grayscale picture** for black-and-white originals with shading, or **Color**, and click **OK**.

See next page

TIP

Setting the DPI
In step 7, the smaller the transparency, the higher the dpi setting should be. For 35mm color slides, set **Resolution** as high as it will go—**1200 dpi** on this scanner.

HINT

It's Not All Black and White
In step 8, avoid the Black and White setting. The only time you'd use it would be for scanning line art, drawings, and text that have no shading.

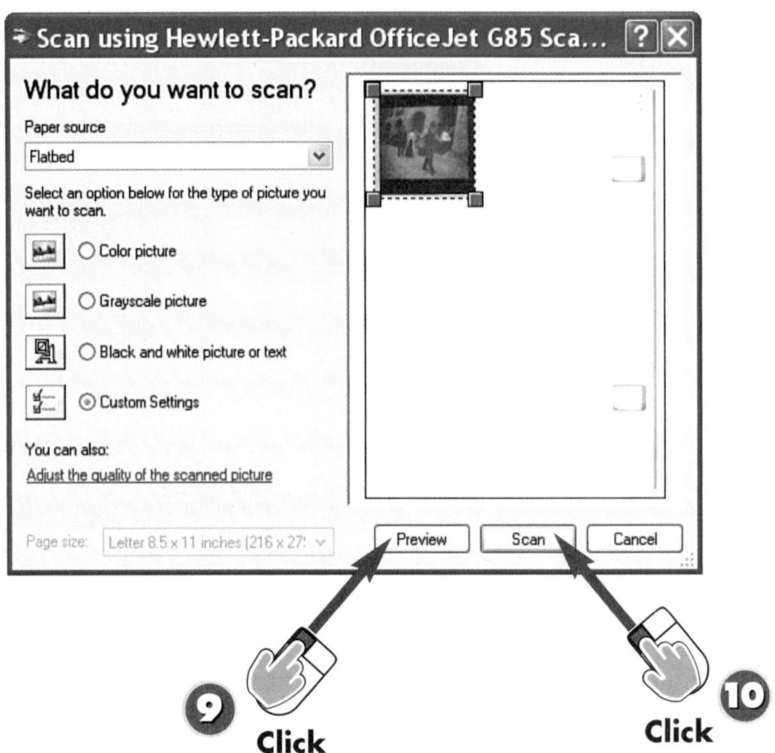

9 Click **Preview** (repeat steps 6–8 and adjust until the preview image looks right).

10 Click **Scan**. The scanned picture appears in the active image window.

HINT

Making Adjustments
Adjusting brightness and contrast can help compensate for not having an adapter to backlight the transparency. Get the best image you can in step 9, and then you can make further adjustments after the picture is in Photoshop Elements.

HINT

Outside Help
If you have a lot of slides, you might consider having your local photo lab convert them all to a photo CD. It'll save you the time and hassle of scanning them individually, and you'll have high-quality digital files.

Making a Positive from a Negative

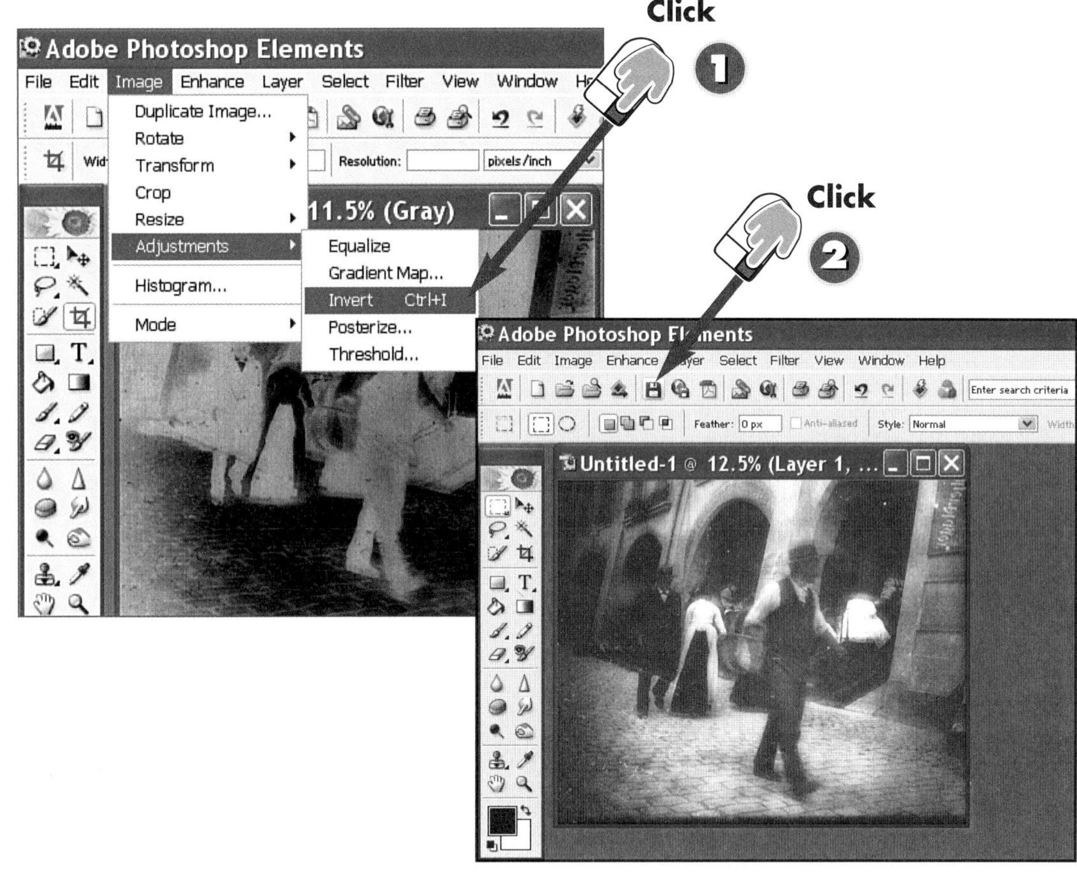

1. After you've scanned the negative, select **Image**, **Adjustments**, **Invert** from the menu bar (or press **Ctrl+I**).

2. Click **Save** on the shortcuts bar to save your work.

INTRODUCTION

It's usually easier to scan photographic prints, but Photoshop Elements can handle negatives, as well. Grayscale images work best. Scanning color negatives won't work very well unless your scanner has settings for eliminating their orange background.

HINT

Color Negatives

If you have a color print, scan that instead. If you don't have a color print and don't want to incur the expense to get one made, consult your scanner's manual to see whether it has settings for color negatives.

Importing an Acrobat Image

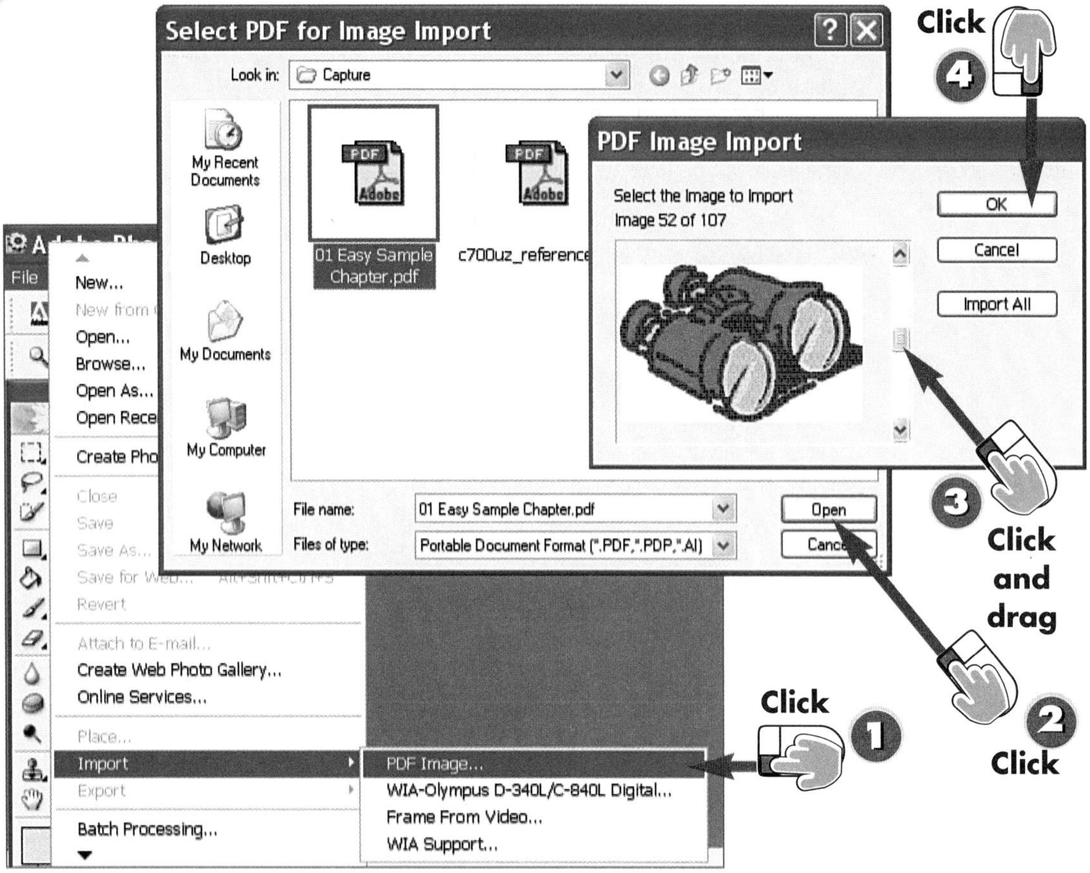

1. From the Photoshop Elements menu bar, select **File**, **Import**, **PDF Image**.
2. Select the file that contains the image you want. (If necessary, navigate the filesystem to open the folder that holds the file.) Click **Open**.
3. In the PDF Image Import window, click and drag the scrollbar to browse through the images in the file.
4. When you see the image you want, click **OK**. It will open for editing in a new active image window.

INTRODUCTION

Adobe's Acrobat Portable Document Format (.pdf extension) makes it possible to distribute printed brochures and manuals in electronic form. Adobe provides Acrobat Reader software free, and PDF files have become very popular on the Web. Photoshop Elements offers this built-in method for extracting pictures easily from downloaded PDF files.

HINT

Well Illustrated

You can also follow these steps to import images from Adobe Illustrator (.ai) documents. Other Adobe graphics applications can read and write Illustrator files, including InDesign, PageMaker, and FrameMaker.

Resizing and Printing an Image

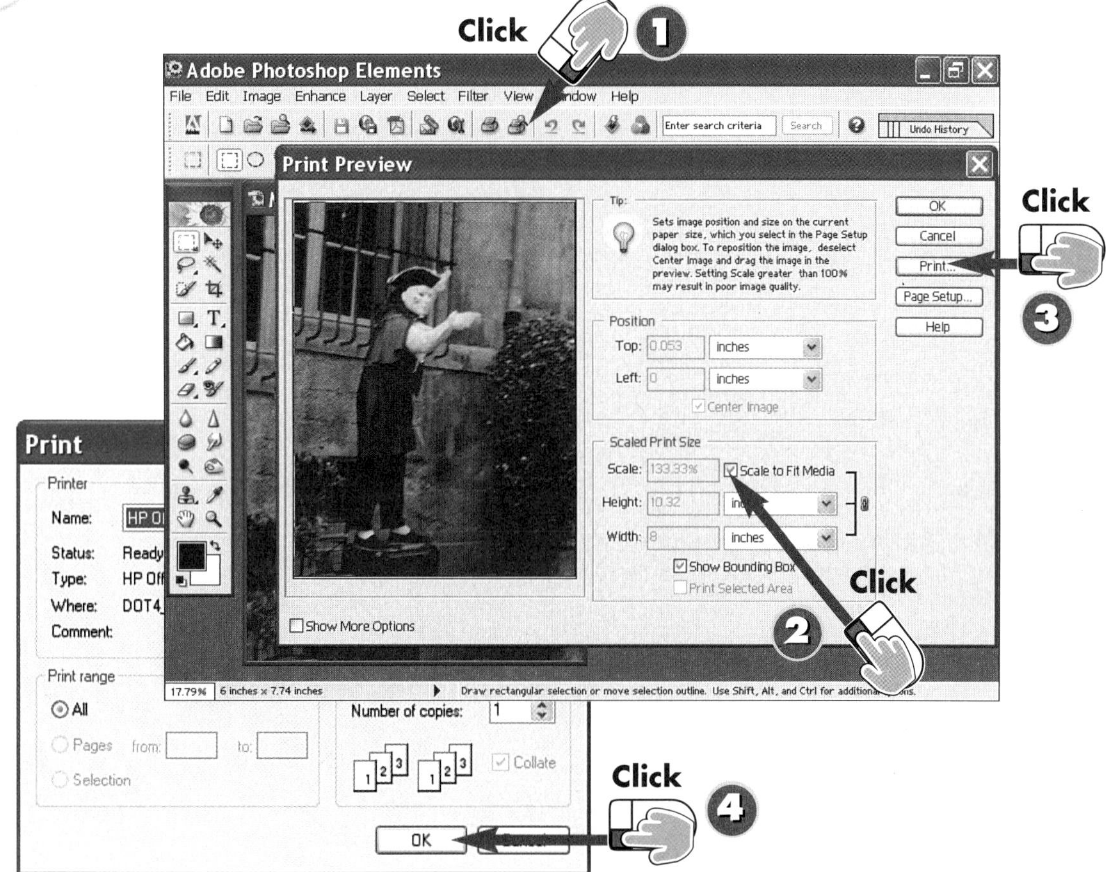

1. Select the **Print Preview** button in the shortcuts bar.

2. Check the **Scale to Fit Media** box.

3. Click **Print**.

4. Click **OK**.

INTRODUCTION

Photoshop Elements reports the current print size of the image in the lower-left corner of the work area. With these few steps, you can resize the image to fit exactly on the printed page. This method uses the default paper size currently set for the printer.

TIP

Switch Orientations
The default printer orientation is Portrait (long side vertical). To switch to Landscape (long side horizontal), after step 2, click the **Page Setup** button, select **Landscape** and **OK**, then go to step 3.

HINT

Glossy Prints
For the best-quality prints on a color inkjet printer, use glossy photo paper. Remove the plain paper and feed just one sheet at a time, because the glossy surface can stick to other sheets and cause jams.

Printing Contact Sheets

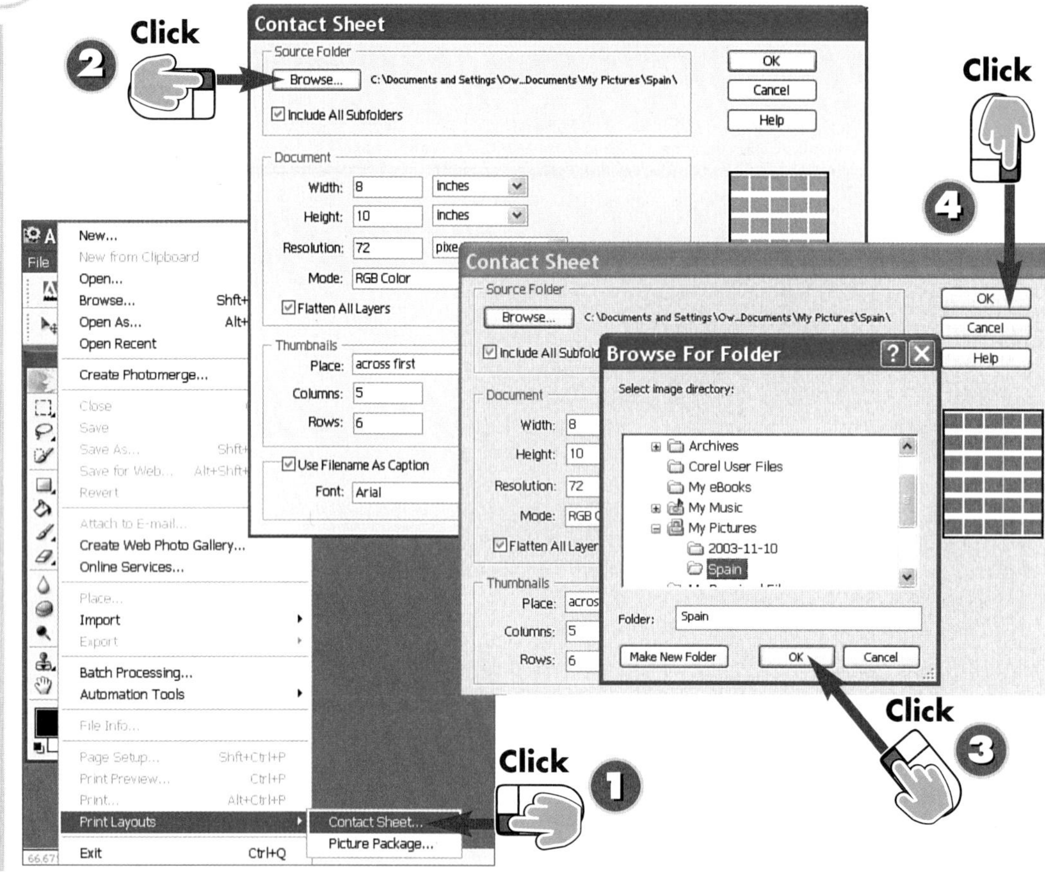

1. From the menu bar, select **File**, **Print Layouts**, **Contact Sheet**.
2. Click **Browse**.
3. Navigate the filesystem to select the folder that contains the images to be printed on the sheet, and click **OK**.
4. In the **Contact Sheet** dialog box, click **OK**.

INTRODUCTION

Professional photographers routinely make *contact sheets* by printing negatives laid directly on photosensitive paper. Their clients review the sheets and mark the shots for which they want to order prints. Photoshop Elements will generate contact sheets that show thumbnails with labels of all files in a specified folder.

HINT

Get the Contact

Print and store contact sheets with each of your photo archive CDs. It's a handy way of browsing the images when they're no longer on your hard drive.

TIP

Grayscale Mode

To conserve color ink when doing reference-quality contact sheets, change the **Mode** setting to **Grayscale** before you select **OK** in step 4.

5. Load your printer with photo paper. From the Shortcuts bar, click **Print**.

6. Click **OK**.

> **HINT**
>
> **Useful Captions**
>
> For more descriptive captions, rename camera files in Windows Explorer or in the Browser before you generate the sheets.

> **HINT**
>
> **Out of a Jam**
>
> The thumbnails of the selected files won't necessarily fit on a single contact sheet. If they don't, Photoshop Elements will print multiple sheets. Remember, to avoid printer jams, load photo paper manually, one sheet at a time.

Changing Paper (Canvas) Size

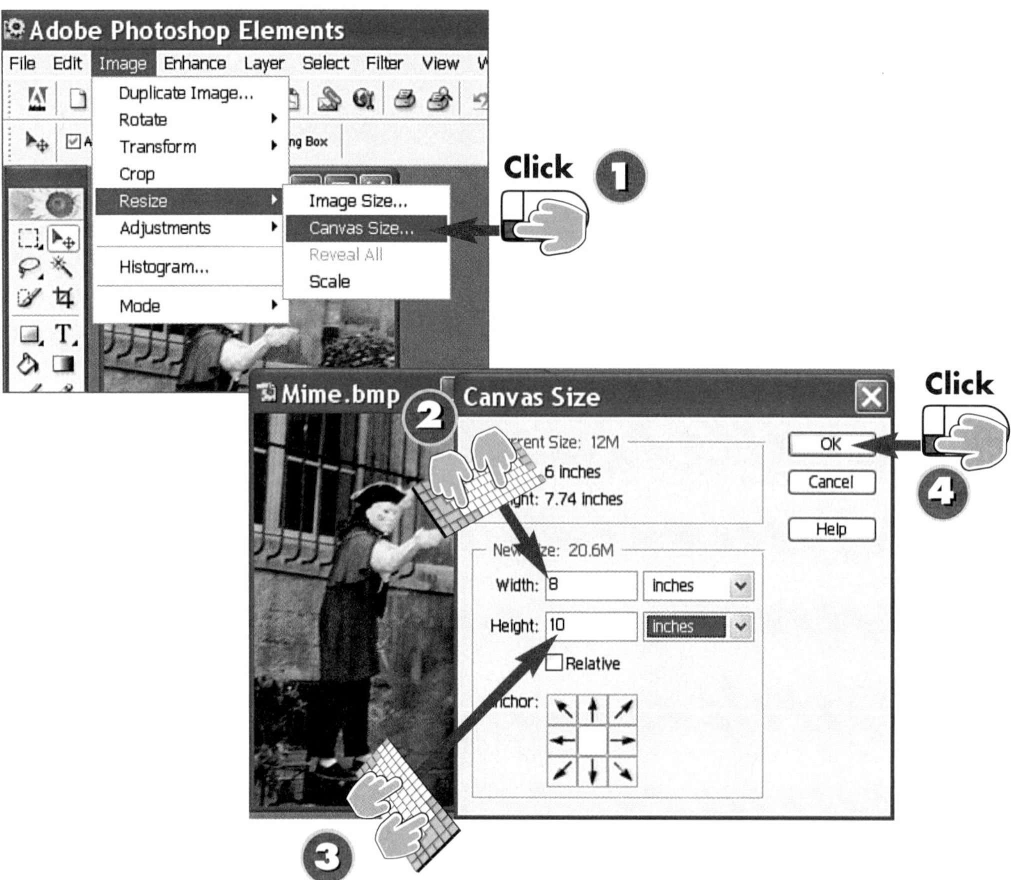

1. From the menu bar, select **Image**, **Resize**, **Canvas Size**.
2. Click in the **Width** box. Type the paper width, using decimals for fractions of an inch.
3. Repeat step 2 for **Height**.
4. Click **OK**.

INTRODUCTION

If you don't want the image to completely fill the printed page, you can size the page (or *canvas*) independently. Normally, the size of the canvas should match the paper size you have in the printer. You might resize the canvas when you're printing greeting cards and postcards individually on small sheets.

TIP

Background Fix
Before you do step 1, if the background color isn't set to white, press **D** to restore default foreground and background colors.

TIP

Resize and Resample
To change the image size within the printed page, select **Image**, **Resize**, **Image Size** from the menu bar. If the resolution falls below 150 pixels/inch, check **Resample Image** and type a value of **150** or greater.

Printing a Picture Package

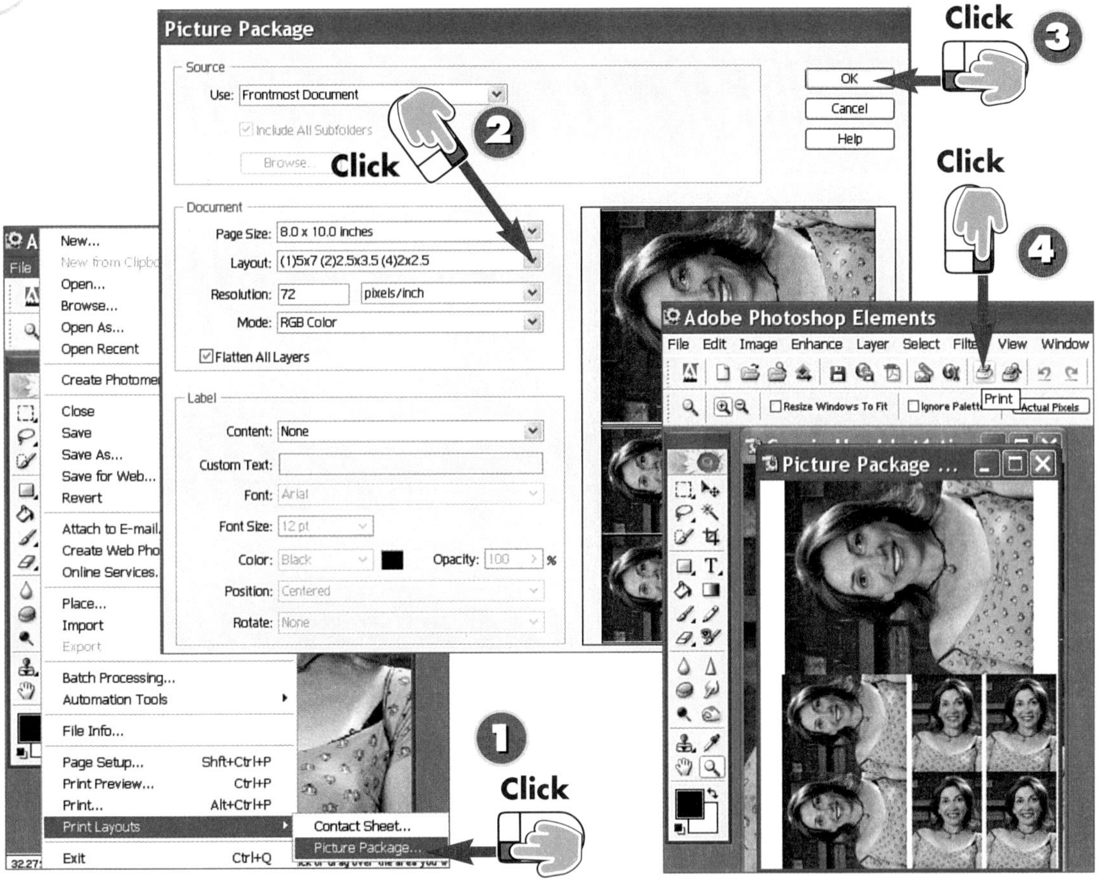

1. With a picture in the active image area, select **File**, **Print Layouts**, **Picture Package**.
2. Select a layout of sizes to fill the printed page, such as **(1)5×7 (2)2.5×3.5 (4)2×2.5**.
3. Click **OK**. The program will generate a page full of different-sized prints.
4. **Print** the page.

INTRODUCTION

Professional photographers who shoot annual school photos, weddings, and social events offer their subjects *picture packages*, prints ranging from wallet size to 8×10s for framing. Photoshop Elements will print a variety of assorted sizes for you on a sheet of photo paper. It's sure to please your "customers."

HINT

Just Like a Pro

Have your subjects pick the shots they want from a contact sheet, then make up their picture packages. Use bright-white, glossy photo paper, and feed one sheet at a time to avoid printer jams.

Saving Your Picture Archive on CD

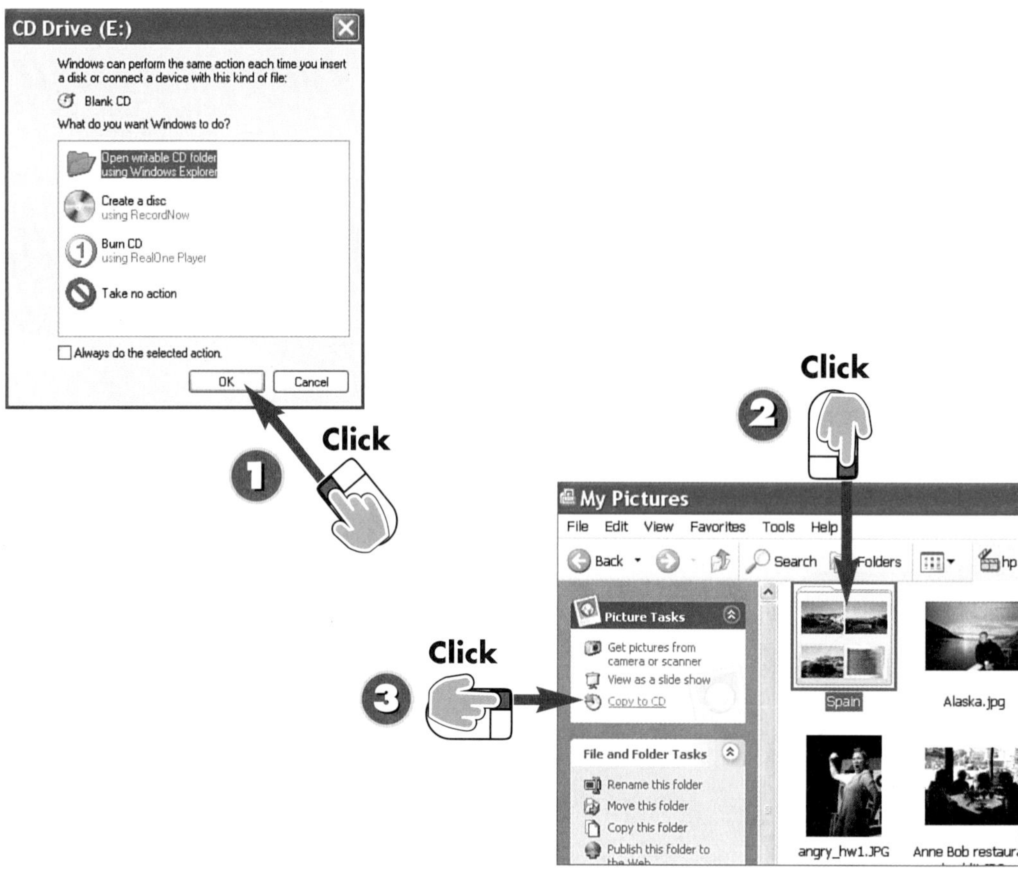

1. Insert a blank CD into your CD-ROM burner and click **OK** to confirm the default choice (**Open writable CD folder using Windows Explorer**).
2. Locate and click the folder that contains the images you want to copy.
3. In the Picture Tasks menu, select **Copy to CD**.

INTRODUCTION

After you've edited your photos and printed them, archive them on CD and delete them from your hard drive. Experienced photographers make a CD right after each shooting session. (You'll need a CD or DVD drive that can write as well as read discs.)

HINT

Just Hold It

The capacity of a typical CD is 700MB, or enough to store 1,400 average-sized JPEG files. If you have a DVD burner, you can put 4GB (about 8,000 shots) on a single DVD-R data disc (but don't put all your precious photos on one disc).

HINT

Write It Again

You can add files to CD-R discs until they are full, if your burner supports *multi-session* capability. You can both add and overwrite files on CD-RW discs (a few times, not indefinitely).

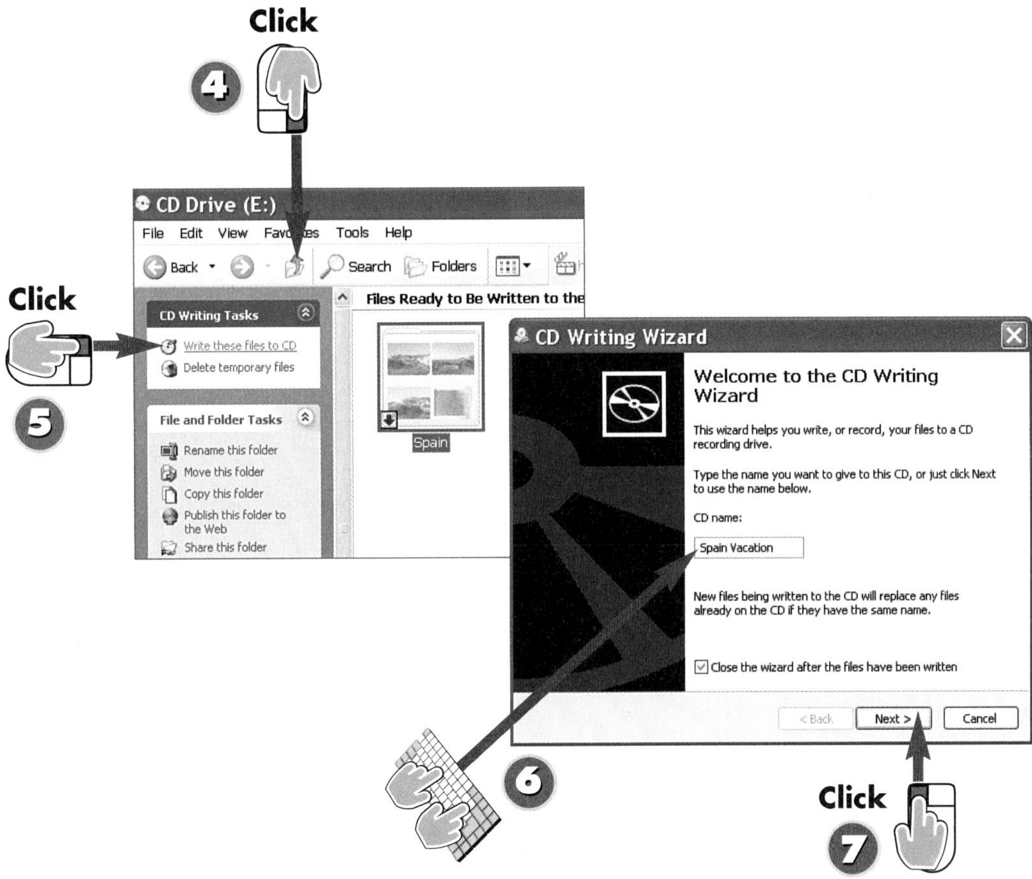

4. In Windows Explorer, navigate the filesystem to reopen the CD directory.
5. In the CD Writing Tasks menu, select **Write these files to CD**.
6. Click the text box and type a label for the CD, such as **Spain Vacation**.
7. Click **Next**. The disc will eject when copying is complete.

TIP

Get It Together
If your photos aren't all in a single folder, copy them all to a single temporary folder first. Alternatively, select a collection of them in Explorer by pressing **Ctrl+click**, and then select **Edit, Copy**, navigate to the CD drive, and select **Edit**, **Paste**.

HINT

Out of the Window
Instead of using the built-in copying functions of Windows XP, you could use a CD-burning application such as Roxio Easy CD Creator or Veritas RecordNow.

PART 3

Basic Photo Fixing

Think of this part of the book as a comfy family restaurant where you could go for your daily bread and never be bored with the same meal twice. It's just not slick, or complicated, or arty. (Oh, we'll go there, too, eventually.) You'd be well served to return here again and again—but these steps are so quick and easy that to do them once is to know them cold.

Up to this point, you've opened files and printed them out, but you haven't changed how they look very much. If you need to fix a photo, come here first. Your quest will probably end here, and you'll be more than satisfied. The shot that looked too dark will perk right up, crooked will become straight, and that unflattering pallor on her face will become a rosy glow.

A particularly handy new feature of Photoshop Elements 2 is the Quick Fix shortcut button, which gives you single-click access to a variety of commonly needed repairs—with automatic corrections. The first task in this part demonstrates its use.

So, if you have time to do only a few of the tasks in this book, choose some of these. You'll be hooked, and you'll recover a lot of shots you thought were duds.

Applying Quick and Easy Fixes

Before

After

Making a Quick Fix

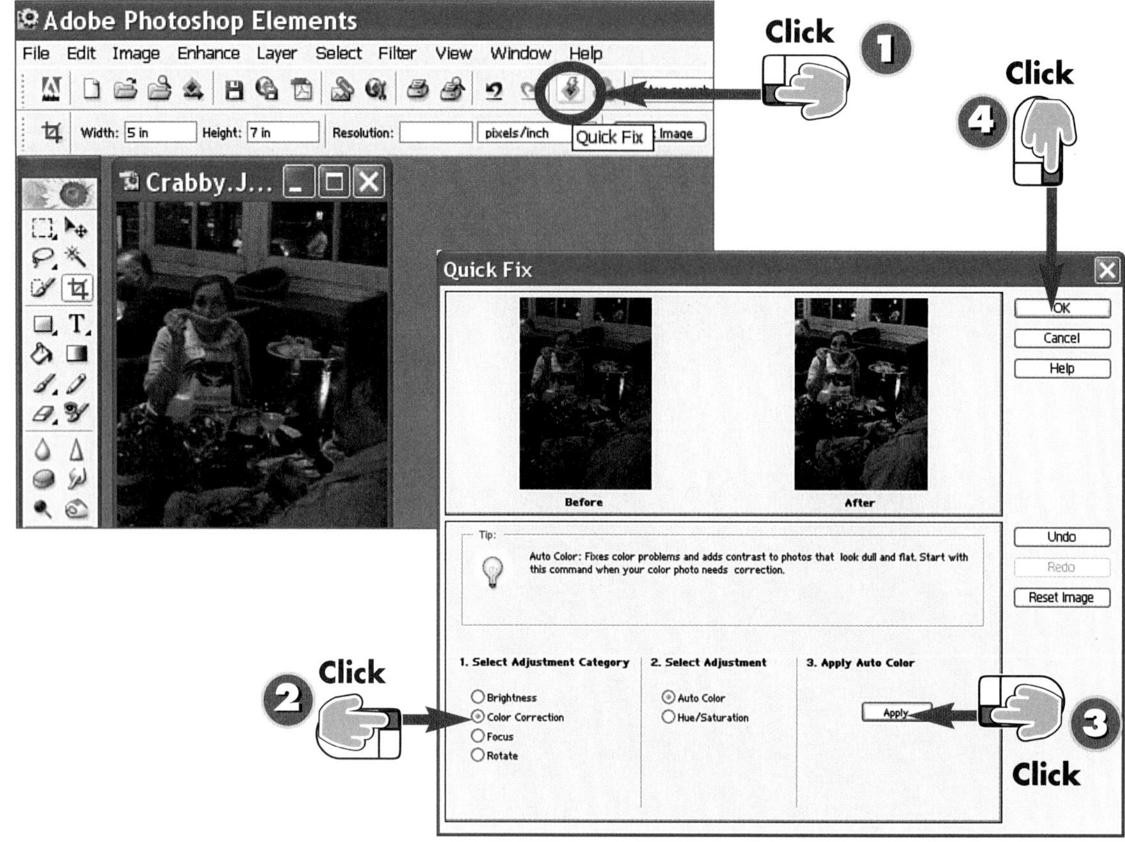

1. With the picture you want to fix in the active image area, click the **Quick Fix** shortcut (or choose **Enhance**, **Quick Fix**).
2. Select an adjustment category, such as **Color Correction** (or accept Brightness, the default).
3. Click **Apply**.
4. Click **OK**.

INTRODUCTION

You can use the Quick Fix dialog box as one-stop-shopping for all the other commands in the Enhance menu, and some others. This multipurpose dialog has commands for adjusting levels (intensity), contrast, overall color correction, lighting, color components, and brightness/contrast, as well as focus and rotation.

HINT

Auto and Semi-Auto Fixes

Any of the Auto adjustments require just a single click of the Apply button, as do Focus/Blur and any of the Rotate or Flip commands. All other commands require some type of slider adjustment (see the next task).

TIP

Don't Like *After?*

If you don't like the result in the After window, click **Undo** and start over. Your changes are cumulative, so you can undo one and then do another until the After image is just right.

Making a Quick Fix with a Slider Adjustment

Start

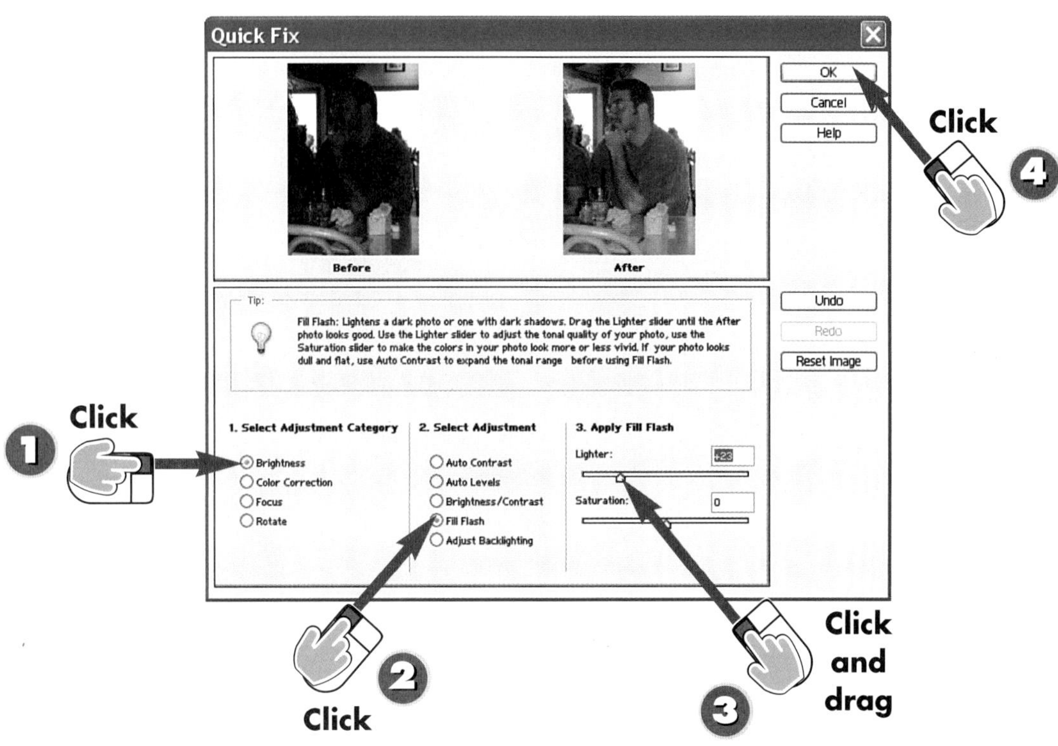

1. In the Quick Fix dialog box, select an adjustment category, such as **Brightness**.
2. Depending on the adjustment category you selected, you'll see related adjustment options. Choose an adjustment, such as **Fill Flash**.
3. If you choose an adjustment that isn't automatic, sliders appear in the third section of the dialog. Adjust them as needed to get the desired result.
4. When you like the result in the After window, click **OK**.

INTRODUCTION

Some commands in the Quick Fix dialog box, such as Auto Contrast, are fully automatic. Others, such as the Brightness/Fill Flash command, require some adjustment. Learn to use the slider controls for these commands so you can get just the effect you want.

HINT

Blown-Out Whites
Applying Fill Flash will probably cause bright background areas such as windows to *blow out*, becoming pure white. Just remember you can't get the detail in blown-out areas back unless you save a copy of the original.

TIP

Applying Backlighting
The command Brightness/Apply Backlighting does the opposite of Fill Flash—it brightens a background that's much darker than the subject (a bad feature of flash photos).

Undoing Your Mistakes

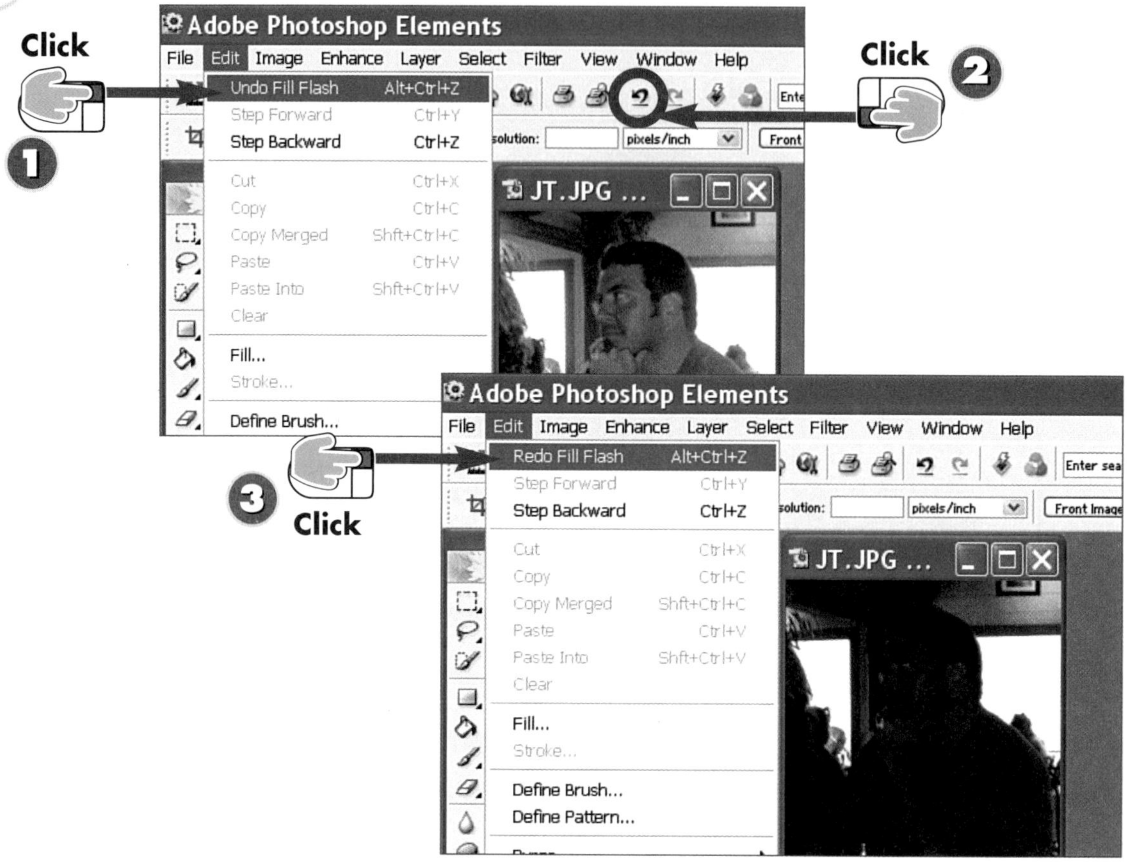

1. Immediately after making any change to the picture in the active image area, choose **Edit**, **Undo**, or press **Alt+Ctrl+Z**.
2. To undo the next-most-recent change, click the **Step Backward** shortcut (or choose **Edit**, **Step Backward**, or press **Ctrl+Z**).
3. To reapply the last change you undid, choose **Edit**, **Redo**, or press **Alt+Ctrl+Z** before you do anything else.

INTRODUCTION

Don't think of any photo-fixing decisions you make as mistakes, for two good reasons: You can always undo them, and experimenting is the only way to learn what works and what doesn't. So, click away—you have nothing to lose but playtime!

TIP

Other Ways to Undo
As alternatives, you can use the Step Backward and Step Forward shortcuts, or open the **Undo History** palette. Right-click the step you want to undo, and select **Delete** (subsequent steps are deleted, too).

TIP

Canceling All Changes
To undo all your changes during a session—*before* you save—choose **File**, **Revert**. The last saved version of the file appears in the active image area.

Cropping a Picture

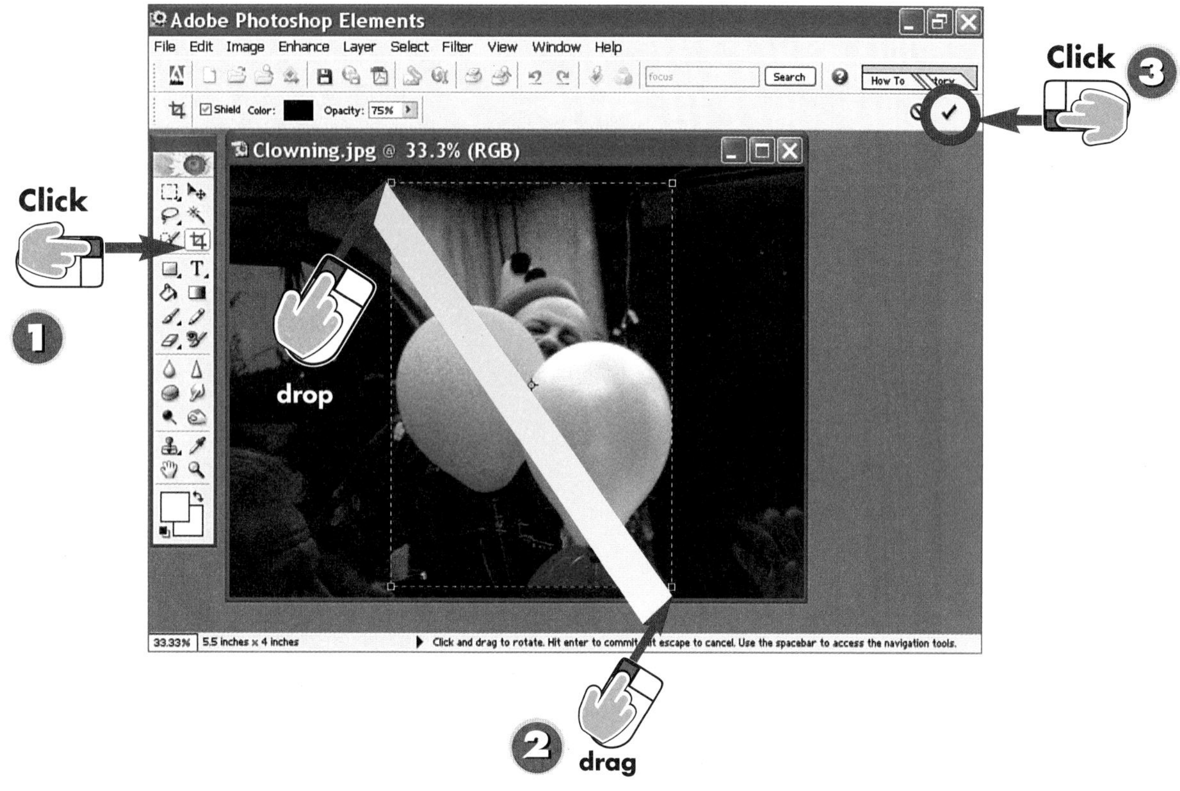

1. Select the **Crop** tool from the toolbox, or press **C**.
2. Within the active image area, drag and drop the corner of a selection box to indicate the new framing.
3. Click the **Commit** button in the options bar, or press **Enter**.

INTRODUCTION

One hallmark of a skilled photographer is pleasing *composition*, or arrangement of the things you're shooting within the picture frame. You can't always take the time to get the composition just right. Cropping used to be one of the most common fixes made in the darkroom—now you can do it with the lights on.

TIP

Adjusting Width and Height

After step 1, type a Width and Height in the options bar to match the proportions (type **5** for Width and **7** for Height for a 5×7 print). Or, pressing **Shift** while dragging forces a perfectly square selection.

TIP

Canceling the Crop

In step 3, to cancel the cropping operation, click the **Cancel** button (just left of the Commit button) in the options bar, or press **Esc**.

Straightening a Crooked Picture

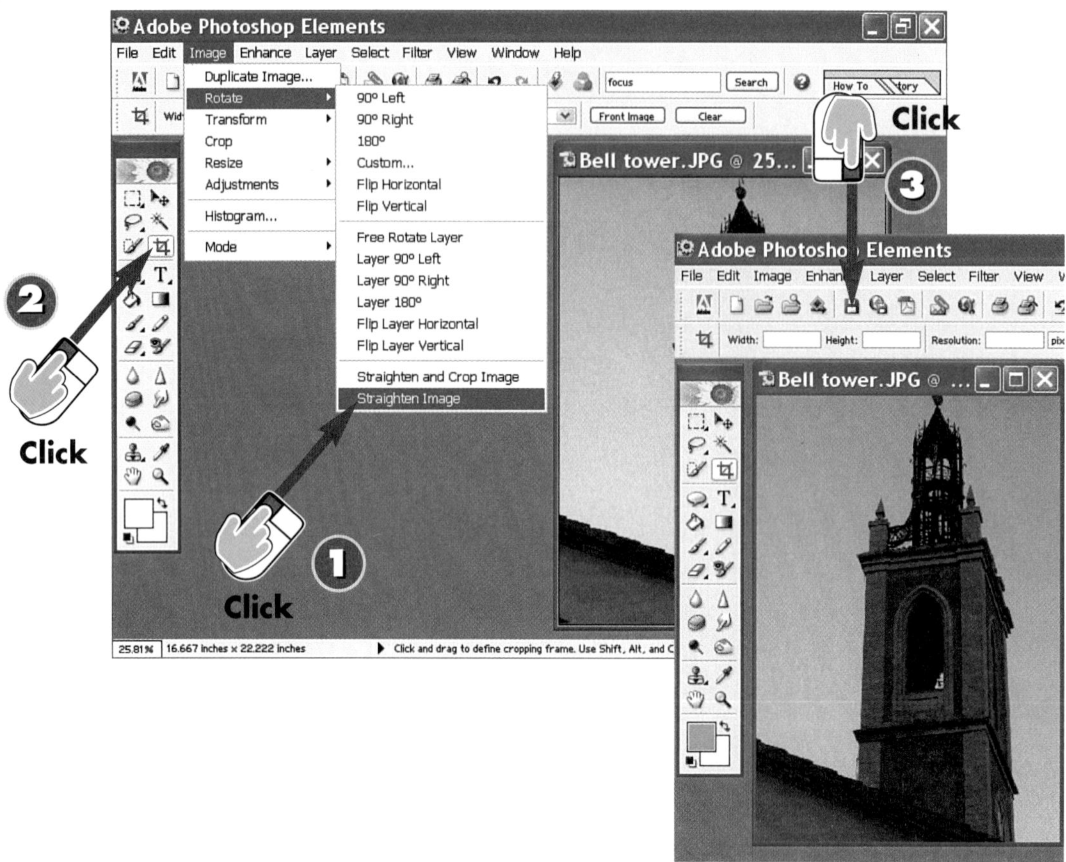

1. With the picture in the active image area, choose **Image**, **Rotate**, **Straighten Image**. The program aligns the image.
2. Crop the photo as desired.
3. Click the **Save** shortcut to save your changes.

INTRODUCTION

This type of automatic straightening works best when the subject is just slightly out of alignment—a tower that appears to be leaning, for example. The program finds a strong vertical or horizontal line in the image and aligns it on the nearest 90° angle.

TIP

Severely Off-Angle?
If the subject is severely off angle, use one of the **Image**, **Rotate** or **Image**, **Transform** commands instead.

TIP

Straighten *and* Crop
As an alternative, the program can both straighten *and* crop automatically (choose **Image**, **Rotate**, **Straighten and Crop Image**). But you'll be happier with the results if you crop it yourself.

Rotating an Image on Opening

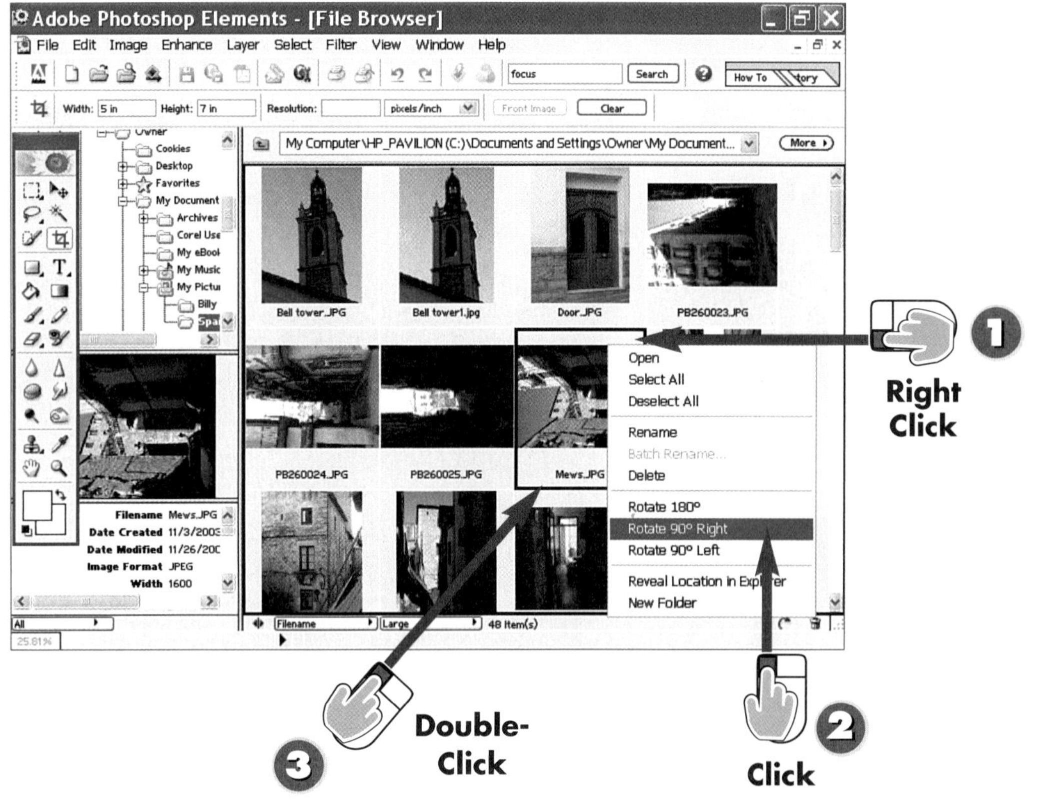

1. In the File Browser, right-click the thumbnail of the picture you want to rotate.
2. Select a rotation angle, such as **Rotate 90° Right**. (If you see a message screen, click **OK**.)
3. Double-click the thumbnail to open the file for editing.

INTRODUCTION

Like film cameras, digital cameras take all pictures in landscape orientation—with the long side of the frame horizontal. To take a portrait, you must physically rotate the camera. The most common reason to rotate an image in Photoshop Elements is so that you can view it correctly for editing and printing.

TIP

Quick and Easy Rotation

This method of rotating a picture has the same effect as selecting one of the **Image**, **Rotate** commands from the menu bar. But you'll find it's more convenient for quickly rotating all your portrait shots.

If you Ctrl+click multiple thumbnails before you do step 1, you can apply the same rotation to multiple shots with a single command. But you must then open the files individually.

Rotating an Image for Artistic Effect

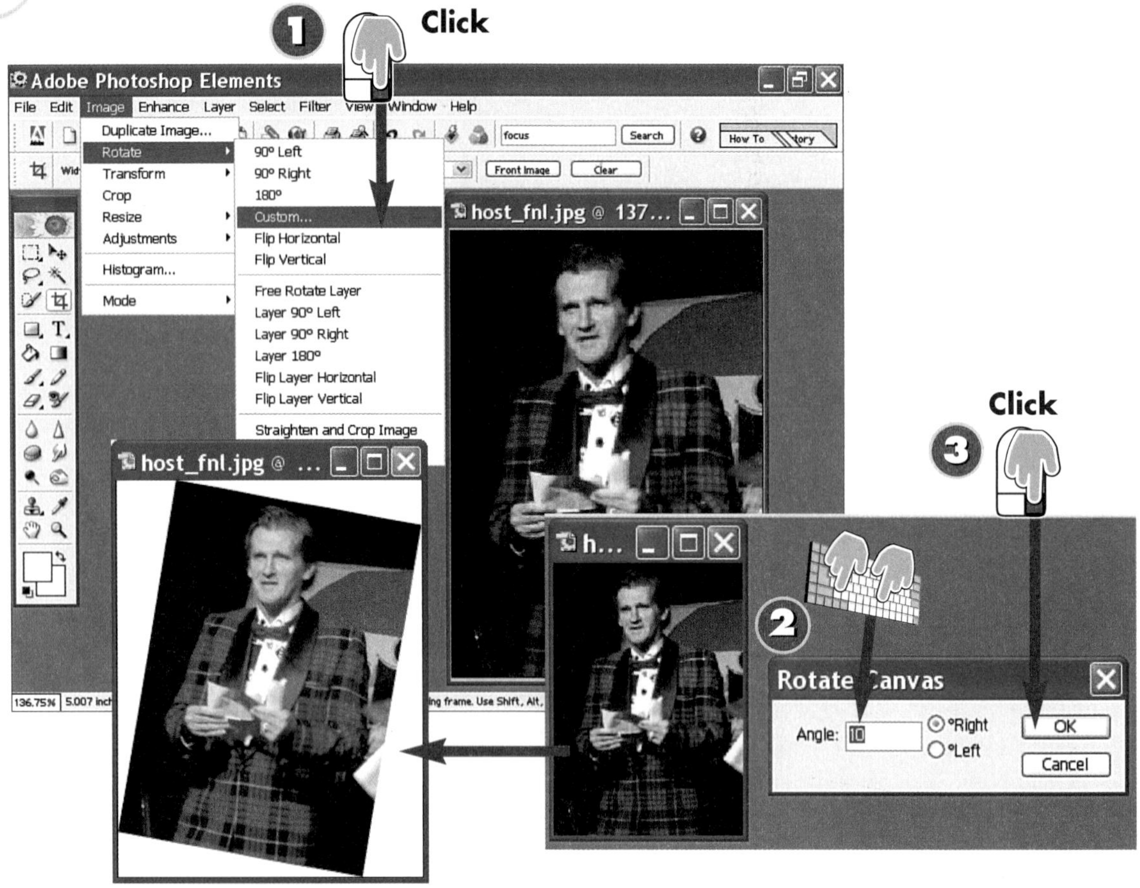

1. With the picture in the active image area, choose **Image**, **Rotate**, **Custom**.
2. In the **Angle** box, type a rotation angle in degrees (clockwise from 12 o'clock; or, click **Left** for counterclockwise rotation).
3. Click **OK**.

INTRODUCTION

Graphic artists call this type of rotation a *Dutch angle*. Perhaps the most familiar example is the nightclub poster with rotated glamour portraits of the performers. It's a great technique for adding flair to greeting cards and family Web pages.

HINT

Auto-Adjust Canvas Size
Photoshop Elements automatically increases the canvas size to create a frame large enough to hold the rotated picture without reducing the image size. The area outside the picture is the current background color.

TIP

Continuous Rotation
As an alternative, you can choose **Image**, **Rotate**, **Free Rotate Layer** and drag a corner to rotate the image continuously. However, this way does *not* increase the canvas size, and some cropping of the picture corners occurs.

Resizing and Resampling an Image

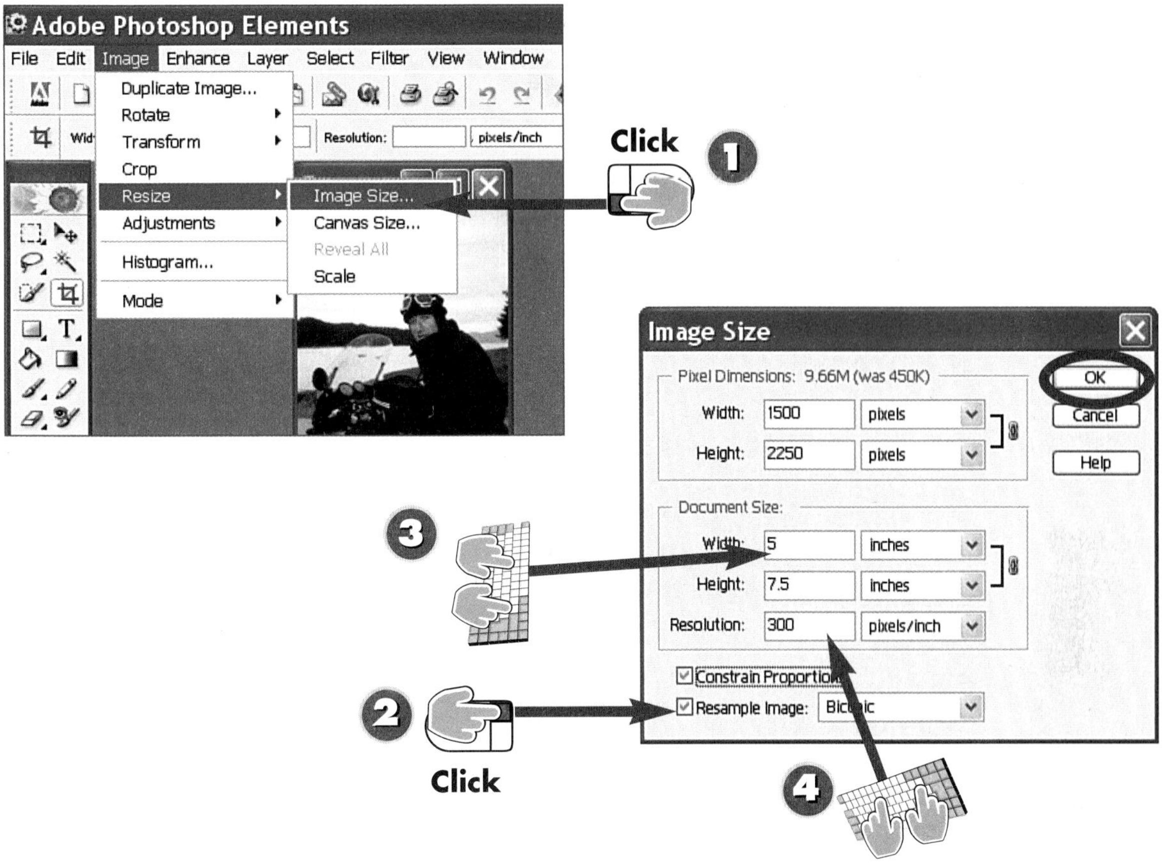

1. With a picture in the active image area, choose **Image**, **Resize**, **Image Size**.

2. Click **Resample Image**.

3. Type a new Width in the box, in decimal units (such as inches).

4. Select the **Resolution** box and type a new numeric value, such as **300** pixels/inch. Click **OK**.

INTRODUCTION

Digital photos are composed of a finite number of pixels. Resizing and resampling often go hand in hand: If you increase the size of an image, the result can look coarse unless you resample it to increase the resolution. If you reduce the image size, it decreases the resolution, resulting in a smaller file size.

HINT

Enter Width *or* Height

In step 3, enter Width or Height, but not both. If you enter one, the program calculates the other so that the image isn't distorted. The Resolution value should be 72 for email or the Web, 150–300 for making prints with a color inkjet.

HINT

Bicubic Is Best

For all but the slowest computers or very large images, leave the Resample Image option set to Bicubic, which gives the highest-quality result. Bilinear, which takes less processing time, is the next-best choice.

Transforming Image Perspective

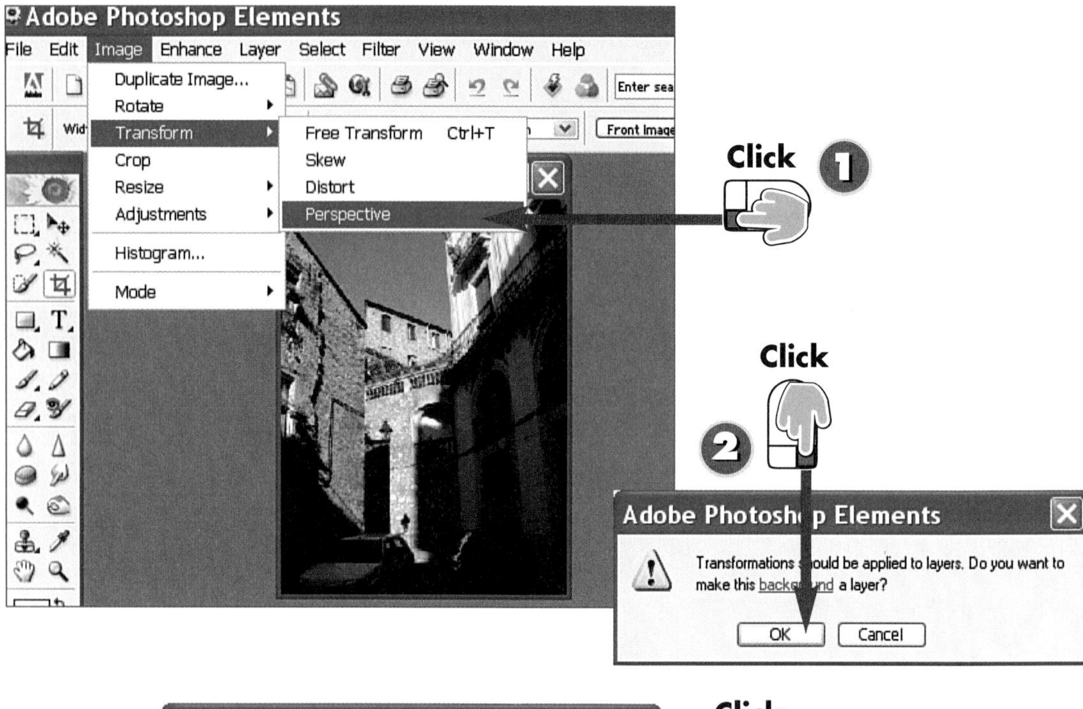

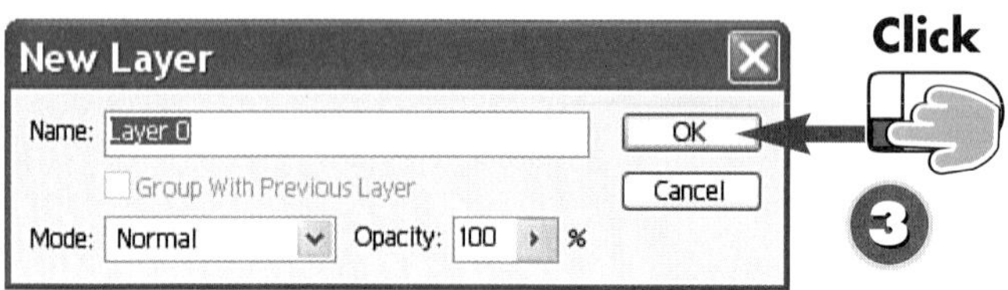

1. With a picture in the active image area, choose **Image**, **Transform**, **Perspective**.
2. Click **OK** on the warning dialog box.
3. The layer is automatically named Layer 0. Click **OK**.

INTRODUCTION

The Image, Transform submenu actually has three other commands besides Perspective: Free Transform, Skew, and Distort. But you apply them all the same way—by dragging picture corners. Try each of them using these steps to see how their effects differ.

TIP

Severe Distortion?
Severe distortion on subjects such as tall buildings results not only from perspective but also from an effect of optical lenses called barrel distortion—which adds curvature.

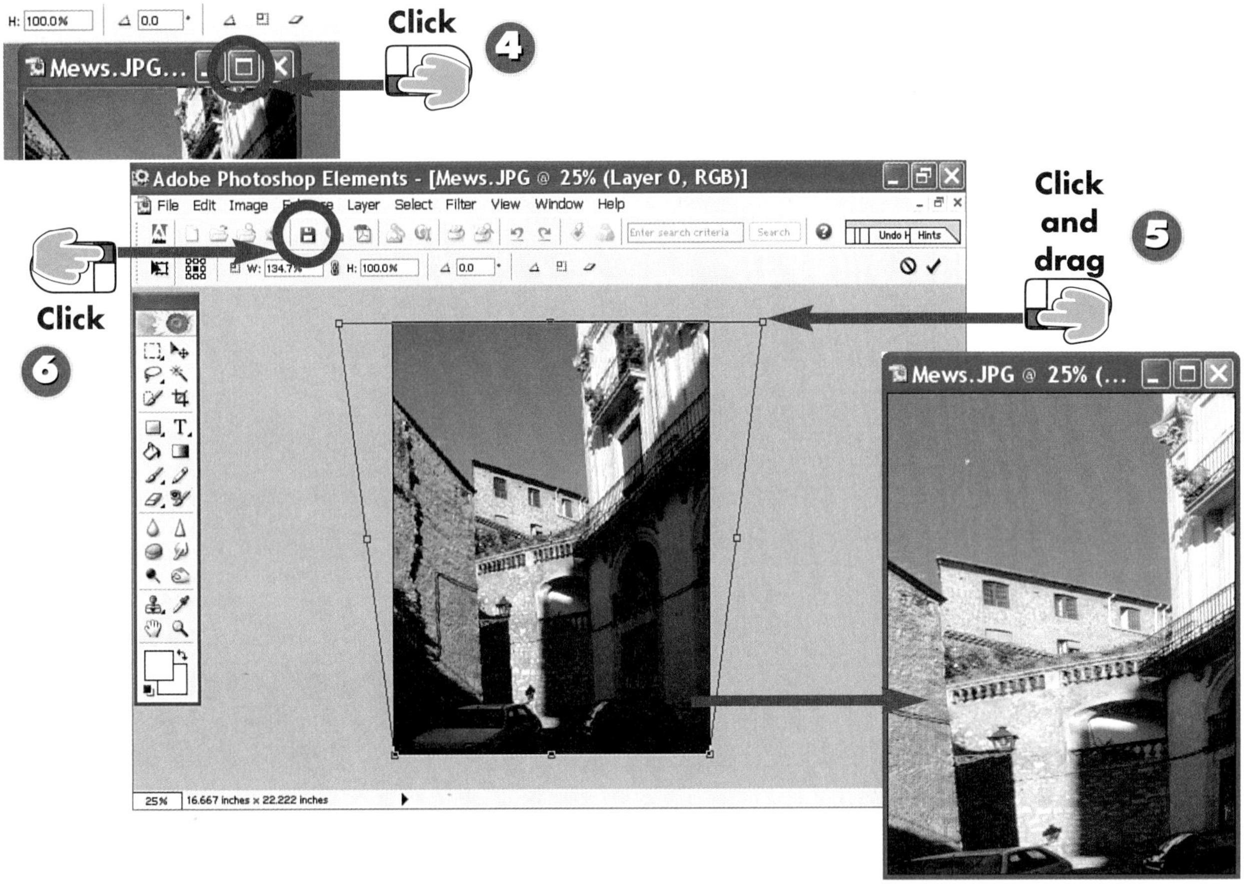

4. Click the **Maximize** button to enlarge the active image area.

5. Click and drag a corner to adjust the perspective.

6. **Save** the transformed image.

HINT

Watch for Keystoning
Keystoning, another type of distortion, results from aiming the camera either up or down at a severe angle. To compensate for keystoning, drag the corner in step 5 that's nearest the pinched end of the subject outward.

HINT

Don't Squish Your Folks
Be careful that in removing distortion from one part of a picture, such as the slope of a building, you don't add distortion in another part—squishing cars or, worse, the faces of your loved ones.

Adding a White Border to Your Prints

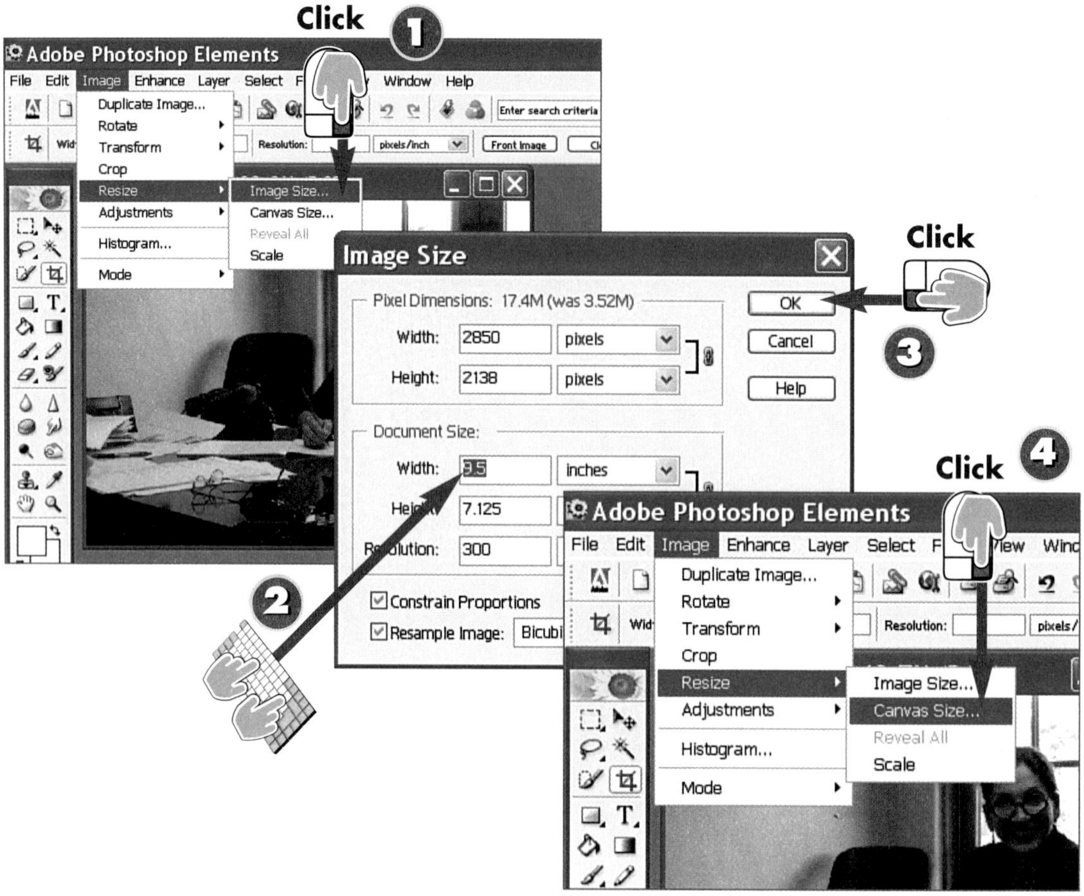

1. With a picture in the active image area, choose **Image**, **Resize**, **Image Size**.
2. Type the new image Width as a decimal, such as **9.5** inches.
3. Click **OK**.
4. Choose **Image**, **Resize**, **Canvas Size**.

INTRODUCTION

A good way to add a white border to your prints involves resizing the image to be smaller than the canvas (paper) size by the amount of the margin you want, and centering the image on the canvas.

TIP

When to Resample
In step 2, check **Resample Image** and increase the resolution if the number in the Resolution field is less than 150. To avoid distorting the image, let the program calculate the height.

TIP

Yet Another Way
To add a white border without resizing the canvas, choose **File**, **Print Preview**. Check the **Show More Options** check box; then click the **Border** button. You can specify the width of the border in inches, millimeters, or points.

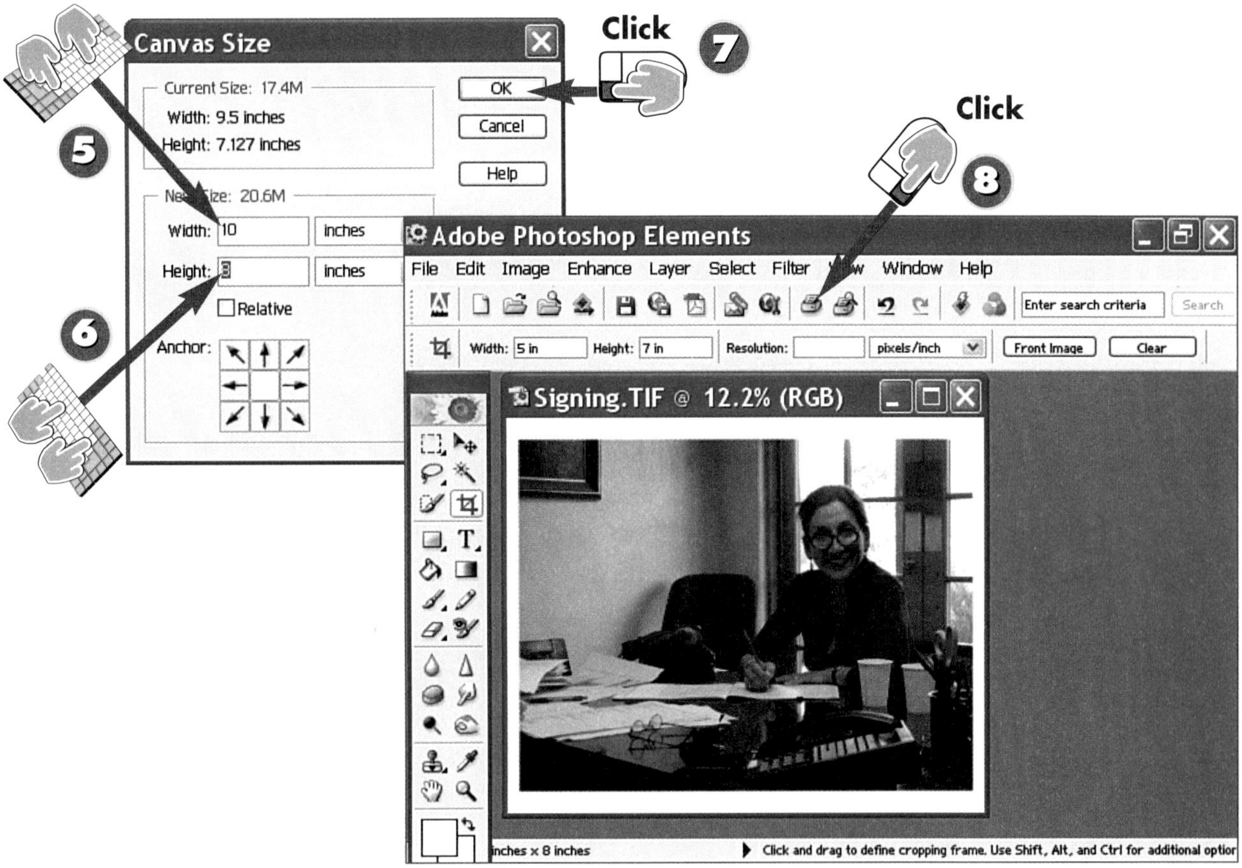

5. In the **Width** box, type the width of the print paper—larger than the image width—such as **10** inches.

6. In the **Height** box, type the height of the paper, such as **8** inches.

7. Click **OK**.

8. Load the printer with photo paper and click **Print**.

HINT

Note the Printable Area
The border becomes part of the image file, so you shouldn't have to adjust print margins as long as the *printable area* of your paper matches the canvas size. Use these steps to add borders to the pictures you print with the File, Print Layouts, Picture Package command, which uses standard print sizes.

HINT

What's the Anchor Point?
The *anchor point* indicates the position of the image relative to the canvas edges. The default is centered. Also remember that most printers can't make borderless prints, so you'll have to allow for the printer's built-in margins.

Removing "Red Eye" in Flash Photos

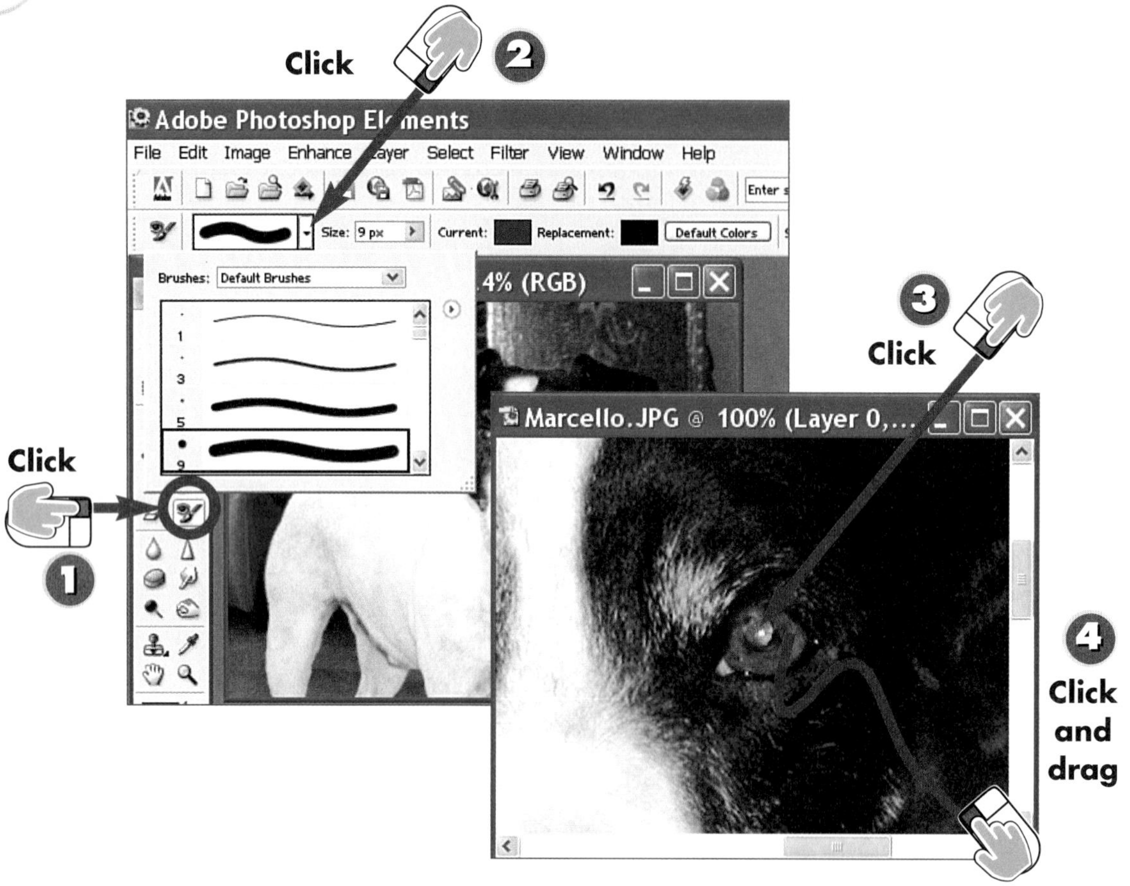

1. With the photo that needs fixing in the active image area, select the **Red Eye Brush** tool, or press **Y**.
2. In the options bar, open the **Brushes** drop-down menu. (Select a brush size slightly larger than the red area in the eye.)
3. Click the red area in the photo to select the color you want to remove.
4. Click and drag over the red area, as if using tiny strokes with an eraser.

INTRODUCTION

The telltale red-eye effect happens when the flash is mounted on or built into the camera and the subject is looking directly into the lens. The retina of the eye bounces the light right back. Take these steps to dispel those smoldering looks.

HINT

Zooming Will Help
This task is much easier if you *zoom* your view of the eye so that you can see the detail before you apply the brush. If the effect is tiny, you may be able to wash it out with a single click—no scrubbing.

HINT

Multicolored Reflections?
Remember that this command only replaces a single color. Red-eye reflections may actually be multicolored. Repeat these steps for each individual color you need to remove.

Correcting a Color Cast

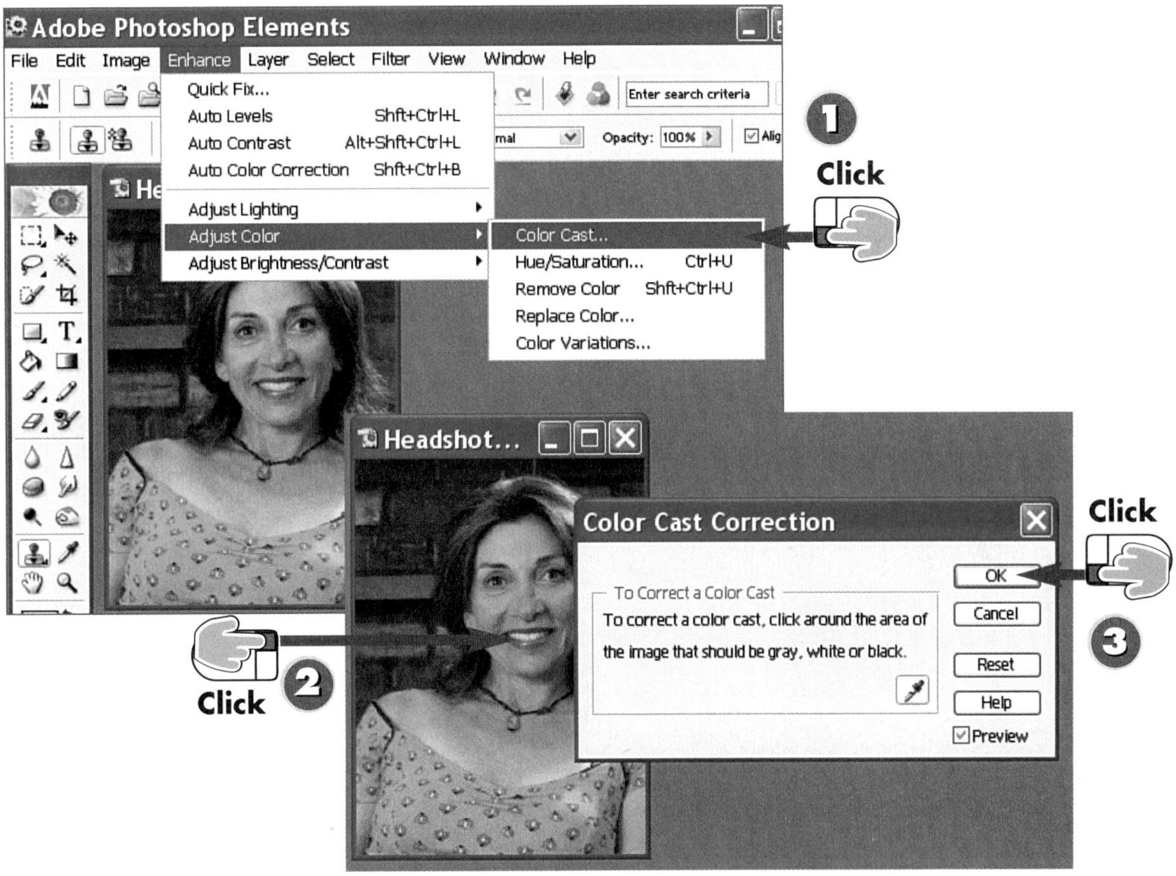

1. With a picture in the active image area, choose **Enhance**, **Adjust Color**, **Color Cast**.

2. Click an area of the image that should be white.

3. Click **OK**.

INTRODUCTION

If a photo has an undesirable overall tint, the camera's *automatic white balance* function didn't do its job well. Daylight has a blue cast, light bulbs indoors make everything orange, and fluorescents can make faces a sickly green. This command compensates by rebalancing all the colors in the picture in relation to pure white.

HINT

Pick Pure White

In step 2, pick an area such as teeth, white of the eye, or a white tablecloth or shirt collar. Any blown-out (overexposed) area usually gives the best result. If there's no white anywhere in the picture, click a neutral area (gray or black).

Selecting Color Variations

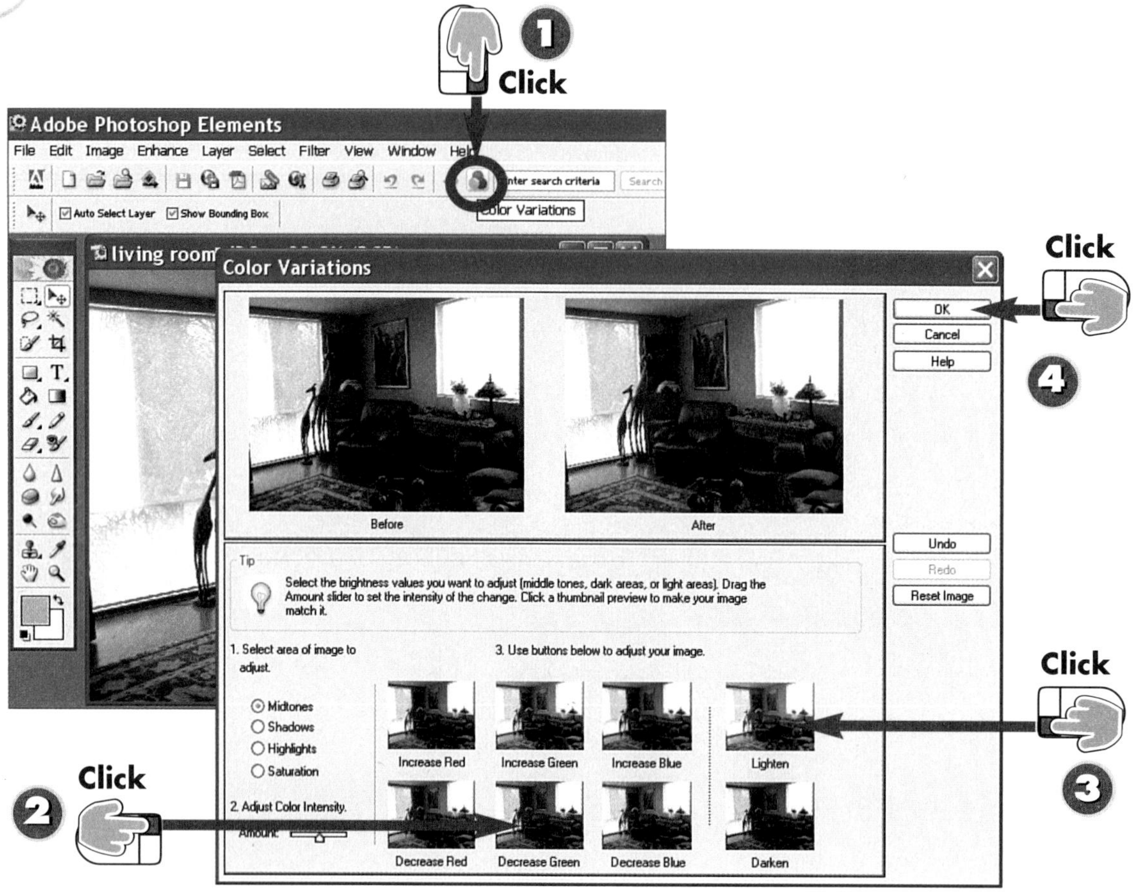

1. With a picture in the active image area, click the **Color Variations** button.
2. Click a thumbnail, such as **Decrease Green**, to change color or brightness in the shot.
3. Repeat the same selection to increase its effect, or make any other selection, such as **Lighten**, for a combined effect.
4. When the After image looks right, click **OK**.

INTRODUCTION

Perhaps it's not that the colors in the picture are wrong, you'd just like to see them different. For example, an interior decorator might want to view a room in a different light or with the decor a different shade. Experiment with color variations, which can be more dramatic than just correcting the overall cast.

TIP

Adjust Midtones First

Of the selections Midtones, Shadows, Highlights, and Saturation, Midtones (values ranging between shadows and highlights) usually give you the most noticeable results. To change the magnitude of an effect, drag the **Adjust Color Intensity** slider before you apply it.

Replacing a Specific Color

Click and drag 3

Click 1

2 Click and drag

4 Click

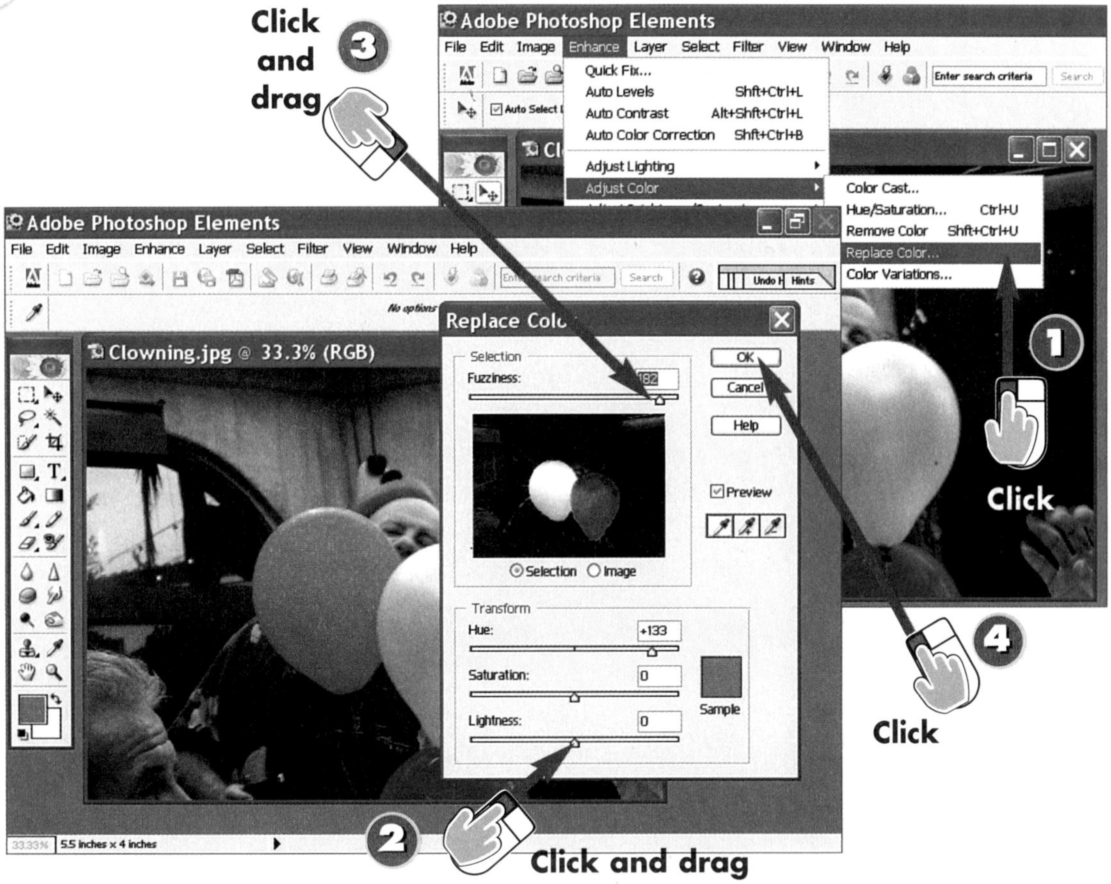

1. With a picture in the active image area, choose **Enhance**, **Adjust Color**, **Replace Color**.
2. Click within an area in the picture; then click and drag the **Transform** sliders until you see the color you want in the Sample box.
3. Click and drag the **Fuzziness** slider to recolor all similar shades in the selection.
4. Click **OK**.

INTRODUCTION

Don't like the color of that dress? Does the sofa clash with the drapes? Want to make the sky pink or the river run green? You can make it so at no extra charge—with your choices limited only by your fashion sense.

TIP

Add or Subtract
Click the **Add to Sample** or **Subtract from Sample** eyedroppers (marked with + and –) and click the area in the picture to add or remove it. Then, dragging the Transform sliders applies the color change to the entire selection.

HINT

What Changes?
These steps change all instances of the same color anywhere in the image, not just on the area you select in step 2.

Adjusting Brightness and Contrast

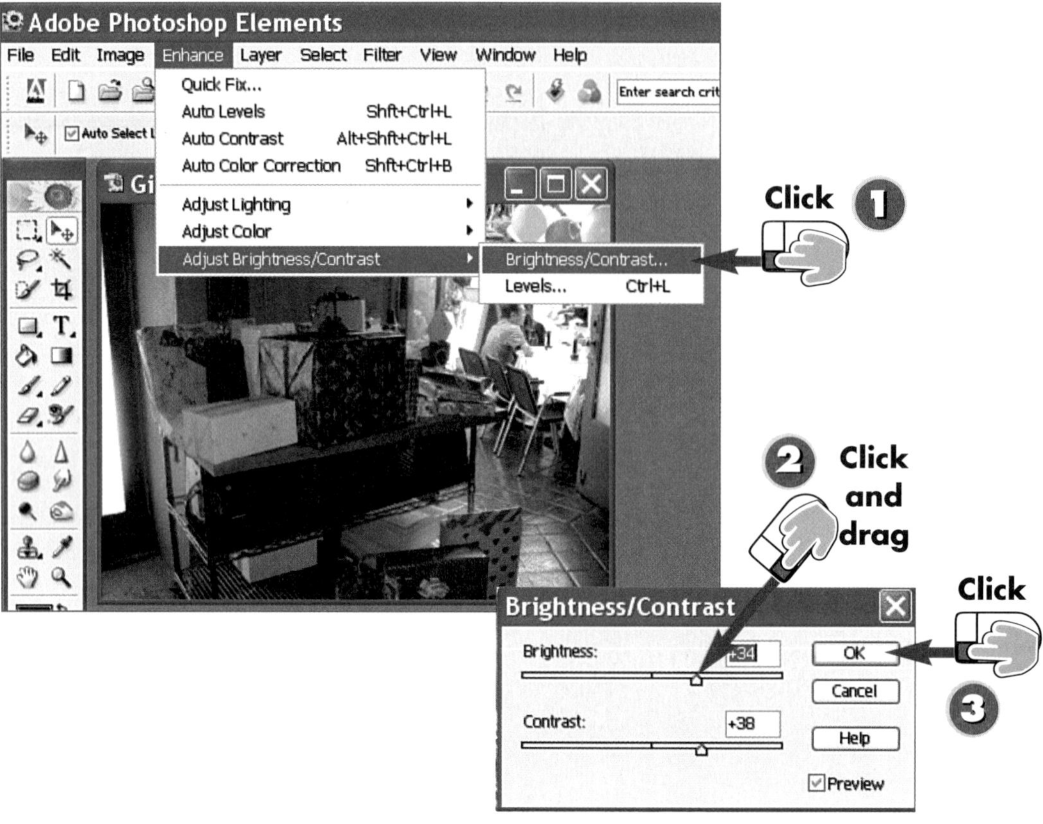

1. With a picture in the active image area, choose **Enhance**, **Adjust Brightness/Contrast**, **Brightness/Contrast**.
2. Click and drag one or both sliders, **Brightness** and/or **Contrast**, until the picture looks right.
3. Click **OK**.

INTRODUCTION

Sometimes a Quick Fix like Auto Contrast just doesn't do the trick—especially if the image has bright highlights, deep shadows, or both. These steps give you more control so that you can make continuous adjustments while previewing the result.

TIP

Overall Change
Changing brightness and contrast affects the entire image unless you select a particular area first. Selection tools are Rectangular Marquee (for rectangular areas), Lasso (for irregular areas), and Magic Wand (for intricate shapes).

HINT

Subject in the Dark?
If your subject is too dark overall (underexposed), try the Fill Flash fix first. It boosts brightness only in the darker areas, leaving the lighter areas—usually, the background—alone.

Changing a Color Photo to Black and White

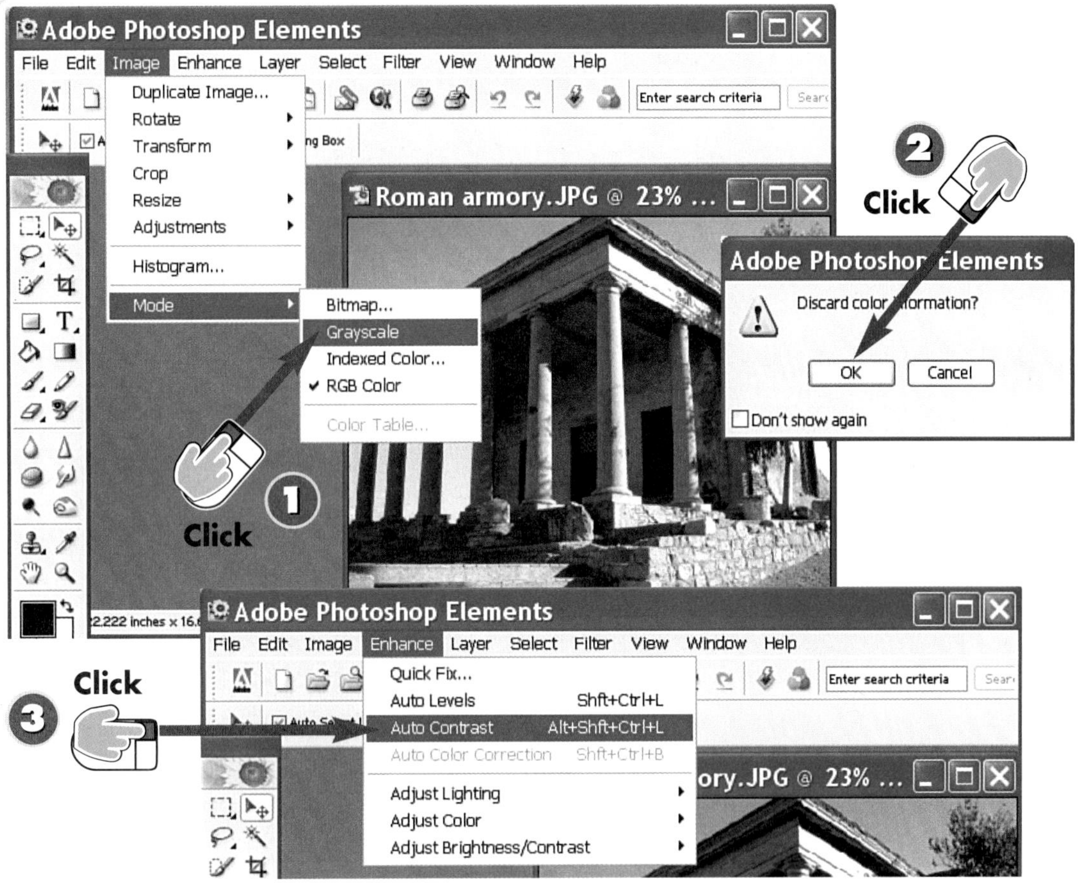

1. With a color picture in the active image area, choose **Image**, **Mode**, **Grayscale**.
2. Click **OK**.
3. Choose **Enhance**, **Auto Contrast**.

INTRODUCTION

You'll occasionally need black-and-white pictures for newsletters that will be printed one-color—or perhaps when you're in a vintage-movie kind of mood. You can easily convert your color shots to B&W, but remember to finish by adjusting the contrast to make them suitably snappy.

TIP

Sepia (a brownish monochrome) is actually a color effect. After converting to B&W and adjusting contrast, repeat the **Image**, **Mode** command and select **RGB Color**; then apply one or more **Color Variations**.

Sharpening Focus

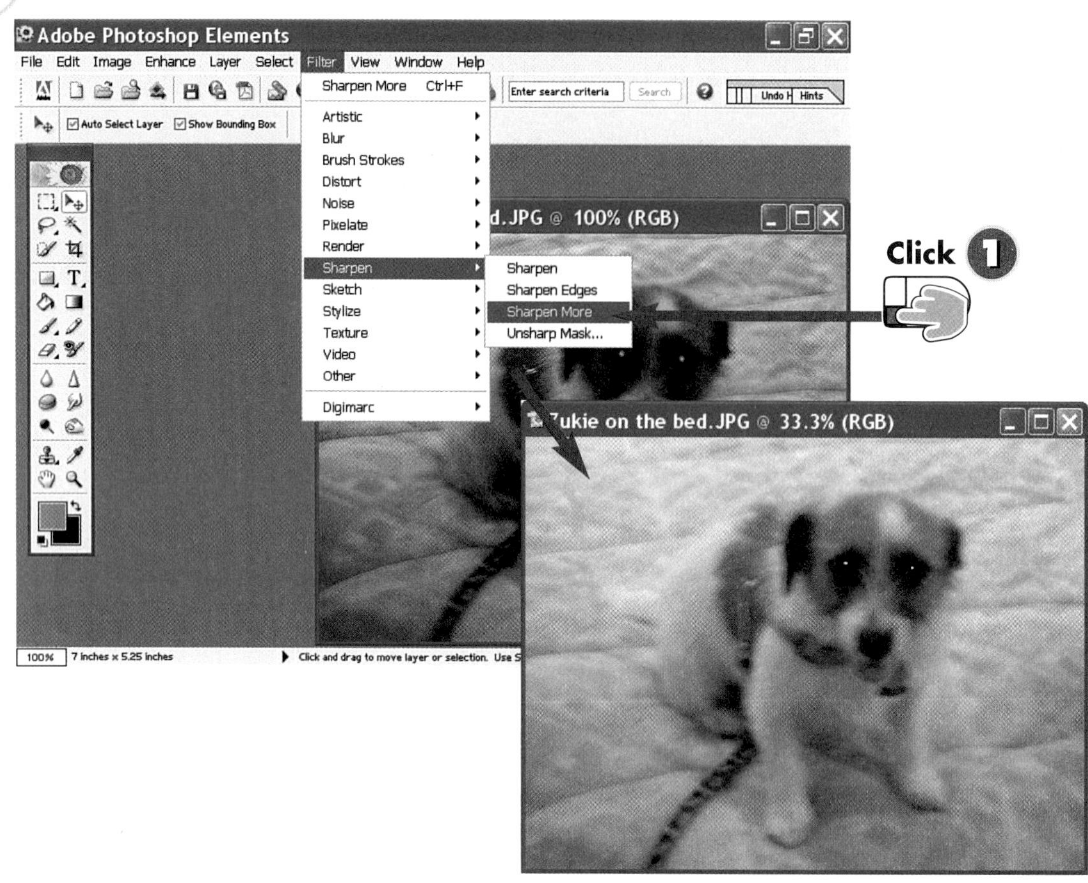

1 With a picture in the active image area, choose **Filter**, **Sharpen**, **Sharpen More**.

INTRODUCTION

Digital cameras have an *auto-focus* feature, which attempts to make the edges of the subject in the center of the frame as sharp as possible. It doesn't always work. For more consistent results, learn how to focus manually. But you can always try this simple step to sharpen shots that are slightly blurred.

HINT

Focus Manually

The Sharpen command can improve the look of a blurred shot somewhat, but it's no substitute for proper manual focusing. That's particularly true when you're doing *closeups*—with the subject less than four feet away.

TIP

Don't Overdo It

This task uses Sharpen More because you might not see much of a difference from the original when you use the Sharpen submenu command. And Sharpen Edges can overdo it.

Making Edges Softer

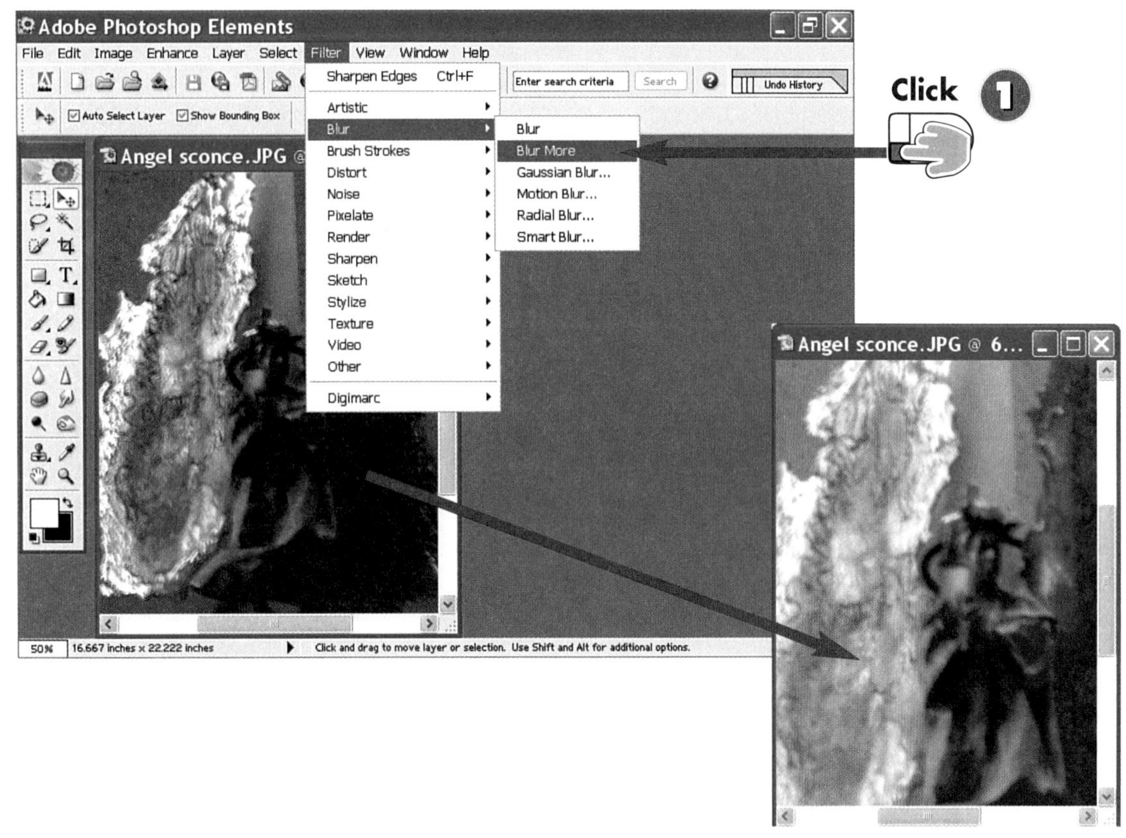

1 With a picture in the active image area, choose **Filter**, **Blur**, **Blur More**.

INTRODUCTION

There are at least two good reasons to soften focus: It can make a portrait look more flattering, blending out lines, pores, and small blemishes; and it can save a shot that's only slightly out of focus—making the softness look more deliberate.

TIP

An Artful Blur

This task uses Blur More because the result of the Blur command in the submenu can be hard to see. The other Blur commands in the submenu are for when you're feeling arty.

Selecting and Coloring Shapes in the Shot

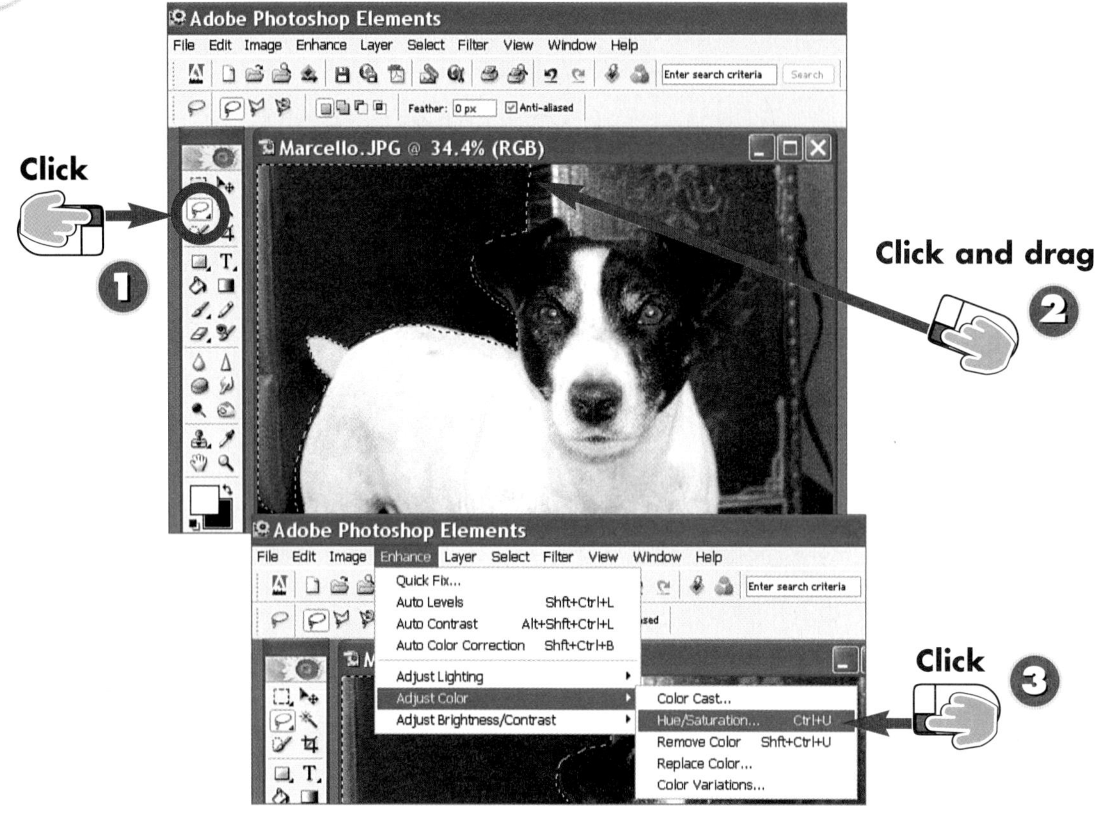

1. With a picture in the active image area, select the **Lasso** tool.
2. Click and drag in the image to trace the outline of the area you want to change.
3. Choose **Enhance**, **Adjust Color**, **Hue/Saturation**.

INTRODUCTION

By using one of the selection tools first, you can apply any of the color, brightness, and level commands to specific areas within an image. In this example, a portion of the background didn't contrast well with the subject, so it was recolored.

HINT

Practice Your Selections

Using the selection tools to capture just the pixels you want to change and no others is a mark of skill with Photoshop Elements. Remember, you can use the selection tools in any sequence for a combined result, to add or subtract from the current selection.

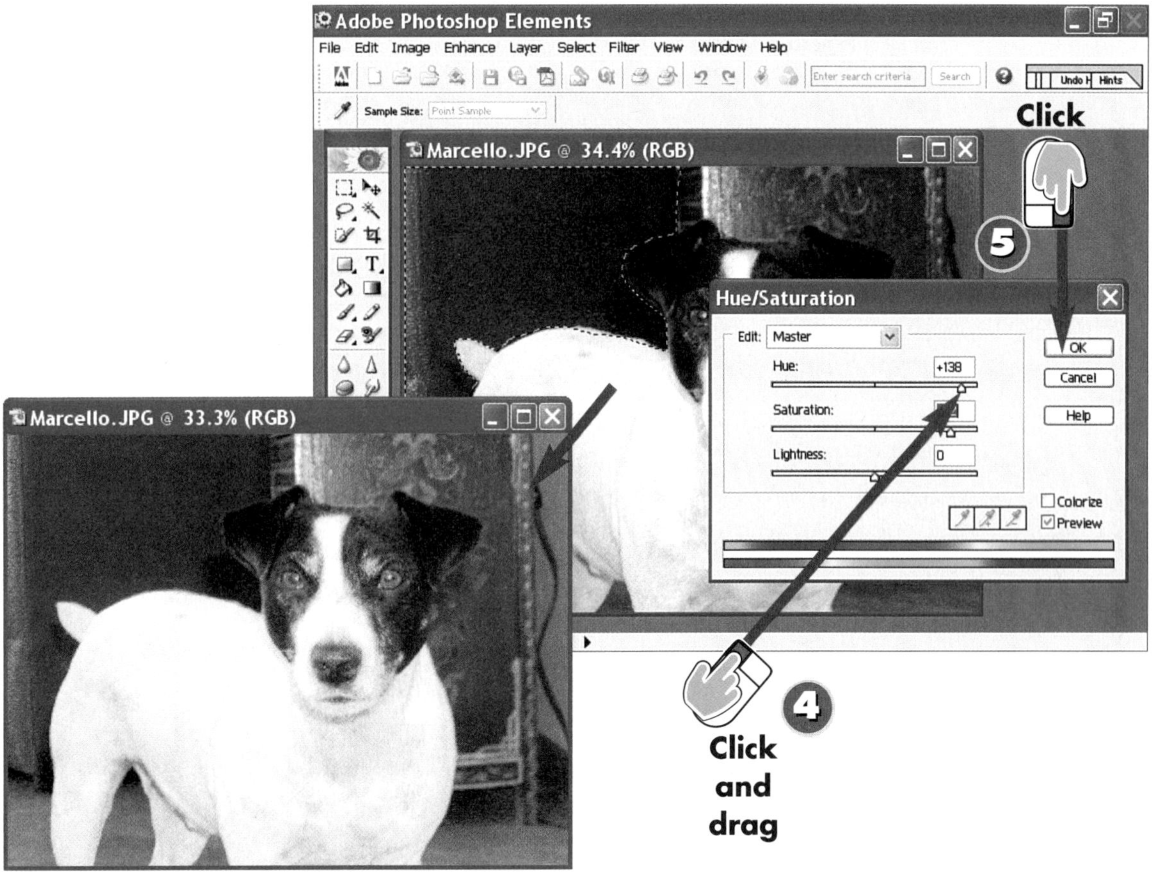

Click

Click and drag

4. Click and drag one or more sliders, such as **Hue**, to adjust the color of the selected area.

5. Click **OK**.

HINT

Colorizing Gets Garish

Checking the Colorize box in the Hue/Saturation window gives you a wider range of colors, many of them garish. By decreasing Saturation, you can also experiment with the Colorize option to create *duo-tone* (two-color) pictures.

HINT

Using the Eyedroppers

In step 4, the eyedroppers become available when you select something other than Master in the Edit drop-down box. Do this to adjust primary colors separately in the image, or to recolor specific areas you sample with the eyedropper.

PART 4

Adding Titles and Text

Being able to print text on your photos can turn your digital snaps into greeting cards, invitations, postcards, or posters.

An interesting photo with a caption can be a news item for a community newsletter or family Web site.

And even if you don't aspire to craft your own greetings or write your own news, including captions in your picture files is a much better way of identifying and describing your photos than writing on the back of the prints with a ballpoint pen.

As you gain skill working with text, you'll want the flexibility of keeping different pieces of text on separate *layers*, which work like clear sheets of acetate you can draw on. Layers permit you to add text and artwork without making any permanent changes to the underlying image. So be sure to take a look at the tasks in Part 9, "Using Layers to Combine Photos and Artwork."

And don't worry. None of this is complicated. Photoshop Element's built-in features help you create professional-looking output, whether it be for a Web site or picture postcard, without having to sweat the technical details.

Say It with Pictures and Words

Adding a caption can give a photo "news value."

Why not think of your life as a movie—and you're the star!

Adding and Printing Photo Captions

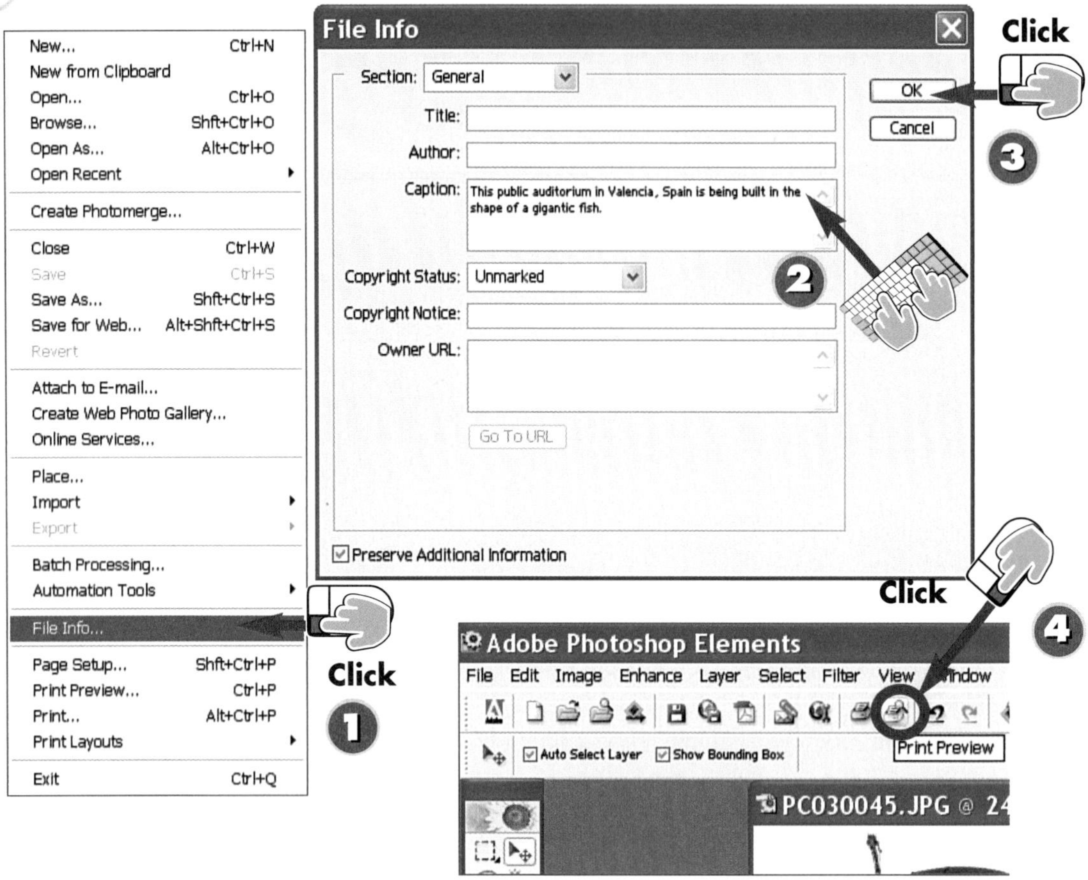

1. With the picture in the active image area, choose **File**, **File Info**.
2. Type a descriptive caption in the **Caption** text box.
3. Click **OK**.
4. From the shortcuts bar, click the **Print Preview** button (or choose **File**, **Print Preview**).

INTRODUCTION

This method of adding a caption to a photo stores the text information with the image file. When you check the Caption check box in the Print Preview dialog box, your photo prints with the caption outside the image area, centered beneath it.

HINT

Dear Diary...
In step 2, the Caption text box can hold about 25 double-spaced pages. That's enough to paste a whole text document from the Clipboard. You could use it to hold your journal entries from a trip, for example.

HINT

Title and Author Boxes
You can also type entries into the Title and Author boxes seen on the File Info dialog. However, only the Caption box is printed by this procedure.

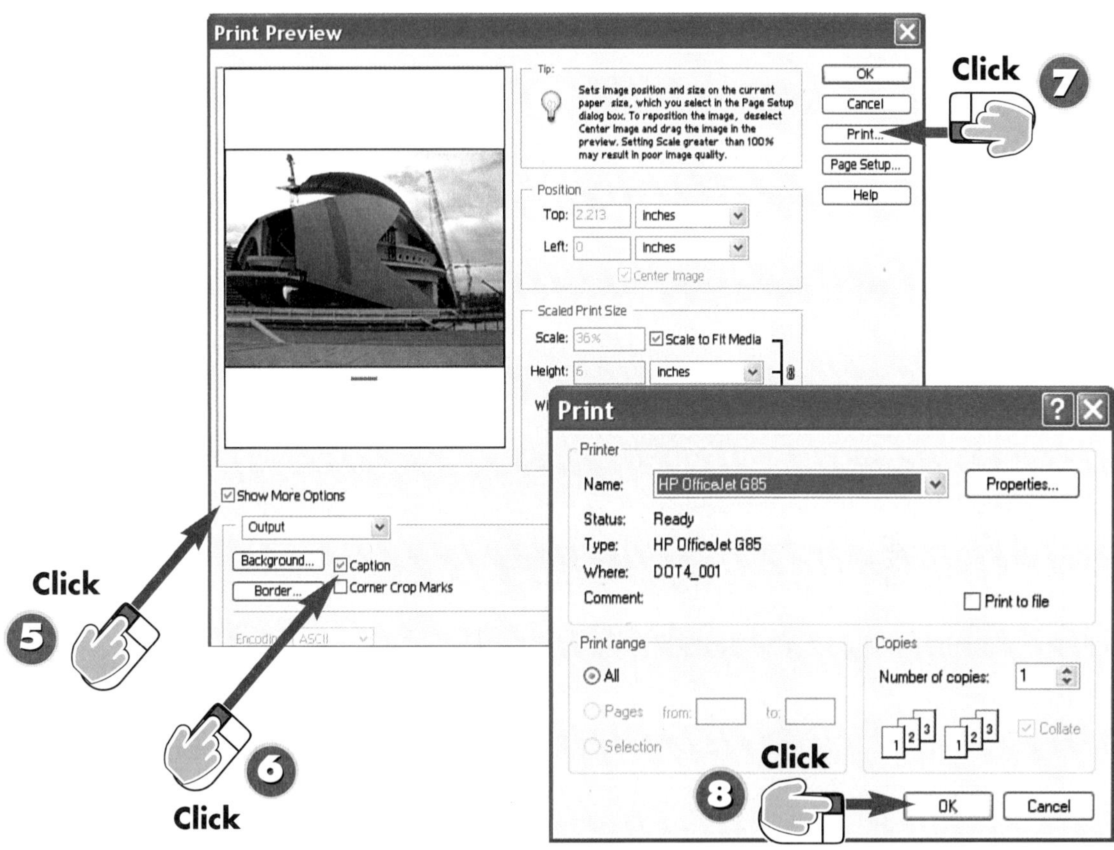

5. Check the **Show More Options** check box.

6. Check the **Caption** check box.

7. Click **Print**.

8. Click **OK** in the Print dialog box.

HINT

Caption Position

The position of the caption as it will appear relative to the image on the printed page appears beneath the thumbnail in the Print Preview dialog box.

HINT

Scale to Fit Media

If you haven't sized the image to fit the canvas and the canvas to the paper size, check **Scale to Fit Media** in the Print Preview dialog box, and Photoshop Elements will fit to the paper size currently selected for the printer.

Adding Text to Prints in a Picture Package

1 Click

2 Click

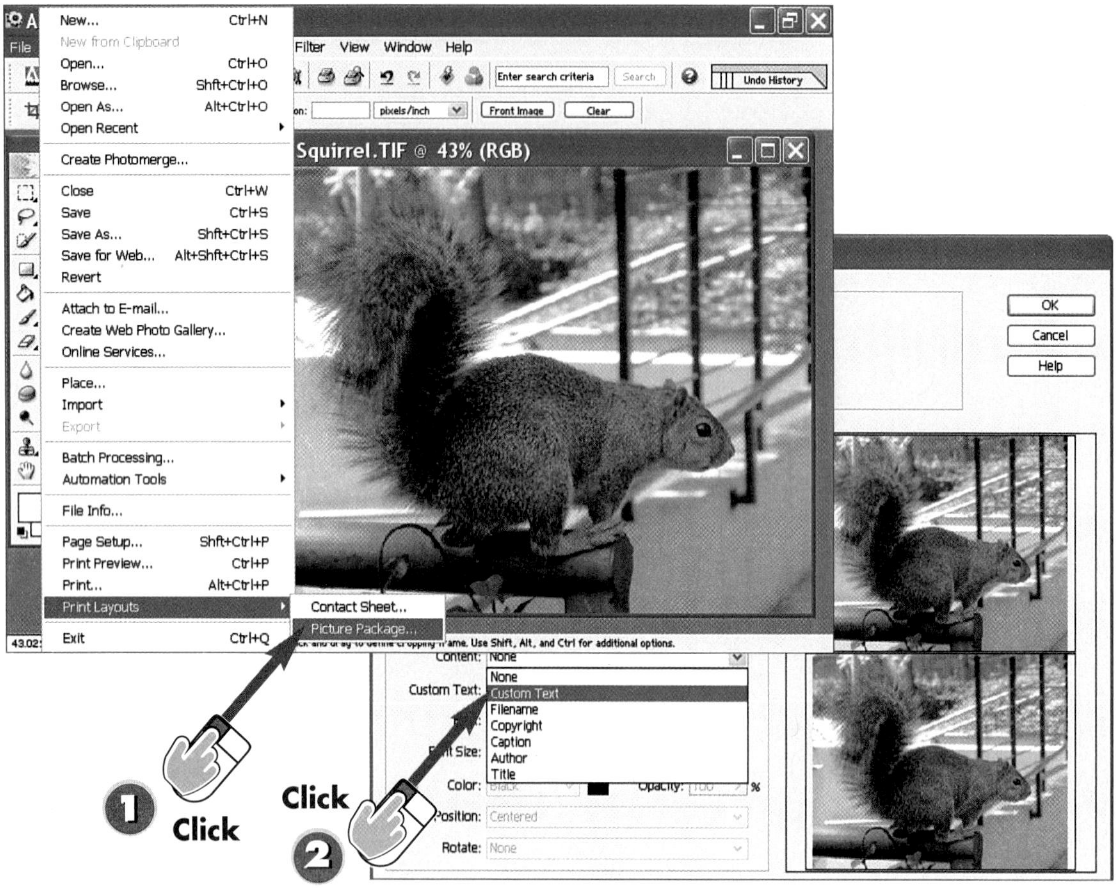

1. With a picture in the active image area, choose **File**, **Print Layouts**, **Picture Package**.

2. Select **Custom Text** from the Content drop-down menu.

INTRODUCTION

Entering Custom Text as described here causes captions to overlay the picture—to be printed inside the image area—when it's printed by the Picture Package command.

TIP

The Caption Option

Selecting Caption instead of Custom Text in step 2 causes the text to be printed outside the image area. But if you do that, you can't enter text here. You must use the File Info procedure described in the preceding task.

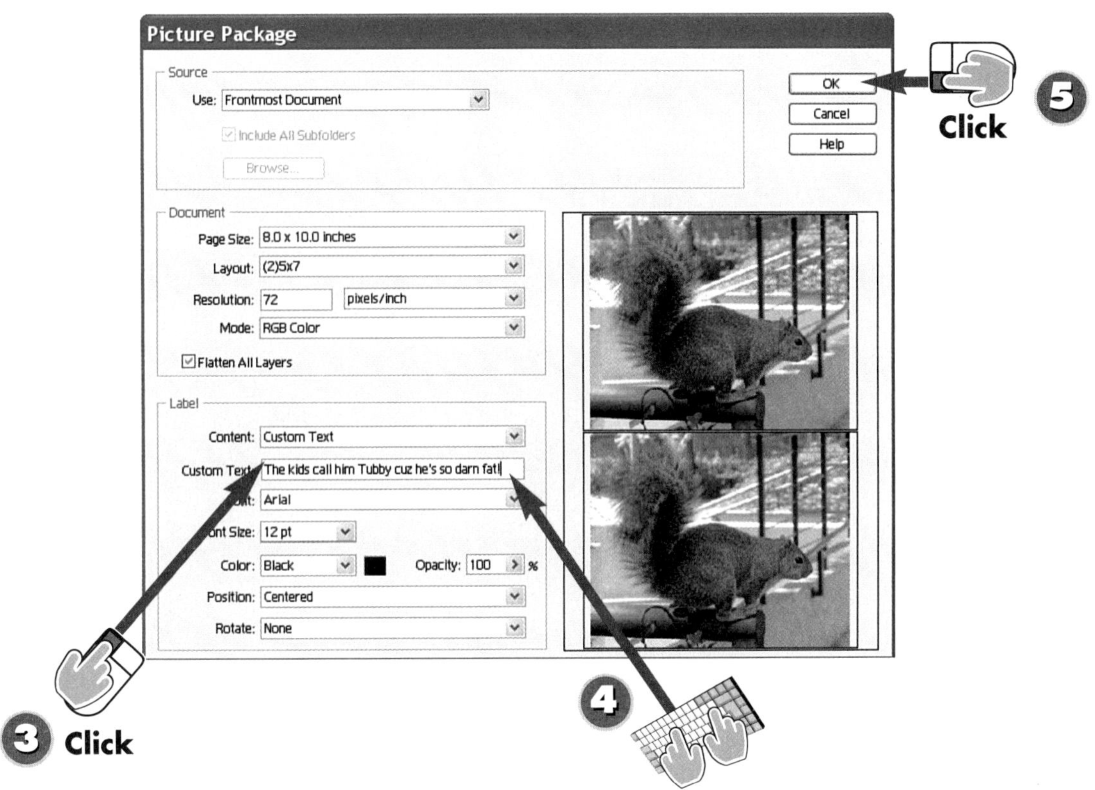

3. Select the **Custom Text** box.

4. Type your description of the picture (100 characters or less).

5. Click **OK**. Text appears superimposed on the shots when you print the package.

TIP

Best Text Color
To make sure that text is visible over any photo, select **Custom** in the Color drop-down box and choose yellow-orange or orange, which contrasts well with almost any background color.

TIP

Best Text Position
Leaving the Position at the default, Centered, places the text in the middle of the picture, right over your subject. A better all-purpose position is Bottom Left.

Overlaying Text on an Image

1. With a picture in the active image area, select the **Horizontal Type** tool.
2. Click the position in the image where the text will begin.
3. Type a line of text. To start a second line, press **Enter**, and keep typing.

INTRODUCTION

Here's the direct approach—just type over an image anywhere you want. You can press Enter between typing multiple lines in the same block of text, or you can click Commit and then repeat these steps to create a separate block that you can move and work with independently. (To move text, see the next task in this part.)

HINT

Alignment Options
The starting point for the text line in step 2 depends on the current Alignment setting in the Options bar (Left Align, Centered, or Right Align).

HINT

New Text Layer
These steps create a new text layer automatically. Think of a layer as a clear sheet you can write or draw on without changing the image underneath.

Selecting and Editing Text

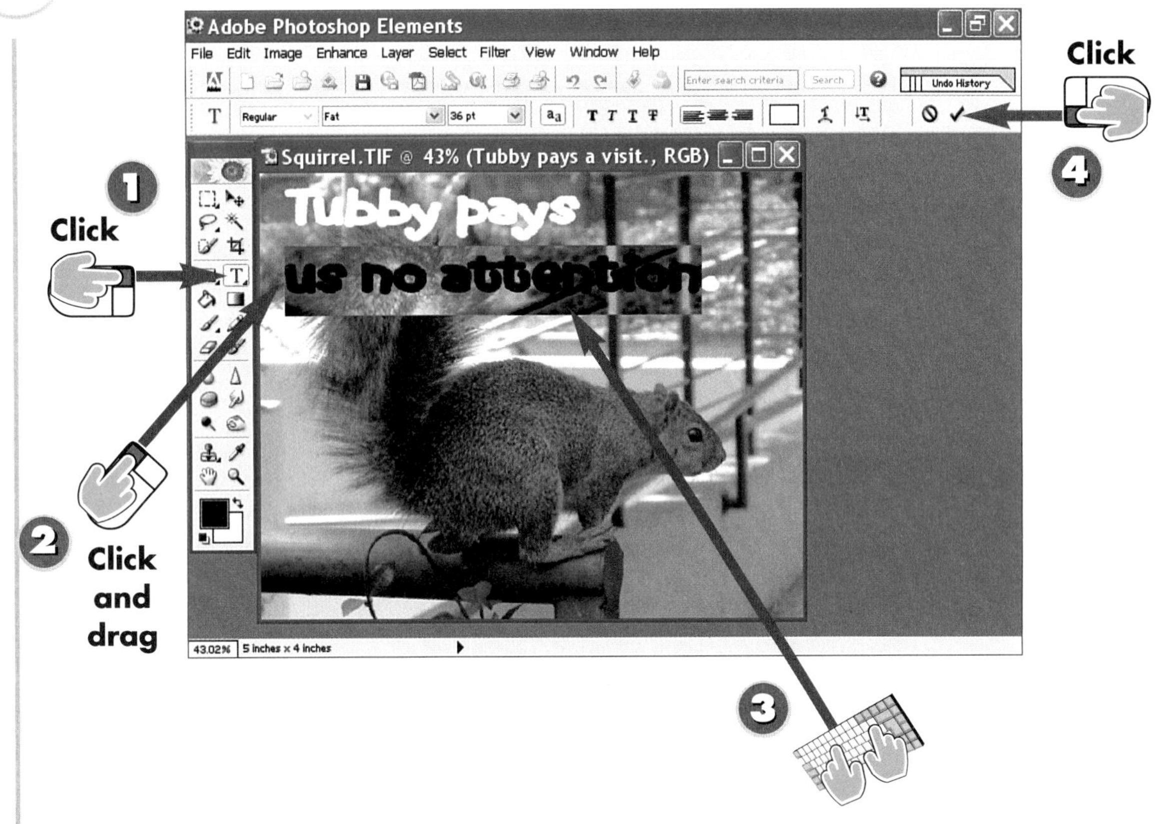

1. Select the **Horizontal Type** tool.
2. Click and drag over the characters you want to replace.
3. Type the replacement characters.
4. Click the **Commit** button in the options bar.

INTRODUCTION

A handy way to remember how to edit text is "swipe and type" because you must first highlight the letters you want to replace.

TIP

Inserting Characters

To insert one or more characters rather than replace some, just click at the insertion point in step 2 and then type.

HINT

Keep Text Editable

You can't edit text after the text layers have been merged with the image (as in a JPEG file, for example). To keep text editable, save your work as a native Photoshop file.

Changing Fonts and Text Properties

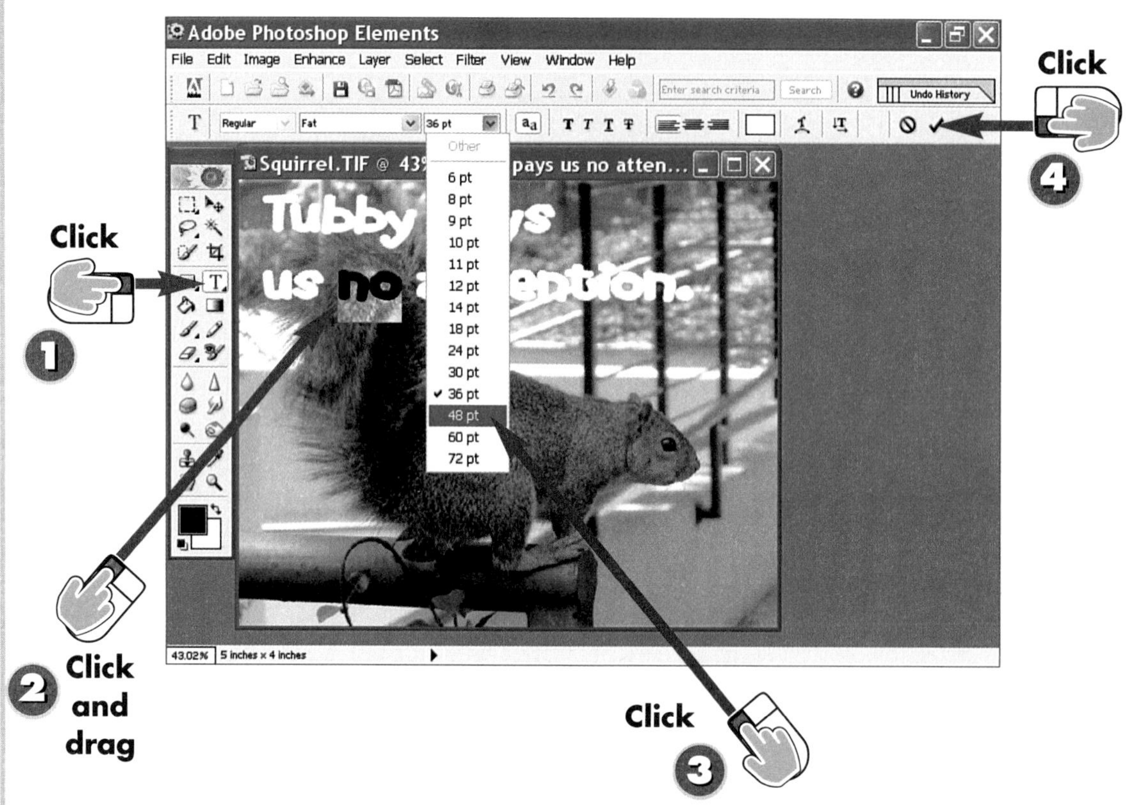

1. Select the **Horizontal Type** tool.
2. Click and drag over the characters you want to change.
3. Select new text properties from the drop-down boxes in the options bar, such as **Font Size**.
4. Click the **Commit** button in the options bar.

INTRODUCTION

Words or even individual characters can have different properties, such as color or font, than adjacent characters in the same block.

TIP

Lines and Blocks of Text
Create the text in a single text block rather than individual ones when you want Photoshop Elements to take care of alignment and spacing between lines.

HINT

Text Properties
Settings for all text properties become available in the options bar when a text object is selected in the active image area.

Moving or Deleting Text

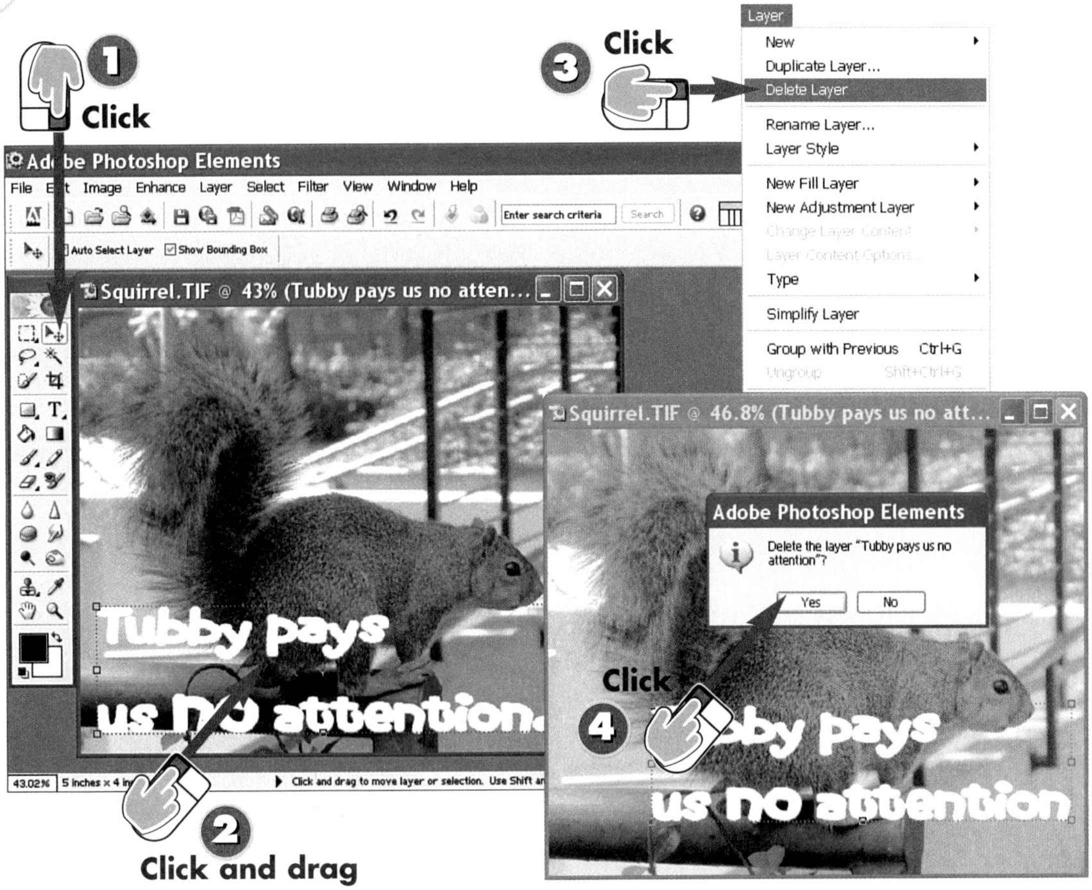

1. Select the **Move** tool, or press **V**.

2. Click and drag the text object to a new position.

3. Or, to delete the entire text layer, choose **Layer**, **Delete Layer**.

4. Click **Yes** to confirm the deletion.

INTRODUCTION

You move a block of text the same way you'd move any other graphic object you create. For example, you should move a line of text out of a cluttered area of the background, to make it more readable.

TIP

Avoid Distortion
To avoid distorting the text, select the center of the object before you drag it around. Press **Shift** while you drag to force horizontal or vertical alignment, or **Alt** to make it diagonal.

Resizing Text

1. Select the **Move** tool, or press **V**.
2. Click the text object you want to resize.
3. Click and drag any handle on the selection box until the box is at the desired size.
4. Click the **Commit** button in the options bar.

INTRODUCTION

This procedure works just like a move, but you drag a handle (corner) rather than the center of the object. It works best for condensing or extending, shrinking or enlarging text by small amounts.

TIP

Best Resizing Results
To enlarge and distort text so that its edges stay smooth, change the **Font Size** first in the options bar and then adjust slightly by dragging object handles. Or, distort with the **Image**, **Transform**, **Free Transform** command instead.

HINT

Auto Select Layer
For step 2 to work, the **Auto Select Layer** box must be checked in the options bar (the usual setting). If it's not checked, you must switch to the corresponding text layer using the Layers palette.

Creating Vertical Text

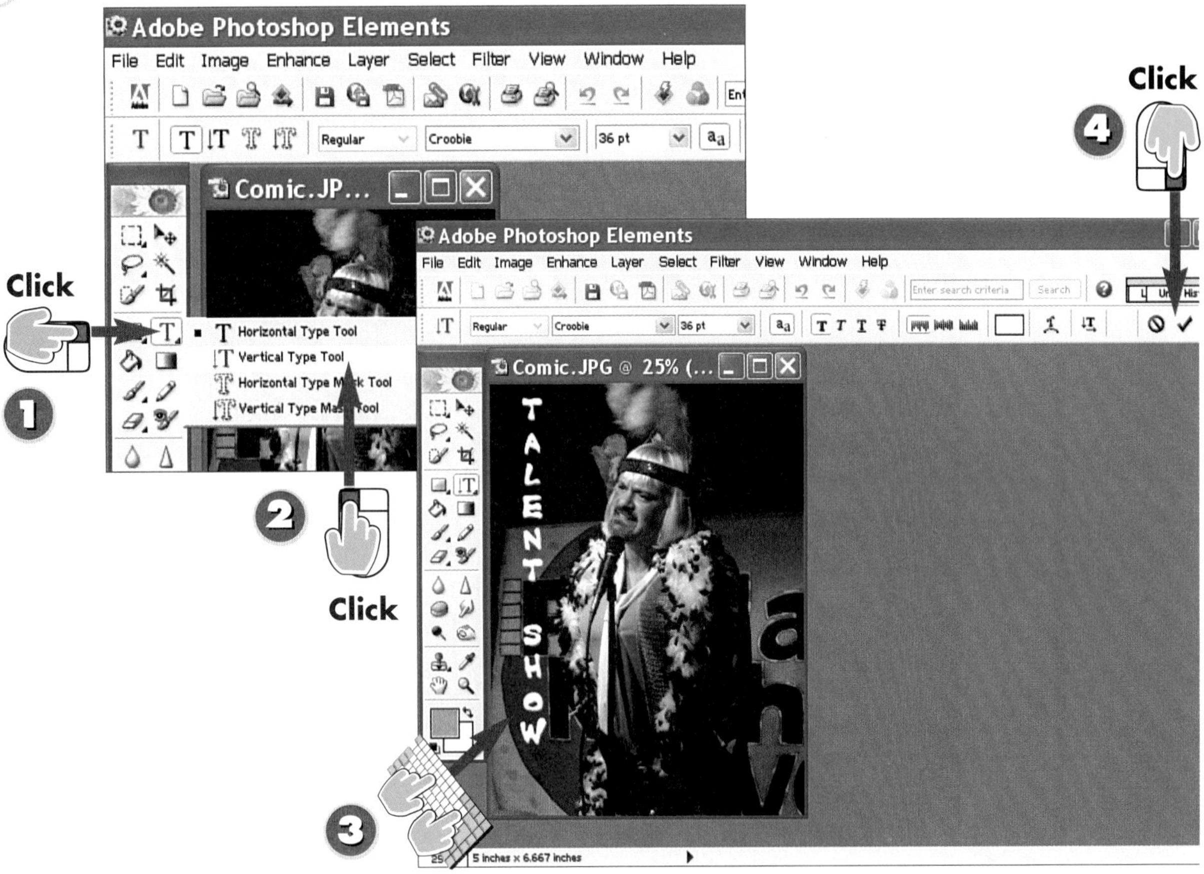

1. Right-click the **Type** tool.
2. Select **Vertical Type Tool** from the submenu.
3. Click the starting point in the image and type some text.
4. Click the **Commit** button in the options bar.

INTRODUCTION

Vertical text can be difficult to read, but there are times when it's the best fit in a tight space. Text created this way reads from the top downward.

TIP

Adding More Text Lines

Press **Enter** after step 3 to add more vertical lines of text to the same block. But for some odd reason, the lines read from right to left. (Enter the second line first if you want them to read from left to right.)

TIP

Vertical Alignment Options

Selections for vertical alignment of text in the options bar are Top Align, Center, and Bottom Align. But in all cases, text reads from the top downward.

Rotating Text

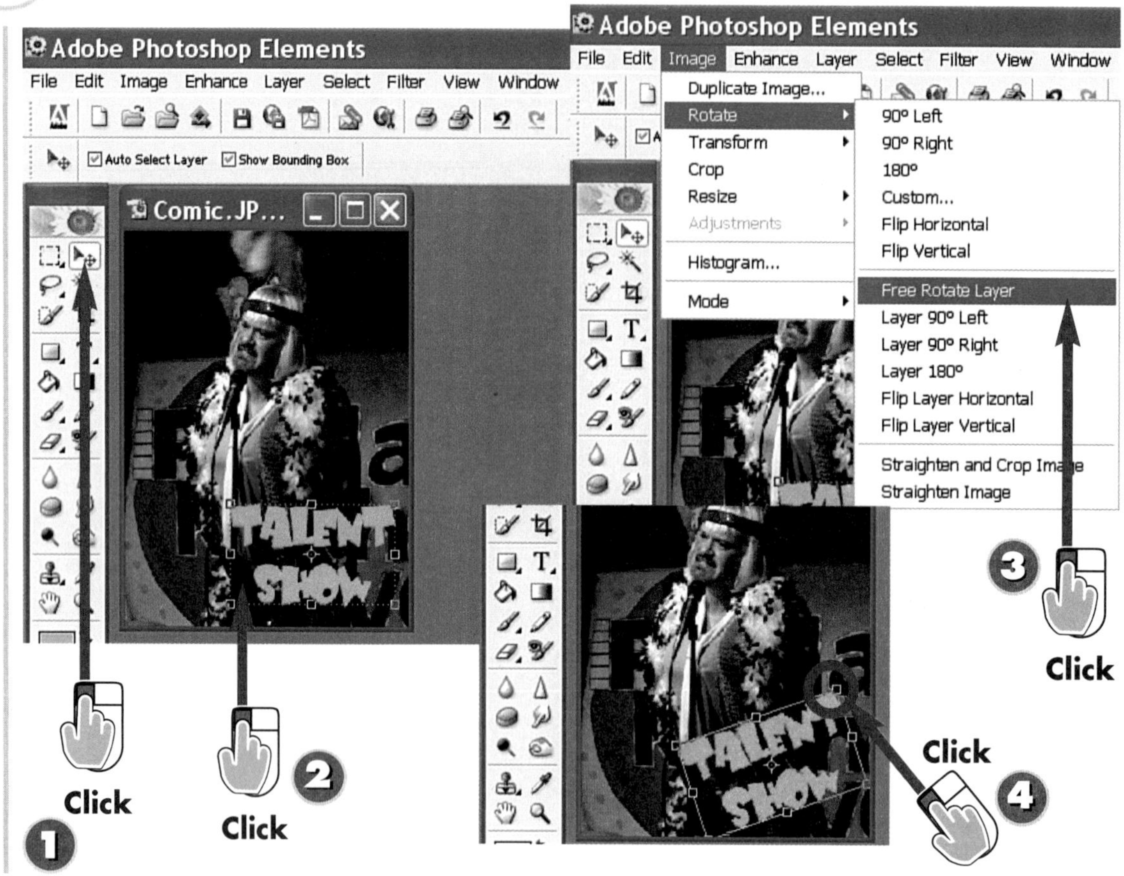

1. Select the **Move** tool, or press **V**.
2. Click the text object you want to rotate.
3. Choose **Image**, **Rotate**, **Free Rotate Layer**.
4. Click and drag a handle on the selection box.

INTRODUCTION

You might want to rotate text to achieve a smarter design or to fit it to an object in the image. Just remember that it might become difficult to read if the angle is too severe.

TIP

Flipping Text
Flipping (creating a mirror-image of) text can be done by choosing **Image**, **Rotate**, **Flip Layer Horizontal** or **Flip Layer Vertical**. (Submenu commands that don't include "Layer" affect the entire image.)

HINT

Auto Select Layer
For step 2 to work, the Auto Select Layer box must be checked in the options bar (the usual setting). If it's not checked, you must switch to the corresponding text layer using the Layers palette.

Transforming and Skewing Text

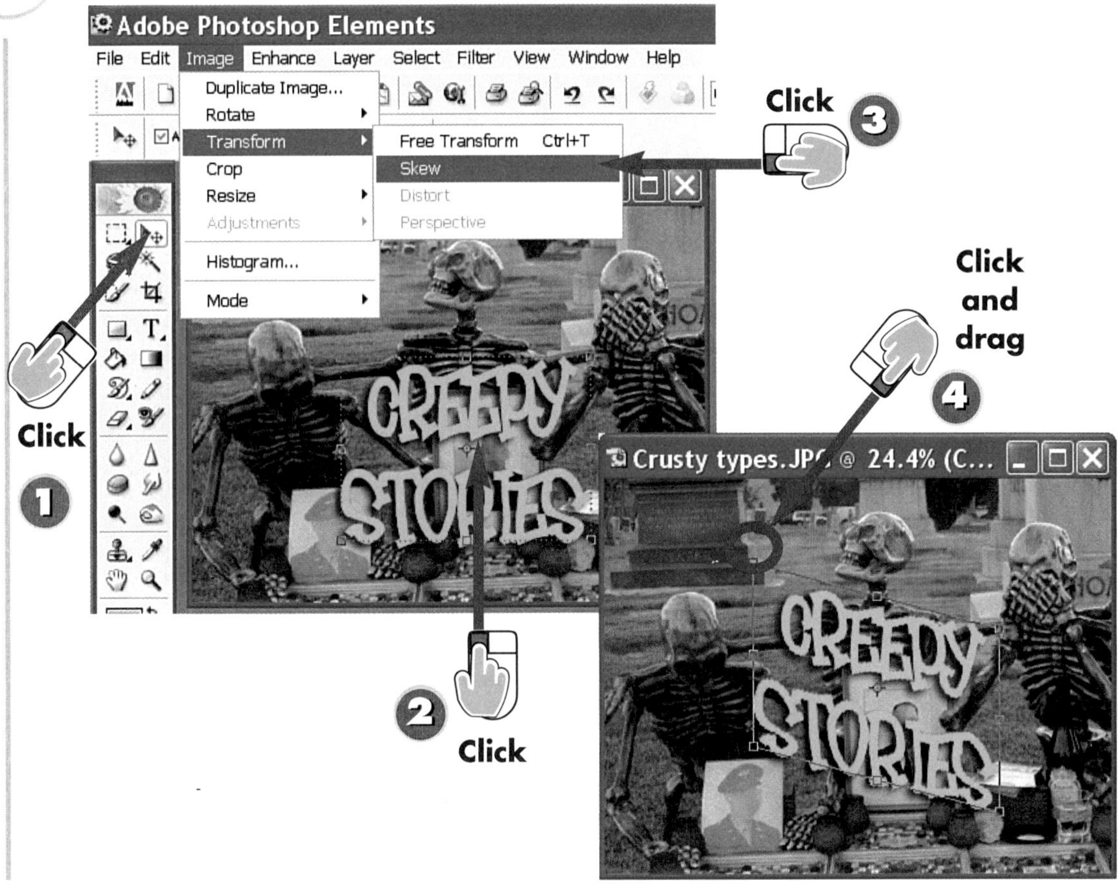

1. Select the **Move** tool, or press **V**.

2. Click the text object you want to transform.

3. Choose **Image**, **Transform**, **Skew**, or press **Ctrl+T**.

4. Click and drag a handle of the selection box to resize and/or distort the text.

INTRODUCTION

Skewing text can give it either an italic or backslanted effect, or make it appear to run up- or downhill. You can also distort it in the process if you want. Free Transform is a similar command, by which you can stretch and squish text in any direction.

TIP

Grow or Distort Text
You can grow or distort text using the same procedure, except choose **Image**, **Transform**, **Free Transform** (or press **Ctrl+T**) in step 3. Try it and notice how this type of transformation differs from Skew.

HINT

Auto Select Layer
For step 2 to work, the Auto Select Layer box must be checked in the options bar (the usual setting). If it's not checked, you must switch to the corresponding text layer using the Layers palette.

Warping Text

1. Select the **Horizontal Type** tool.
2. Click the text you want to warp.
3. In the options bar, click the **Create Warped Text** button.

INTRODUCTION

You can apply all kinds of fancy effects to text by this method, which is great for adding dramatic or comic touches to titles of albums and slideshows.

HINT

Auto Select Layer

For step 2 to work, the Auto Select Layer box must be checked in the options bar (the usual setting). If it's not checked, you must switch to the corresponding text layer using the Layers palette.

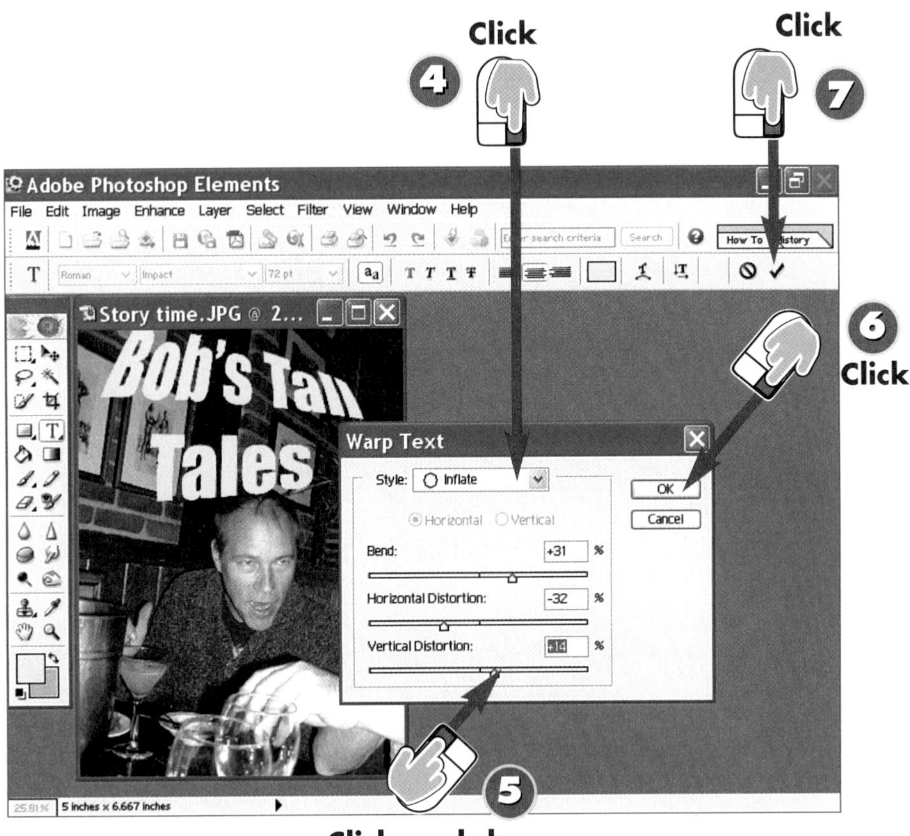

4 Select a style from the drop-down menu, such as **Inflate**.

5 Click and drag one or more sliders to adjust the degree of the effect.

6 Click **OK**.

7 Click the **Commit** button in the options bar.

TIP

Another Way to Warp
Here's an alternative method for warping your words: Right-click the text and select **Warp Text** from the pop-up menu.

HINT

Warped, Not Crazy
Warping text is usually done for comic effect. For best results, choose a font with fat letters. Some fonts don't warp well. For example, Old English and cursive fonts can become downright unreadable.

Adding a Talk Bubble

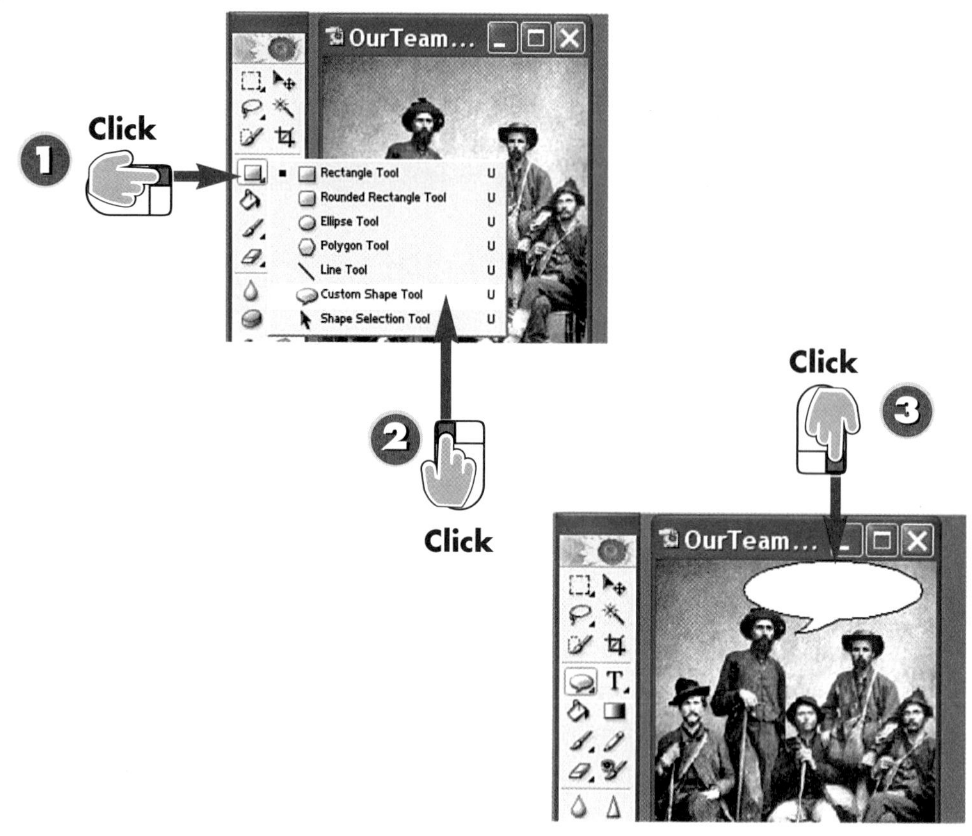

1. Right-click the **Rectangle** tool.
2. Select **Custom Shape Tool**.
3. Click and drag to size the shape in the image area.

INTRODUCTION

Oh, those wacky relatives and the wild things they say! A *talk bubble* can add a whimsical touch to your greeting cards and Webmail. It's actually just one of many shapes that Photoshop Elements can draw so that you don't have to create them freehand.

TIP

Hearts and Flowers

The talk bubble—or *speech balloon*—is just one of an assortment of custom shapes. To pick one, after selecting the Custom Shape tool, select the **Shape** drop-down menu in the options bar.

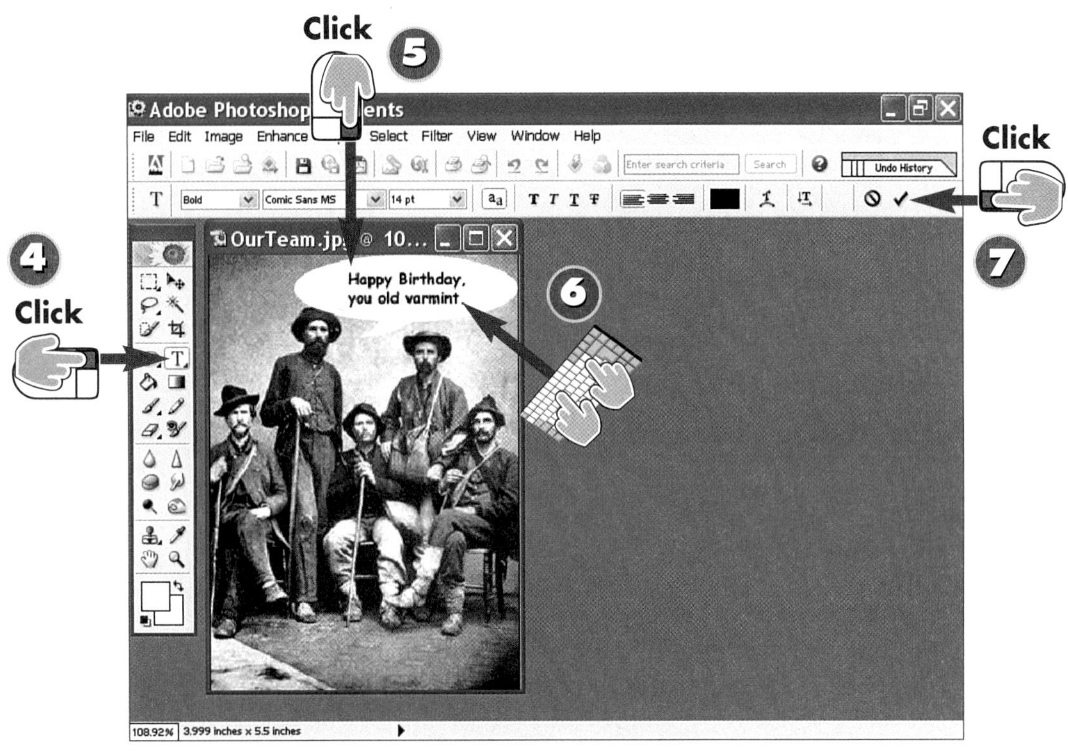

4. Select the **Horizontal Type** tool.
5. Click the start of a text line inside the talk bubble.
6. Type some text.
7. Click the **Commit** button in the options bar.

TIP

Don't See a Talk Bubble?
The toolbar shows the Custom Shape tool you used last. If the Talk Bubble isn't there, select the Custom Shape tool and choose the shape you want from the Shape box in the options bar.

HINT

Other Shape Tools
Besides custom shapes, other tools in the Shape submenu in the toolbar are Rectangle, Rounded Rectangle, Ellipse, Polygon, and Line.

Applying a Text Effect

1. Select the **Move** tool, or press **V**.

2. Click the text that needs the effect (Auto Select Layer must be checked).

3. Choose **Window**, **Effects**.

4. Select the effect you want, such as **Bold Outline**, and click **Apply**.

INTRODUCTION

Thumbnails in the Effects palette marked ABC are text effects, which you can apply to selected text with a click. If Photoshop Elements didn't include these "canned" effects, you'd have to be a skilled graphic artist, and it would take a lot more work to reproduce them.

TIP

Effects Palette Open?
To clear your work area, you may want to close or dock the Effects palette when you're finished. If it's not in the palette well, you can always get it back by choosing **Window**, **Effects**.

HINT

Applying Text Effects
Use only effects marked ABC. The others will affect the entire image, not just text. You can also apply text effects by dragging an effect from the palette and dropping it on the text.

Adding a Drop Shadow to Text

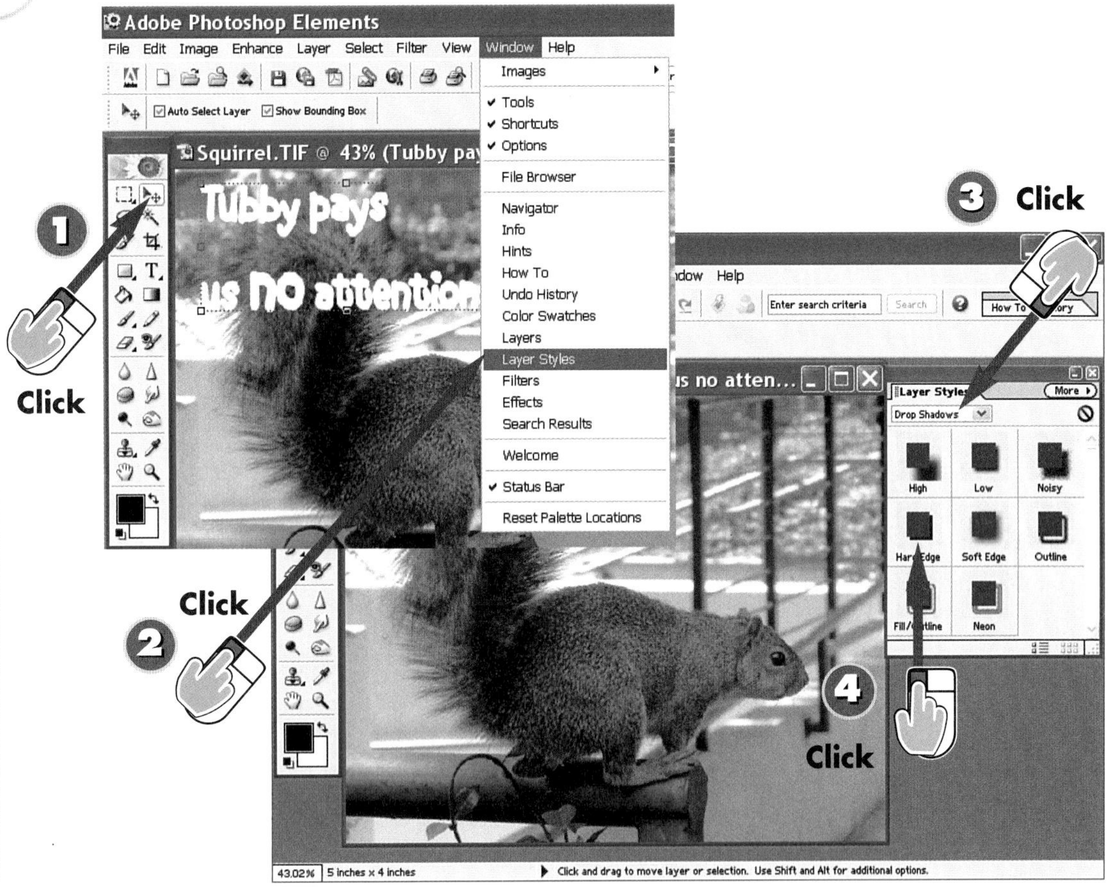

1. Select the **Move** tool, or press **V**.

2. Click the text to which the drop shadow will be added (Auto Select Layer must be checked). Choose **Window**, **Layer Styles**.

3. From the Style Libraries drop-down menu, select **Drop Shadows**.

4. Select a drop-shadow effect, such as **Hard Edge**.

INTRODUCTION

Place a drop shadow behind text to make it appear to "pop" out from the background so that it's more readable. This is particularly handy when the background has both light and dark areas and you can't find a solid area to serve as a background for the text that gives enough contrast.

HINT

Auto Select Layer
For step 2 to work, the Auto Select Layer box must be checked in the Options bar (the usual setting). If it's not checked, you must switch to the corresponding text layer using the Layers palette.

HINT

Make Your Own?
You can experiment with creating your own drop shadow effects if you know this: A drop shadow is actually a duplicate of the text object, in a contrasting color, positioned behind it and offset slightly.

Creating "Hollow" Text

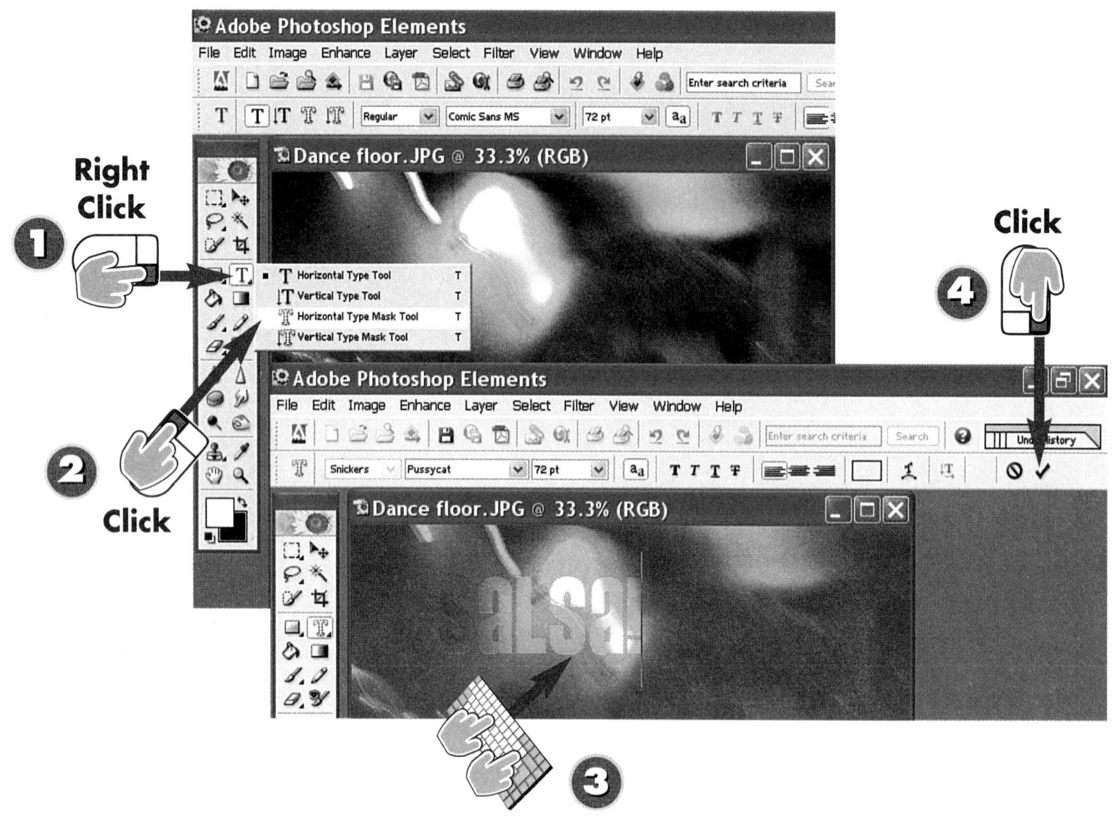

1. Right-click the **Type** tool.
2. Select **Horizontal Type Mask Tool**.
3. Click the starting point of the text in the image. Type some text.
4. Click the **Commit** button in the Options bar.

INTRODUCTION

A *type mask* makes a text object appear to be hollow so that the background (or the next layer) shows through. It's not an effect you'll use every day, but it could add just the right touch to your new CD album cover—whether it's the school choir or a garage band!

TIP

Use Fat Letters

A type mask works best with big, fat letters. Use it on titles for a decorative effect. If you apply it to smaller text or to a block of words, the result probably won't be readable.

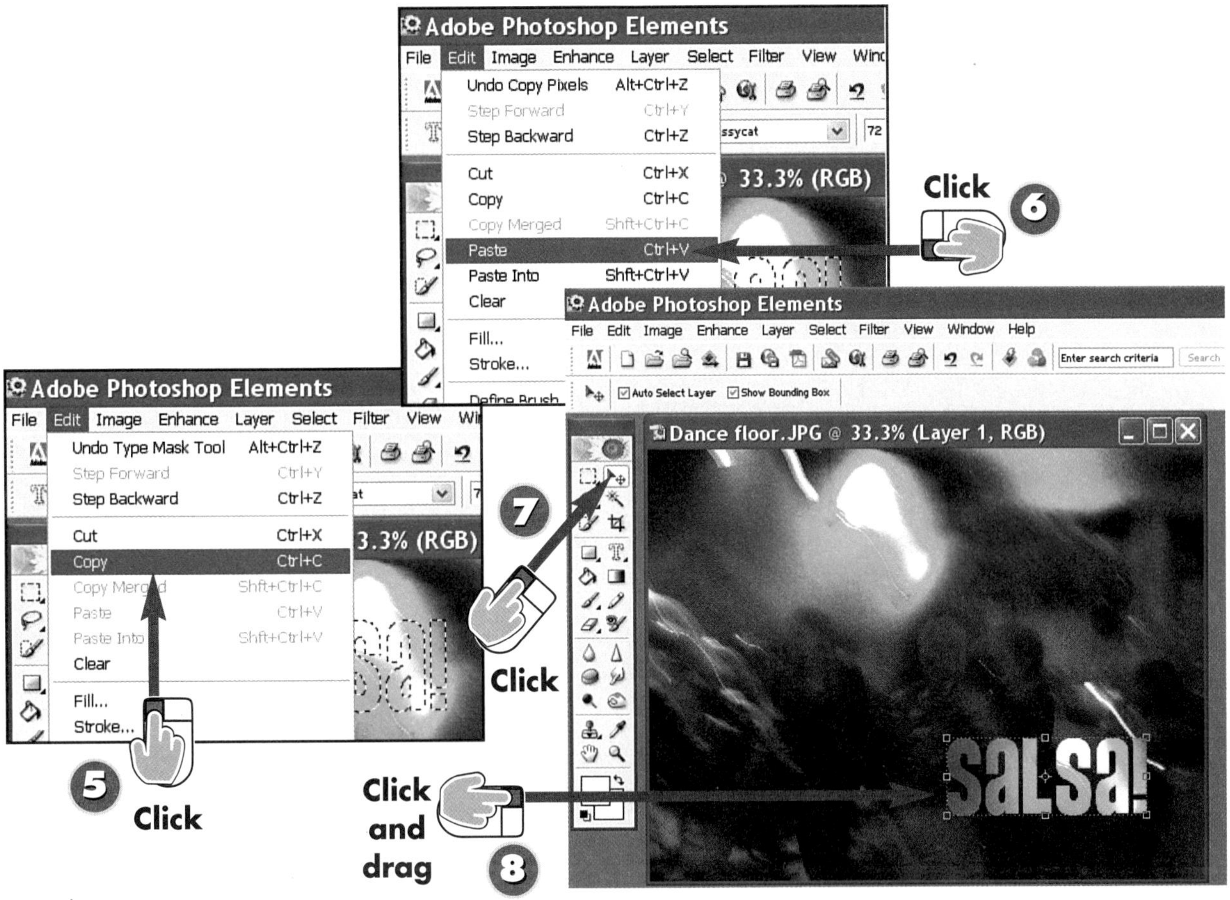

5 Choose **Edit**, **Copy**, or press **Ctrl+C**.

6 Choose **Edit**, **Paste**, or press **Ctrl+V**.

7 Select the **Move** tool, or press **V**.

8 Click and drag the copy of the masked text to reposition it in the image. The background from the original position shows through the hollow text.

HINT

Use a Variegated Background

This effect works best on variegated backgrounds, cutting and pasting from a lighter to a darker area, or vice versa. If the background is too uniform, the effect won't be obvious.

HINT

What's Behind the Mask?

A type mask utilizes the characteristic of Photoshop layers to affect the visibility of all layers beneath them. In this case, because the text is hollow (actually, transparent), the lower layer—the background—shows through.

PART 5

Creating Snazzy Effects

With the invention of the electronic calculator, schoolchildren are the only ones who fret over doing arithmetic by hand. Similarly, you might be surprised at how many commercial artists don't draw from scratch anymore. Many of them earn their daily bread using computer graphics software like Photoshop Elements to make photos *look* like fine art.

When you've worked through the tasks in this part, you'll know many of their secrets. You can make greeting cards and party invitations look as if they were hand-drawn by a skilled sketch artist, create photo-realistic illustrations for flyers and newsletters, and add expensive-looking graphics that will give a professional touch to your personal Web site.

Photoshop Elements helps you achieve artistic effects by way of *filters* that can transform an image with a click, but in complex ways. The program comes with a wide variety of filters, and you can download even more of them (called *plug-ins*) from **www.adobe.com** and other vendors' Web sites. There are far too many filters to cover them all here, but you'll see enough to show you how easy they are to apply—and to start you thinking about all the creative possibilities.

How Did You Do *That*?

Before It helps to start with a photo that has an interesting composition, and some bright colors and contrasts.

After Here's some "fine art" that took less than a minute to make. It's the result of adding both the Palette Knife artistic filter and a Sandstone texture, finally adjusting Hue for brighter greenery.

Adding a Decorative Border

Start

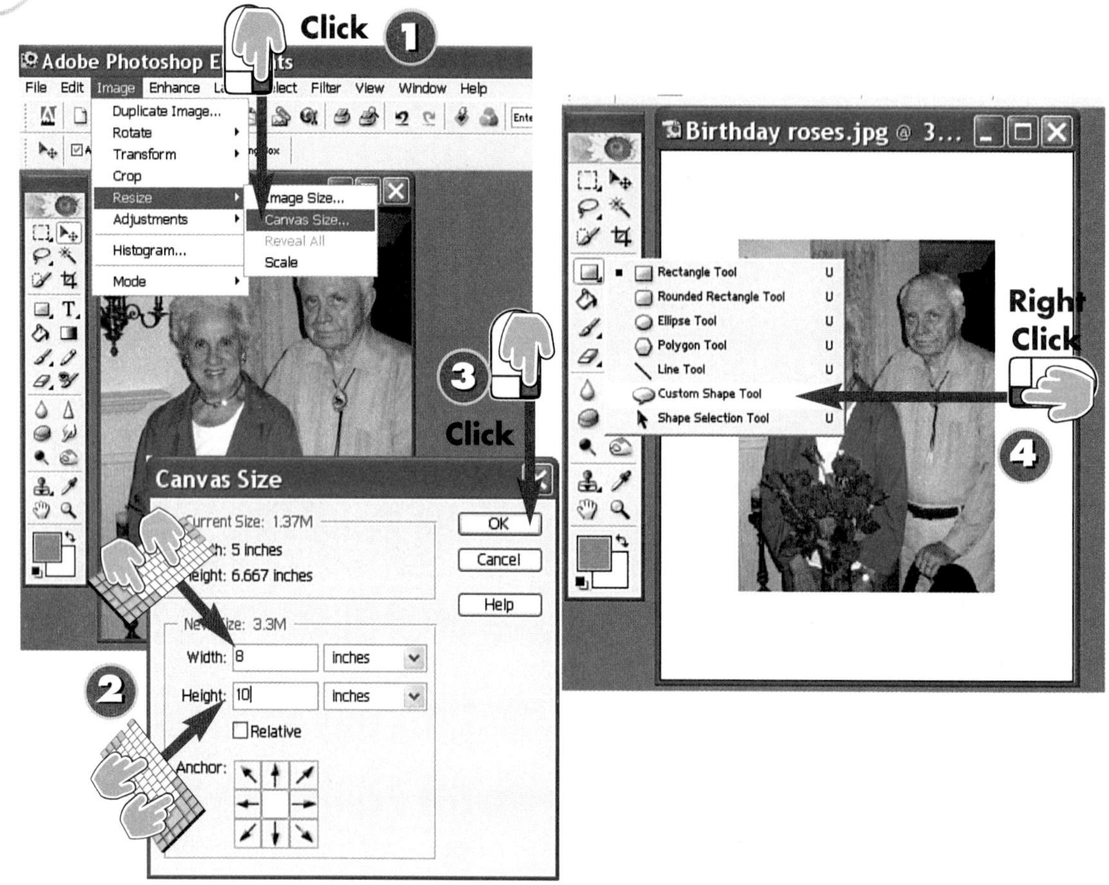

1. With a picture in the active image area, choose **Image**, **Resize**, **Canvas Size**.
2. Type a Width the same as the print size and about 2 inches wider than the current image size. Do the same for Height.
3. Click **OK**.
4. Right-click the **Shape** tool in the toolbar and select **Custom Shape Tool**.

INTRODUCTION

A frame is just one example of the wide variety of custom, prebuilt shapes available in Photoshop Elements. To make the frame even fancier, this example applies a Craquelure filter to give the frame a rich, dimensional look.

HINT

Know the Image Size
In this example, the image size of the photo is about 5×7 inches. Placing it on an 8×10 canvas adds just the right amount of border for the decorative frame.

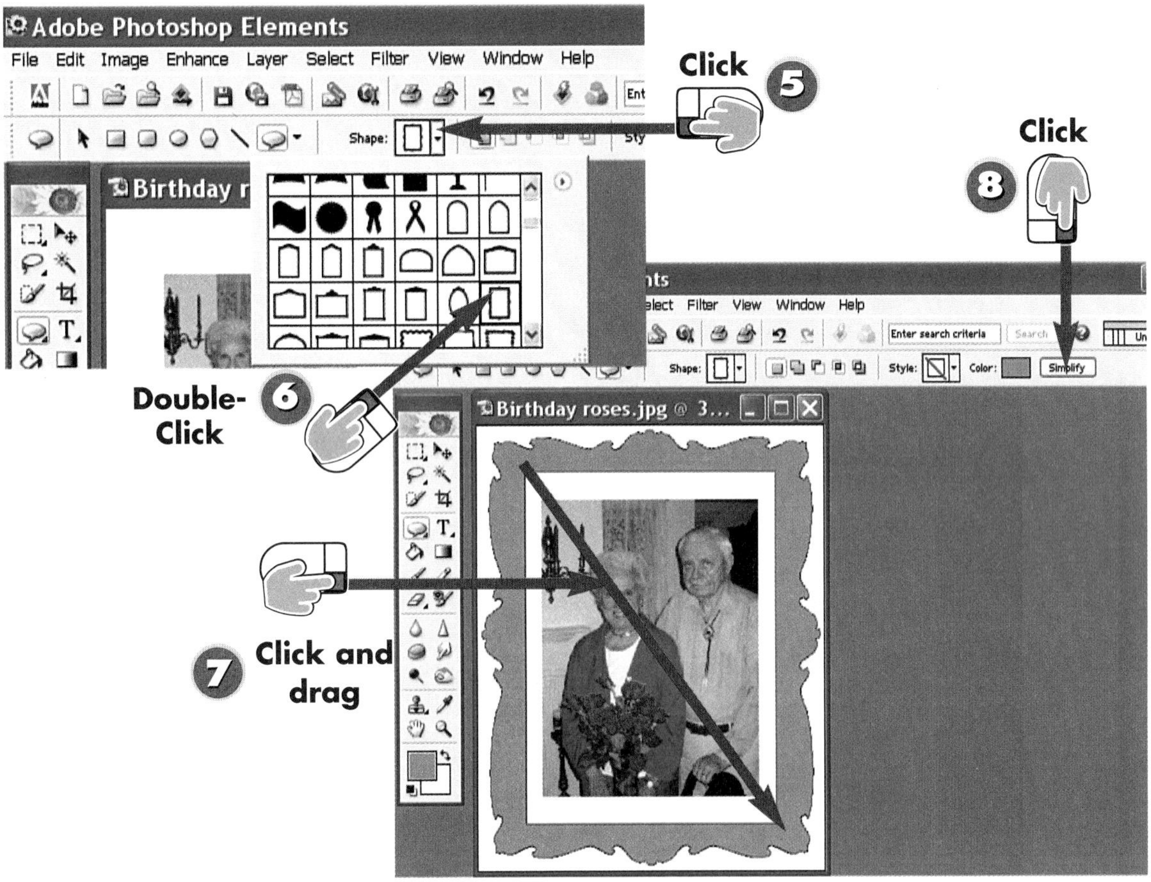

5 In the Options bar, open the **Shape** drop-down menu.

6 Double-click any **Frame** shape.

7 Click and drag in the image to surround the photo with the frame.

8 Click the **Simplify** button.

See next page

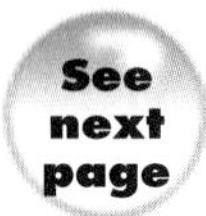

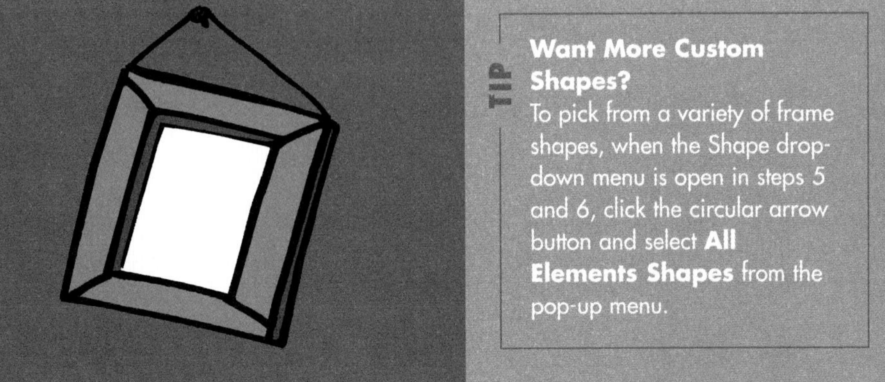

TIP

Want More Custom Shapes?

To pick from a variety of frame shapes, when the Shape drop-down menu is open in steps 5 and 6, click the circular arrow button and select **All Elements Shapes** from the pop-up menu.

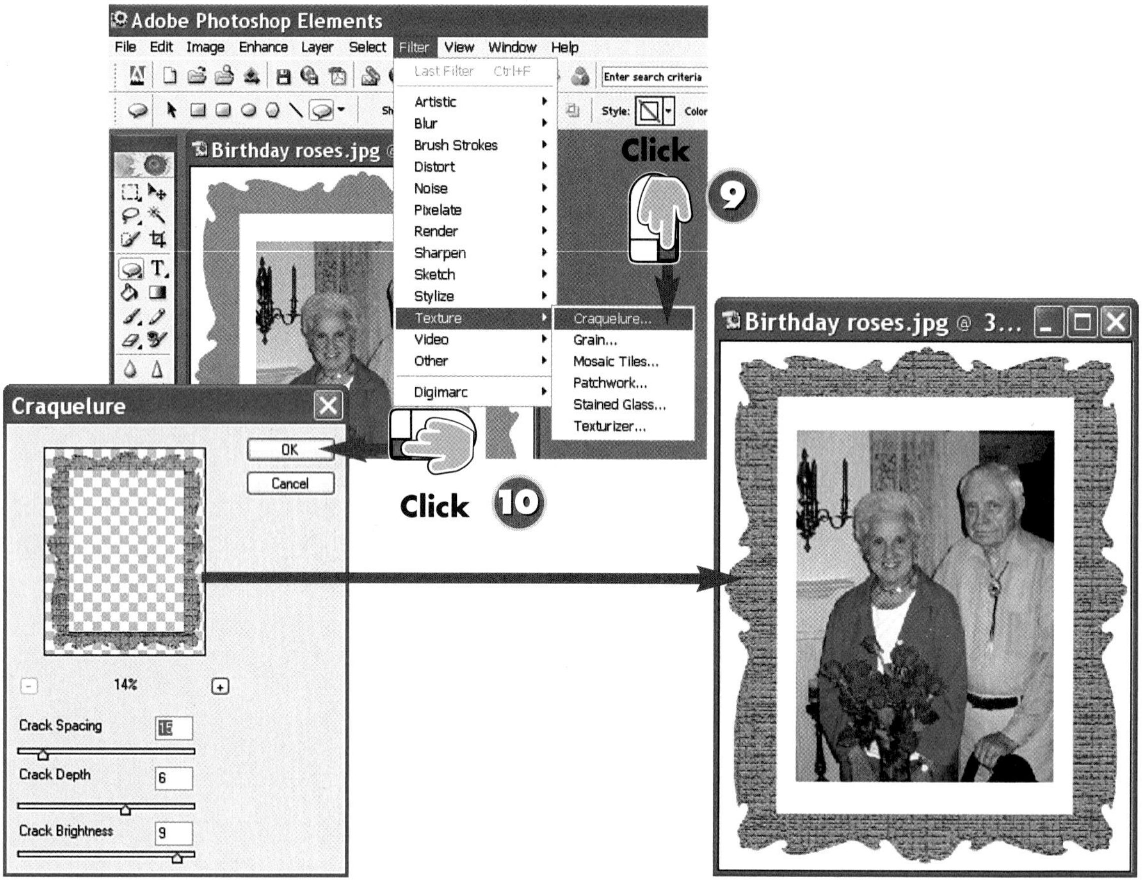

Choose **Filter**, **Texture**, **Craquelure**.

Click **OK**.

INTRODUCTION The frame used here is just one of many Custom Shapes, which are ready-made so you don't have to do any freehand drawing. Categories include Animals, Arrows, Banners and Awards, Characters, Default, Frames, Fruit, Music, Nature, Objects, Ornaments, Shapes, Signs, Symbols, Talk Bubbles, and Tiles.

TIP

Craquelure Not Your Style?

Instead of applying the Craquelure filter in step 9, try any other effect or combination of effects from the **Filter** menu.

TIP

Don't See the Preview?

For the preview of the whole frame to be visible in the Craquelure dialog box in step 10, click the – button several times to reduce the view percentage from 100 to 14 percent.

Creating a Gradient Fill

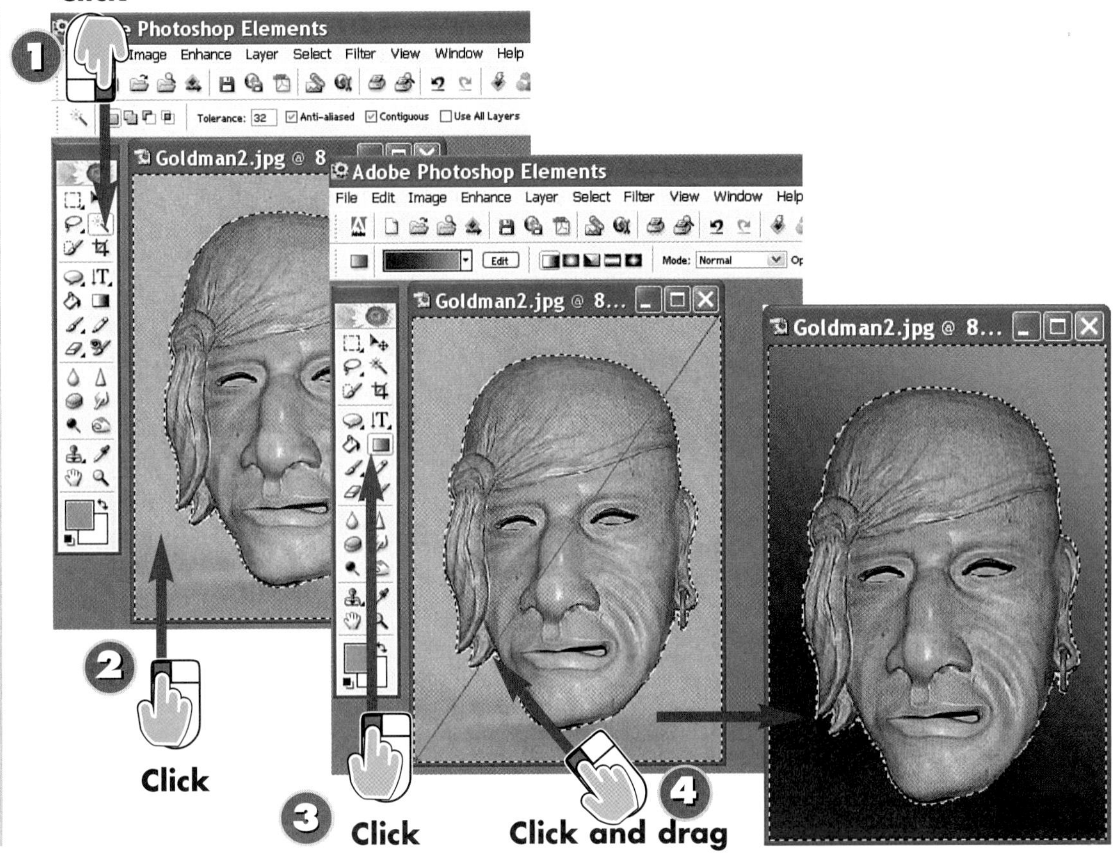

1. With the picture in the active image area, select the **Magic Wand** tool, or press **W**.
2. Click to select the area in the image to which the effect will be applied.
3. Select the **Gradient** tool, or press **G**.
4. Click and drag across the area to be filled in the direction you want the color gradation to take. (Press **Ctrl+D** to release the selection.)

INTRODUCTION

A *gradient fill* is a blended transition—usually between two colors—within a selected area. In this example, the gradient is applied to the entire background, but it could also be used to fill any object you select, even hollow text.

TIP

Making Your Selection
Use any combination of selection tools in step 1 (Move, Magic Wand, Lassos, or Marquees). Press **Shift** as you select with a tool to add an area to the current selection, **Alt** to subtract.

TIP

Mix Your Own Gradients
After selecting the Gradient tool, clicking the **Edit** button in the Options bar opens the Gradient Editor, which contains options for creating custom gradients.

Mounting a Photo on a Fancy Background

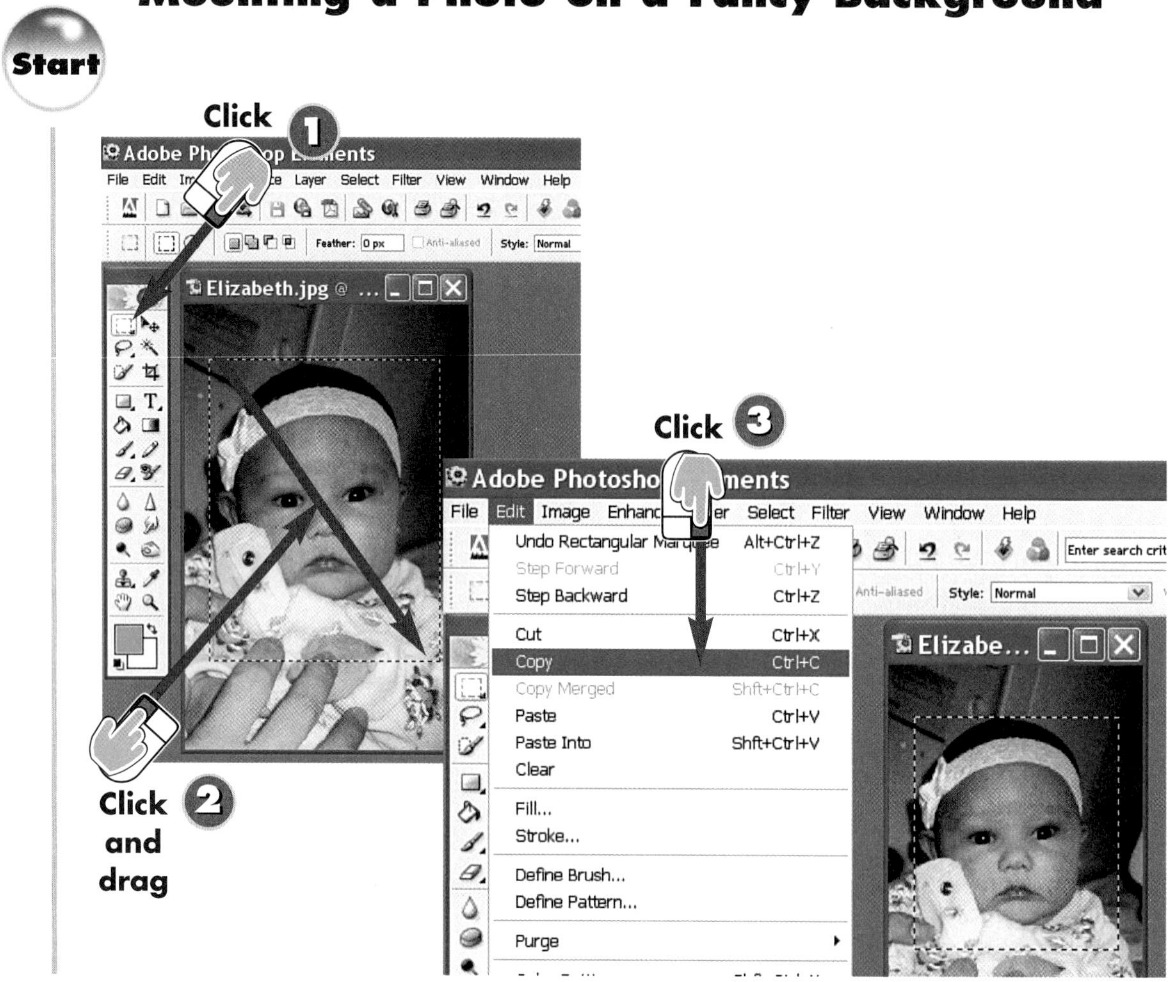

Click 1

Click 2 and drag

Click 3

1. With the photo open in the active image window, select the **Rectangular Marquee** tool, or press **M**.
2. Click and drag to frame the image.
3. Choose **Edit**, **Copy**, or press **Ctrl+C**.

INTRODUCTION

Putting a cherished family photo in an expensive frame is a fine idea, but the price of a custom matte is a needless expense. Create your own fancy background, and it won't cost you any more than a little extra printer ink. And yours will probably be prettier than any you can buy.

HINT

Crop, While You're at It
You don't need to crop your photo first, because selecting the area to copy has the same result. But if the selection is too small in relation to the fancy background image, resample the image first to increase resolution.

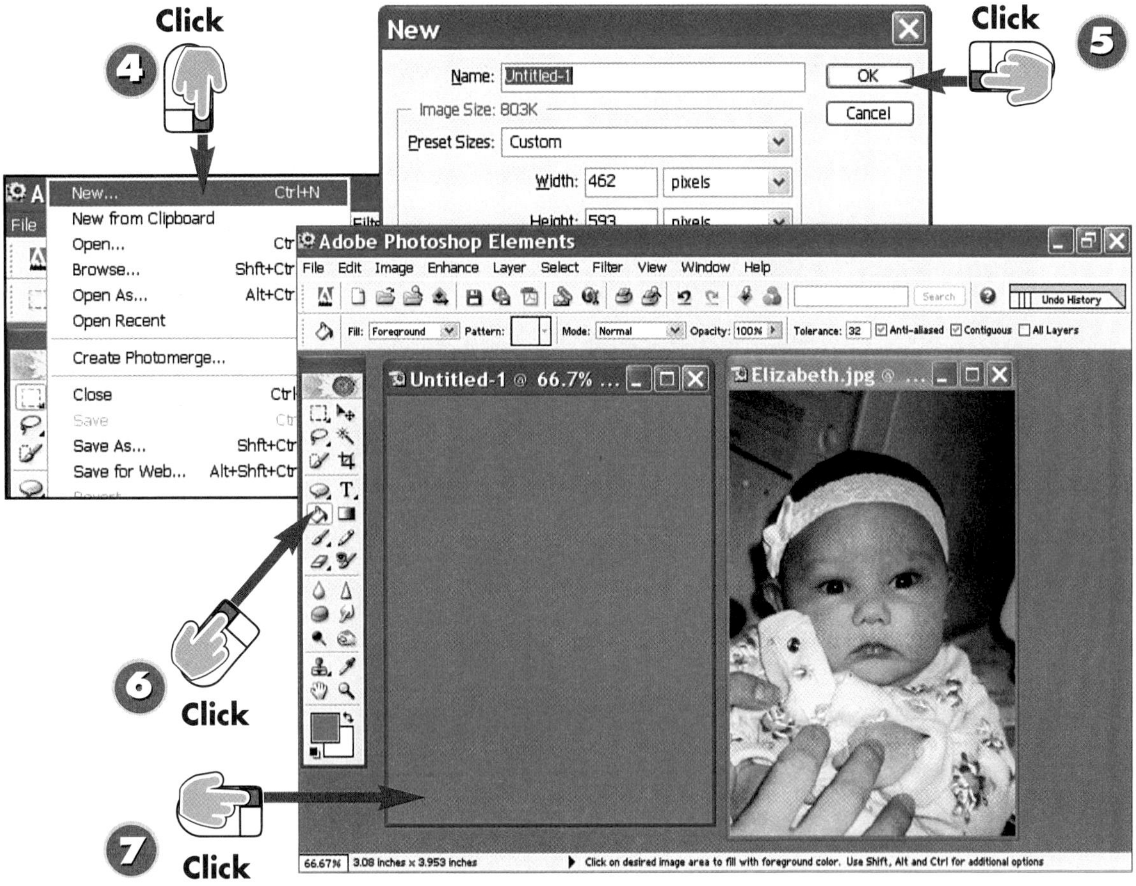

4 Choose **File**, **New**, or press **Ctrl+N**.

5 Click **OK**.

6 Select the **Paint Bucket** tool, or press **K**.

7 Click in the new image area to fill it with color.

TIP

What Color Do You Prefer?

The Paint Bucket tool deposits the currently selected foreground color. To make a different choice, click the topmost color patch at the bottom of the toolbar, and make a new selection from the Color Picker.

TIP

You're Not Stuck

In step 6, for a different look, after selecting the **Paint Bucket** tool, choose **Pattern** in the Fill box in the Options bar, select a pattern, and click inside the image area to fill the background with the pattern.

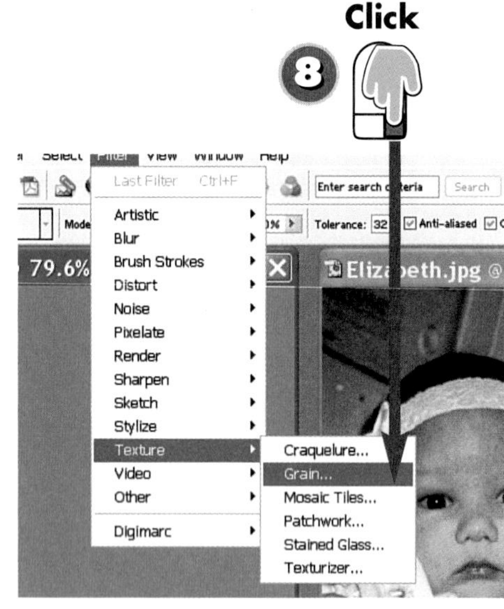

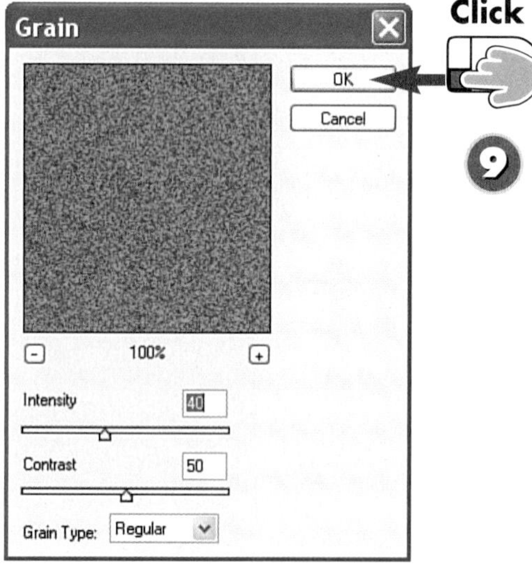

8 Choose **Filter**, **Texture**, **Grain**.

9 Click **OK**.

INTRODUCTION

By adding a frame using Photoshop Elements, you can begin to think of every photo you shoot as just the starting point for a piece of attractive, personalized artwork. Traditionally, film photographers didn't get involved in such artistic cutting and pasting, but in today's digital realm, it's just so easy.

HINT

Varying Textures
Like the Craquelure filter shown previously, you can vary Grain by adjusting sliders after step 8. Other available textures are Mosaic Tiles, Patchwork, Stained Glass, and Texturizer (for surface effects such as Canvas and Burlap).

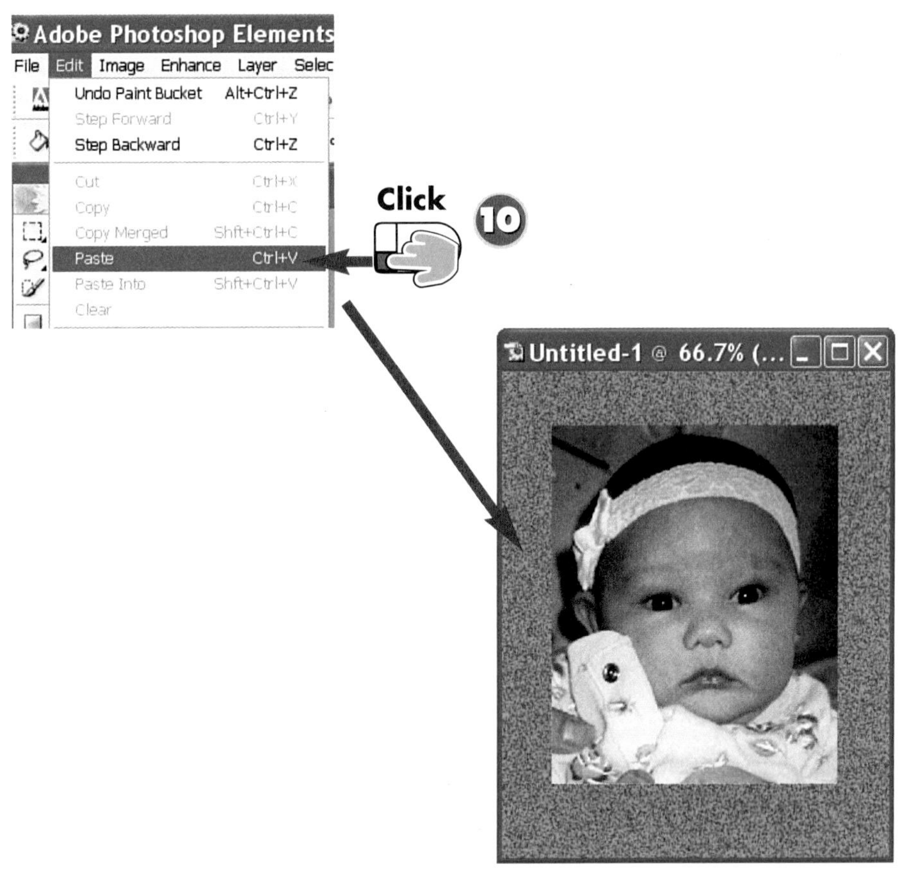

10 Choose **Edit**, **Paste** from the menu bar, or press **Ctrl+V**.

HINT

Metal or Paper?
Applying a gradient effect to the background instead of the grainy texture can give the impression of a metallic picture frame.

TIP

Didn't Work as Advertised?
The size of the pasted photo in the new window depends on the relative image sizes of the two pictures. If the photo size needs adjustment, select the **Move** tool after step 9 and reposition/resize it.

Adding a Beautiful Sky

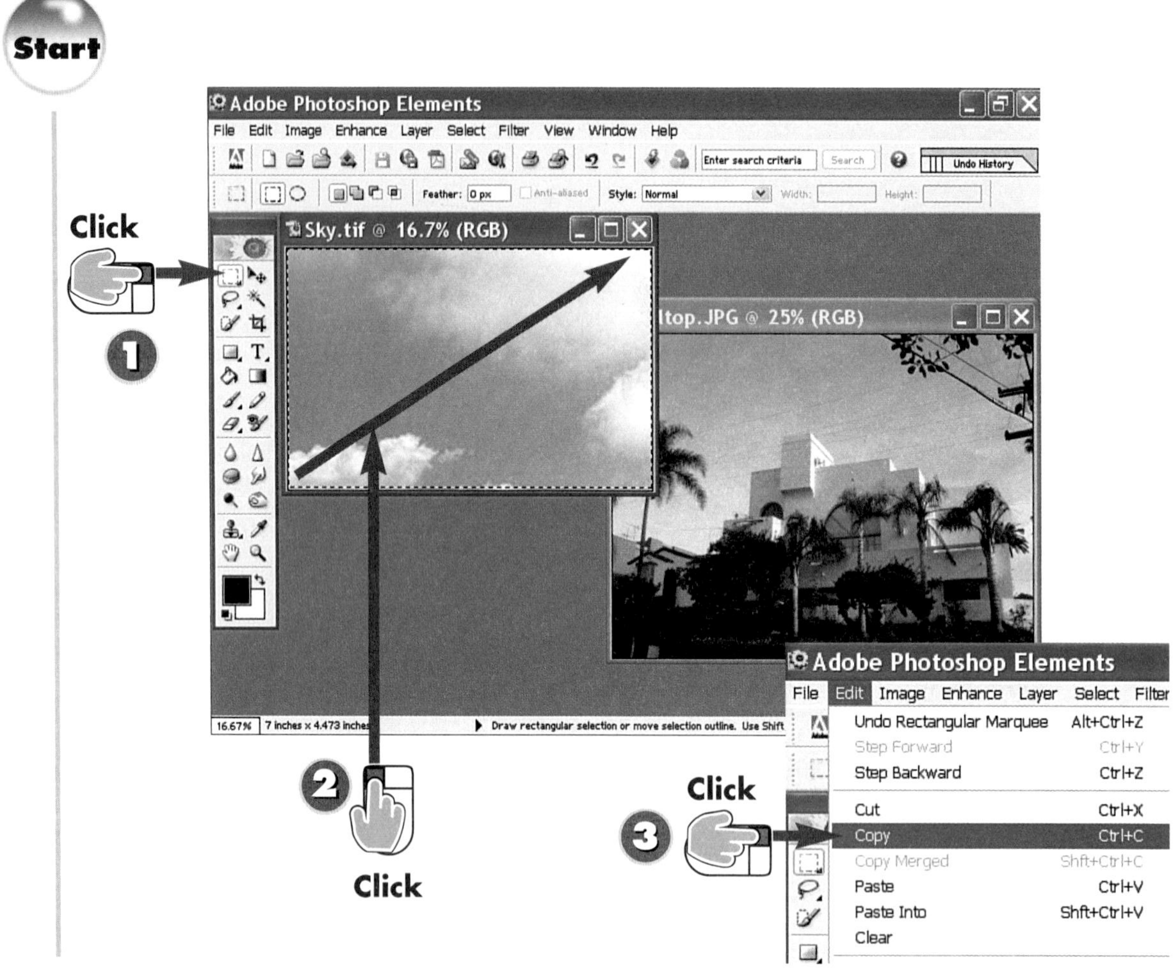

1. Start with two images open: a pretty sky and a scene with sky you want to replace. Select the **Rectangular Marquee** tool.
2. Click and drag in the pretty sky window to select a large rectangular piece.
3. Choose **Edit**, **Copy**, or press **Ctrl+C**.

INTRODUCTION

Replacing the sky is a particularly neat trick, permitting you to scoff at overcast days, not to mention getting rid of power lines and intrusive foliage. Add a gorgeous sunset and forget it was raining that day.

TIP

Be Sure to Grab It All
In step 2, use any combination of selection tools. The Lasso tool is particularly handy for irregular areas, followed by several Shift-clicks with **Magic Wand** to get the rest.

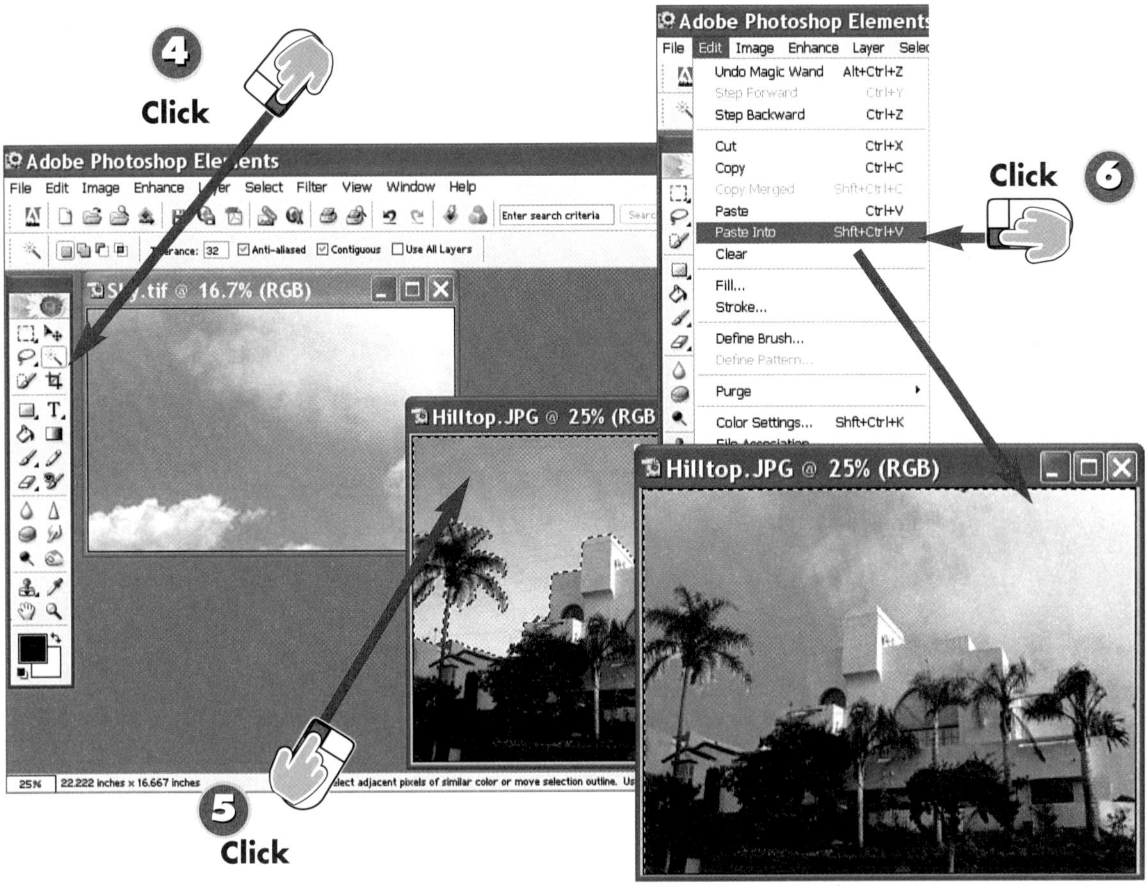

4 Click

5 Click

Click 6

4. Select the **Magic Wand** tool, or press **W**.

5. In the scene window, click to select the sky that needs replacing. (Shift+click to add other areas to the selection.)

6. Choose **Edit**, **Paste Into**, or press **Shift+Ctrl+V**.

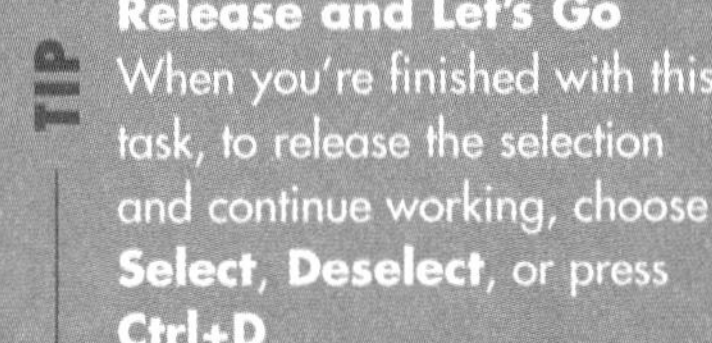

TIP

Release and Let's Go
When you're finished with this task, to release the selection and continue working, choose **Select**, **Deselect**, or press **Ctrl+D**.

HINT

But Don't Leave Home
You can try the same technique used here for replacing sky to replace the background of any photo with any other shot. Keep your subjects in place and take them to some exotic locale—at no expense!

Start

Creating a High-Contrast Black-and-White Picture

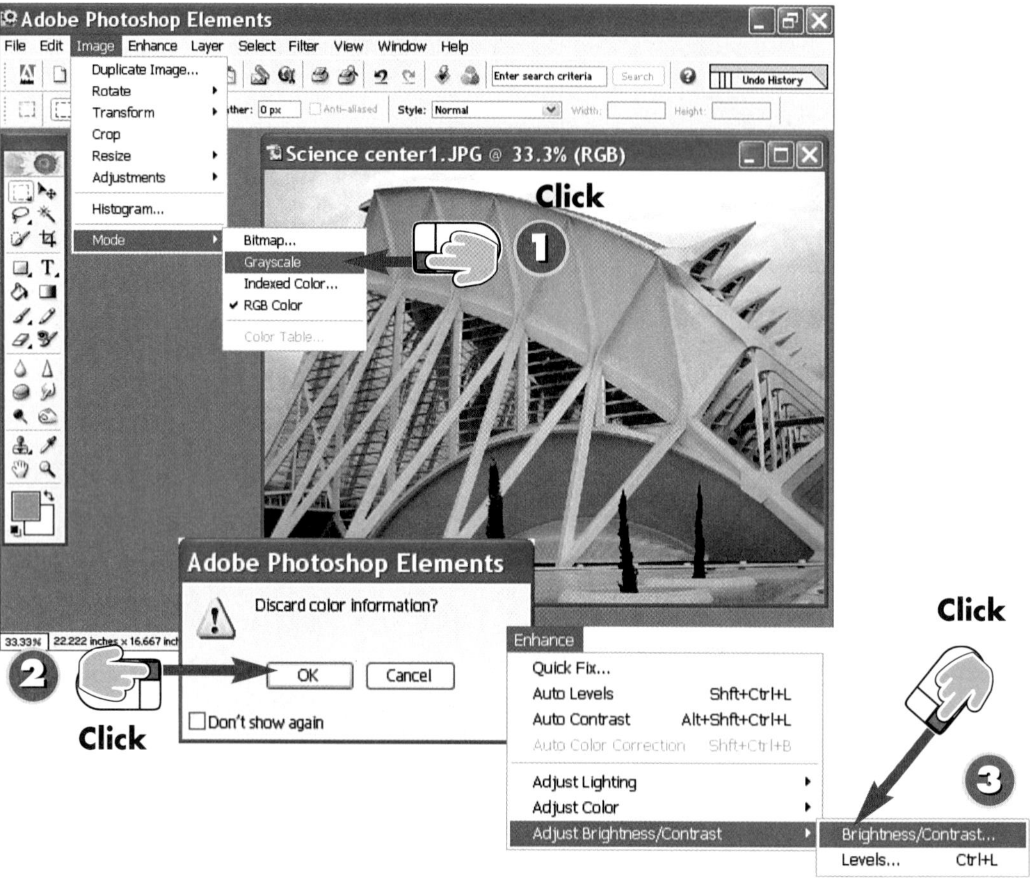

1. With a picture in the active image area, choose **Image**, **Mode**, **Grayscale**.
2. Click **OK**.
3. Choose **Enhance**, **Adjust Brightness/Contrast**, **Brightness/Contrast**.

INTRODUCTION

Back in the ancient days of film, high-contrast (hi-con) transparencies were called *Kodaliths*, the name of a Kodak product for mastering printing plates. You can create some dramatic artistic effects doing the same thing digitally—by converting a photo to black-and-white, with no shading.

HINT

Don't Do This to Your Boss

Hi-con doesn't make flattering portraits. Clean-shaven men with five o'clock shadow end up with real stubble trouble, and wispy laugh lines become deep trenches.

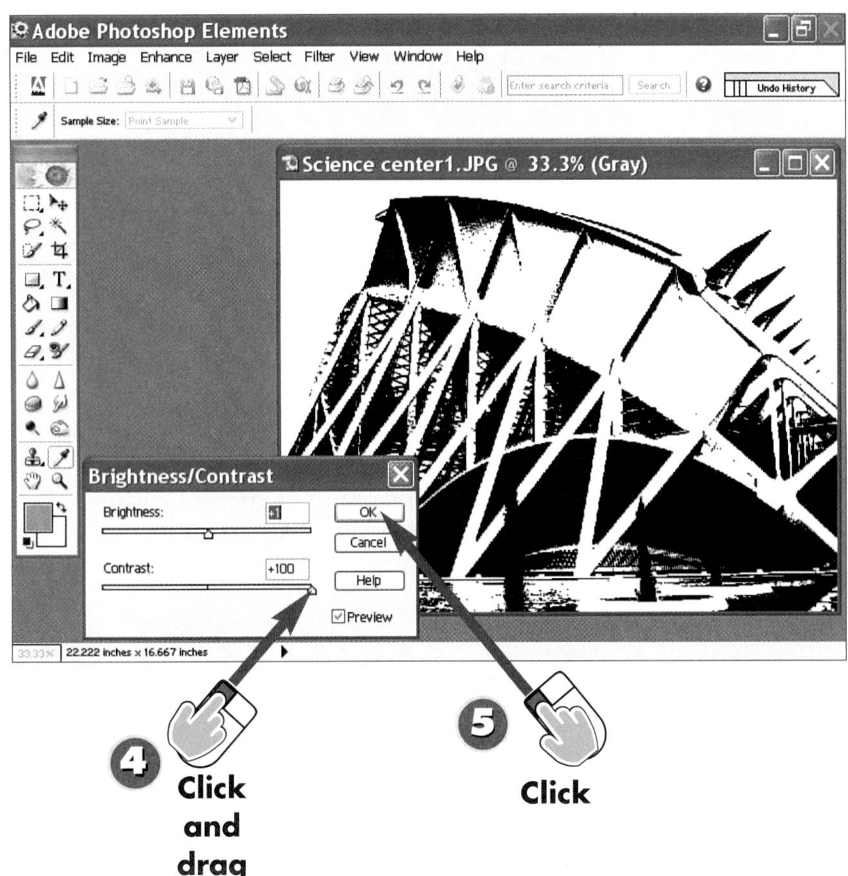

4. Adjust the **Contrast** slider to **100**.

5. Click **OK**.

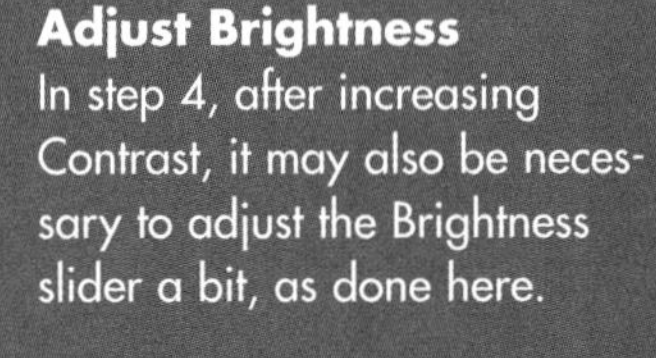

HINT

Adjust Brightness
In step 4, after increasing Contrast, it may also be necessary to adjust the Brightness slider a bit, as done here.

HINT

Consider the Source
Hi-con effects work best on images with smooth surfaces and sharp edges, such as architectural views. If the source photo has shaded areas, keep the Contrast setting below 80 percent to preserve some grayscale.

Making a Photo Look Like an Oil Painting

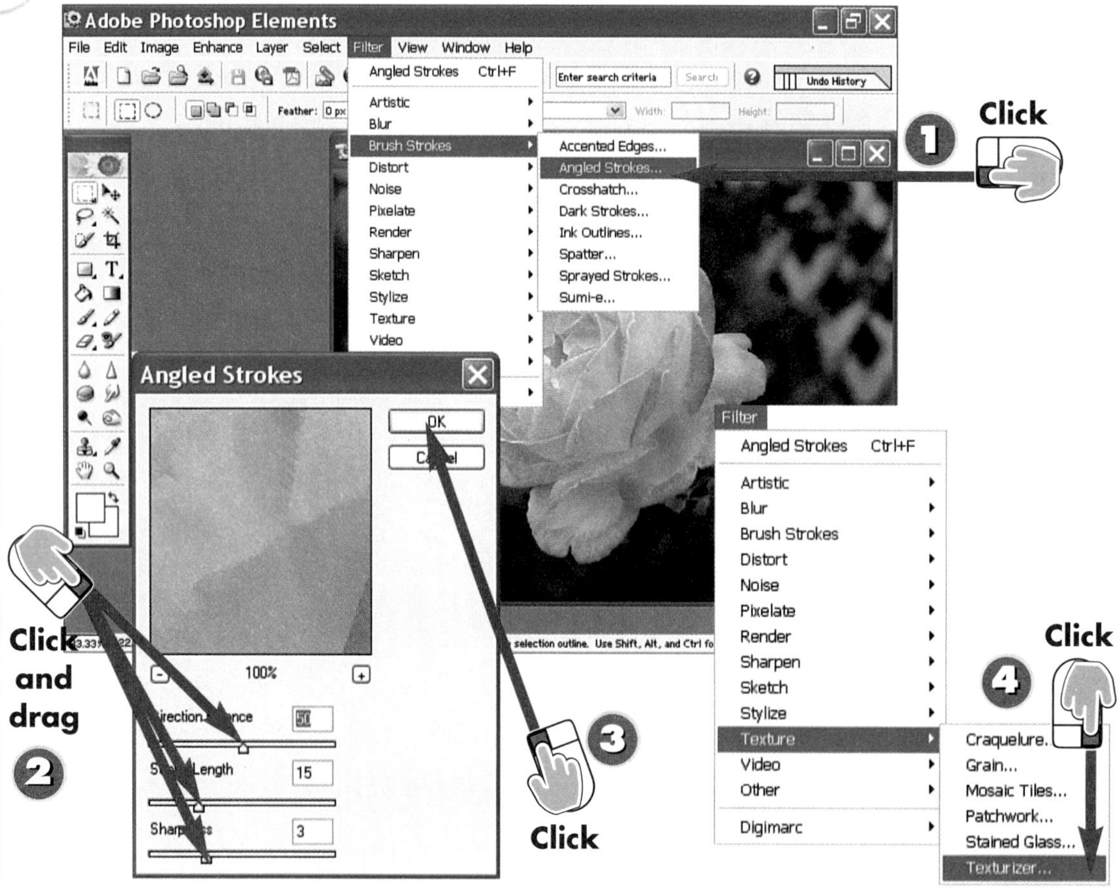

1. With a photo in the active image area, choose **Filter**, **Brush Strokes**, **Angled Strokes**.
2. Optionally, adjust the **Direction Balance**, **Stroke Length**, and **Sharpness** sliders.
3. When you see the desired effect in the Preview window, click **OK**.
4. Choose **Filter**, **Texture**, **Texturizer**.

INTRODUCTION

No one's proposing you start cranking out fake Rembrandts, but there's something about brush-strokes on canvas that says high class. Try this with the family portrait and pretend you sat for a Dutch master.

HINT

Tuning Your Strokes

The slider options in step 2 control the magnitude of the effect. You want to balance making the brushstrokes obvious enough to be seen, yet not so much as to obliterate fine detail in the picture.

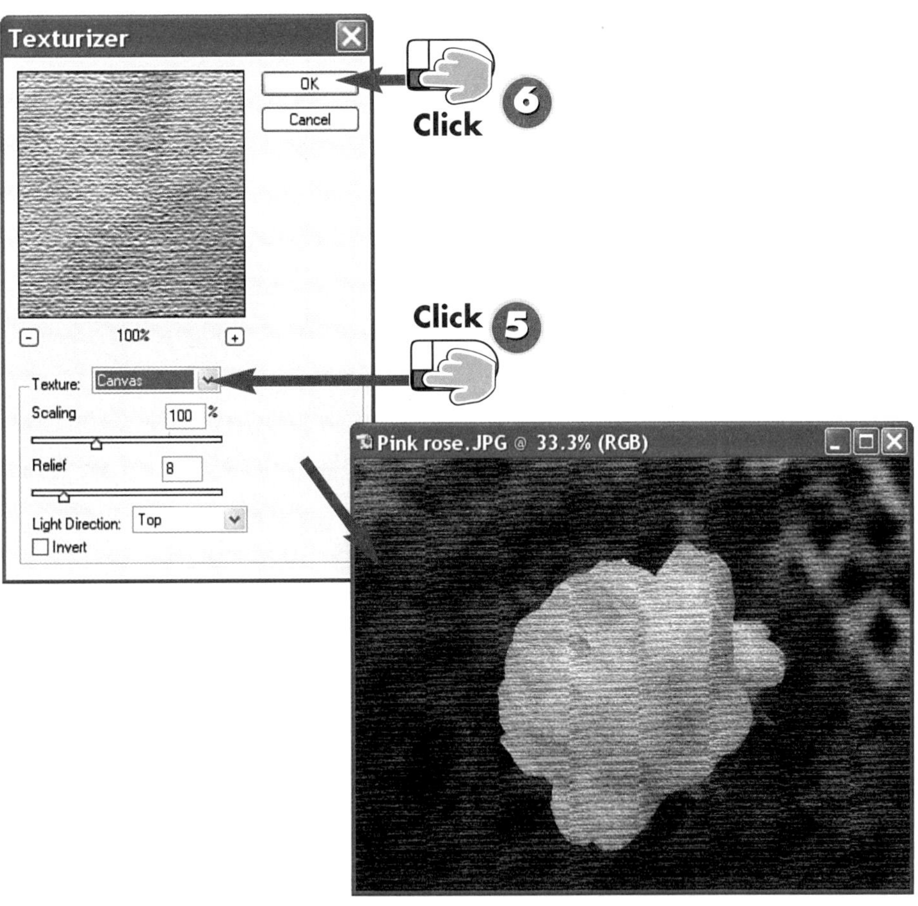

5 In the Texture box, select **Canvas**.

6 Click **OK**.

HINT

How Rough Is Your Canvas?
As with brushstrokes, you can adjust Texturizer options to control roughness and lighting on the canvas: Scaling, Relief, and Light Direction. The Invert option reverses light and dark effects.

TIP

No Rules
There are no rules for applying artistic effects. Be guided by your own taste. For example, instead of a Canvas texture, try Burlap or Sandstone. And remember, results vary depending on the source material.

Posterizing a Picture

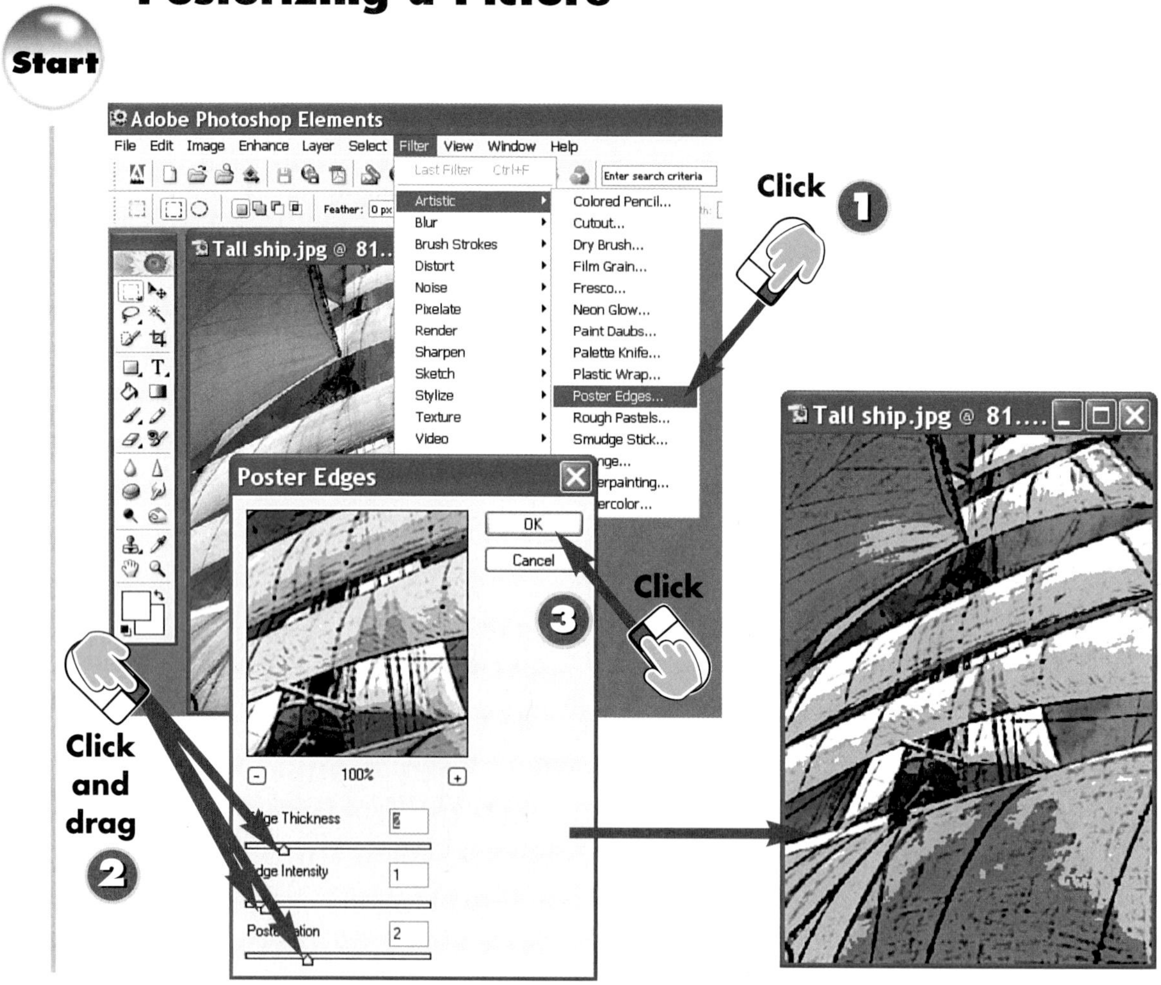

1. With a picture in the active image area, choose **Filter**, **Artistic**, **Poster Edges**.

2. Optionally, adjust sliders for **Edge Thickness**, **Edge Intensity**, and **Posterization**.

3. Click **OK**.

INTRODUCTION

Posterization became popular in the psychedelic movement of the 1960s as a way of making images seem more intense. Photoshop Elements includes a filter called Poster Edges to create this effect.

HINT

Ideas for Greeting Cards?

Applying the Poster Edges effect to a photo can make it look like a fine watercolor and ink drawing, or an elaborate illustration in a children's book.

Making a Photo Look Like a Sketch

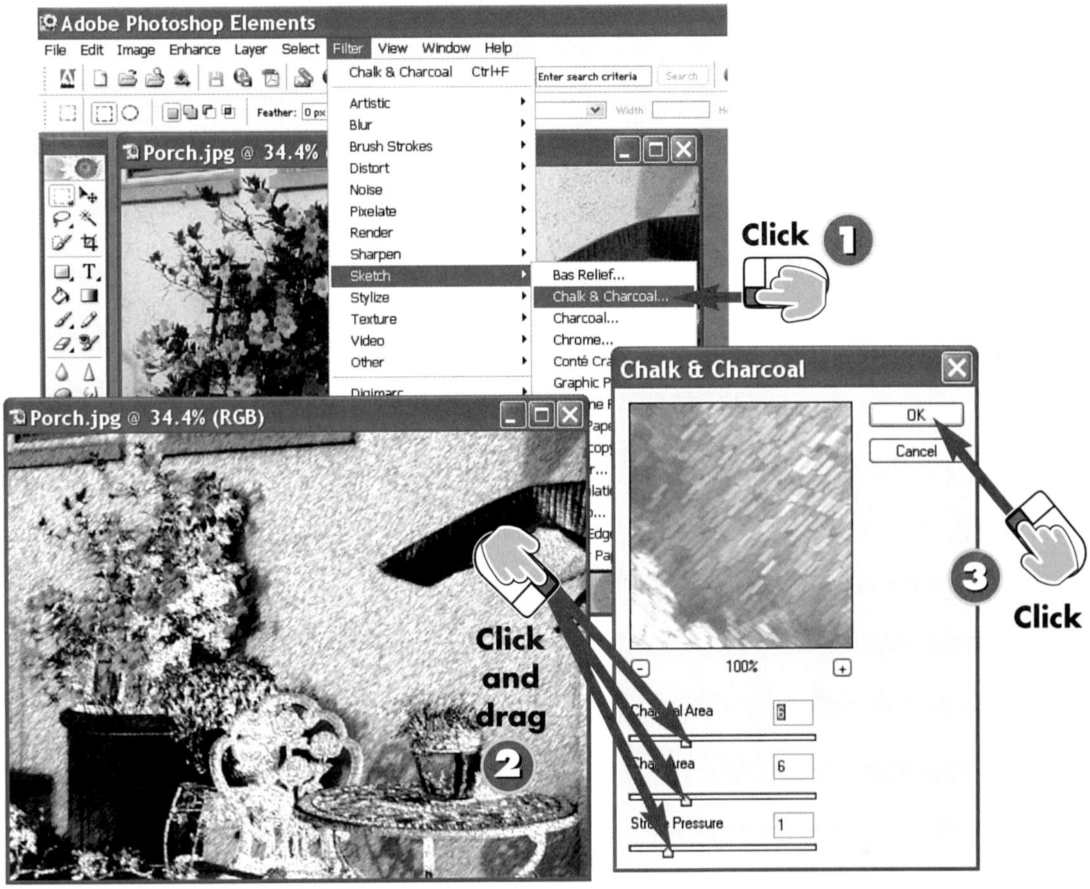

1. With a photo in the active image area, choose **Filter**, **Sketch**, **Chalk & Charcoal**.
2. Optionally, adjust sliders for **Charcoal Area**, **Chalk Area**, and **Stroke Pressure**.
3. Click **OK**.

Whether your drawings look like stick figures or you're just in too big a hurry to sit down with your sketchpad, Photoshop Elements can make any photo look hand-drawn. For example, take a photo of the curbside view of your home, convert it to a sketch, and use it to illustrate personalized party invitations or stationery.

HINT

Make It Snappy

Although level correction isn't a required step, it's applied to this example to darken the lines so that the result reproduces better in print.

Applying the Pointillize Filter

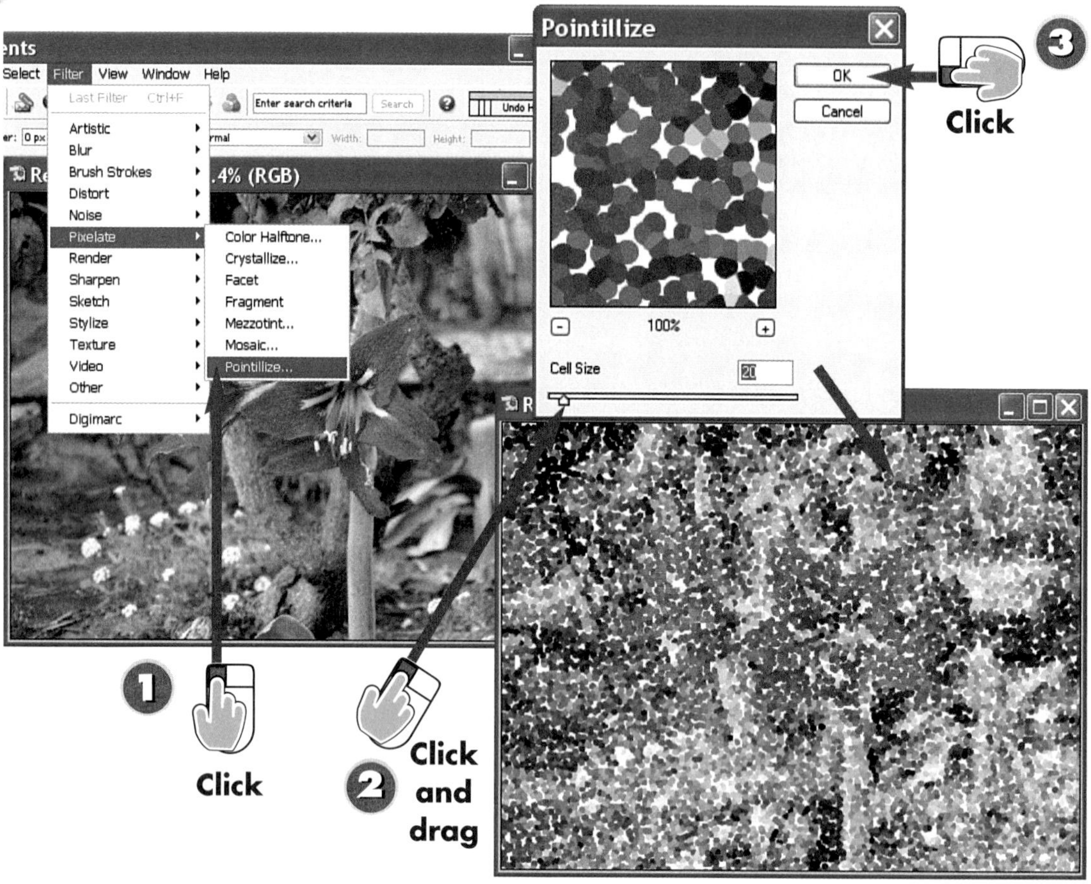

1. With a photo in the active image area, choose **Filter**, **Pixelate**, **Pointillize**.
2. Optionally, adjust the **Cell Size** slider to get the look you want.
3. Click **OK**.

INTRODUCTION

Pointillism is a technique pioneered by French Impressionist painter Georges Seurat more than a century ago. His paintings are composed of thousands of tiny dots of bright colors—and the overall effect was apparent only when viewing the work from a distance. In a sense, he invented pixels, which are the building blocks of today's computerized, digital images.

TIP

How Big Is a Cell?
Cell size in step 2 controls the size of the picture dots and the magnitude of the effect. You want it large enough to make the effect visible, small enough to preserve important picture details.

Using a Blur Filter

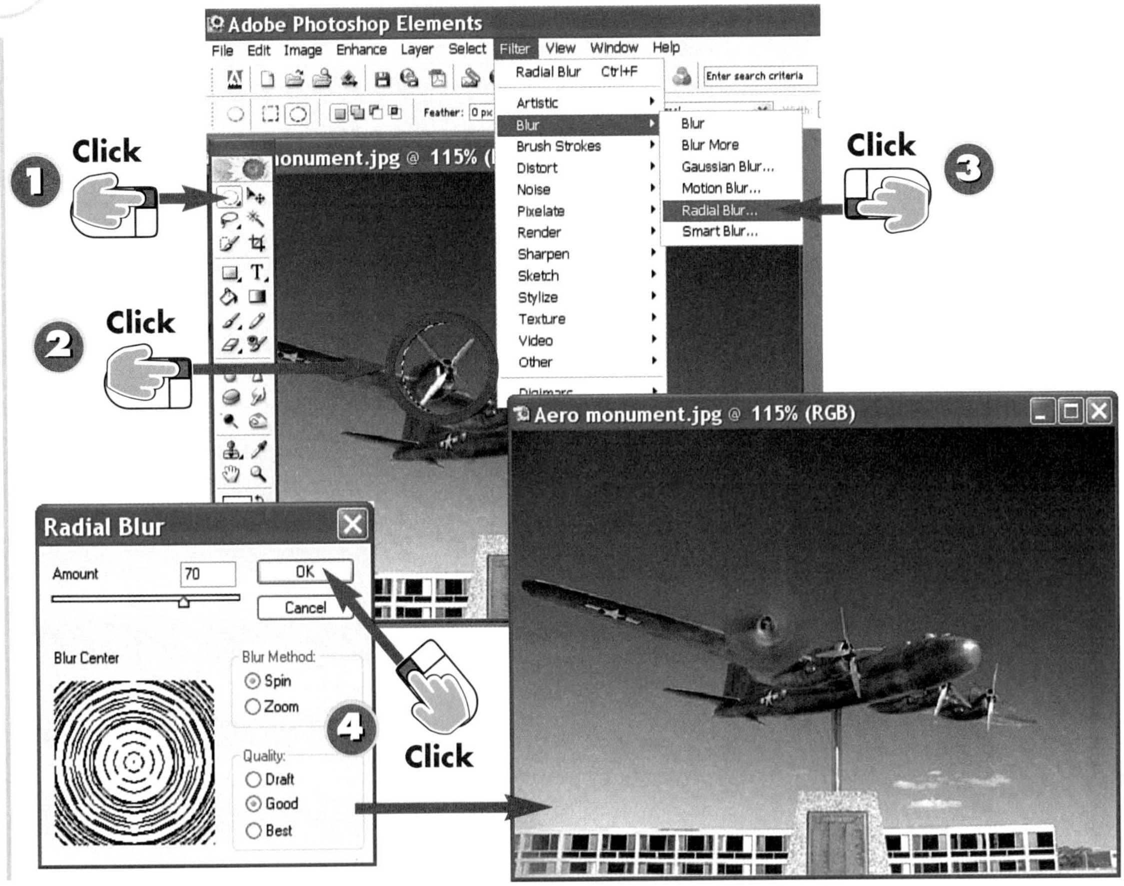

1. With a photo in the active image area, click a selection tool, such as **Elliptical Marquee**.
2. Click and drag to select the area in the image to which you want the blurring effect applied.
3. Choose **Filter**, **Blur**, **Radial Blur**.
4. Click **OK**. (To keep working on the photo, press **Ctrl+D** to release your selection.)

INTRODUCTION

Many of the artistic filters in Photoshop Elements might well be applied to the whole picture. Blurring is an example of a filter you'd normally apply only to a selected portion of an image, such as the propeller of this aircraft replica.

TIP

Blur or Zoom—and How Fast?

Options in the Radial Blur window include Amount (magnitude of the effect), Blur Method (Spin or Zoom), and Quality (Draft, Good, or Best). You can drag the **Blur Center** to reposition it.

PART

Painting and Drawing

Many people think of Photoshop Elements mainly as a digital photo lab, but it's also an art studio. So, welcome to your all-electronic work-and-play room—where you never have to wear a smock, clean a brush, or deal with that nasty turpentine.

Those of you who start with a photo as a background may have a more practical purpose in mind—such as making ads and brochures.

And along with adding text, combining your photos with your original artwork gives a wonderfully personal touch. Recipients of your greeting cards, party invitations, photo email, and newsletters will appreciate the care you took—even though none of this is nearly as hard as they might imagine!

Getting a bit more serious, you can also illustrate business presentations, school reports, and instructional materials with professional-looking diagrams and drawings. No more crude pencil sketches, and good-bye forever to stick figures!

But don't stop there. Set aside a rainy Saturday afternoon to discover the joy of digital painting and drawing. Vincent Van Gogh never had such a rich and varied set of tools!

Look What I Made!

Paint and draw over a photo to create your own custom graphics for postcards.

Or just paint and draw from scratch for the pure joy of it!

Creating a Shape

Start

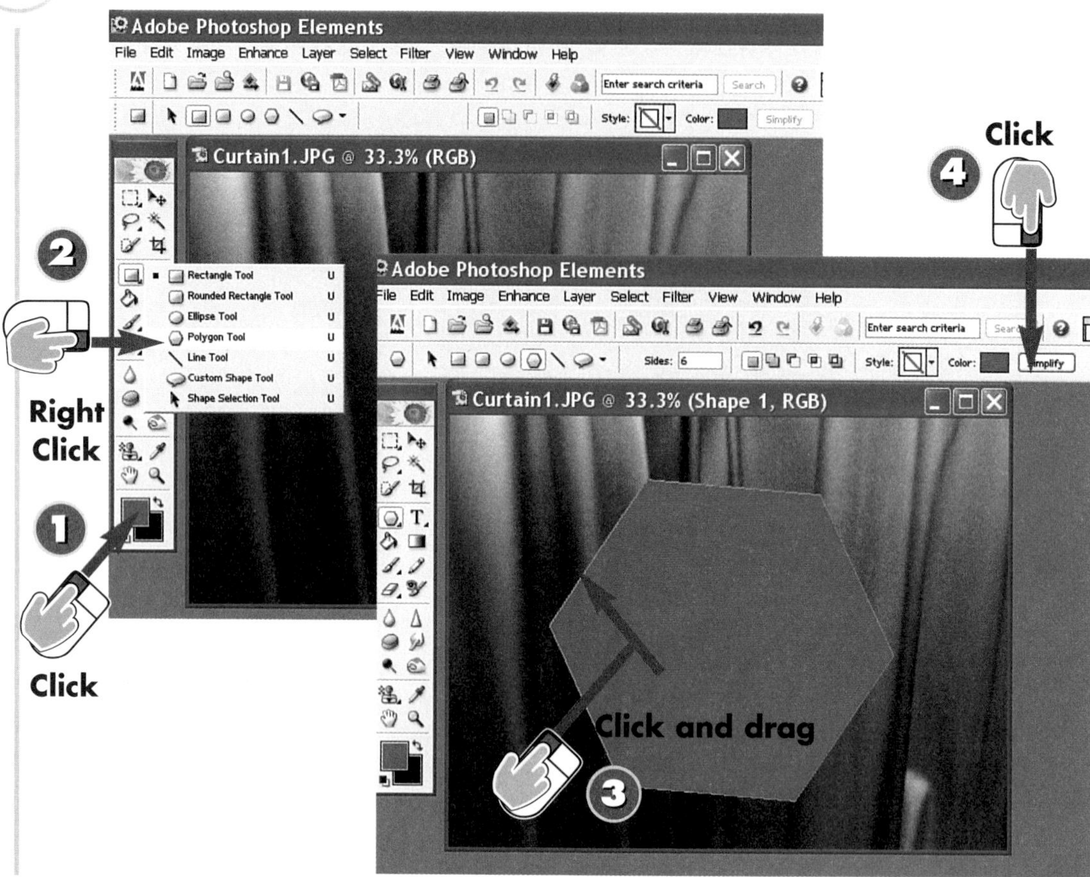

1. Click to select a foreground color.
2. Right-click the **Shape** tool and select the shape tool you want, such as Polygon Tool.
3. Click and drag in the image area to adjust the size and proportions of the shape.
4. To make the pixels of the shape editable, click the **Simplify** button.

INTRODUCTION

Photoshop Elements generates a variety of geometric shapes for you. Here we show drawing over an image. You can also start by choosing File, New to draw on a blank canvas.

TIP

Shift to Get Regular
Hold down the **Shift** key while you draw to make Rectangles square, Ellipses circular. Lines follow the closest 45-degree angle.

HINT

Moving and Resizing
To move or resize a shape before it's simplified, use the Shape Selection tool. When simplified, use the Move tool instead. For best-quality shapes, always try to resize before you simplify.

Adding a Bevel to a Shape

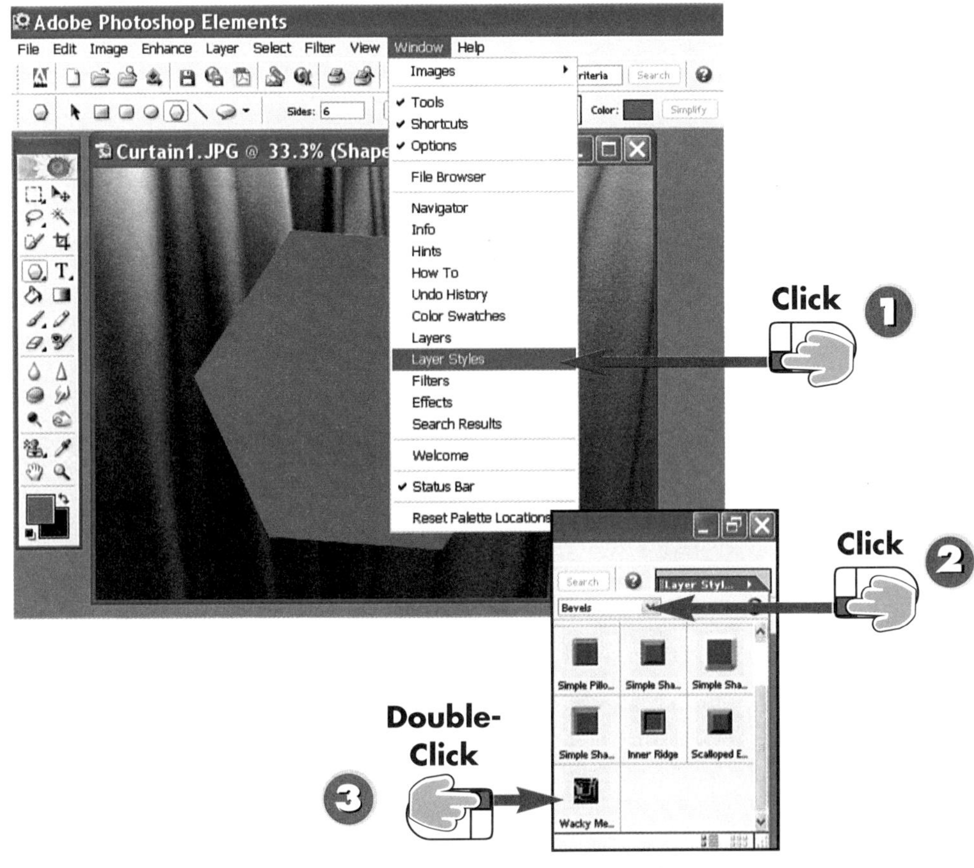

1. Having created or selected a shape, choose **Window**, **Layer Styles**.
2. In the Layer Styles palette, select **Bevels** in the Style Libraries drop-down menu.
3. Double-click the bevel style you want to apply.

INTRODUCTION

New shapes can look plain and flat. Adding a bevel gives the shape a dimensional quality that can also make it stand out from the background. Photoshop Elements provides a nice selection of bevel styles that can give your object a bold, dimensional look. Just click the one you like, and it's applied automatically.

TIP

Close It Quick!
If the palette is open but docked, as shown, click anywhere outside the palette to close it after step 3.

TIP

Selecting Shapes
If the shape you want isn't the most recent one you created, select it with the **Move** tool before you do step 1 (Auto Select Layer must be checked). If the shape is one of many on a layer, use the **Shape Selection** tool instead.

Filling a Shape with Color

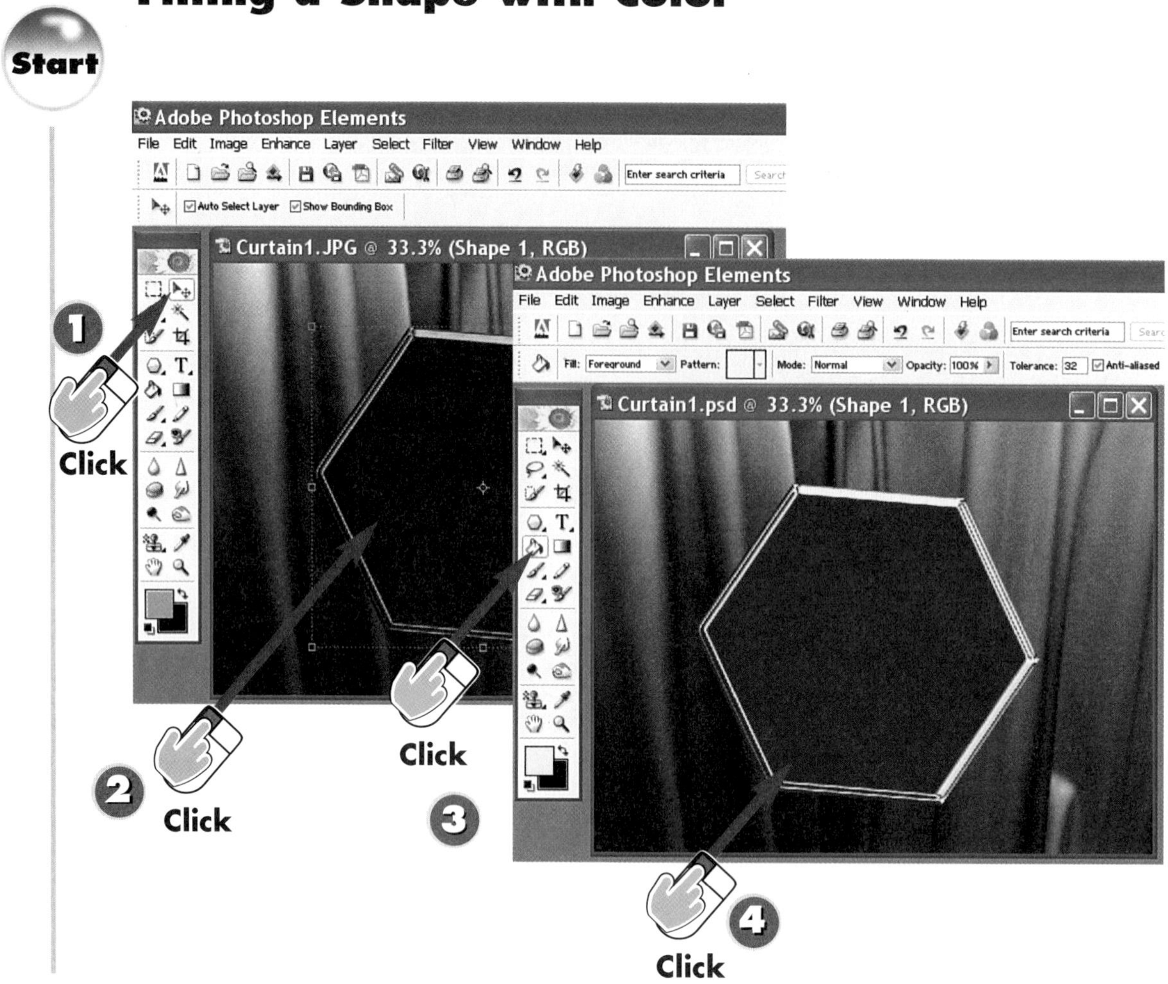

Click

Click

Click

Click

1 Having chosen the foreground color, select the **Move** tool, or press **V**. (**Auto Select Layer** must be checked.)

2 Select the shape.

3 Select the **Paint Bucket** tool, or press **K**.

4 Click inside the shape to apply the color.

INTRODUCTION

If you've worked through the tasks to this point, this won't be the first time you've used the Paint Bucket tool. But notice how quickly and easily you can recolor a shape. Always remember that the Paint Bucket—and other painting tools—use whatever you've selected as the current foreground color.

TIP

Change the Fill Color
Before you do step 1, click the Foreground color swatch at the bottom of the toolbar and make a selection from the **Color Picker**.

TIP

Fill with a Pattern
If you prefer a pattern rather than a color, before doing step 2, select **Pattern** from the **Fill** drop-down menu in the Options bar; then make a selection from the **Pattern** menu.

Using the Eyedropper to Pick a Color

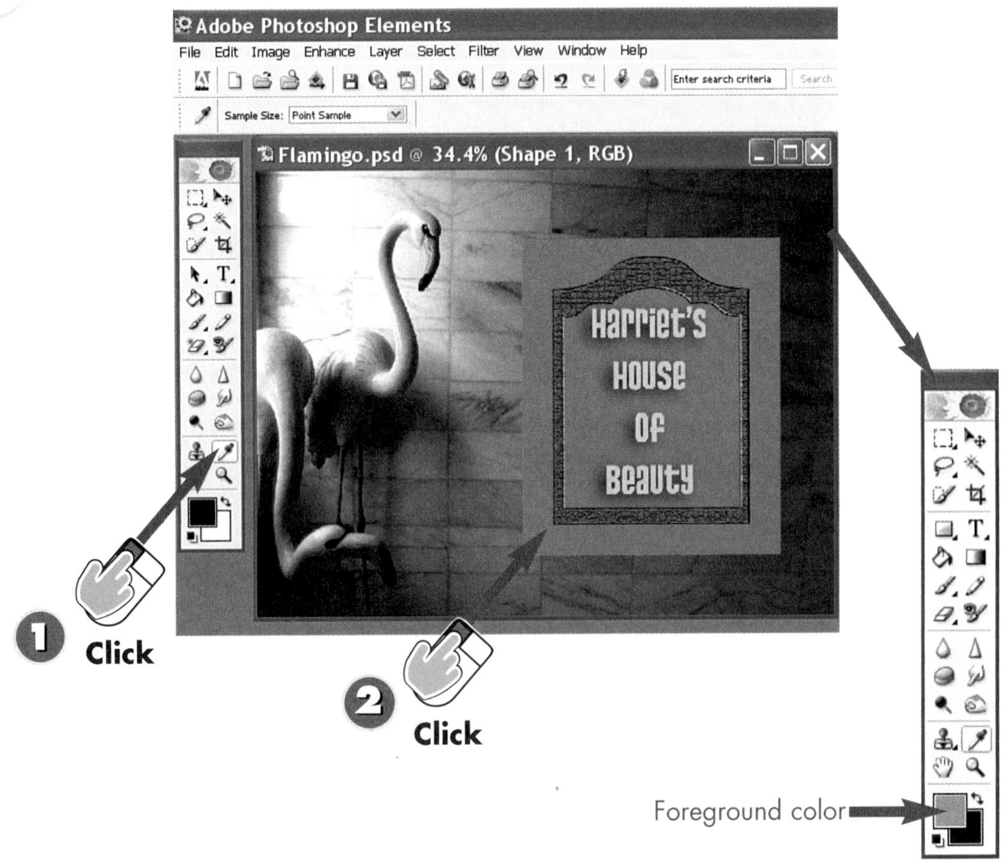

1. Select the **Eyedropper** tool, or press **I**.

2. Click a color you want to match in the image area. The foreground color changes to the color of your sample, and you can now use any tool that applies color.

INTRODUCTION

Want to pick a color for a new shape or brush stroke that exactly matches some color in the image? The Eyedropper tool sucks up the color you click and loads it as the current foreground color. Whatever painting or drawing tool you use next applies that color.

TIP

Changing Sample Size
Before step 2, you can choose **3 x 3 Average** or **5 x 5 Average** to set the number of pixels in the area the Eyedropper will sample. (Remember, it's an average, so the resulting color may be a blend of the sampled pixels.)

HINT

Whenever You See It
Photoshop Elements uses the Eyedropper pointer in other places, such as the Color Swatches palette, and it always works as a color selector.

Using the Color Swatches Palette

Start

1 Click

2 Click

New Foreground color

1. Choose **Window**, **Color Swatches**.

2. Click the color you want to use next. The foreground color changes to the color of your sample, and you are ready to use any tool that applies color.

INTRODUCTION

If you've ever browsed through color swatches at the paint store, you know how handy it can be to see a coordinated selection of choices. It's generally quicker and easier to make a choice from preset Color Swatches than to use the Color Picker (which, for most folks, has way too many).

TIP

Swatches for Different Purposes
The drop-down menu in the Swatches palette has sets of colors for both creative and practical purposes. For example, choose **Web Safe Colors** when creating graphics for use on the Internet.

Painting and Drawing with a Brush and Pencil

Start

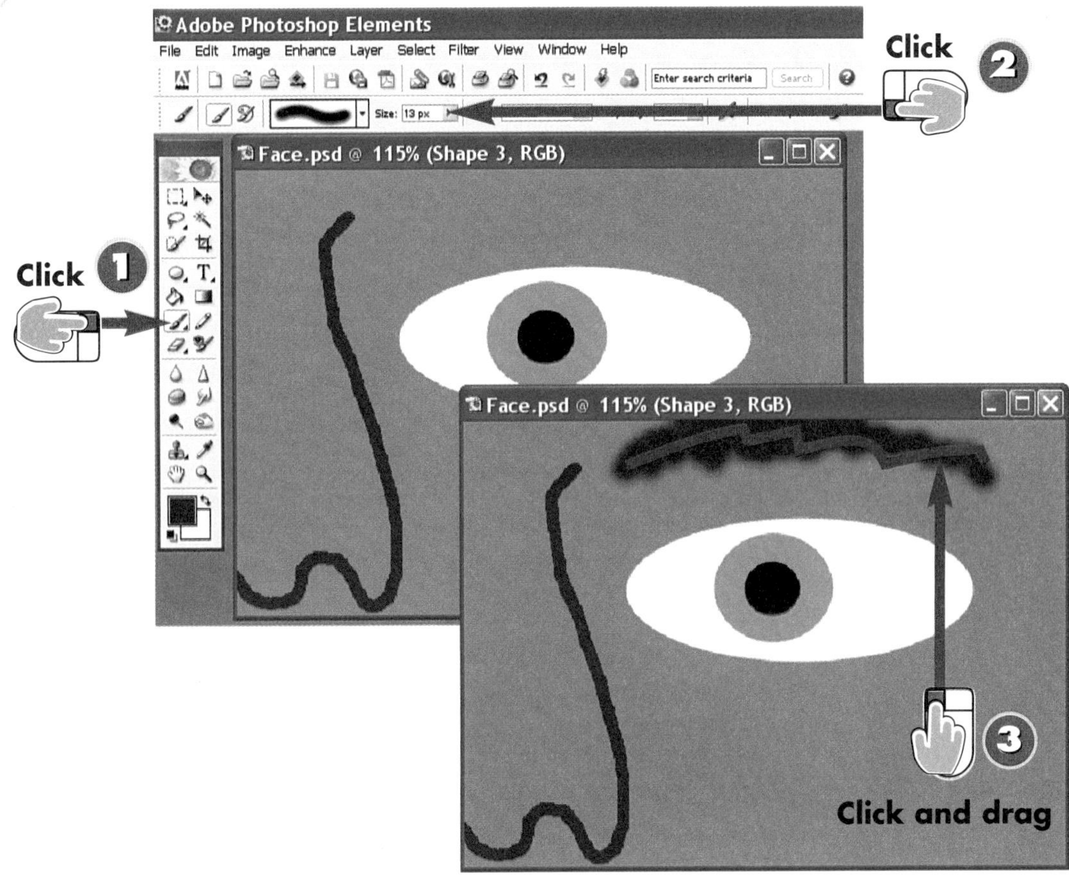

1. Select the **Brush** tool.
2. Set brush properties in the options bar, such as **Size**.
3. Click and drag in the image area to apply each brush stroke.

INTRODUCTION

Use the Brush tool to do freehand painting (or Impressionist Brush to paint over and blur). The Pencil tool right beside it in the toolbar works much the same, except pencil lines don't have soft edges.

HINT

Brush Stroke Technique

Keep holding down the mouse button and paint with a scrubbing motion to apply a single, continuous brush stroke. Or, click and release the mouse button frequently as you paint to apply dabs of color.

TIP

A Tip on Brush Tips

Select the tip size and brush stroke properties in the options bar before you do step 2. Pick one of the preset brushes or adjust the other options to create your own.

Controlling How Brushes Behave

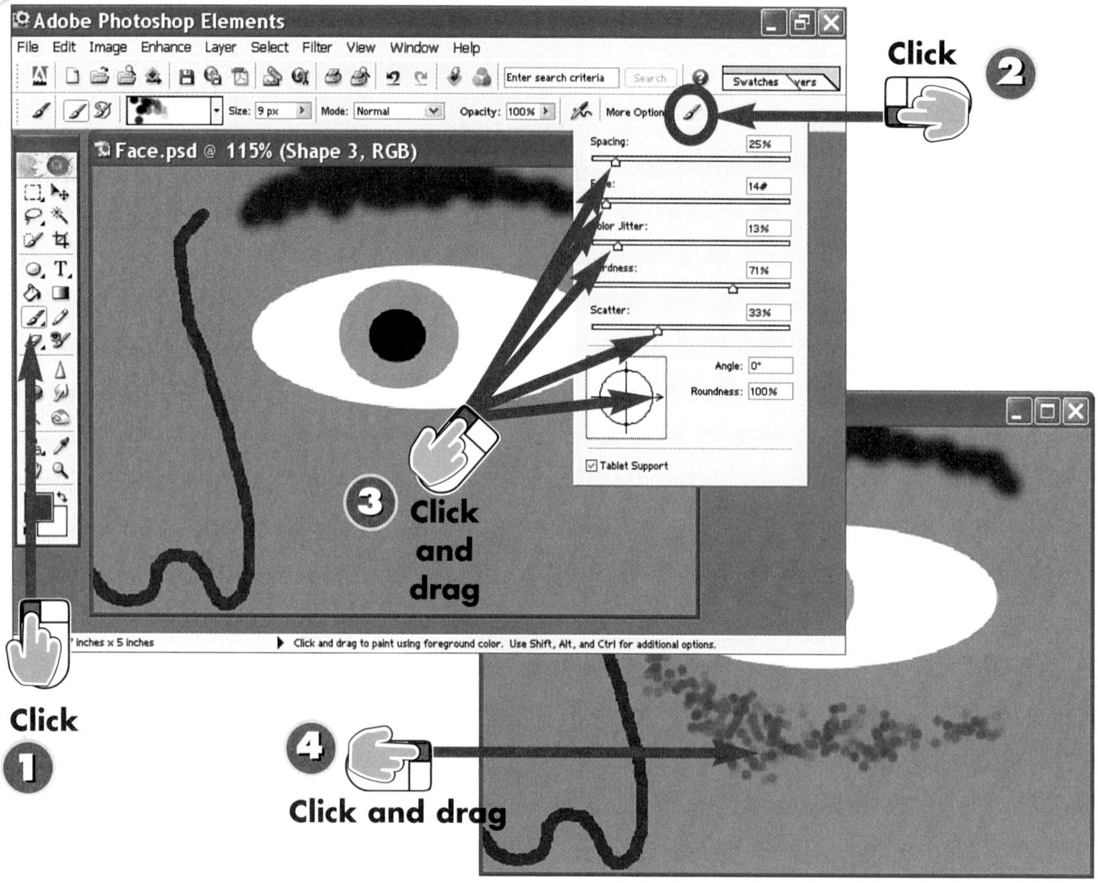

1. Select the **Brush** tool.
2. Click **More Options** in the options bar.
3. Adjust how the brush works by dragging a slider or typing a new percentage for one or more options.
4. Click and drag in the image area to apply each brush stroke.

INTRODUCTION

If you really want to get arty with brush tips, you can make all kinds of adjustments in the options bar, before you start painting. Also located there is the Airbrush button, which generates a spray of pixels at the brush tip. (Access the full range of options from the More Options drop-down menu.)

HINT

Lots to Choose From
There are more than a dozen categories of preset brushes in the options bar, and you have the choice of fine-tuning any of them by making adjustments using the More Options drop-down menu.

TIP

Still More Options
In the options bar, Mode controls effects for artistic purposes, as well as for doing fine photo retouching. Opacity, in effect, is paint thickness—lower numbers are more like watercolor.

Painting with the Pattern Stamp

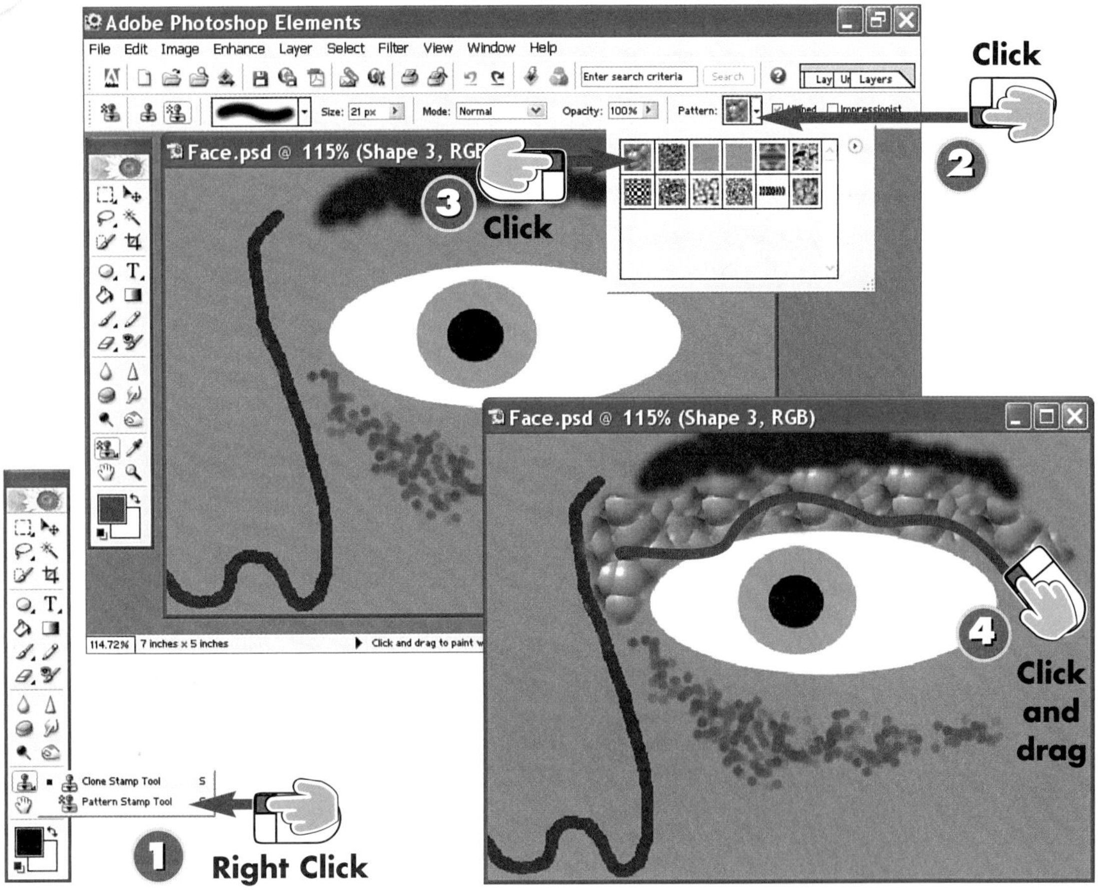

1. Right-click the **Stamp** tool and select the **Pattern Stamp** tool.
2. Open the **Pattern** menu in the options bar.
3. Double-click to select a pattern from the Pattern drop-down menu.
4. Click and drag in the image area to paint, just as you would with the Brush tool.

INTRODUCTION

Painting with a pattern is lots of fun—and something you can't do nearly as easily with physical paint and paper. The result is more like making cutouts of wallpaper or fabric and pasting them down—much like art techniques *collage* and *mixed media.*

HINT

The Other Stamp Tool
The Pattern Stamp's roommate in the toolbar, the Clone Stamp, isn't so much for painting as it is a tool for removing unwanted details, such as facial blemishes, from photos.

HINT

Options, Options
Notice that there are all kinds of choices in the options bar. Make your selections before doing step 2, just as you would with a brush.

Using the Erasers

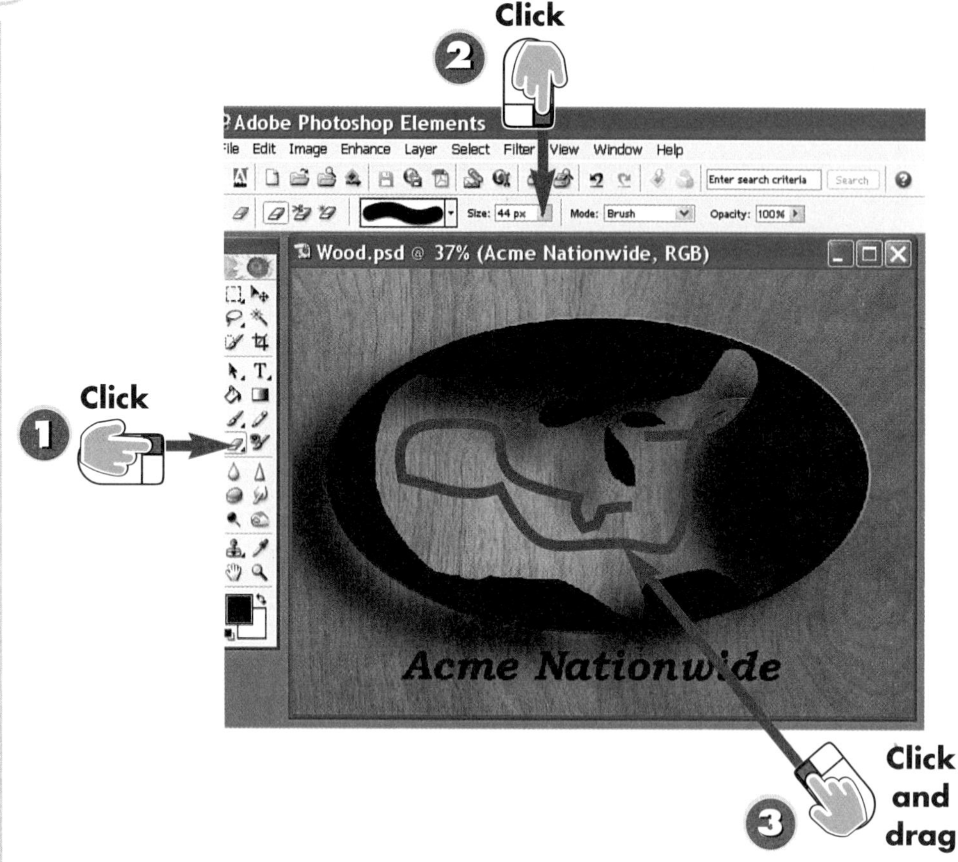

1. Select the **Eraser** tool, or press **E**.
2. If you want, change the tool properties in the options bar.
3. Click and drag over the pixels you want to erase.

INTRODUCTION

The Eraser tool works just like a brush—but removes pixels in its path rather than depositing them. It only affects shapes on the layer currently selected, so you may want to open the Layers palette first to get your bearings.

TIP

Undo Instead?
Use the Eraser tool for partial erasures of shapes. To simply get rid of painting mistakes, **Edit**, **Undo** or **Edit**, **Step Backward** may be faster and cleaner.

TIP

Other Eraser Tools
Right-click in step 1 to select **Background Eraser**, which deletes a single color sampled from the center of a brush, or **Magic Eraser**, which deletes areas of similar-colored pixels with a click (like Magic Wand does for selections).

Softening Edges

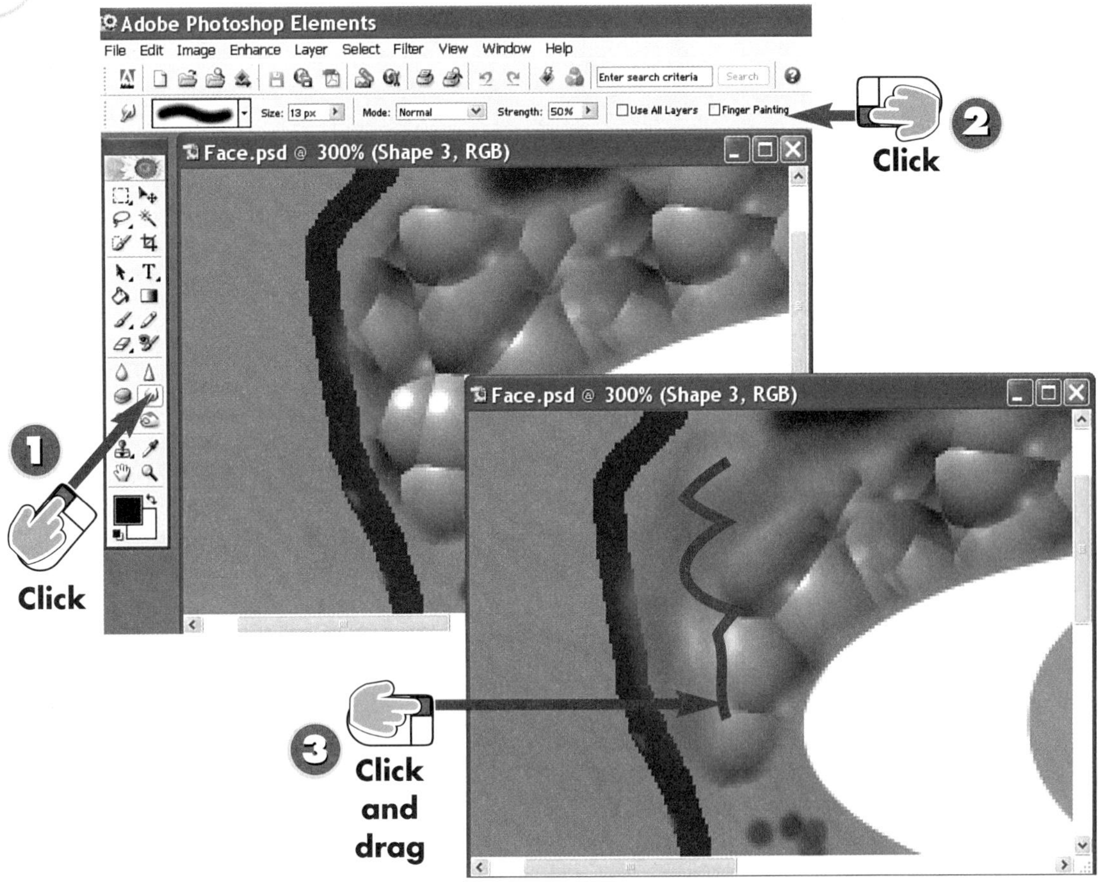

1. With the edge you want to soften zoomed in the image area, select the **Smudge** tool, or press **F**.
2. If you want, change the tool properties in the options bar.
3. Click and drag along the edge to soften it.

INTRODUCTION

Some of the painting tools can be used either for painting or for retouching details in photos, and the Smudge tool is one of these. Artists who've worked with pastels will be familiar with the technique of rubbing chalk edges to soften them.

TIP

Finger Paint, Oh Boy!
If you're tempted to make a creative mess the clean, electronic way, check the **Finger Paint** box in the options bar before you do step 2.

HINT

Impressionist Brush Instead?
The effect of the Smudge tool may be too subtle for your taste. For more pronounced blurring, use the Impressionist Brush tool in one of the smaller brush sizes. Also try effects in the Filter, Blur submenu.

PART 7

Flattering Your Subjects

Okay, in other parts of this book we've talked about Photoshop Elements being your photo lab and your art studio—but why not also think of it as a one-stop health and beauty spa? Digital retouching, if not overdone, can perk up your friends and loved ones, making them appear to shed pounds, revitalizing their complexions, and putting that old sparkle in their eyes—all without risky fad diets, treatments, or pills!

But let's emphasize—*don't overdo it.* As a good rule of thumb, try to soften rather than erase. Leave some lines, freckles, and whatever other imperfections give your beloved her unique character and winning charm. Go too far, and you'll have a slick beauty shot of a lifeless mannequin.

Many of the techniques described in this part were applied to the photo on the facing page. Retouching included correcting a color cast, desaturating the background with the Sponge tool, softening facial lines with the Smudge tool, removing a bra strap and tan line with the Clone Stamp tool, adding eyelight with a brush tool, emphasizing eyebrows with Sharpen, adding a Gaussian blur to soften skin overall, and increasing hair-color highlights with the Sponge tool set to Saturate.

The transformation took about 10 minutes. But, go figure, she still wants a trip to the spa.

You Look Simply Marvelous, Darling!

Before

After

Adding Eyelight for Personality

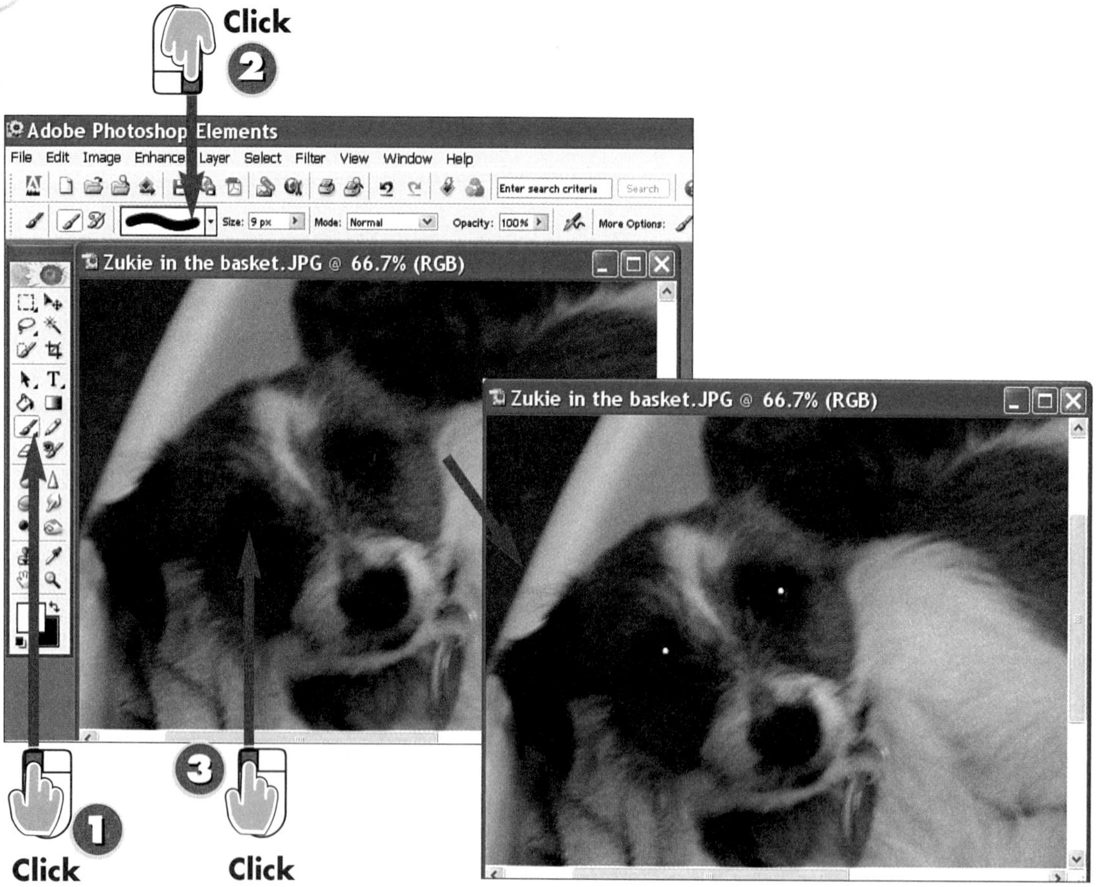

1. With white as the current foreground color, select the **Brush** tool.
2. In the options bar, select a brush tip smaller than the iris of the eye.
3. Click inside the eye lens, at the edge of the iris. (Repeat to match position in the other eye.)

INTRODUCTION

Eyelight is a trick of Hollywood cinematographers, who aim a small spotlight directly at the star's eyes to add sparkle. They don't give movie villains eyelight, and somehow you instinctively know they are shiftless, not to be trusted.

HINT

Eyelight Is a Reflection

Instead of being centered in the eye, the position of the eyelight should match the direction of the main light source (called *key light*). If the key is high and to the left, put the white dot in the top-left center of the eye.

HINT

Get It Right

Besides indicating the direction of the light source, the positions of the eyelights in each eye should match exactly. If not, your star could look either cross- or wall-eyed.

Fixing Dark and Light Areas in a Photo

Click

Click

Click and drag

Click and drag

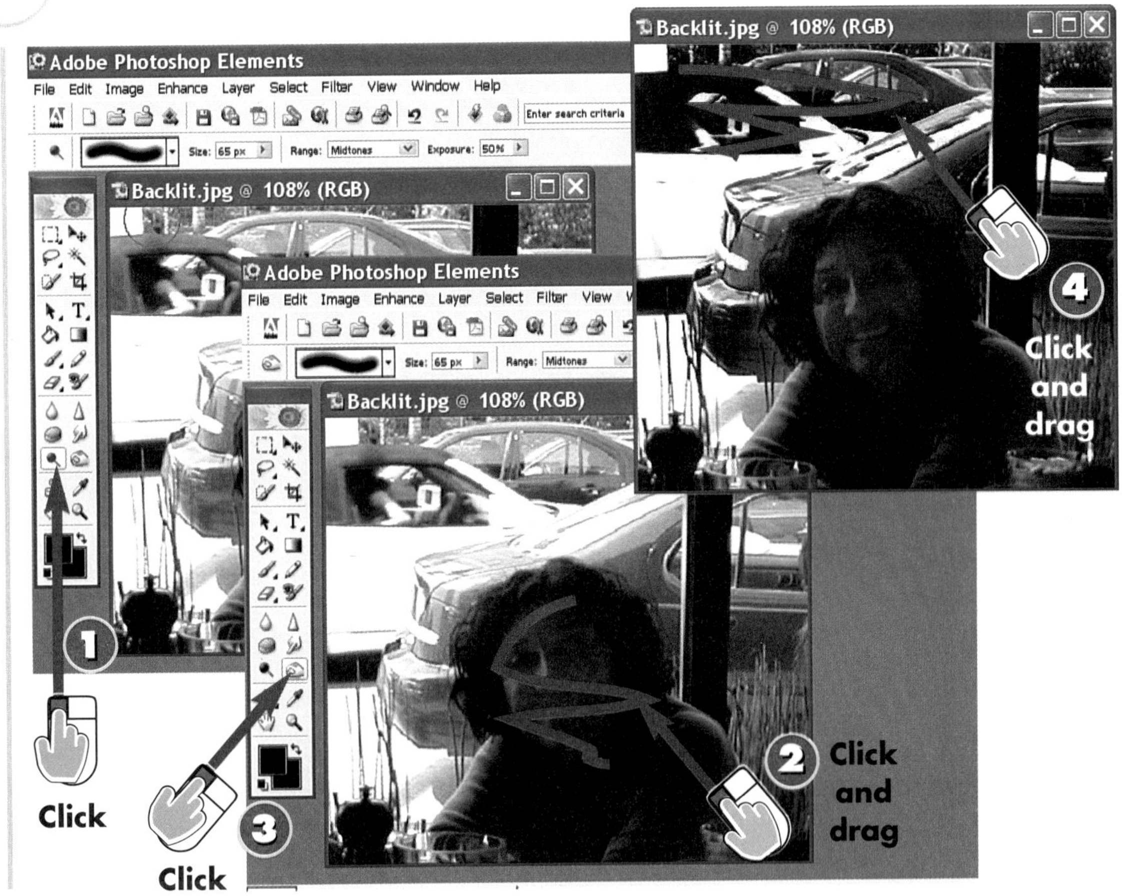

1. With the photo in the active image area, select the **Dodge** tool, or press **O**.
2. Click and drag to paint an area to recover detail from its shadows.
3. Select the **Burn** tool, or press **J**.
4. Click and drag to paint an area that needs detail recovered from its highlights.

INTRODUCTION

Dodge and Burn are *toning* tools with names carried over from traditional darkroom techniques for increasing or decreasing exposure in areas of shadow or highlight when printing film *negatives*. The Dodge tool lightens dark areas (overexposed), and the Burn tool darkens light areas (underexposed).

HINT

Crushed or Blown Out?
Dark areas that are totally black are said to be *crushed*, and totally white areas are *blown out*. Neither has any detail you can recover by using these steps. Try to light the shot better next time before you take it.

TIP

Dodge/Burn Options
Besides a selection of brush tips, the options bar contains settings for Mode (Shadows, Midtones, or Highlights) and Strength (similar to print light intensity in the darkroom).

Removing or Softening Facial Lines

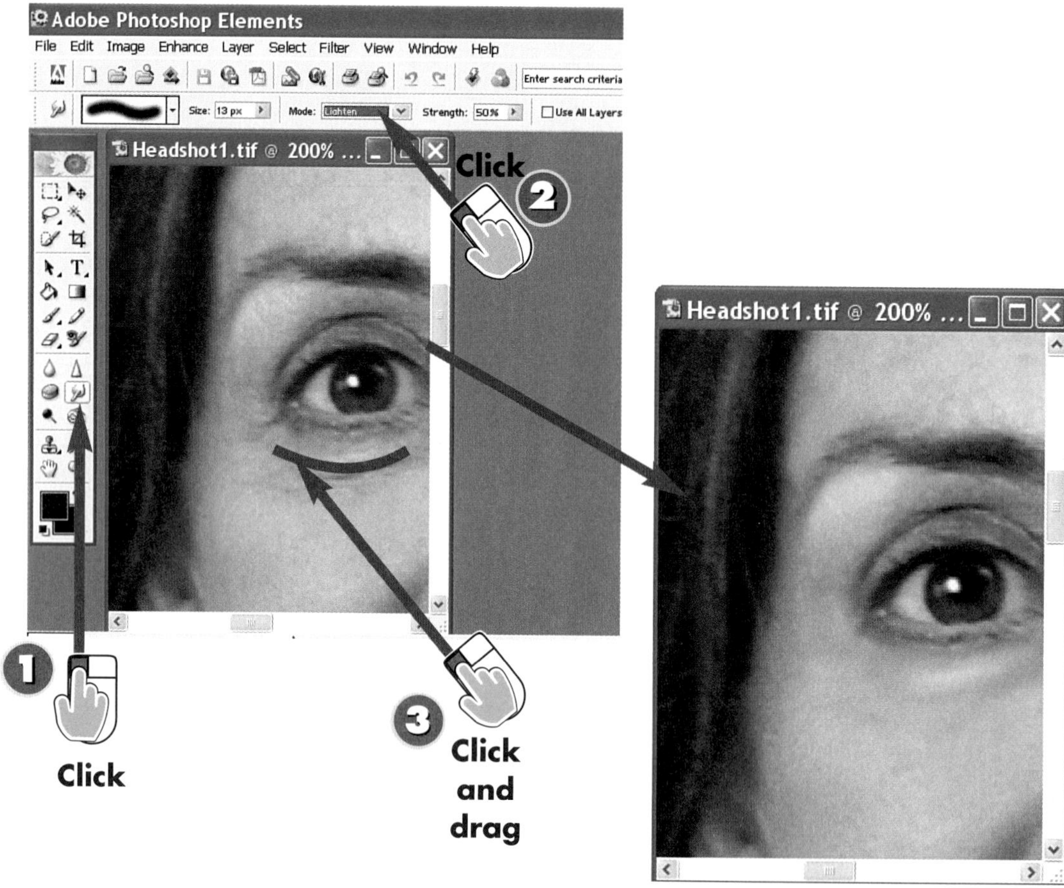

1. With a zoomed photo in the active image area, select the **Smudge** tool, or press **F**.
2. In the options bar, select **Lighten** from the **Mode** drop-down menu.
3. Click and drag over a facial line to blend it away.

INTRODUCTION

This one's sure to please—the wrinkle remover. Remember, the lines in the face convey expressiveness, so don't paint them all out. Ask yourself: Are these crow's feet or laugh lines? (To work in even finer detail, you can use the Blur tool much the same way.)

HINT

Mode Options
The Smudge tool can be versatile, depending on this setting. Besides Normal, Darken, and Lighten (used here), the effect can be confined to Hue, Saturation, Color, or Luminosity.

TIP

To Be Precise About It
For best results, pick a Soft Round brush tip in the options bar with a Size just slightly larger than the facial lines you're retouching—and trace along the line as you paint.

Removing Facial Blemishes

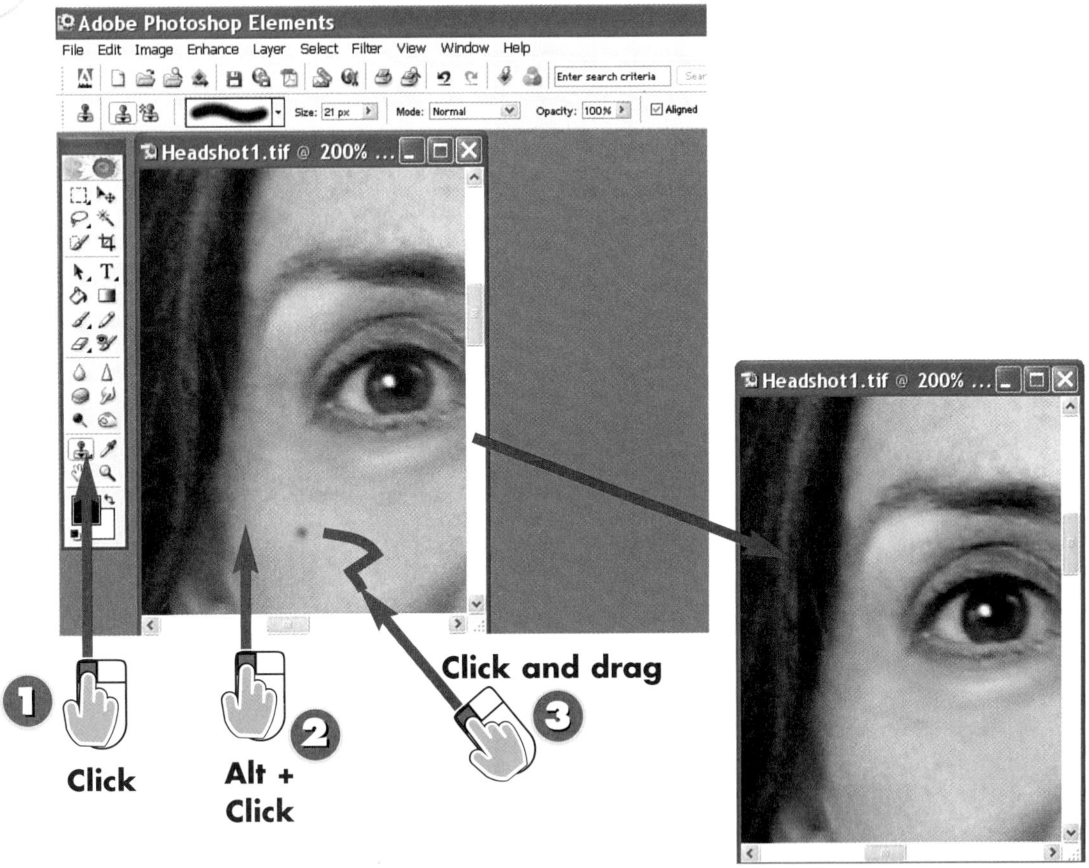

1. With a zoomed photo in the active image area, select the **Clone Stamp** tool, or press **S**.

2. Press **Alt** as you click a clear area of skin near the blemish.

3. Click and drag over the blemish to replace it with the sampled texture.

INTRODUCTION

That's right—the Clone Stamp tool is a painless zit zapper. But its marvels don't stop there. Use it to paint over any part of a picture with a texture you've sampled from another part. So take a clear patch of skin and graft it over an age spot, tan line, or even paint out a tattoo.

HINT

Practice, Practice
The distance of the sample from your pointer stays the same as you paint—unless you Alt+click again. Try to pick a sample that steers clear of unwanted textures, such as a string of beads when you're cloning skin on a neckline.

TIP

Aligned Option
If Align is unchecked in the options bar, you can apply multiple copies of the selection with several strokes; if checked, you get one stroke and one copy.

Changing Hair Color

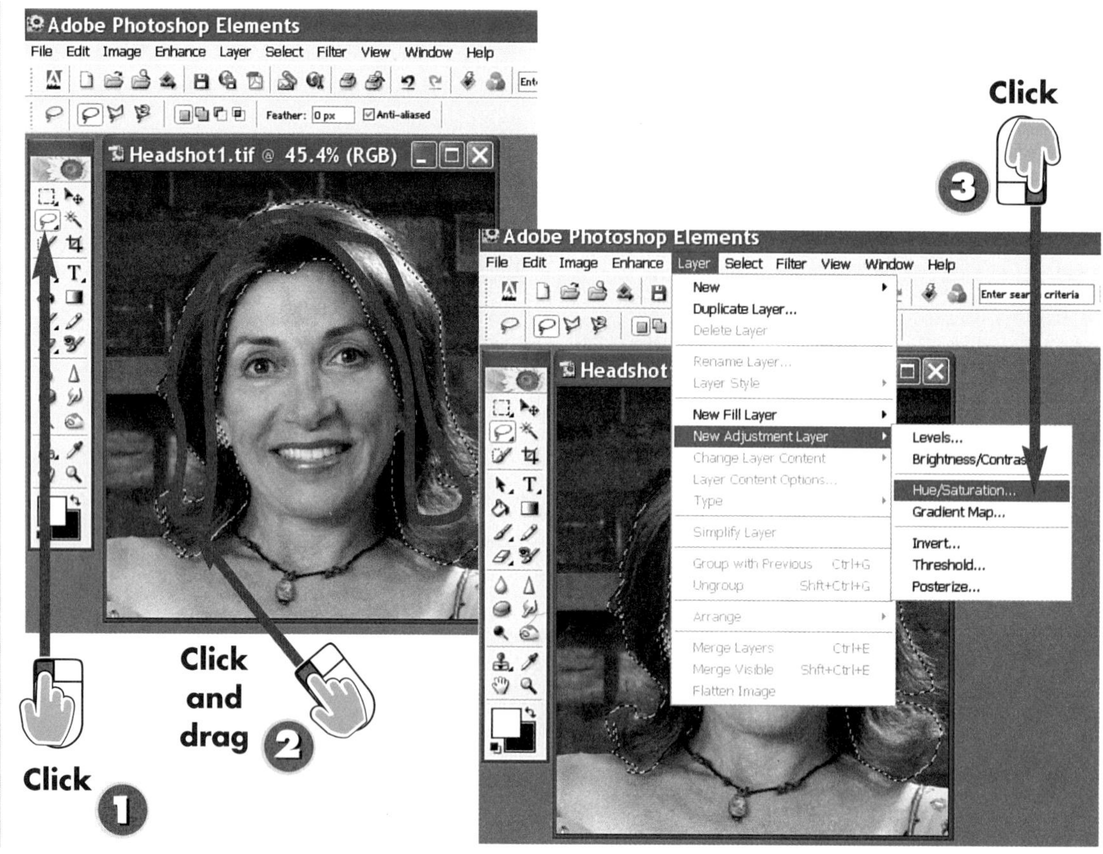

1. Select the **Lasso** tool, or press **L**.
2. Click and drag to trace the outline of the hair.
3. Choose **Layer**, **New Adjustment Layer**, **Hue/Saturation**.

INTRODUCTION

Being able to digitally recolor hair opens up all kinds of possibilities. Try on new looks and print them out to show the colorist at your hair salon. Change your Web photo because an ardent admirer has a thing for redheaded dudes. Or—go blue, pink, or green without fear of social stigma.

HINT

It's Cake, It's a Sandwich

There's a lot more about layers in a later part, but in these steps you're creating a separate copy of the hair on another layer that you can change without affecting the underlying picture.

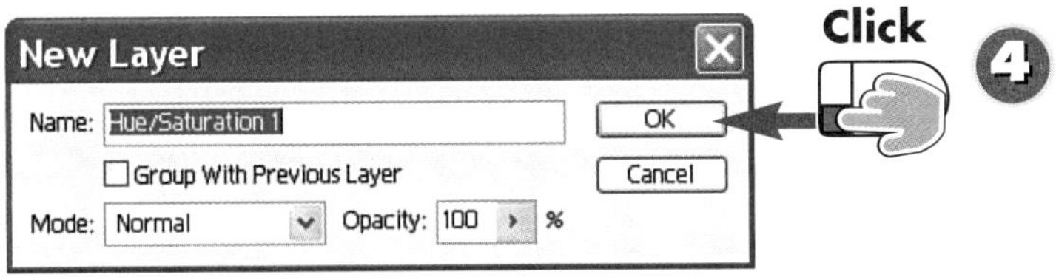

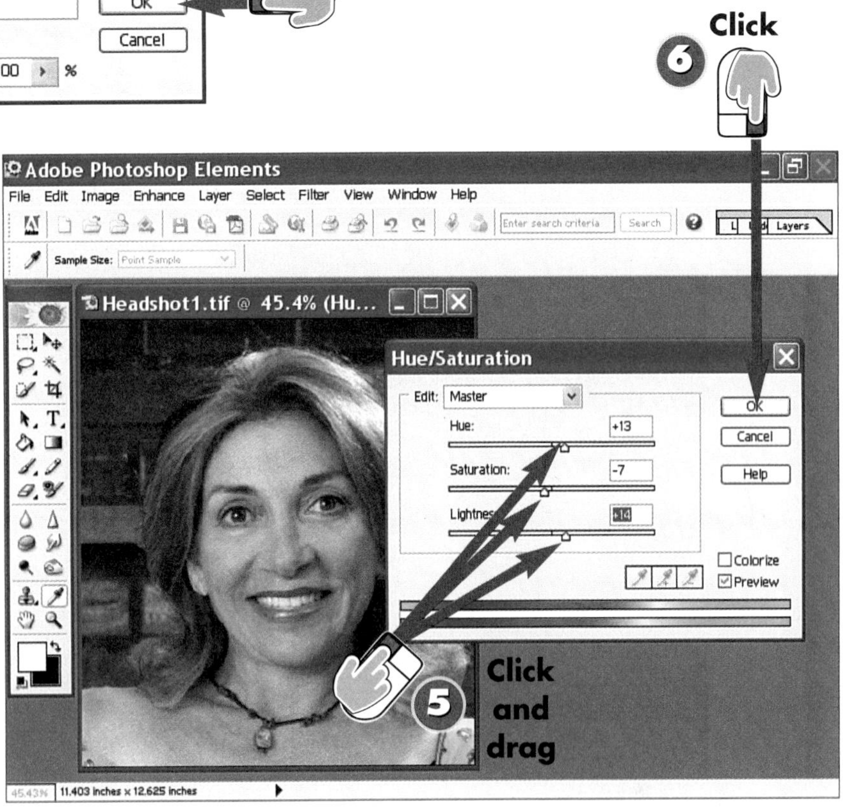

4 Click **OK**.

5 Adjust sliders to change the hair color.

6 Click **OK**.

TIP

Want Subtler Color?
To soften the effect of the Hue/Saturation layer on the underlying hair color, decrease the value of **Opacity** for the new layer in the Layers palette.

TIP

Keep Those Layers
To keep a version of the image that contains editable layers, save your file as a Photoshop (.psd) file.

Flattering by Softening Focus

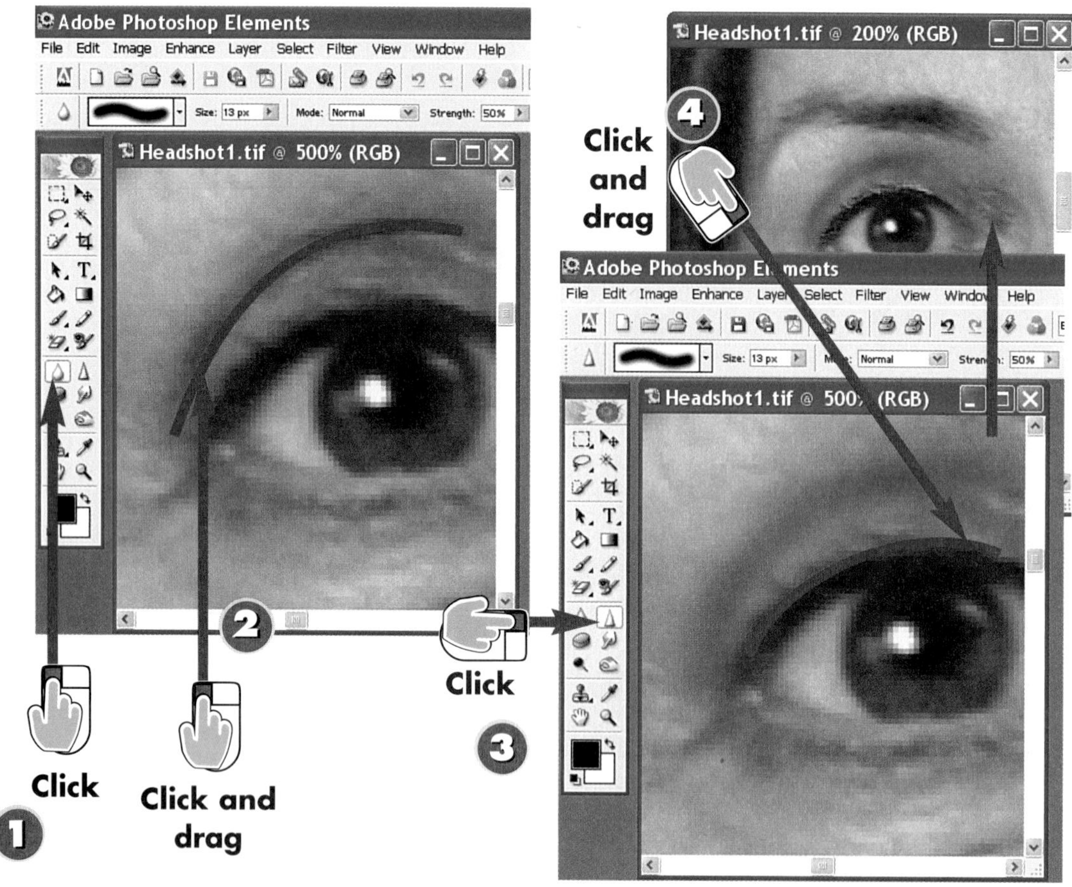

1. With the edge you want to work on zoomed in the active image window, select the **Blur** tool, or press **R**.

2. Click and drag over an edge to blur and soften it.

3. Select the **Sharpen** tool, or press **P**.

4. Click and drag over an edge to sharpen and accentuate it.

INTRODUCTION

In a sharp photo, you can selectively soften the focus on any detail by using the Blur tool. However, the Sharpen tool can't actually fix an out-of-focus photo. But you can use Sharpen to heighten contrast at edges, which can help emphasize some details, such as the eyeliner on an eyelid.

TIP

Blur or Smudge?
Use **Blur** for fine detail work, especially when you're zoomed in close. For a bolder effect, try the **Smudge** tool with the Mode set to **Lighten** or **Darken**.

Enhancing or Toning Down a Color

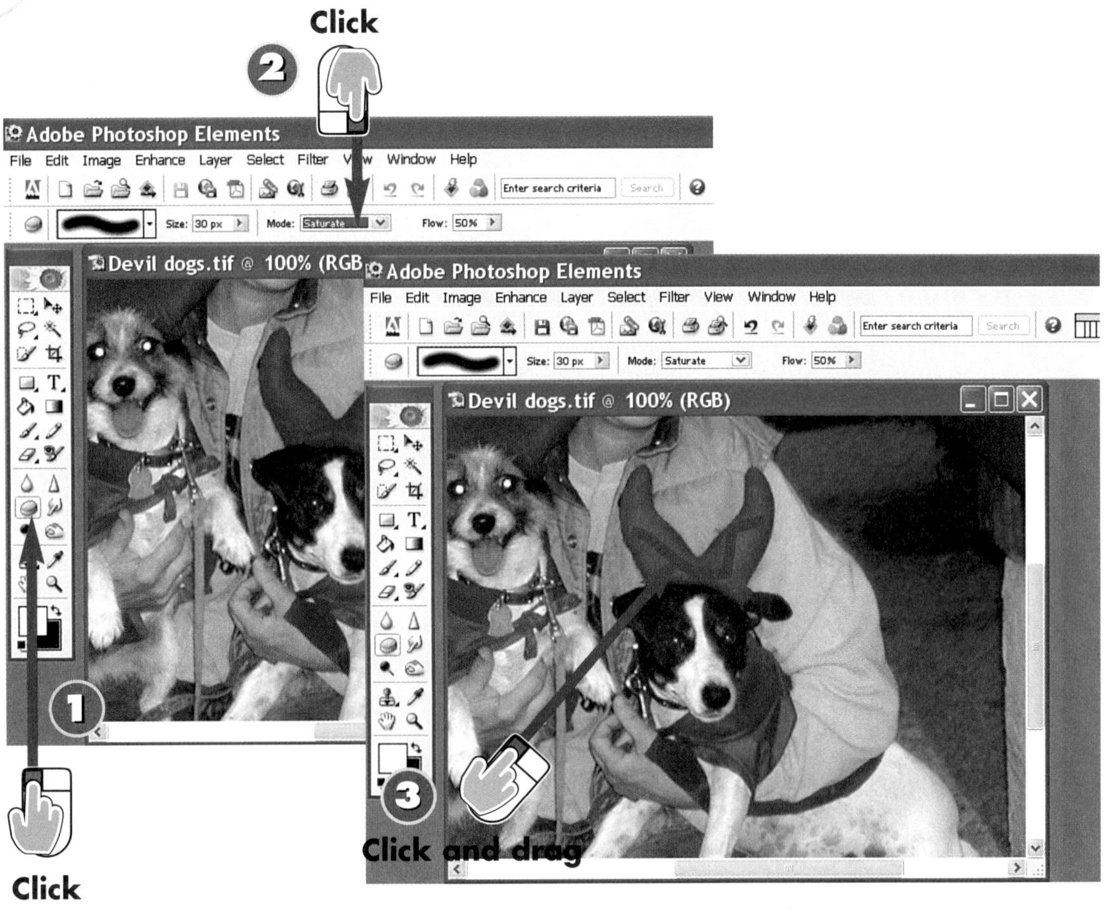

1. With a photo in the active image area, select the **Sponge** tool, or press **Q**.
2. To enhance color, select **Saturate** from the **Mode** drop-down menu in the options bar.
3. Click and drag over an area to heighten its color.

INTRODUCTION

The Sponge tool doesn't actually change the color of a selection, it just intensifies (saturates) or reduces (desaturates) it. It can come in handy for brightening up a wardrobe, such as neck scarves, or for toning down a too-colorful background that's competing with your subject.

TIP

Sponge Options
As with many other tools, the options bar offers a selection of brush tip sizes. The Flow setting controls the rate at which pixels become saturated or desaturated as you paint over them.

HINT

Dishwater Results?
If you overuse the Sponge in Desaturate mode, you'll remove all color from the area. That's fine if you're going for a selective monochrome look—or to make skin look downright ghostly.

Adding a Vignette to a Portrait

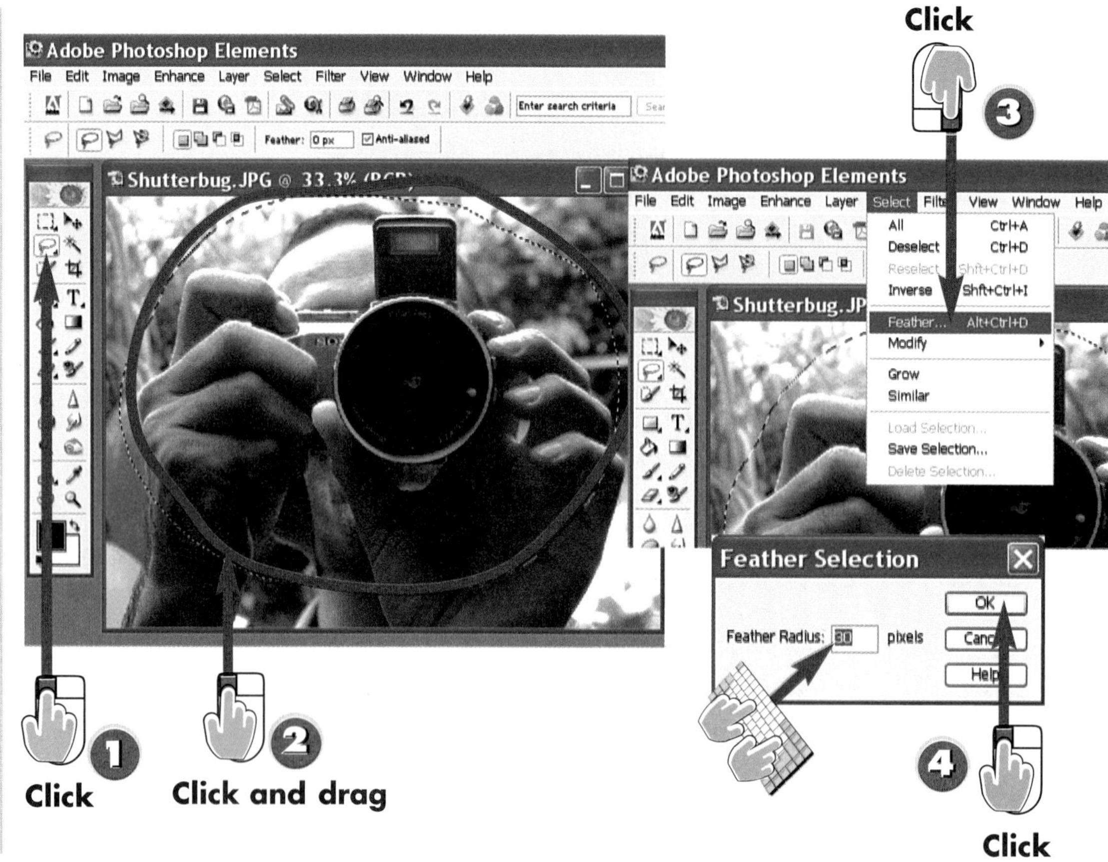

1. Select the **Lasso** tool.

2. Click and drag to trace around the subject of the portrait.

3. Choose **Select**, **Feather**, or press **Alt+Ctrl+D**.

4. Type a large **Feather Radius** (such as **30** pixels for a 5-inch 300 pixel/inch image). Click **OK**.

INTRODUCTION

Professional portraitists call a feathered photo a *vignette*, and it's been around ever since Matthew Brady aimed his camera at Civil War soldiers in the 1860s. Although you can use feathering to soften the edges of any selected area, its usual purpose is to convey sentimental feeling for the subject.

HINT

Noticeable Feather Radius

In step 4, the higher the resolution of the picture, the greater the Feather Radius should be. You might need to increase the setting to make the feathered edge large enough to be obvious.

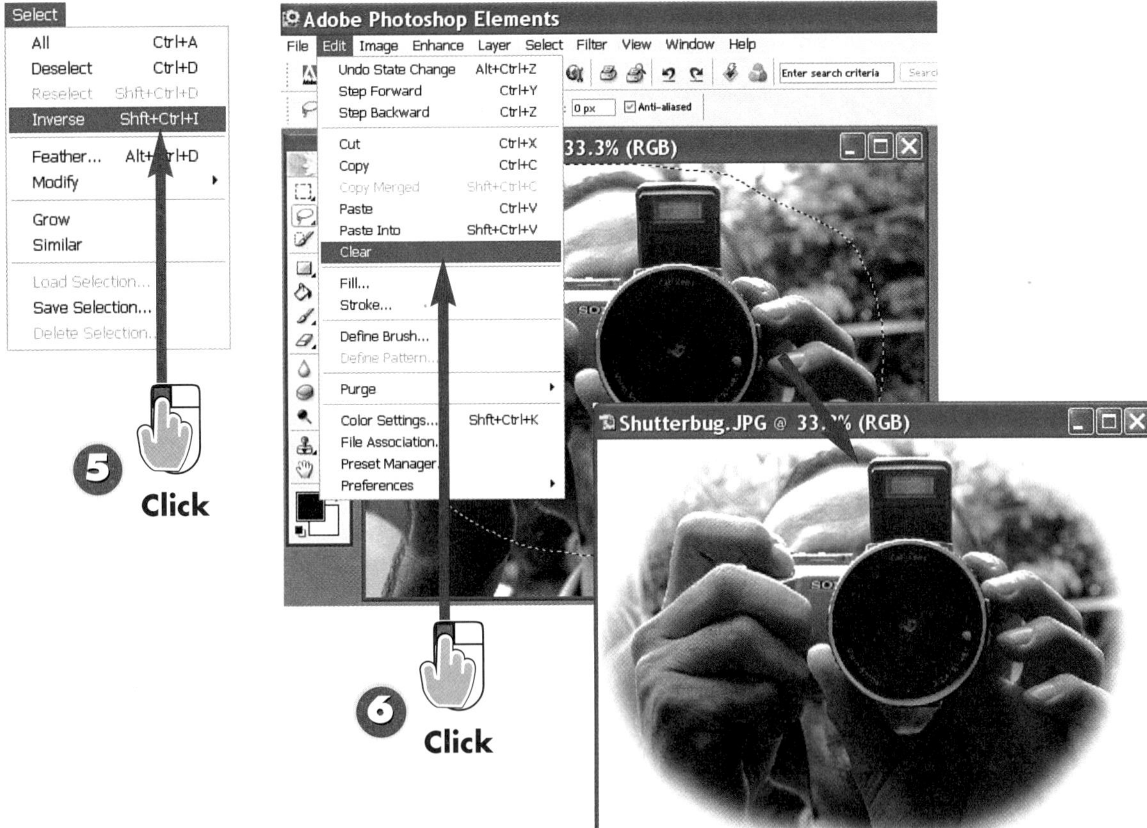

5 Choose **Select**, **Inverse**, or press **Shift+Ctrl+I**.

6 Choose **Edit**, **Clear**, or Press **Del**.

HINT

When to Use?
Vignette portraits can be particularly attractive when you frame them in oval or circular mattes and/or frames. And if you're going for an antique look, such as a sepia print, a vignette is the right finishing touch.

HINT

Selection Shape
Using the Rectangular Marquee or Elliptical Marquee tools gives more regular results than the Lasso and so might be a better choice if you're trying to fit your vignette image neatly inside a frame.

Adding a Soft Glow

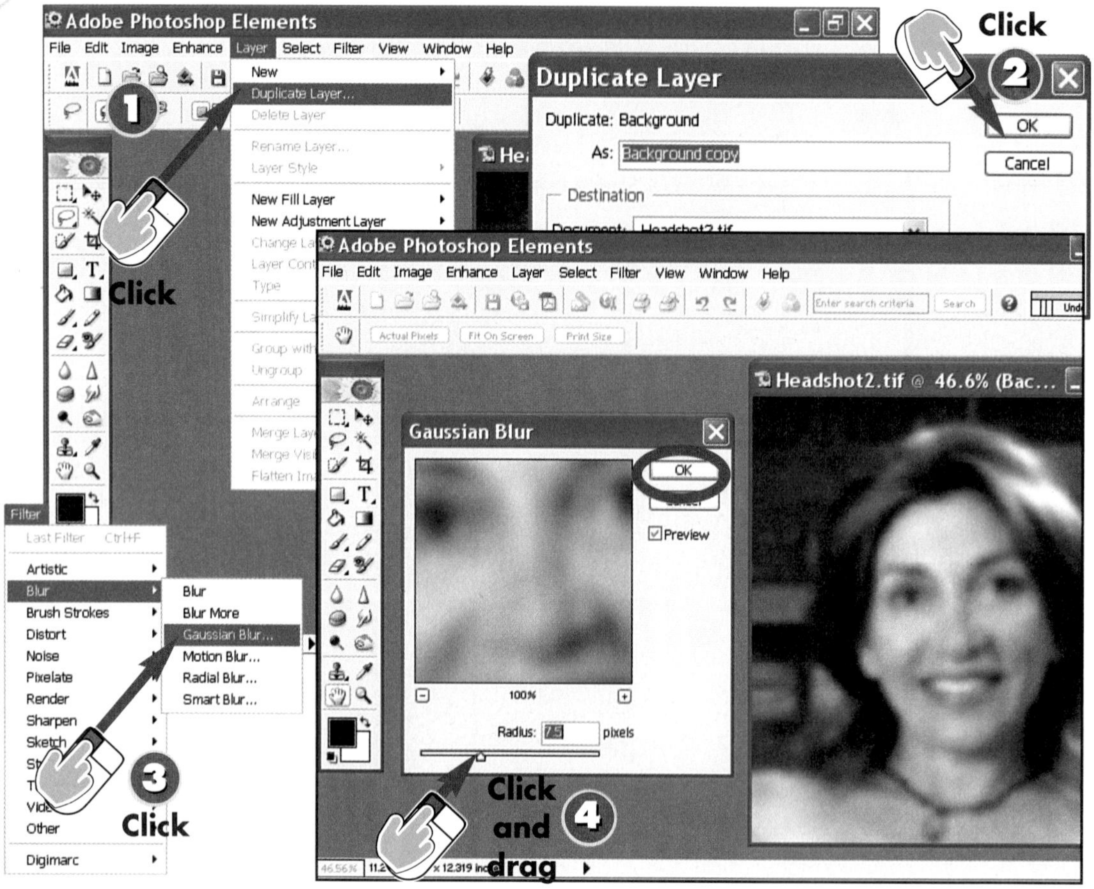

1. With a portrait in the active image area, choose **Layer**, **Duplicate Layer**.
2. Click **OK**.
3. Choose **Filter**, **Blur**, **Gaussian Blur**.
4. Adjust the **Radius** of the blur for the amount of softening you want. Click **OK**.

INTRODUCTION

Ever notice the glow around starlets in black-and-white movies of the 20s and 30s? This *halation effect* was actually a flaw of early film, but audiences equated it with glamour. Soft focus is still a wonderful way to soften skin and hide pores.

HINT

Gaussian Blur Radius
The Gaussian Blur option controls the extent of blurring. The image changes as you adjust the slider. Make it blurred enough to lose unwanted detail, but sharp enough so the viewer can't immediately tell it's out of focus.

HINT

Preserving Layers
To preserve editable layers so you can return to the original image, save your work as a Photoshop (.psd) file. TIFF (.tif) files also have an option for saving layers.

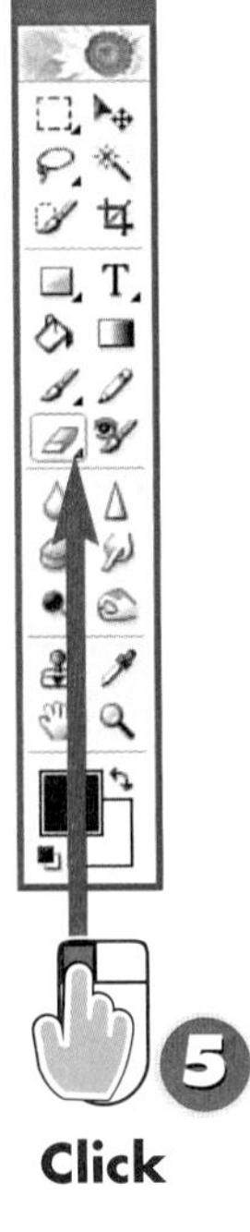

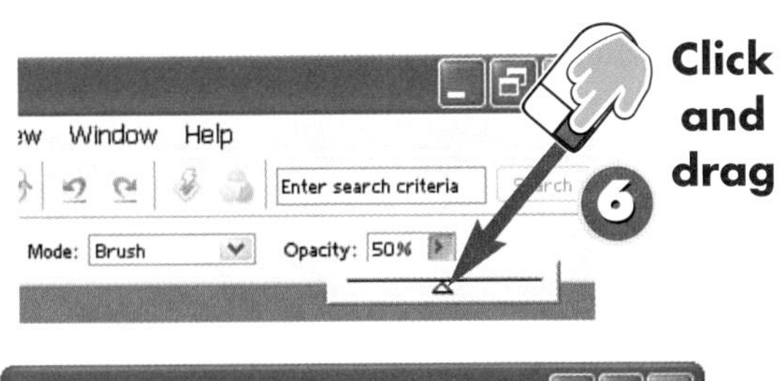

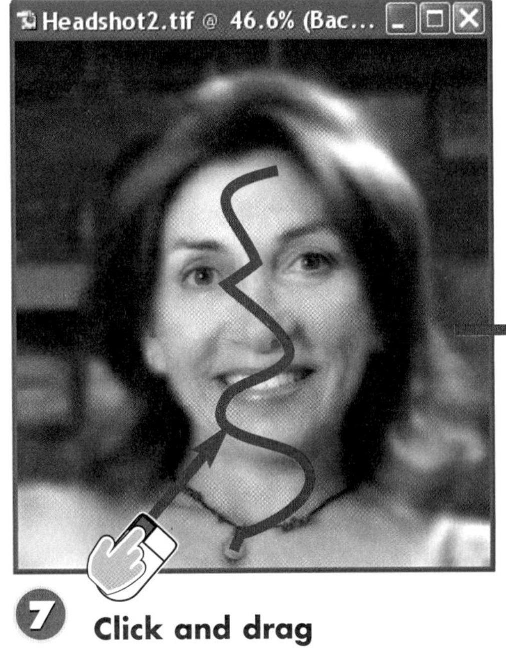

5. Select the **Eraser** tool, or press **E**.

6. Adjust **Opacity** to **50%**.

7. Click and drag in the image to paint over and reveal facial details you want to remain sharp.

HINT

Clarify Important Details
If you sharpen facial features—such as eyes, nose, and mouth—viewers won't necessarily notice the rest is out of focus. Don't forget to sharpen important details, such as the necklace, in this case.

TIP

Do This Last
If you're doing a thorough retouching job on a portrait, use the other techniques described in this part first to reduce lines, and so on; then add the Gaussian blur last.

Trimming Contours on the Face or Body

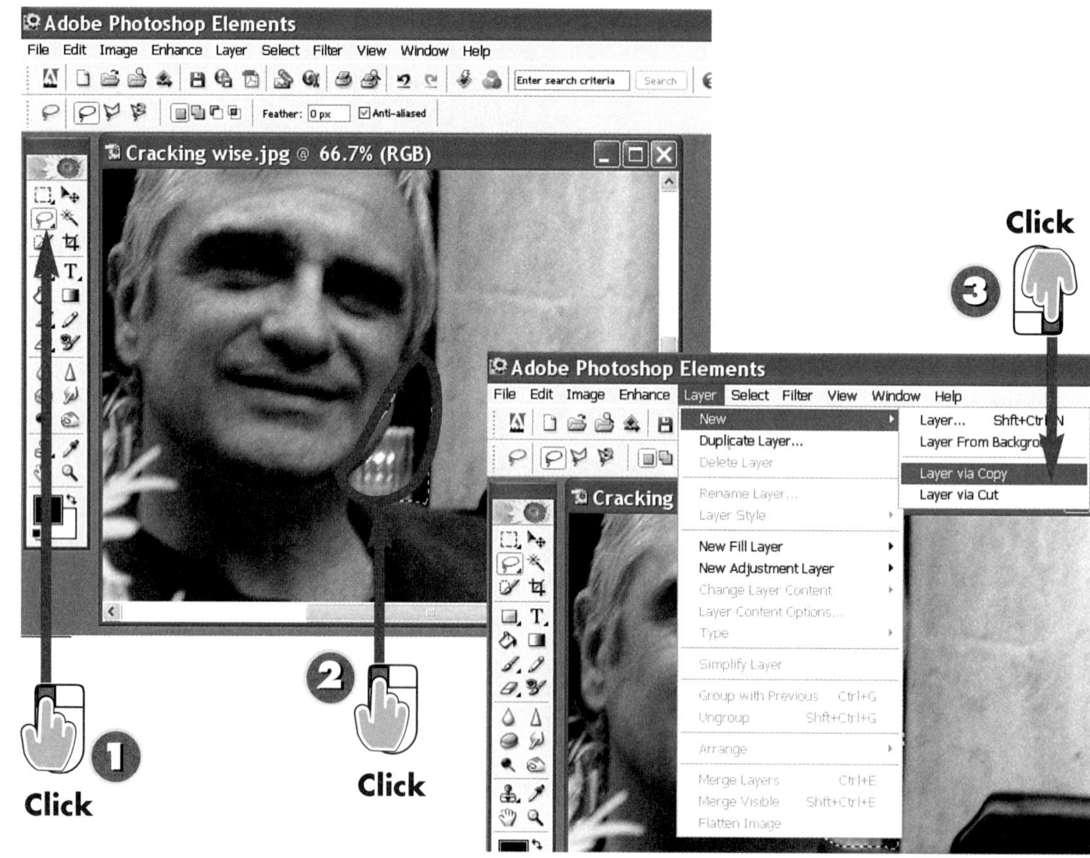

1. Select the **Lasso** tool.
2. Click and drag around the contour to be reduced, including the area on either side of the edge.
3. Choose **Layer**, **New**, **Layer via Copy**.

INTRODUCTION

Rather than carving off love handles or slimming hips with the result of embarrassing a dear relative, the author chose to lop off his own jowl. The surgery was quick and painless, and it took a few years off!

HINT

Surgical Technique
The trick here is to cut an area that includes either side of an edge, such as a jaw or waistline, and then move it inward—toward the center of the face or body.

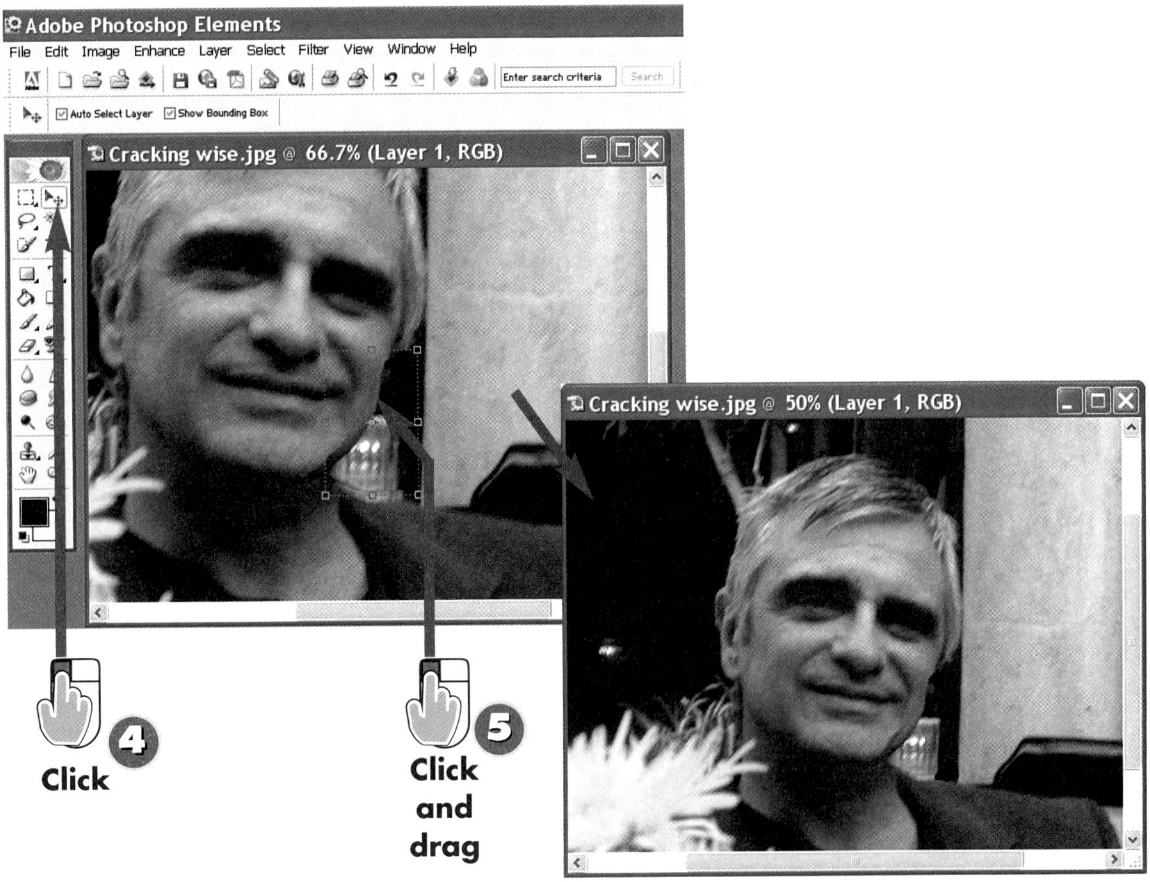

4 Click

5 Click and drag

4. Select the **Move** tool, or press **V**.

5. Move the selection closer to the face (or body) to reposition the edge.

TIP

Move By Itty Bits
To move the selection by small, more controllable increments, use the **Arrow** keys on your keyboard instead of clicking and dragging in step 5. This is called *nudging*.

HINT

Tidy Up
For a seamless transplant, you may need to use other retouching tools, such as Smudge or Clone Stamp, to clean up the edges.

Building Albums and Presentations

For some of us, it's all about getting published. It's all very well to learn how to retouch those family photos and tart them up with cute drawings, but if you don't show them to anybody—what's the point?

Photoshop Elements 2 has a feature called Web Photo Gallery that generates personal photo Web sites with very little effort. To publish your work to the Web, you'll need to get a Web hosting account. Many Internet service providers (ISPs) offer space for personal Web pages as part of their basic service, so if you have an account with an ISP, you might already have this available to you.

To venture further into the realm of multimedia and Internet publishing, you need to load your finished digital images into some other applications. Microsoft PowerPoint for slideshows and Microsoft Word for printed documents (and Web pages) come to mind right away because so many people rely on them.

You can get a variety of even more impressive outputs from Adobe Photoshop Album 2, a companion product that publishes catalogs of images on paper and onscreen, as well as 3D-Album, which makes dazzling screensavers and self-running shows.

Thanks for the Memories

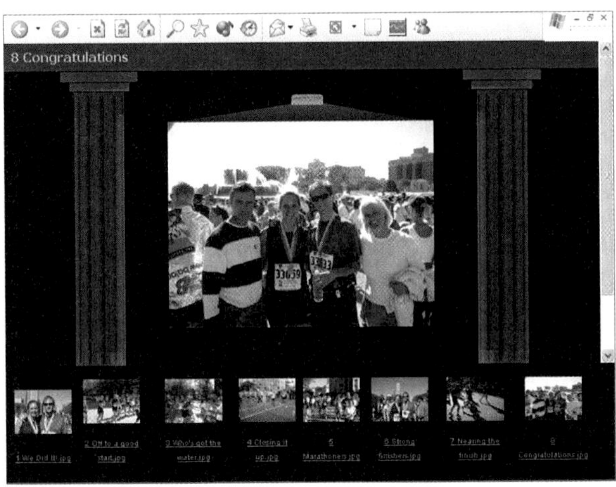

Web Photo Gallery

3D-Album™ Screensaver

Photoshop® Album Greeting Card

Making a Web Photo Gallery

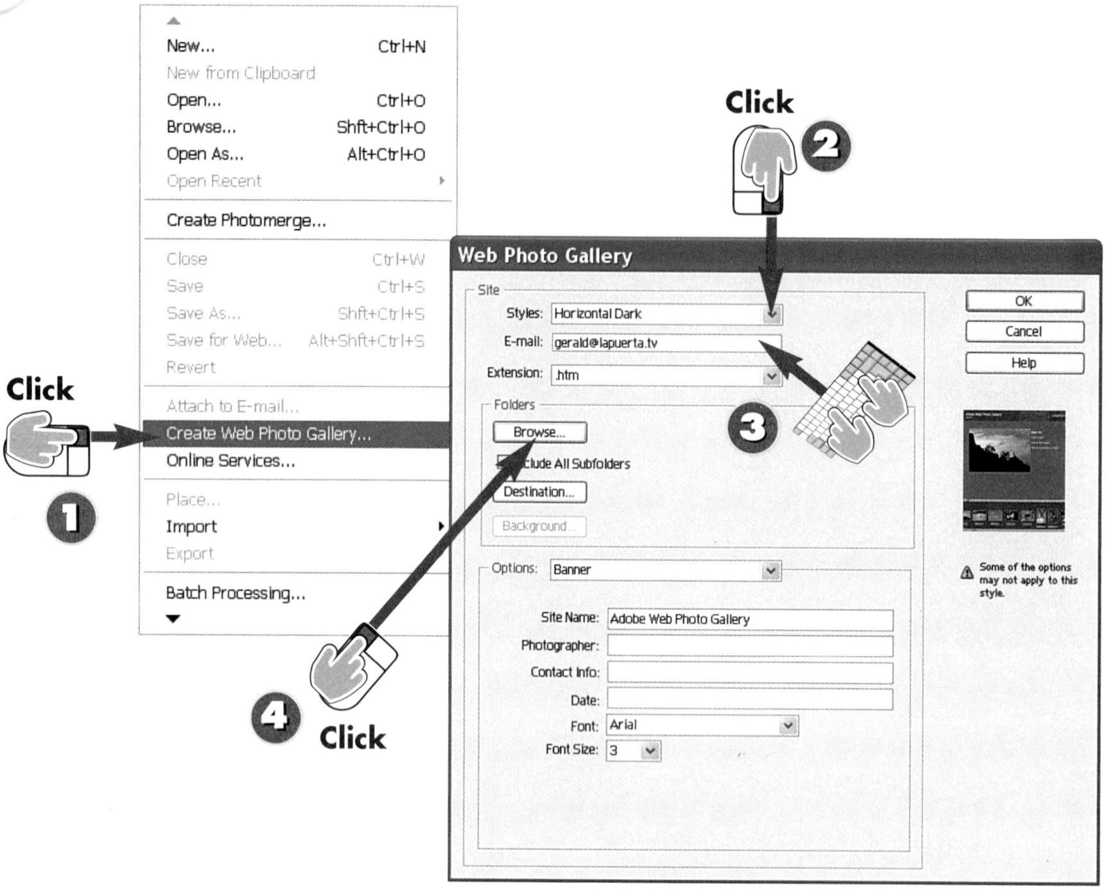

1. Choose **File**, **Create Web Photo Gallery**.
2. From the **Styles** drop-down menu, select a Gallery Style, such as **Horizontal Dark**.
3. Type your email address if you want it displayed on your Web pages. (Some of the styles don't show it.)
4. Click **Browse**.

INTRODUCTION

Photoshop Elements 2 has pre-designed photo Web pages and can insert your photos and descriptive text with just a few clicks. It then generates completed pages ready for uploading to your Web hosting service or ISP.

HINT

Folder Your Photos

For quickest results, start by putting the photos you want to use in a separate folder. The order of the pictures on the pages will be alphabetical by filename.

HINT

Filenames as Labels

Filenames of your pictures are picked up as photo labels on the Web page, so rename each with some descriptive text before you create the gallery.

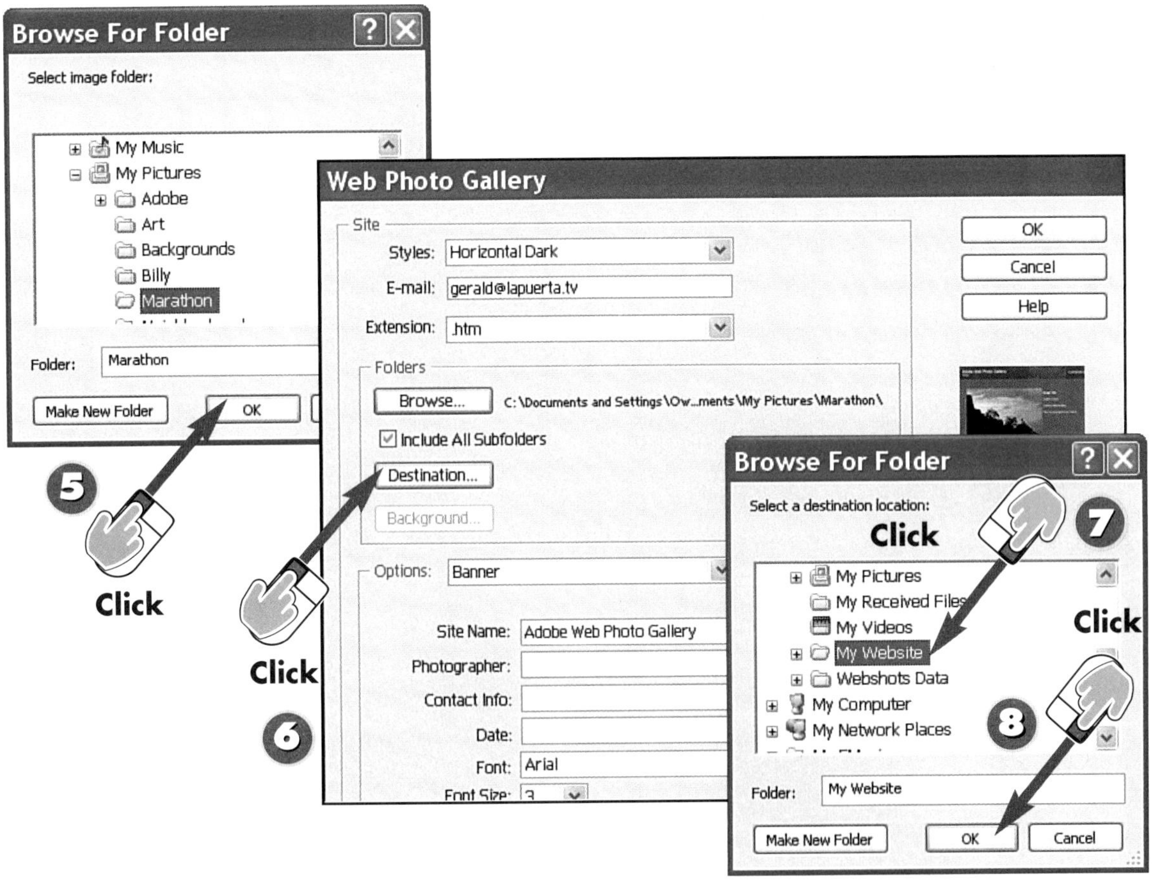

5. Navigate to select the folder that contains the photos you want to appear in your gallery, and click **OK**.
6. Click the **Destination** button.
7. Navigate to select an empty folder to hold your Web pages. (Or click **Make New Folder** to create one.)
8. Click **OK**.

See next page

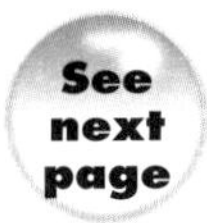

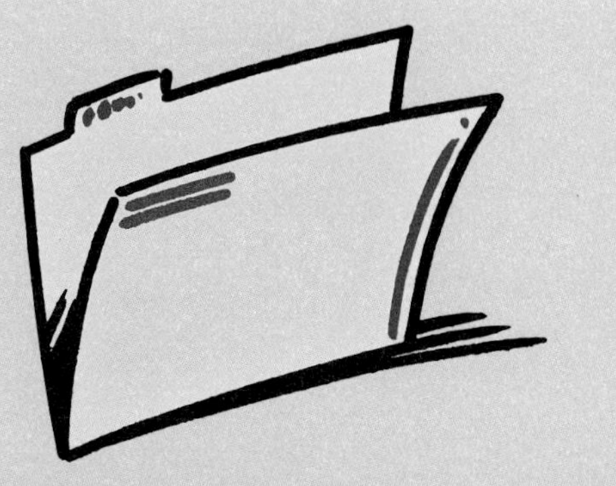

TIP

Want Mail?

Entering an email address in step 3 isn't mandatory, so just leave it blank if you don't want site visitors to contact you. If the E-mail text box is grayed, the style you selected can't display an address.

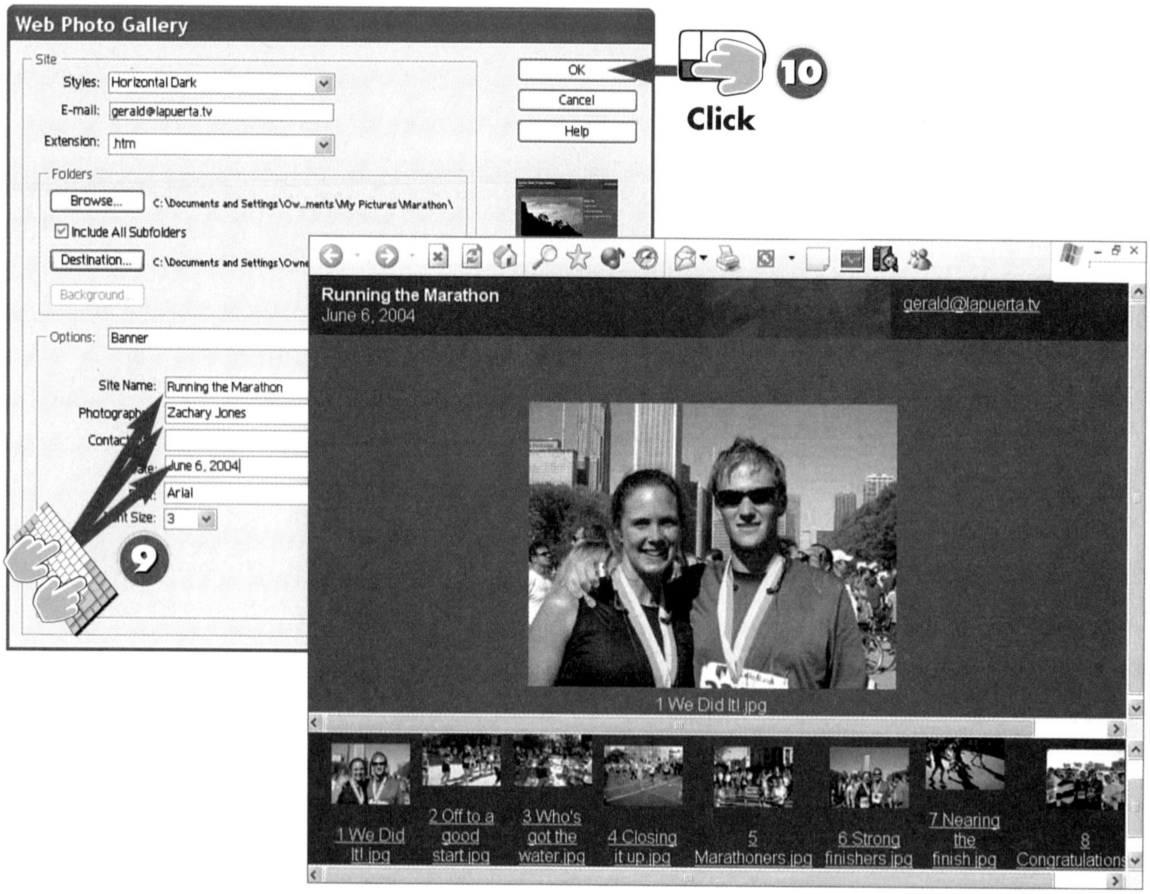

Type entries for **Site Name**, **Photographer**, **Contact Info**, and **Date**. (Omit information you don't want displayed.)

Click **OK**. The program generates the photos as Web pages and places them in the destination folder you chose in step 7.

INTRODUCTION

Follow instructions of your Web hosting service for uploading—*publishing*—your files. The usual method is via *file transfer protocol (FTP)*. A handy and inexpensive program for doing this is GlobalSCAPE CuteFTP.

TIP

Table Background Image
In the Folders section of the Web Photo Gallery dialog box, the Background button is available only for the Table style. Click it to select an image file (must be JPEG) for the table's background.

TIP

Other Options
Besides Banner, other categories you can select from the Options drop-down menu are **Large Images** and **Thumbnails** (dimensions, labels, and quality), **Custom Colors**, and **Security**.

Loading Your Photos into Photoshop Album

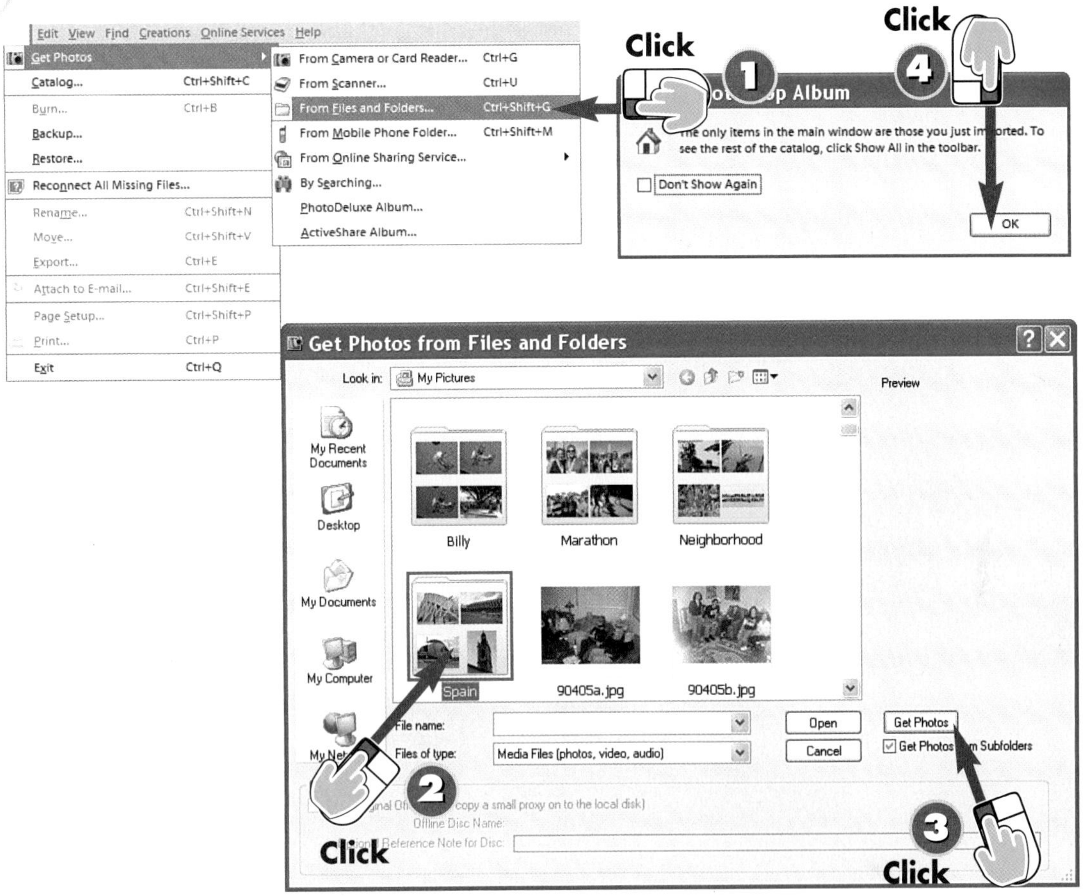

1. From the Photoshop Album menu bar, choose **File**, **Get Photos**, **From Files or Folders**, or press **Ctrl+Shift+G**.

2. Navigate to the folder that contains your pictures, and click its thumbnail (or filename).

3. Click the **Get Photos** button.

4. Click **OK**. The photos in the selected folder are loaded into a new catalog. You can now create an album or presentation.

INTRODUCTION

With Adobe Photoshop Album 2, you can create albums, slideshows, greeting cards, Web galleries, video CDs, e-cards, calendars, photo books, and 3D galleries. But to do any of this, you must first load your pictures into the application to create a *catalog*.

HINT

Get Organized
Photoshop Album also provides ways of organizing your growing photo collection. But the easiest way to create an album or show is to put all the photos in a folder on your hard drive (or other media) first, as suggested here.

Building an Album with Photoshop Album

1. In Photoshop Album, after loading pictures to create a catalog as described in the previous task, choose **Creations**, **Album**.
2. Click to select an Album Style, such as **Classic**.
3. Click **Next**.

INTRODUCTION

A traditional-style printed photo album is just one of Photoshop Album's Creations choices. The other selections that have much the same steps as Album are Slideshow, Video CD, Greeting Card, eCard, Calendar, and Photo Book.

HINT

Web Presentations

The Creations, Web Photo Gallery menu option produces much the same result as the File, Create Web Photo Gallery in Photoshop Elements—a set of Web pages ready for uploading to the Internet.

4 Type a title for your album.

5 Click **Next**.

6 If your collection of pictures is complete, click **Next**. (Otherwise, click **Add Photos** to select some more.)

7 Optionally, to vary page layouts within your album, click the **Next Page** button.

INTRODUCTION

Remember that you can't do much at all in Photoshop Album until you build a catalog of photos within the application. See the preceding task for the easiest way to do this—by creating a folder that contains only the photos you want to be in your album or presentation. However, the **File**, **Catalog** command can be a powerful tool for organizing your entire digital photo collection.

HINT

Selecting Photos

If you start with all the photos you need in the same folder, you won't need to make any changes in step 6. However, you have the option to add, duplicate, or delete photos from the catalog by using the buttons above the images.

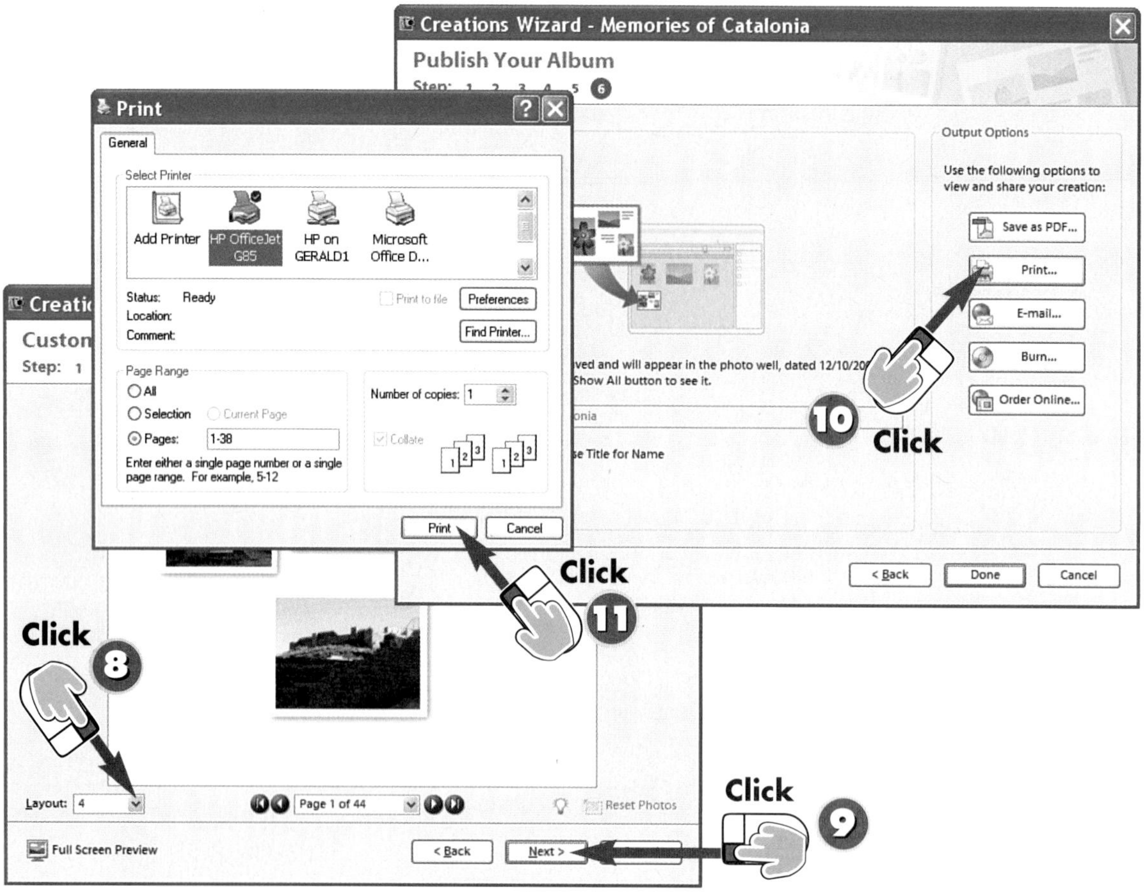

8 Select the number of photos per page in the **Layout** drop-down menu. (Repeat steps 7 and 8 to lay out the other pages.)

9 Click **Next**.

10 Click **Print**.

11 Load your printer with photo paper; then click **Print**.

TIP

Output Options
In step 10, regardless of the type of presentation you've created, you also have the options of saving in Adobe Reader (.pdf) format, sending as an email attachment, burning a CD, or ordering professional photo prints online.

Creating a PowerPoint Photo Slideshow

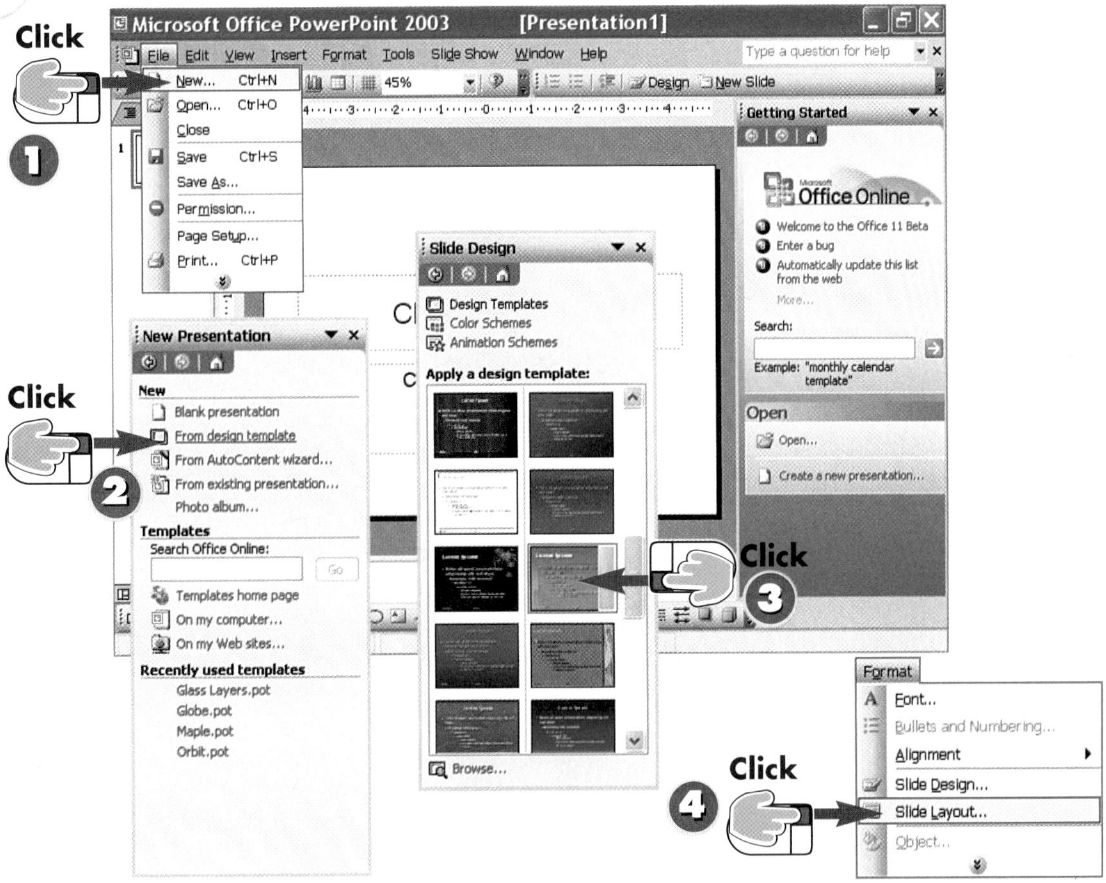

1. In Microsoft PowerPoint, choose **File**, **New**, or press **Ctrl+N**.
2. In the New Presentation task pane, select **From design template**.
3. Click a design template in a style you like.
4. Choose **Format**, **Slide Layout**.

See next page

INTRODUCTION

Adobe offers Photoshop Album, a separate application, for creating electronic slideshows. But many folks already have PowerPoint (part of the Office suite), so here's how to make a series of photo slides with titles in just a few steps.

HINT

PowerPoint's Graphics

PowerPoint has its own graphics tools for adding text and drawings to your slides. If you want to modify the image itself, use Photoshop Elements. For objects that surround it on the slide, use the PowerPoint tools.

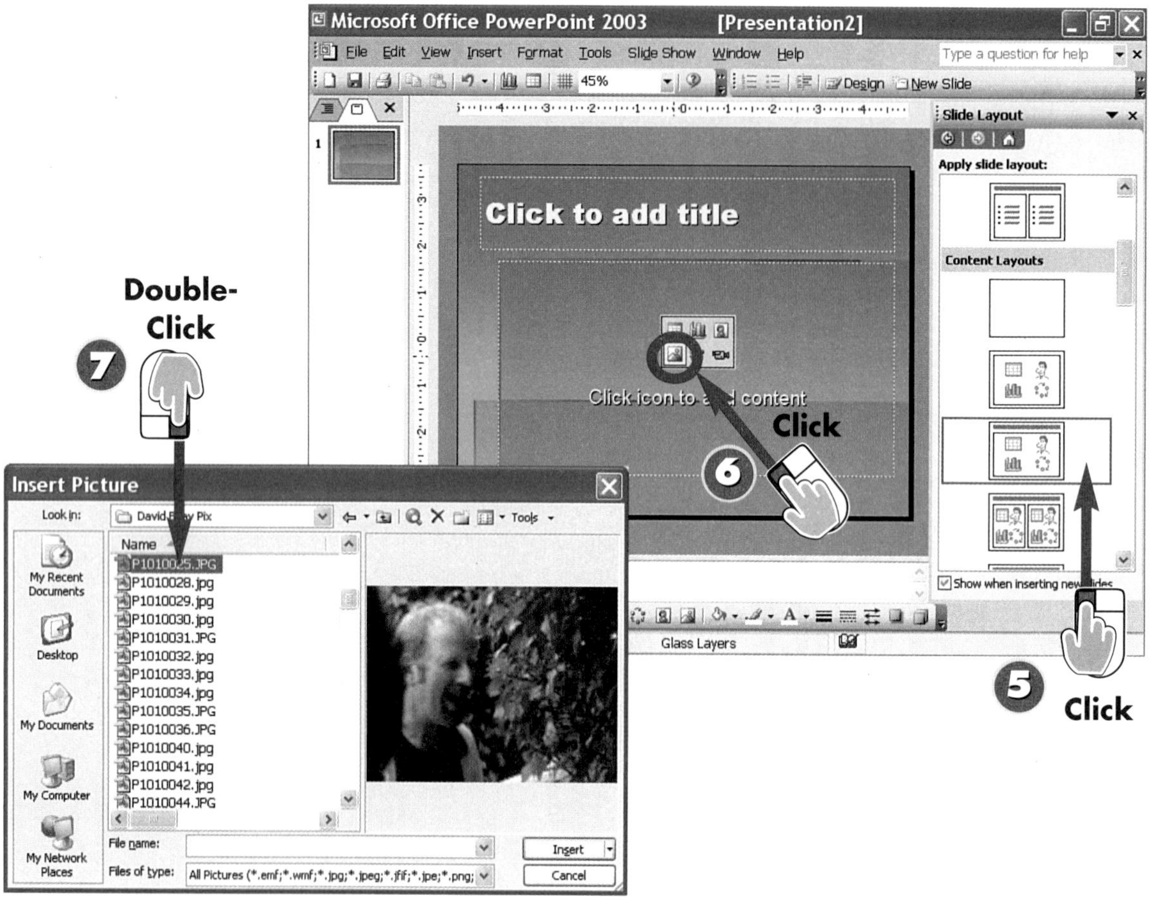

5. Click a Content Layout in the Slide Layout task pane, such as **Title with Content**.

6. In the slide area, click **Insert Picture**.

7. Navigate to the folder that contains the picture, and double-click its filename. The picture is inserted into the slide.

TIP

Insert in Any Slide

Any of the content layouts are best for making slides that contain photos, but you can add a picture from an external file to any slide by choosing **Insert**, **Picture**, **From File**.

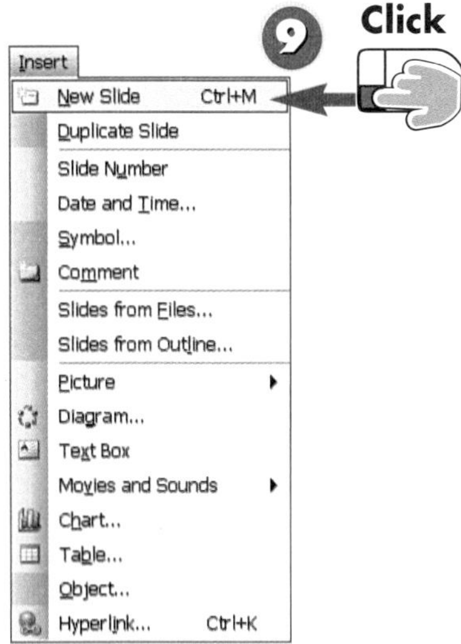

8 Select the default title text field and then type a title for the slide.

9 Choose **Insert**, **New Slide**, or press **Ctrl+M**. (Repeat these steps for every slide in the presentation; then save your work.)

INTRODUCTION

This task was done using PowerPoint 2003. Even though their screens look different, earlier versions of PowerPoint (97 and 2000) work much the same way. As an alternative, Photoshop Album 2 can also generate slideshows.

TIP

Running Your Show
After you're finished, save your work. Then choose **View**, **Slide Show** (or press F5) to display the show on your computer screen. Press **Spacebar** or **PageDown** to advance to the next slide. Press **Esc** to exit the show.

HINT

Emailing Your Show
To create a show that's viewable on most PCs that don't have the PowerPoint software on them, choose **File**, **Save As** and select the **PowerPoint Show** (.pps) file type.

Start

Creating a Screensaver Show with 3D-Album

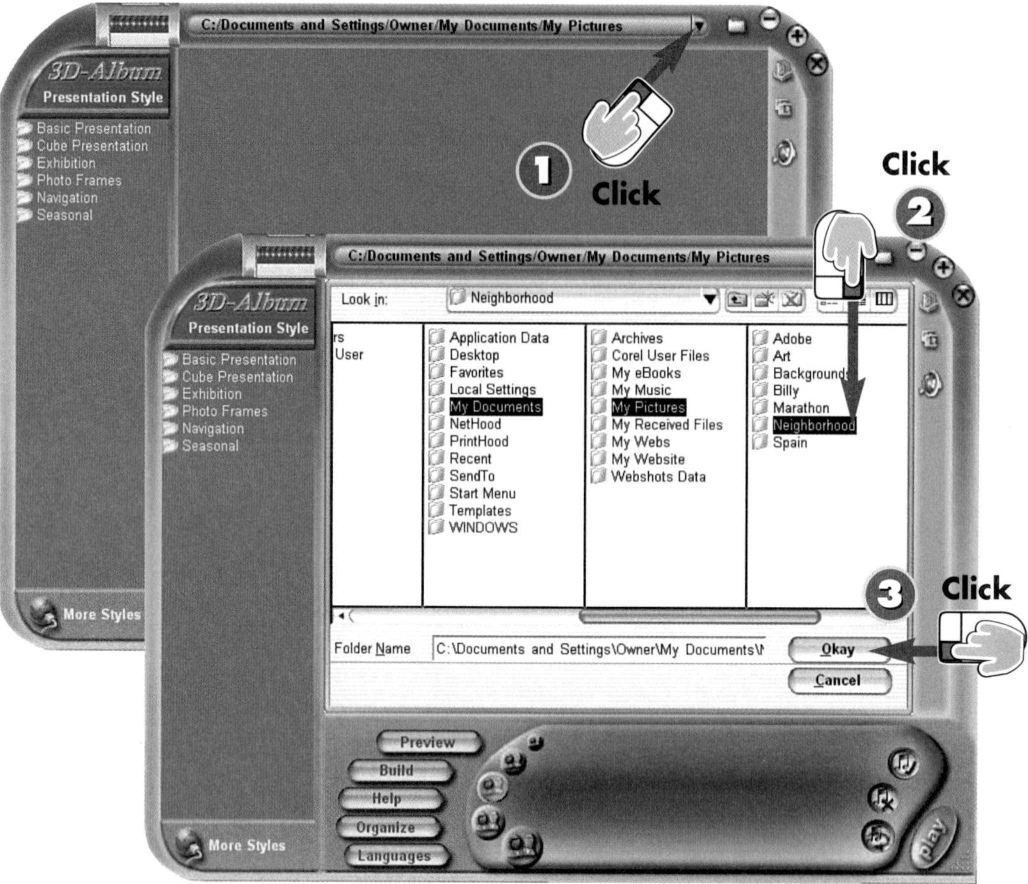

1. In 3D-Album, click the **Album Folder** drop-down menu.
2. Select the folder that contains the photos you want to use.
3. Click **Okay**.

INTRODUCTION

Micro Research Institute 3D-Album™ can generate self-running slideshows, screensavers, Web pages, and email attachments. You'll find a version of 3D-Album on the companion CD. Its animated screensavers are particularly cool.

HINT

Adobe's 3D Shows
Photoshop Album's output options include Atmosphere 3D Gallery, which generates an animated *virtual walkthrough*, a tour of imaginary rooms as a series of Web pages. But it doesn't make screensavers or self-running shows.

4 Select a Presentation Style, such as **Exhibition**, **Exhibit Island**. Click **Build**.

5 Select **Create presentation as a screensaver**.

6 Type an identifying name for the screensaver selection.

7 Click **Build**.

TIP

Finishing Up
After the screensaver has been built, you see a message dialog box. Click **Okay** and close 3D-Album. Your new screensaver is now the current setting for the Windows Desktop.

TIP

Screensaver Settings
To change your screensaver, right-click an empty space on the Windows Desktop, select **Properties**, click the **Screen Saver** tab, make a new selection in the **Screen Saver** drop-down menu, and click **OK**.

PART 9

Using Layers to Combine Photos and Artwork

If you know how animated movies were made in the days before computer generation, you're already familiar with the concept of layers. Animation artists traditionally used a process called *ink-and-paint* to draw cartoon characters on transparent sheets of celluloid, or *cels*. One new cel had to be created for each time a character moved. Cels were then placed over elaborate painted backgrounds, such as witches' castles or the decks of pirate ships. Painting on separate layers—the animated character on the cel and the background beneath—made it possible to reuse the same background throughout a long scene.

Layers in Photoshop Elements work much the same way. The image you begin with is the Background layer. Every layer you add starts out as transparent until you change its color, change its adjustment properties, or add objects to it.

If you've done any of the tasks in other parts involving shapes or text, you were working with layers, whether you realized it or not. Understand, building more complex layered images isn't for beginners. But you should learn some of this if you want to graduate to more ambitious tasks.

The postcard on the facing page is actually built from 10 layers, including the background. Photoshop Elements permits you as many as 8,000 layers—provided you don't run out of computer memory first!

A Ten-Layered Image

Painting on a New Layer

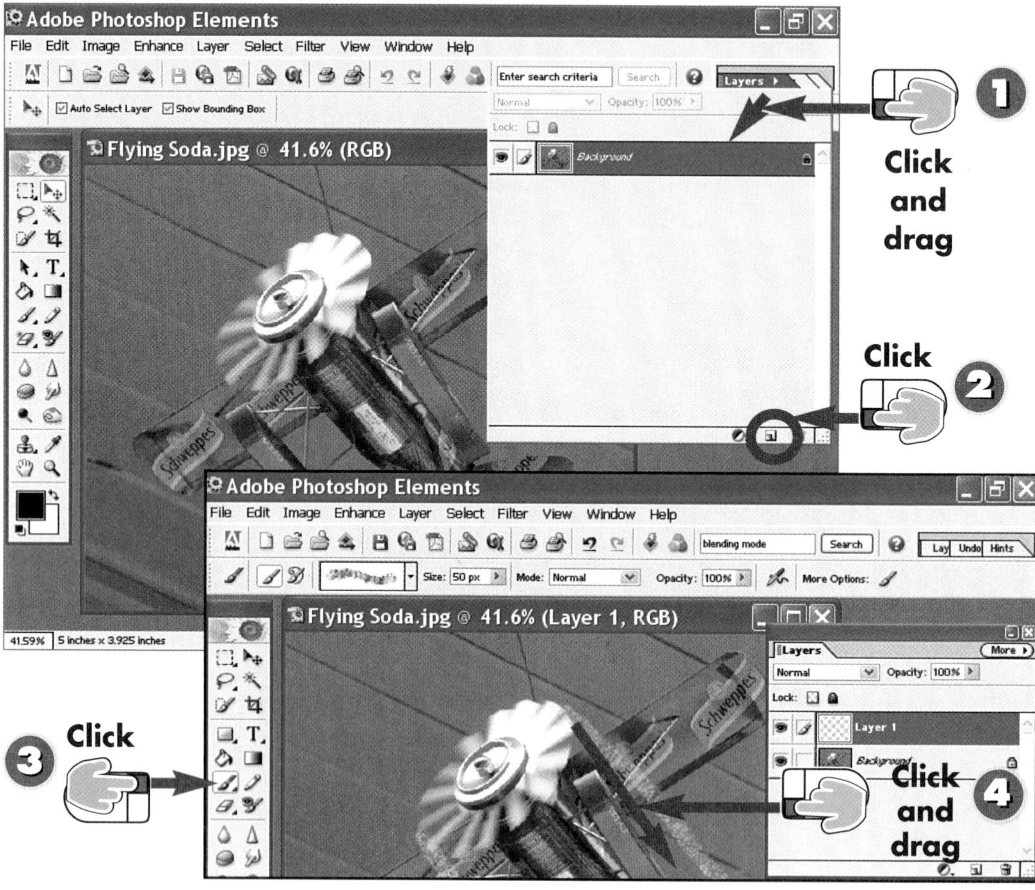

1. Open or undock the **Layers** palette (or choose **Window**, **Layers**).
2. Click the **Create a New Layer** button (or choose **Layer**, **New**, **Layer**).
3. Select a tool, such as **Brush**.
4. Paint on the layer.

INTRODUCTION

You should create a new layer for painting, drawing, or adding new shapes to your photo. However, a new layer is created automatically whenever you use the Shape or Type tools—also, whenever you paste (choose **Edit**, **Paste**) or select certain other commands on the Layers menu.

TIP

Simplify and Merge

Simplifying changes vector shapes and text (based on geometry) to pixels—editable as dots, not as shapes. Merging both simplifies the active (selected) layer and combines it with the layer beneath.

You can't manipulate text and shapes as objects after merging. If you see a warning that the layer must be simplified before proceeding with a tool, choose **Cancel** and create a new layer using these steps; then reselect the tool and paint or draw.

Copying an Object to a New Layer

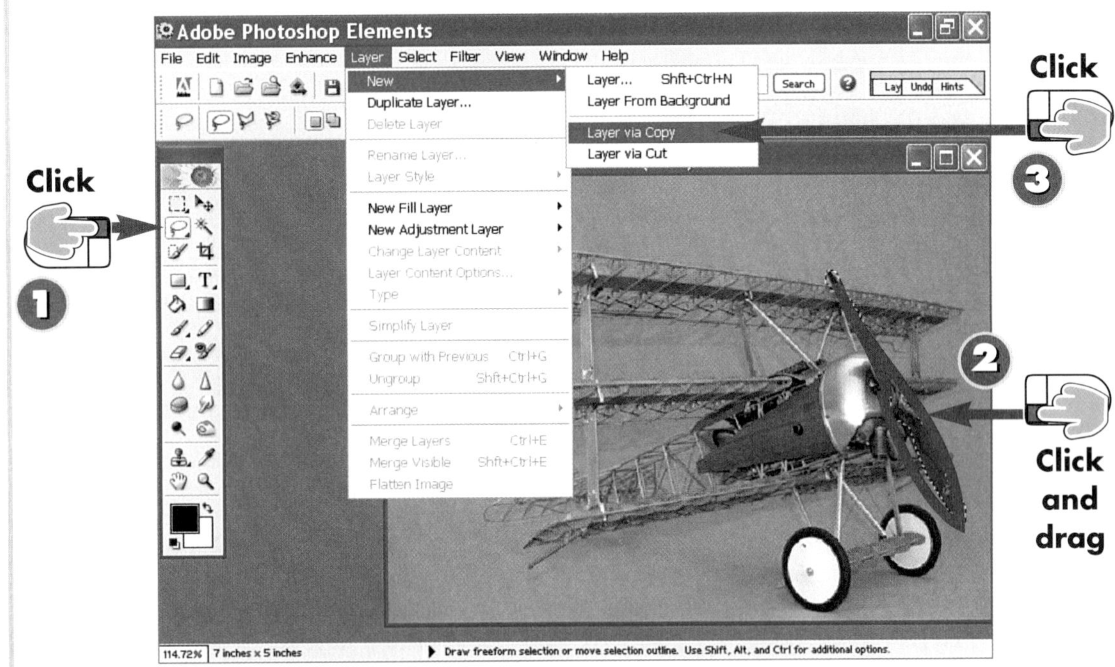

1. Click a selection tool, such as **Lasso**.

2. Select the object to be copied to a new layer.

3. Choose **Layer**, **New**, **Layer via Copy**.

INTRODUCTION

Selecting an object on the background layer, making changes, and then saving your work, changes the original image forever. Instead, use these steps to copy a selected object to a new layer, leaving the background layer unchanged.

TIP

Cutting a Selection
The command **Layer**, **New**, **Layer via Cut** works just the same way, but it also deletes the selection from the original layer. Especially if the original layer is the Background, use **Layer via Copy** instead.

TIP

Deleting or Hiding
As long as the original layer is intact, you can always hide or delete the copied layer (**Layer**, **Delete Layer**) to cancel all its changes with a click.

Repositioning a Layer

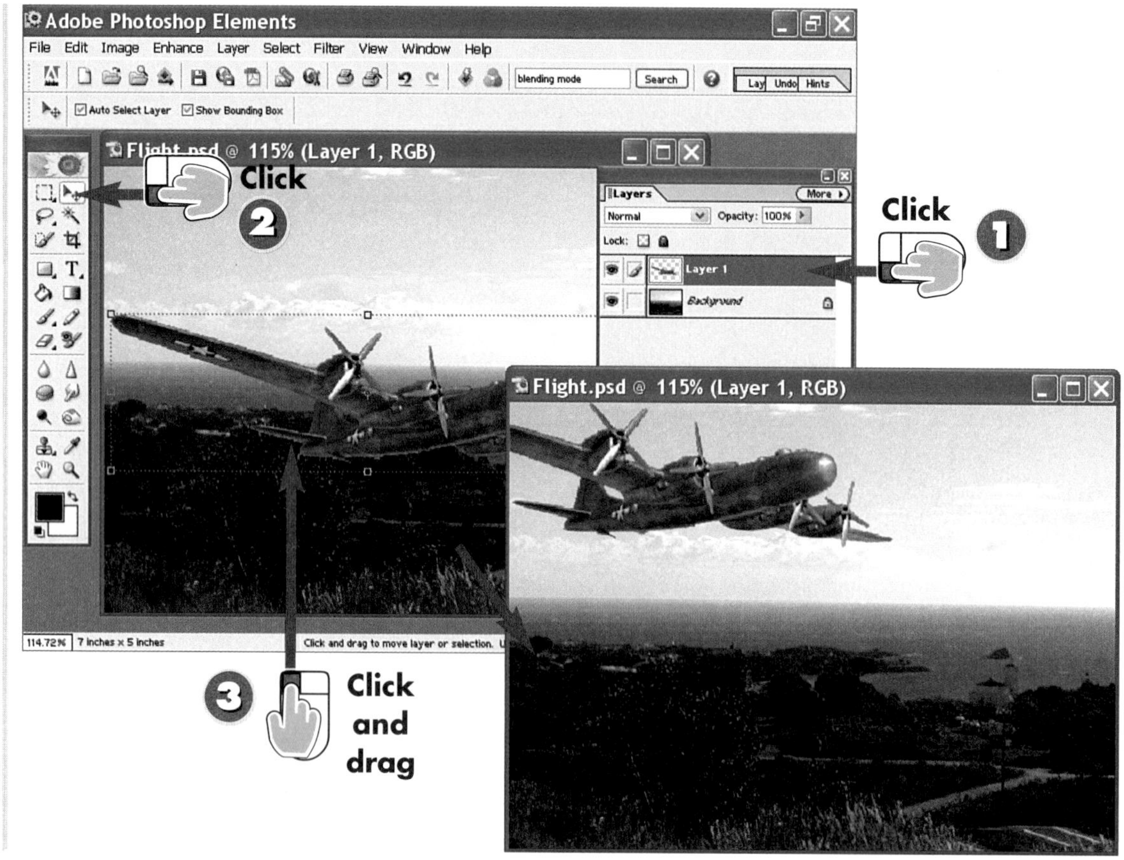

1. Select the name of the layer in the Layers palette.

2. Select the **Move** tool.

3. Click and drag the layer to reposition it in relation to the image area (or nudge with Arrow keys, or **Click+Shift** to constrain as you drag).

End

INTRODUCTION

When you moved text and shapes in previous tasks, you might not have realized you were actually repositioning an entire layer, including not only the selection but also the transparent pixels surrounding it. In this image, the plane and the sky are on separate layers, and the task moves the entire layer higher in the sky.

HINT

Auto Select Layer

If Auto Select Layer is checked in the Move tool's options bar, the layer selection (the active layer) changes automatically when you click an object that resides on it. Remember that doing so actually moves the entire layer, not just the object.

TIP

More Button

Clicking **More** in the top-right corner of the Layers palette brings up a menu of commands that affect layers (handy alternative to the Layers menu).

Controlling Layers

Click 1

Click and drag 2

Click 3

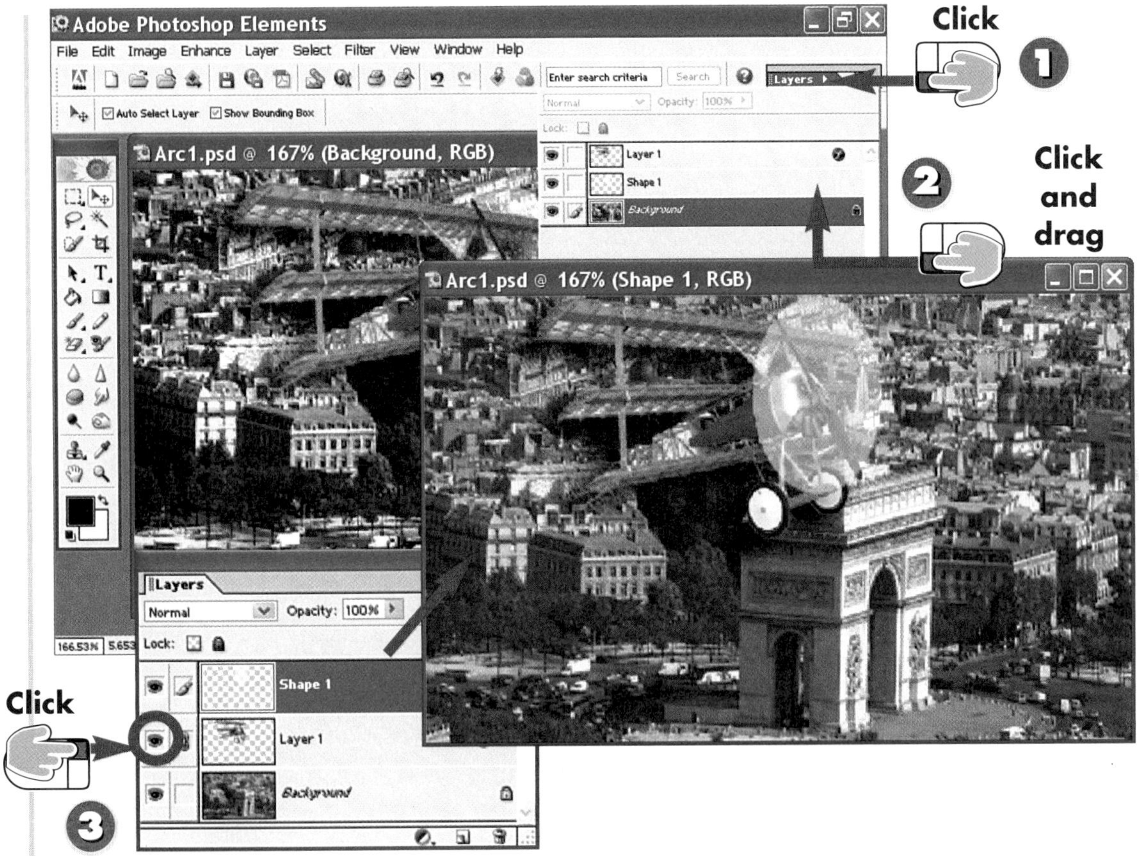

1. Open or undock the Layers palette (or choose **Window**, **Layers**).

2. To change the order of layers, click and drag the layer name to a new position, higher or lower on the list.

3. To hide any layer, causing it not to display or print, click the **Eye** icon. (To restore its visibility, click the Eye icon again.)

INTRODUCTION

The icons in the columns to the left of the layers in the palette control various layer behaviors such as locking a layer (preventing changes), creating and deleting a layer, hiding/unhiding a layer, new fill/adjustment layers, and *linking* layers.

TIP

Linking Layers

Link any layer to the active one by clicking the column to the left of the layer name in the Layers palette. A Link icon appears there. Some commands and operations, such as the Move tool, affect all linked layers at once.

TIP

Grouping Layers

The purpose of grouping layers is to control visibility of their objects according to a *base* layer. To group a layer with the one below, choose **Layer**, **Group with Previous**.

Creating a Fill Layer and Adjusting Layer Opacity

Start

1. Select the layer in the Layers palette above which the new layer will be inserted.
2. Choose **Layer**, **New Fill Layer**, **Solid Color**.
3. Click and drag the **Opacity** slider to change how transparent the new layer is.
4. Click **OK**.

INTRODUCTION

One way to change how layers look is to adjust the *opacity* of a fill layer above them. Think of a *semitransparent* fill layer (less than 100 percent opacity) as a colored photographic filter—tinting and dimming the layers beneath it. (The more opaque, the less transparent, and vice versa.)

TIP

Gradient and Pattern Fills
Besides Solid Color, other submenu selections available in step 2 are Gradient and Pattern, which have the same options as the Gradient tool and the Pattern settings of the Paint Bucket tool.

HINT

Well Adjusted
Continuing to add other adjustment and fill layers, each with its own properties, will have a combined effect. Remember that an adjustment layer only affects the appearance of the layers *beneath* it; all affect the background.

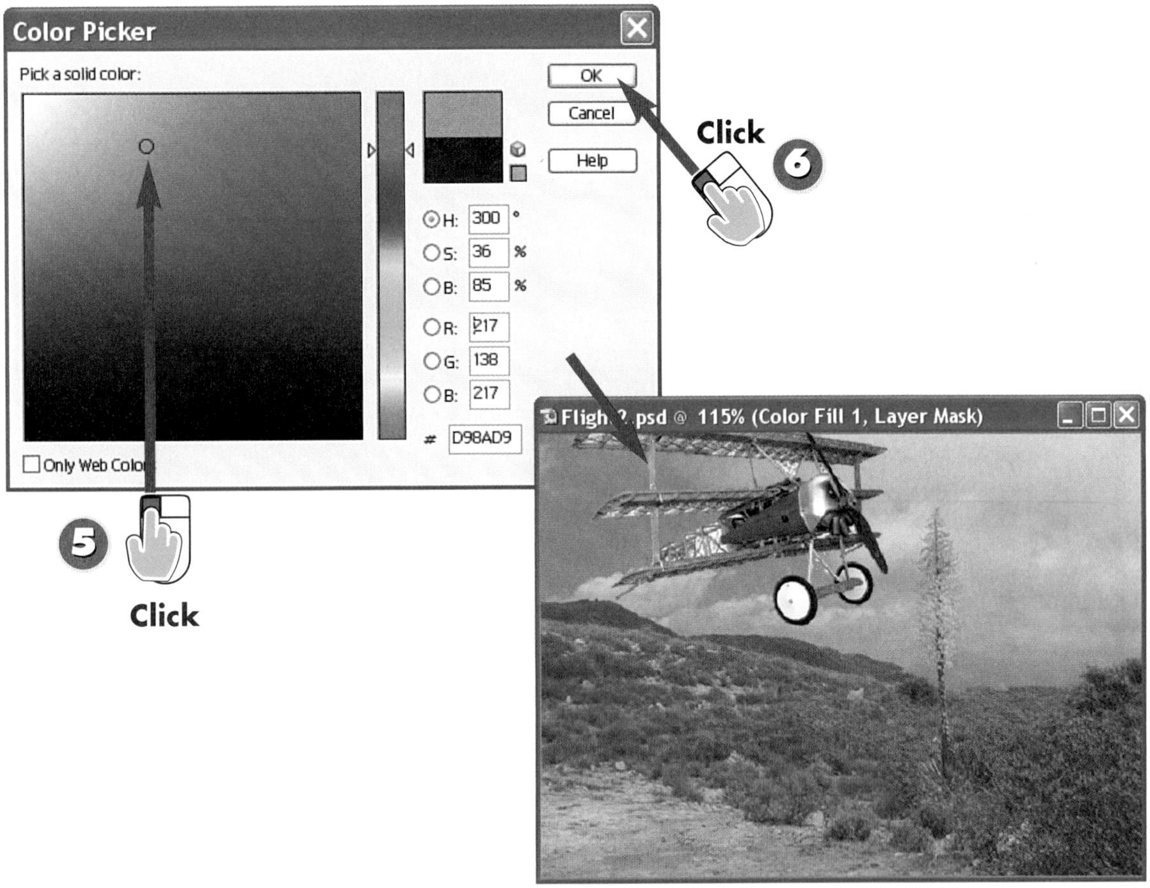

5 Click to select a fill color.

6 Click **OK**.

TIP

Special Effects

By using either the Gradient or Pattern submenu commands instead of Solid Color, you can create variegated effects: Gradient could cause the filtration effect to fade across the background; Pattern could give it a texture, like a dust storm.

Flipping or Rotating a Layer

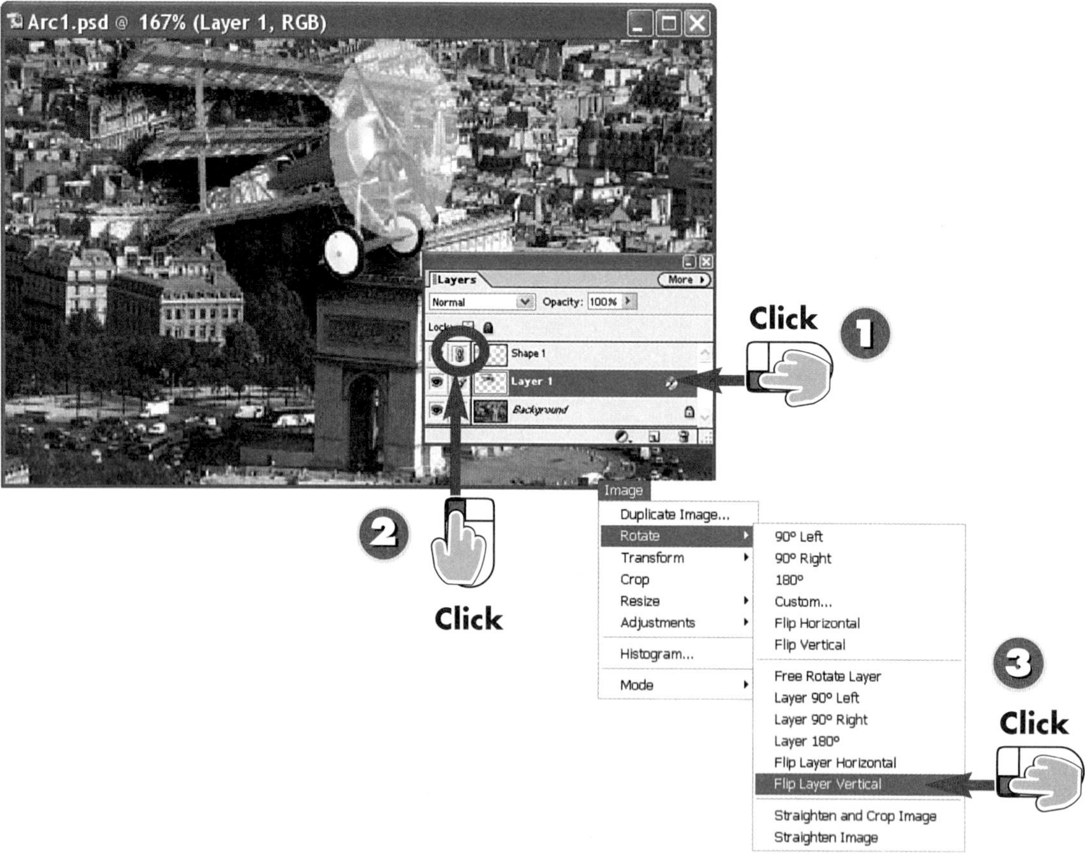

1. Select the layer name in the Layers palette to make it the *active*, or current, layer.
2. Click the **Link** icon in the Layers palette to link any other layers that must be included in the operation.
3. Choose **Image**, **Rotate** and choose from the submenu commands.

INTRODUCTION

The purpose of flipping or rotating a layer can be either to change the position of the objects on the layer or to vary the effect of a gradient or pattern layer. The Image, Rotate command has a submenu section for such operations performed on entire layers.

TIP

Selections or Layers?
To flip or rotate an individual selection—such as a shape or text—within a layer, but not the whole layer, use the set of commands in the top half of the Image, Rotate submenu.

Using an Adjustment Layer

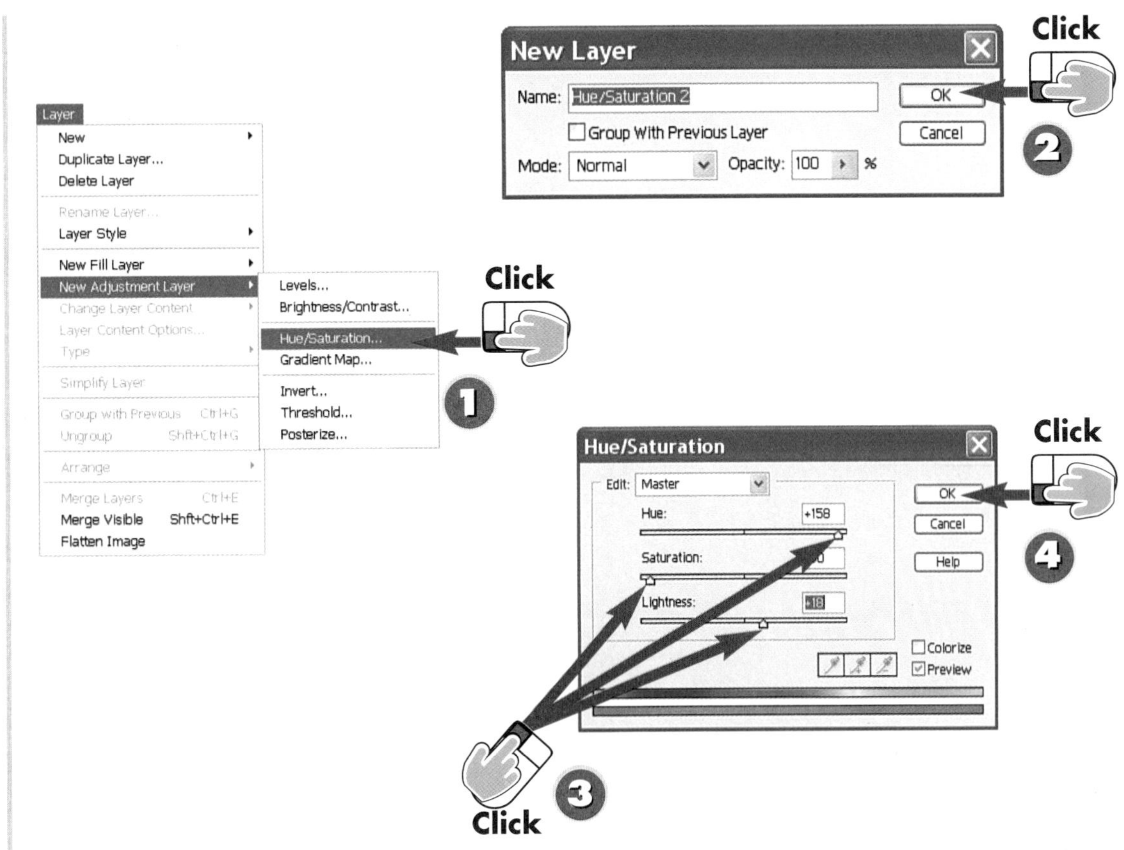

1. Having selected the layer you want to control, choose **Layer**, **New Adjustment Layer** and select from the submenu commands.
2. Click **OK**.
3. Make adjustments using the options in the dialog box and see the effect on your image in the background.
4. When you are satisfied with the effect, click **OK**.

INTRODUCTION

An adjustment layer has no color of its own but lets you control color, brightness/contrast, and other factors on layers beneath without making changes directly to them. The adjustment layer has no effect on layers above it unless you link or group them to the layer or layers below it.

TIP

Select a Layer First
The new adjustment layer will be inserted just above the layer that's active when you begin step 1. So if you want to adjust the background image, select that layer first and then do these steps.

HINT

Blending Mode
As described in the next task, the effect of any fill or adjustment layer can also be controlled by selecting a Blending Mode from the More menu in the Layers palette (or Mode menu in the New Layer dialog box).

Using Blending Modes on Layers

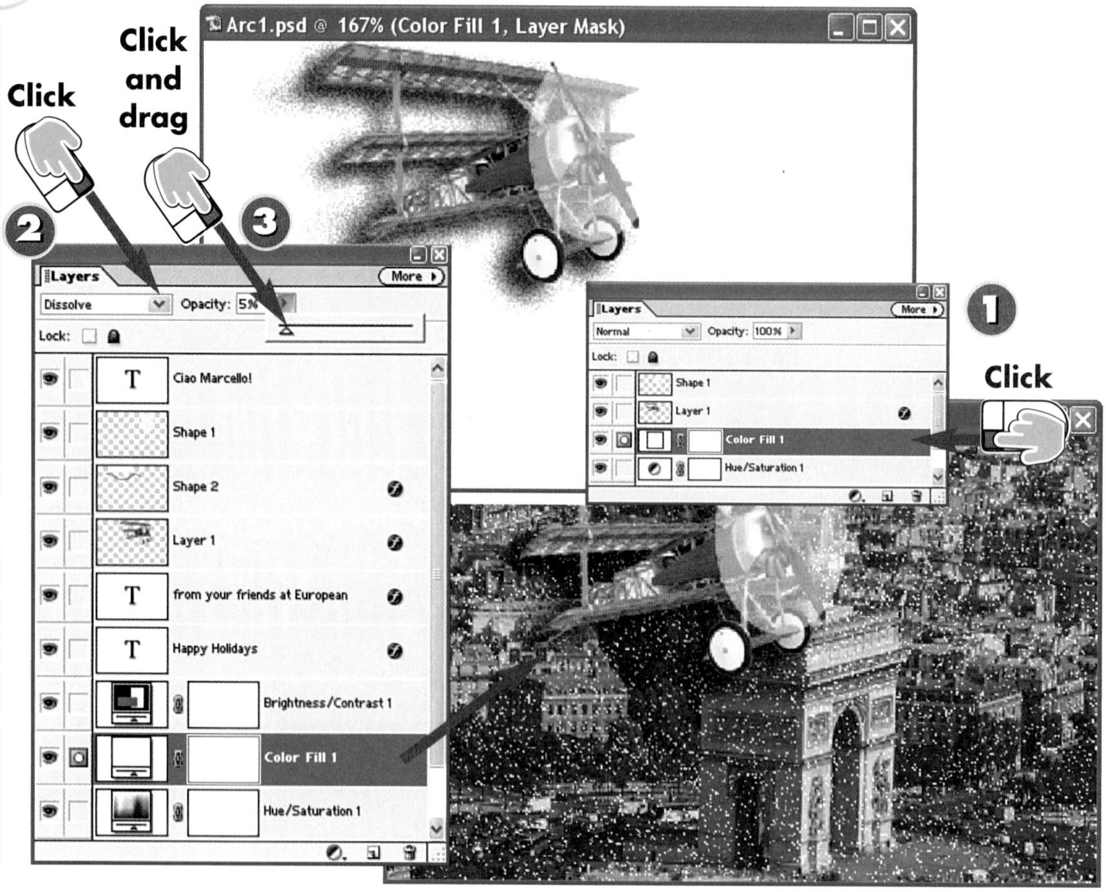

1. Select the layer name in the Layers palette to make it the active layer.
2. Select a blending mode, such as **Dissolve**.
3. Adjust the **Opacity** setting to control the extent of blending.

INTRODUCTION

Blending mode controls how pixel values within a layer are blended with those of the layers beneath. The default is Normal. Other modes include Dissolve, several Dodge or Burn effects, quality of light (such as Soft or Hard), adding (Exclusion) or subtracting (Difference) pixel values, or individual elements of color.

TIP

Try 'Em On
After making a selection from the blending mode list in step 2, press the **Up** or **Down** arrow keys to step through the other modes and preview their effects on the image.

TIP

Controlling Blending Mode
To turn off a blending mode, change the setting back to **Normal** for that layer in the drop-down box in the top-left corner of the Layers palette.

Copying and Pasting a Layer Style

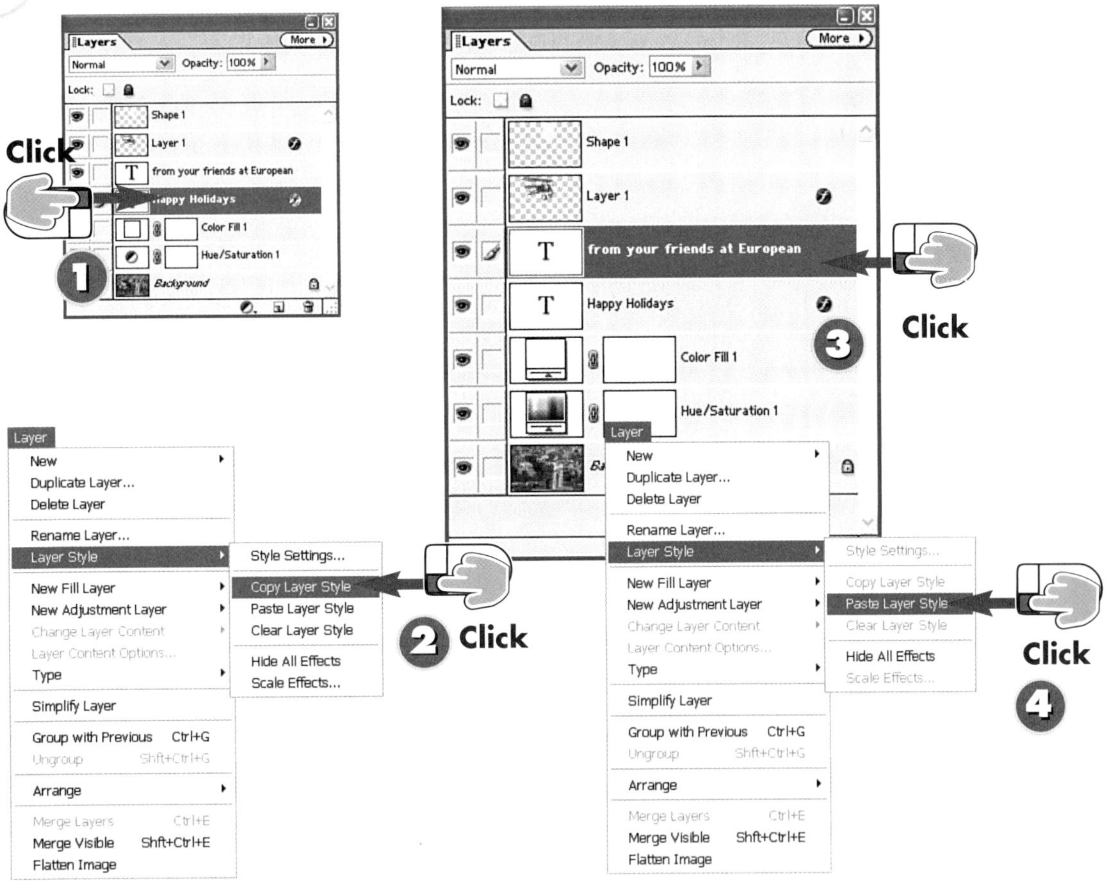

1. Select the name in the Layers palette of a layer that contains a layer style, such as **Drop Shadow**.
2. Choose **Layer**, **Layer Style**, **Copy Layer Style**.
3. Select the name of a layer to which the style will be applied.
4. Choose **Layer**, **Layer Style**, **Paste Layer Style**.

INTRODUCTION

Copying layer styles is particularly convenient when you've made several style changes on one layer and want to apply them with a click to all objects on another layer—also if you've taken pains to fine-tune a style, such as adjusted the angle of a drop-shadow.

TIP

Fine-Tuning Styles
To fine-tune a layer style on the active layer, such as Bevel or Drop Shadow, choose **Layer**, **Layer Style**, **Style Settings**. Make adjustments by clicking and dragging the sliders; and then click **OK**.

Preparing to Publish

With Photoshop Elements, a digital camera, a computer, and an inexpensive color inkjet printer, you can be your own one-stop shop for most of your photography needs. But there's a whole wide world out there—including a giant color printing industry—ready to serve you.

Need custom-printed tee shirts? Color posters? Banners? A thousand color postcards? These days, most commercial printers accept—and actually prefer—your Photoshop image files as source artwork for these kinds of printing jobs. You can even submit your orders online at sites such as **www.vistaprint.com**, **www.inkchaser.com**, and **www.kinkos.com**.

Admittedly, preparing files for commercial printing is a major reason why some serious graphic artists consider upgrading to "big Photoshop" (Adobe Photoshop CS). Specifically, that application has extensive *color management* capabilities that Photoshop Elements lacks.

But there's still a lot you can do in Photoshop Elements to improve the quality of the results when you decide to "send it out"—whether you're publishing on paper or via electronic media.

How Do I Get from Here to There?

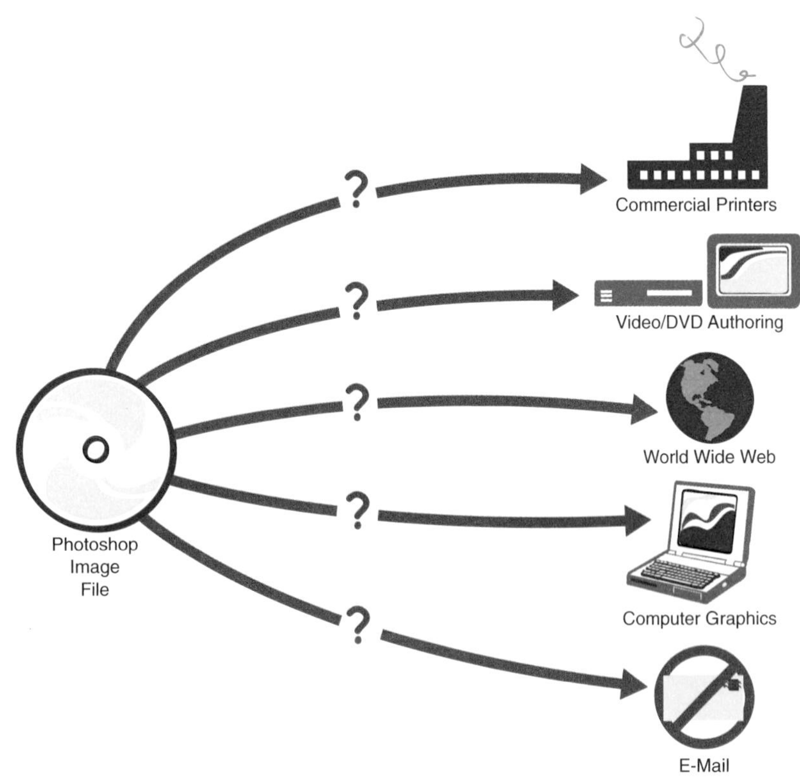

Start

Previewing a Halftone Image for Color Printing

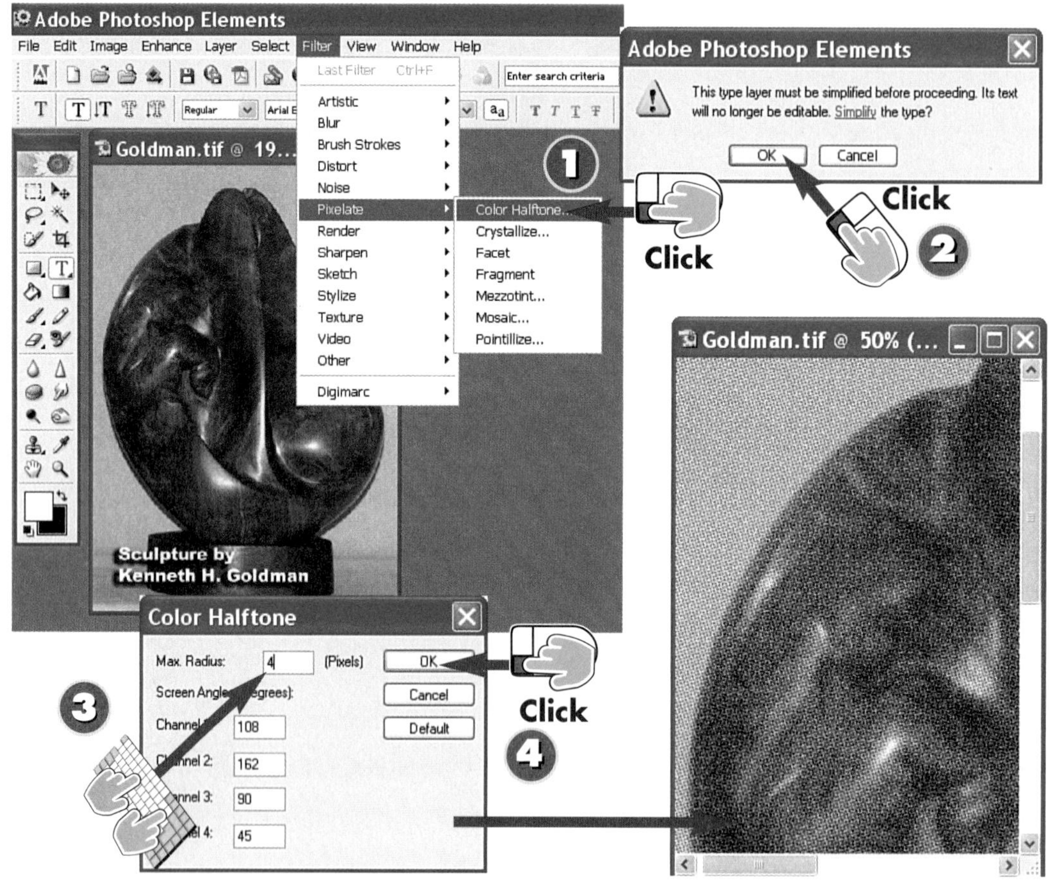

1. With a color picture in the active image area, choose **Filter**, **Pixelate**, **Color Halftone**.
2. If a Simplify warning appears, click **OK**.
3. Type a number between **4–127** for **Max. Radius** to control the size of the halftone dots.
4. Click **OK**.

INTRODUCTION

Halftone screens break images into collections of tiny dots for conventional printing. Photoshop Elements lacks the features to convert imagery to true halftones but can show you how images would look if reproduced by this method. The printing service to which you submit your files can convert them.

HINT

Resolution and Radius

The lower the resolution of your image, the lower the Max Radius setting must be. A setting of 4 is about right for a 300 dpi image.

HINT

Don't Sweat the Angles

Don't mess with the Screen Angles settings unless your printer tells you to vary them.

Previewing a Halftone Image for B&W Printing

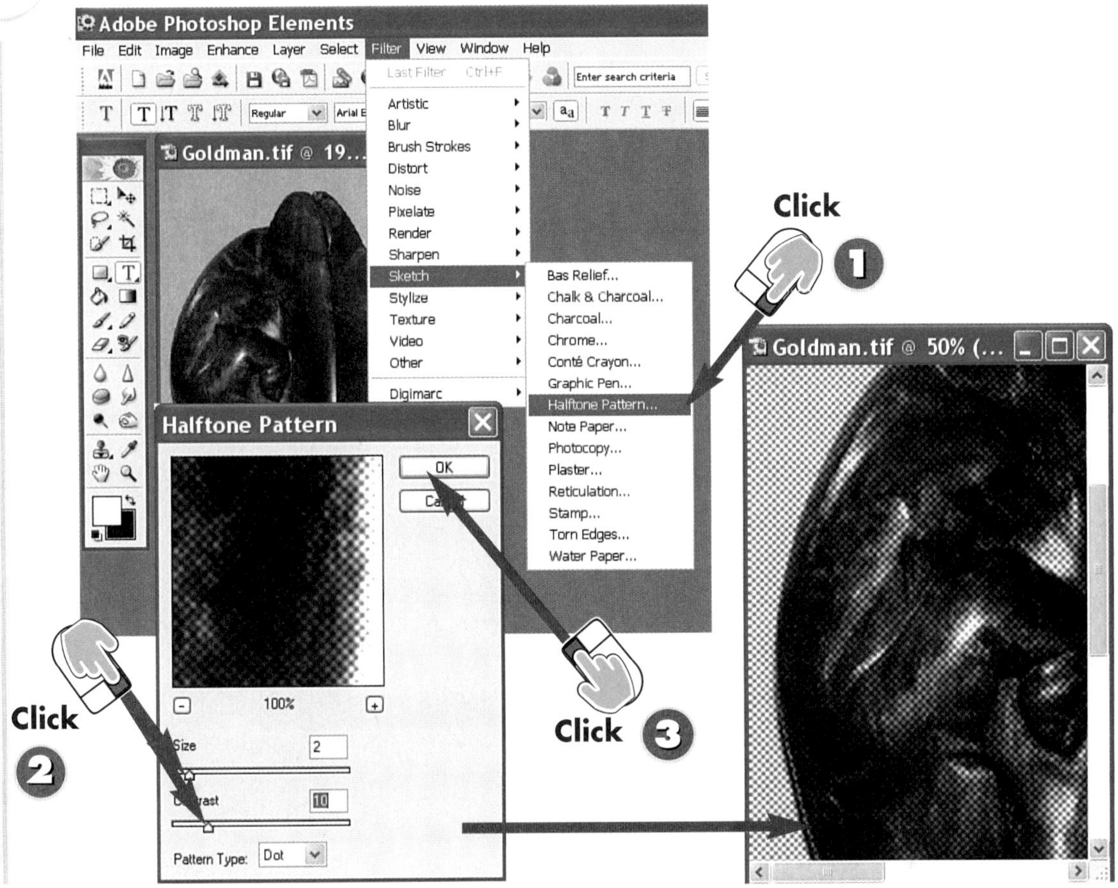

1. With a grayscale picture in the active image area, choose **Filter**, **Sketch**, **Halftone Pattern**.
2. Adjust the sliders to control dot **Size** and **Contrast**.
3. Click **OK**.

INTRODUCTION

As with color halftones, this Sketch filter is simply a way of previewing how a grayscale image would look in print. Some designers also use it as an artistic effect. The main thing to remember about a halftone image is that, although it appears to have grayscale shading, every dot in the image is pure black.

HINT

Other Pattern Types

Most conventional printing processes use the Dot pattern. Alternatives are Circle and Line.

Using Color Management for Commercial Printing

Start

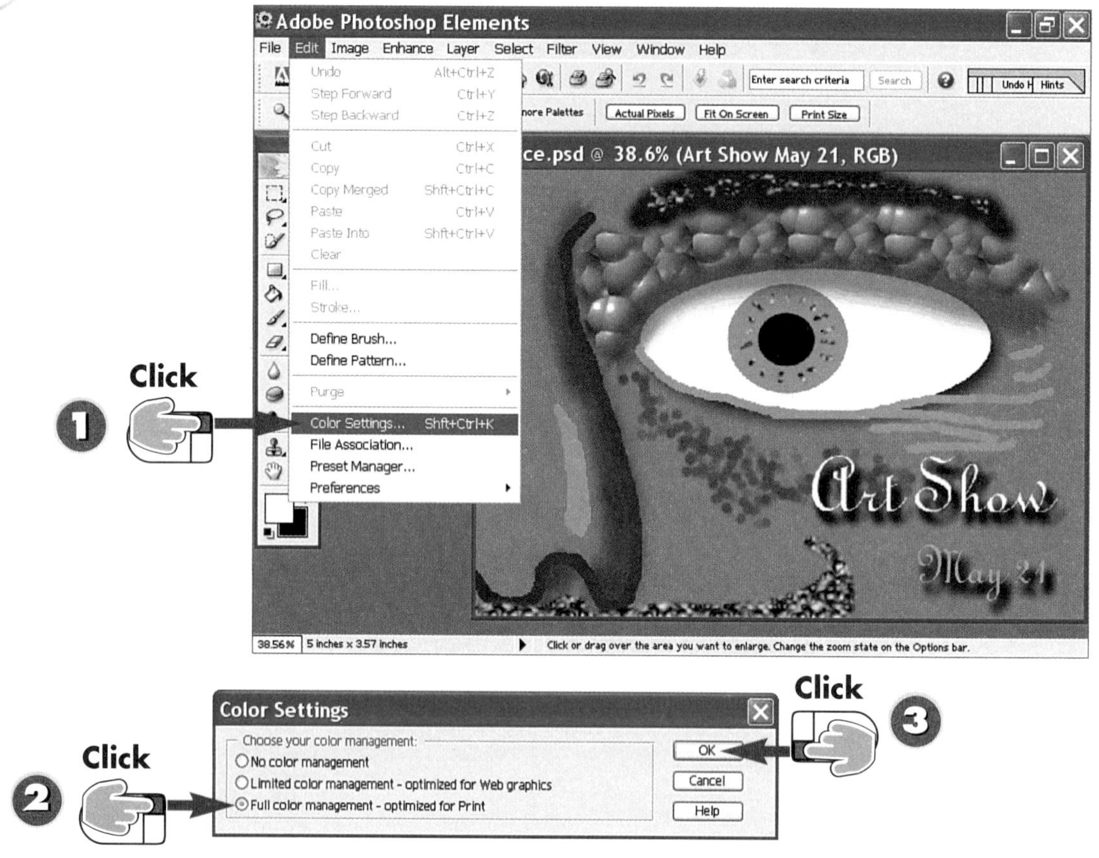

1. With a picture in the active image area, choose **Edit**, **Color Settings**, or press **Shift+Ctrl+K**.
2. Click **Full Color Management**.
3. Click **OK**.

INTRODUCTION

An important part of submitting your digital files for color printing is to be able to match color accurately. Apply color management to any file you send out to a commercial printer. To adjust CMYK color and to generate Prepress PDF files, you'll have to upgrade to Photoshop CS.

TIP

Paper or Screen?
In step 2, select **Limited Color Management** if you will be publishing on the Web instead of in print.

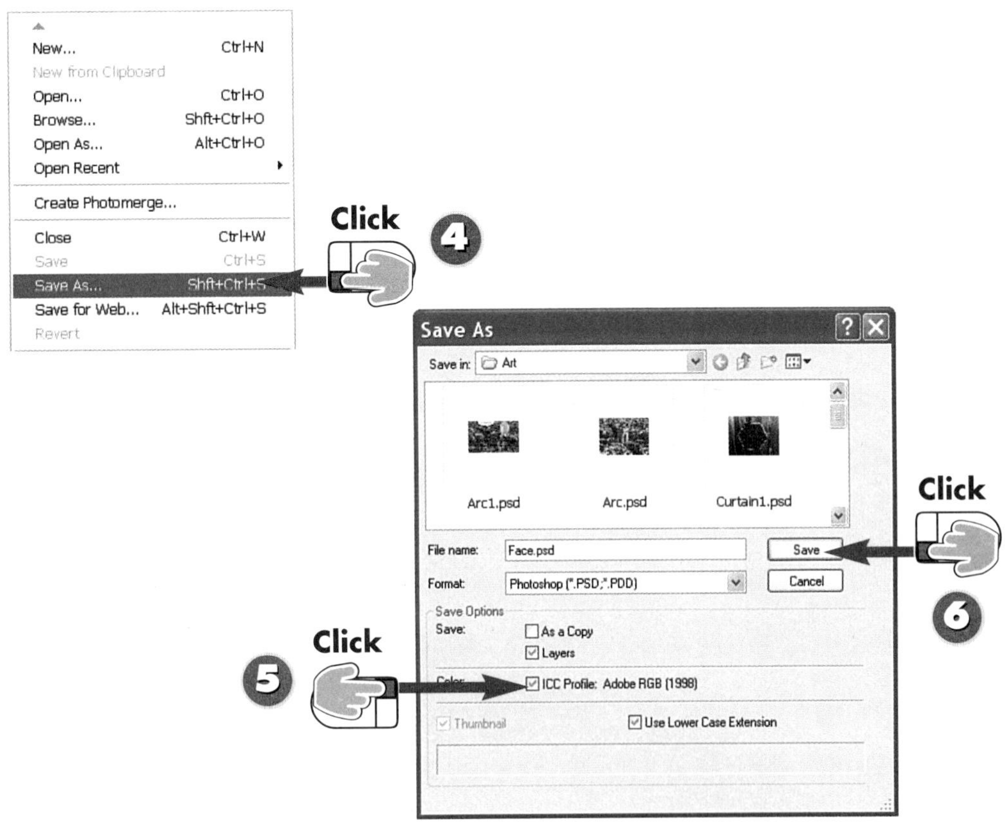

4. Choose **File**, **Save As**, or press **Shift+Ctrl+S**.
5. Check the **ICC Profile** box.
6. Click **Save**.

TIP

What's Your Profile?
Profiles are standardized color tables used by the printing industry. Adobe has been an industry leader in making it possible to match digital outputs with conventional printing methods.

HINT

Why Bother?
Important reasons to worry about *color matching* are when you are trying to reproduce product photography (particularly food, which must look realistic and appetizing) and company logos, which have precise color requirements.

Preparing a Still Image for Video

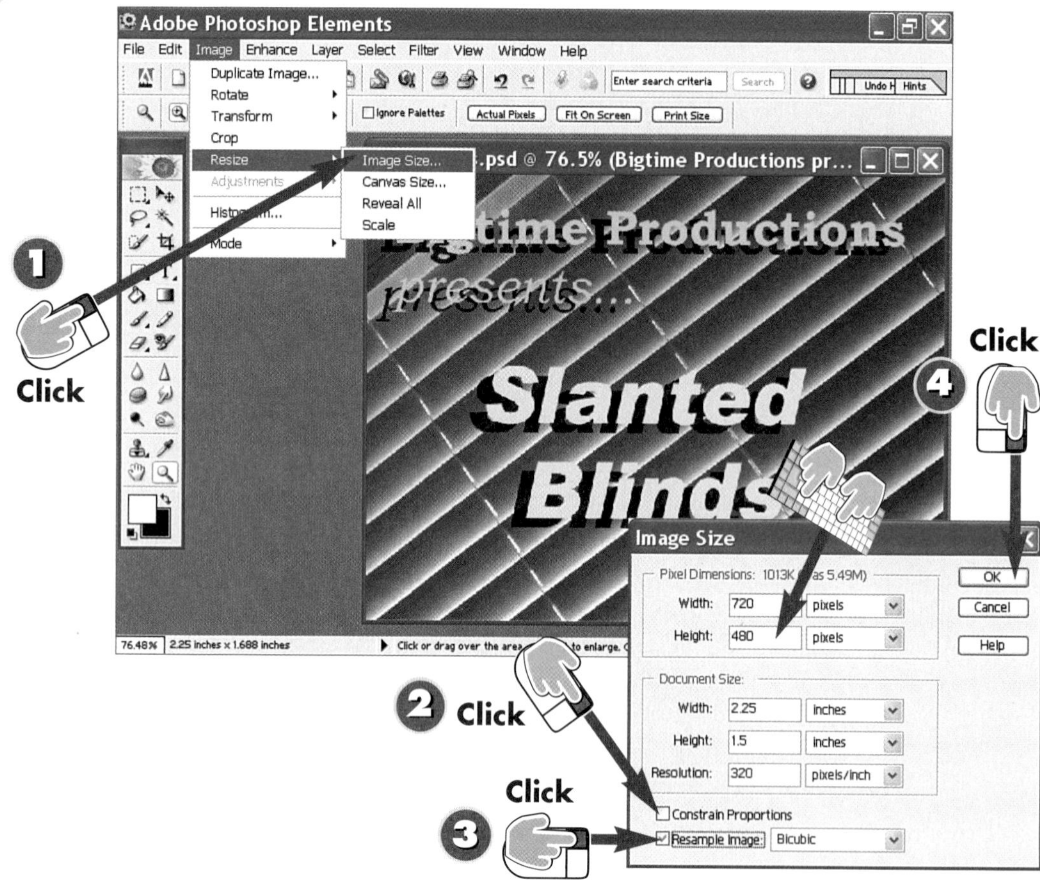

1. Start with an image that's 720×540 pixels open in the active image area. Choose **Image**, **Resize**, **Image Size**.
2. Uncheck **Constrain Proportions**.
3. Check **Resample Image**.
4. Keeping the Width at 720, change **Height** to **480** pixels and click **OK**.

INTRODUCTION

A curious problem arises from the fact that computer images have square pixels, but in digital video they're rectangular. You might think this an odd technicality, but if you make video titles or *DVD menus* in Photoshop Elements and don't follow these steps, the images will look squished when you convert them to video.

TIP

What's Your System?
Digital video (DV) editing is coming to a PC near you. Windows Movie Maker, Apple iMovie, and Pinnacle Studio are examples of the many applications available for assembling your home movie footage in creative ways.

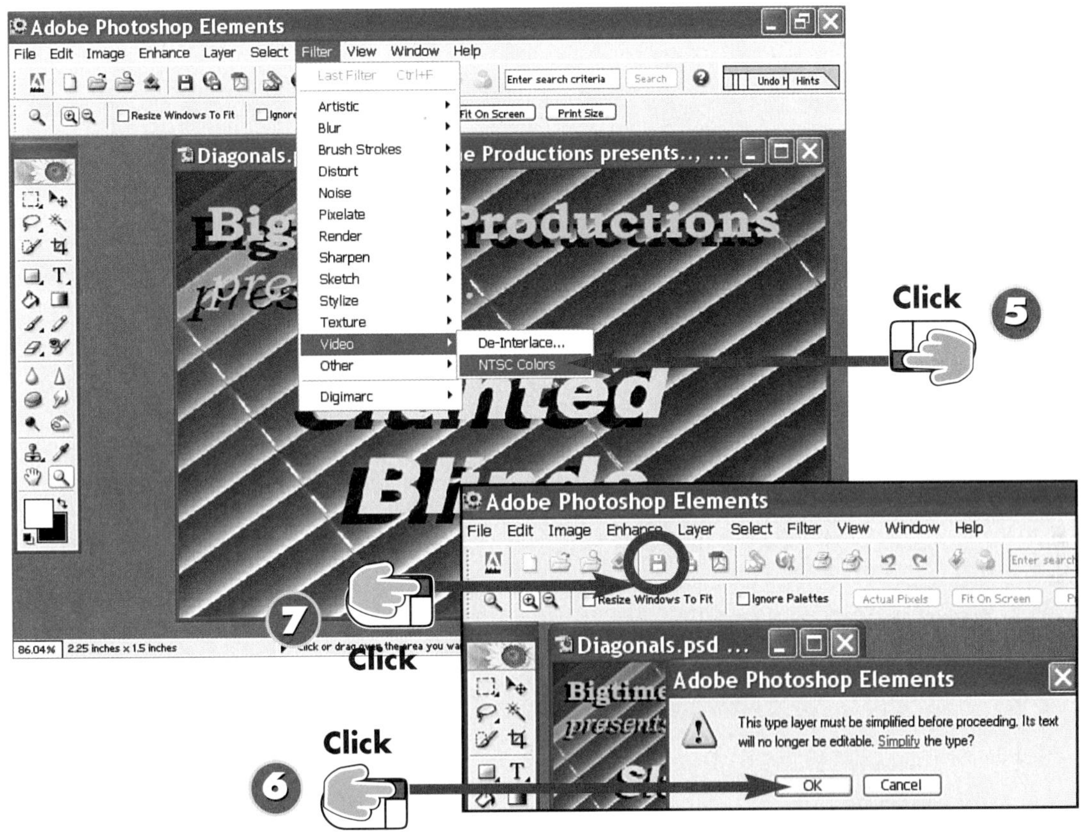

5 Choose **Filter**, **Video**, **NTSC Colors**.

6 If you see a Simplify warning, click **OK**.

7 Click **Save**.

TIP

DVD Menus
One challenge of creating a DVD is to build the menu system by which users can make program selections. Many DVD authoring programs can use still imagery you create as Photoshop files for menus.

HINT

NTSC Color
This color model applies to broadcast television in North America. You'll need a different plug-in for the UK or France/Asia.

Sending a Picture via Email

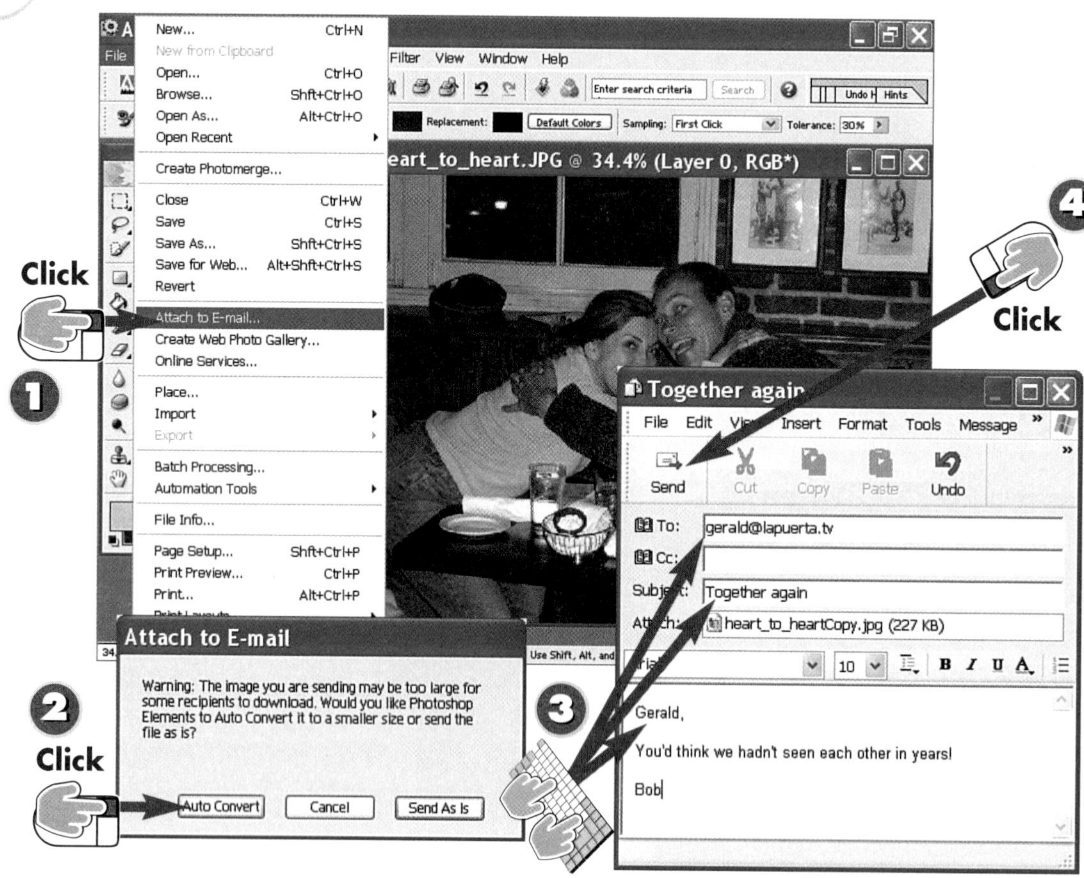

1. With a JPEG picture in the active image area, choose **File**, **Attach to E-mail**.
2. If you see this warning, click **Auto Convert**.
3. Type the recipient's email address in the **To** field. (Or click **To:** to select from your Address Book.) Also type a **Subject** and **Message.**
4. Click **Send**.

INTRODUCTION

The secret to sending pictures via email is to make the files compact without sacrificing too much quality. Even though any file converted for the Web will also do nicely for email, Photoshop Elements 2 has this handy built-in feature that both automatically resizes the photo and attaches it to an outgoing email message.

TIP

Sender Beware!
Certain types of computer viruses can hide out in image files, so install virus protection such as Norton Antivirus or McAfee VirusScan and set it to check all outgoing email attachments automatically.

Converting to Indexed Color for the Web

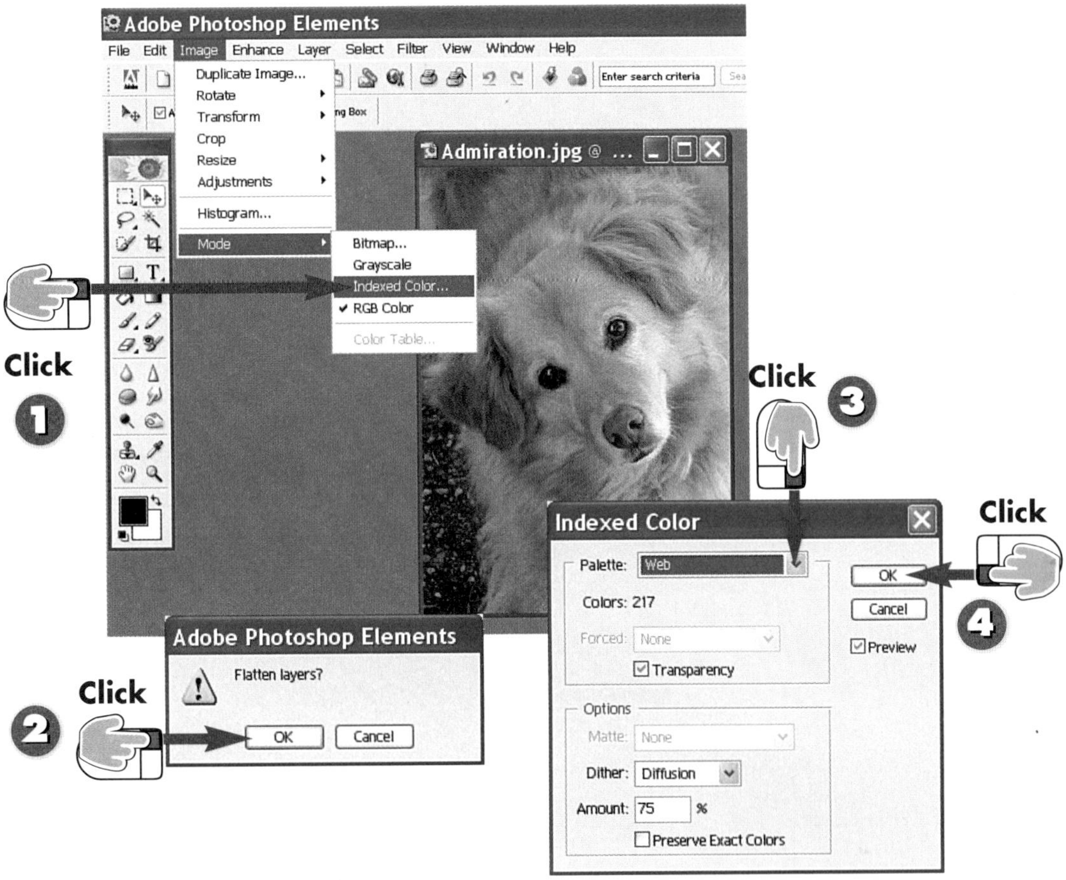

1. Choose **Image**, **Mode**, **Indexed Color**.
2. If this warning appears, click **OK** to flatten all layers.
3. Set Palette to **Web**.
4. Click **OK**.

INTRODUCTION

Desktop computers of various vintages differ in the number of video colors they can show. To ensure that Web imagery can be viewed on most of them, Photoshop Elements has this feature for converting and restricting an image to the 256 colors most computers can display.

HINT

Palette Types

As long as you are creating for the Web (the main reason for using indexed color), the other palette types needn't concern you. If you're making graphics for use in a Windows program, select **System**.

TIP

Index Color Options

Selecting the **Diffusion** option for Dithering should make the best Web pictures. *Dithering* groups dots of two or more indexed colors together to simulate subtler colors.

Optimizing a Picture for the Web

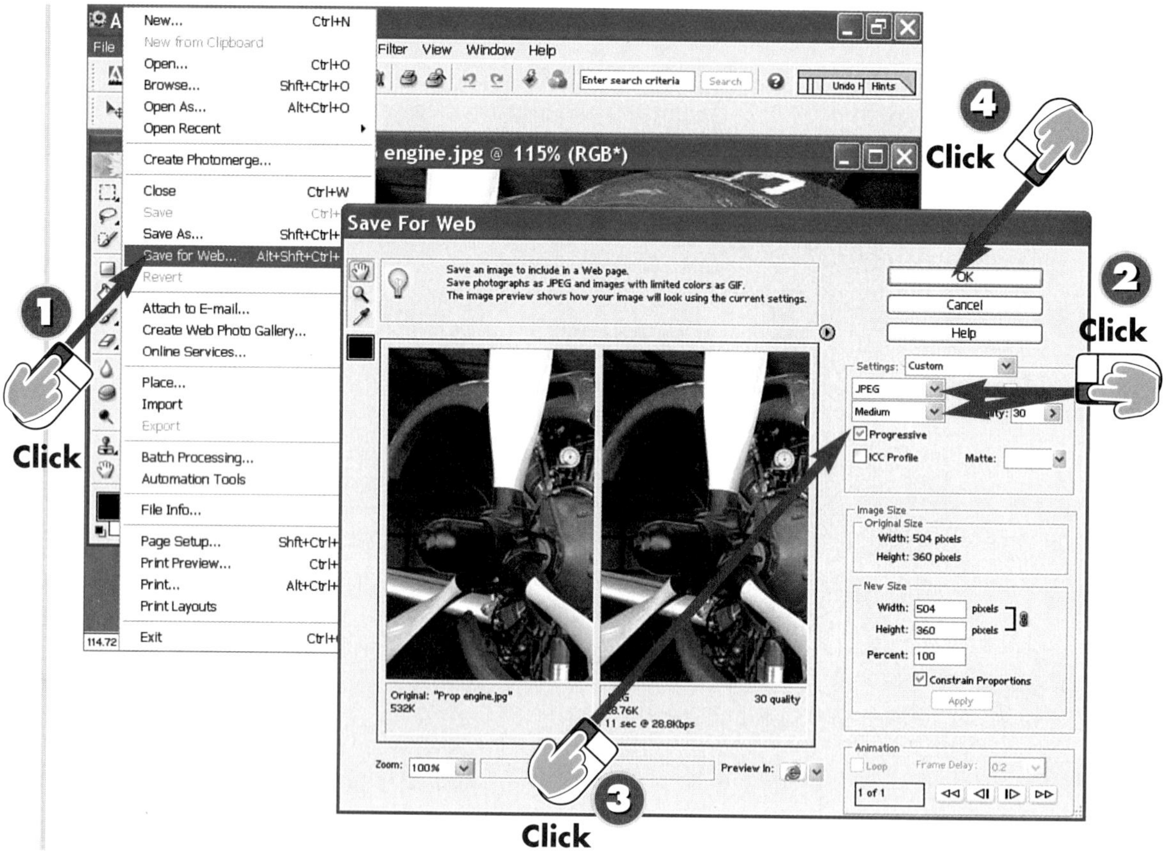

1. With your finished picture in the active image area, choose **File**, **Save for Web**.
2. In the Settings box, select a picture format and quality, such as **JPEG Medium**.
3. Optionally, check the **Progressive** box.
4. Click **OK**.

INTRODUCTION

Preparing an image for the Web involves converting its file type to JPEG, GIF, or PNG; restricting its colors to 256; reducing its size to a few inches wide; and limiting its resolution to 72 pixels/inch.

HINT

Control File Size
You can use the Image, Resize, Image Size command to size the image to the computer screen (typically, 2–4 inches wide), with resolution of 72 pixels/inch.

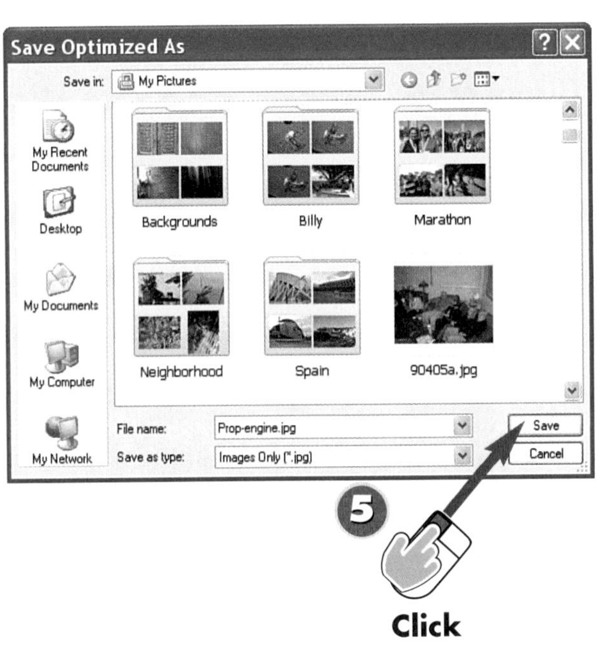

5 Click **Save**.

TIP

Progressive Mode
Selecting **Progressive** mode for a JPEG file causes it to be displayed in stages as it downloads, resulting in a more pleasing experience for users with relatively slow (dial-up) connections.

HINT

Control Image Size
To capture the interest of Web surfers, you want your home page to load as quickly as possible. Keep images there to thumbnail size; then permit interested viewers to click on them to download higher-resolution pictures.

Saving As an Animated Picture for the Web

Start

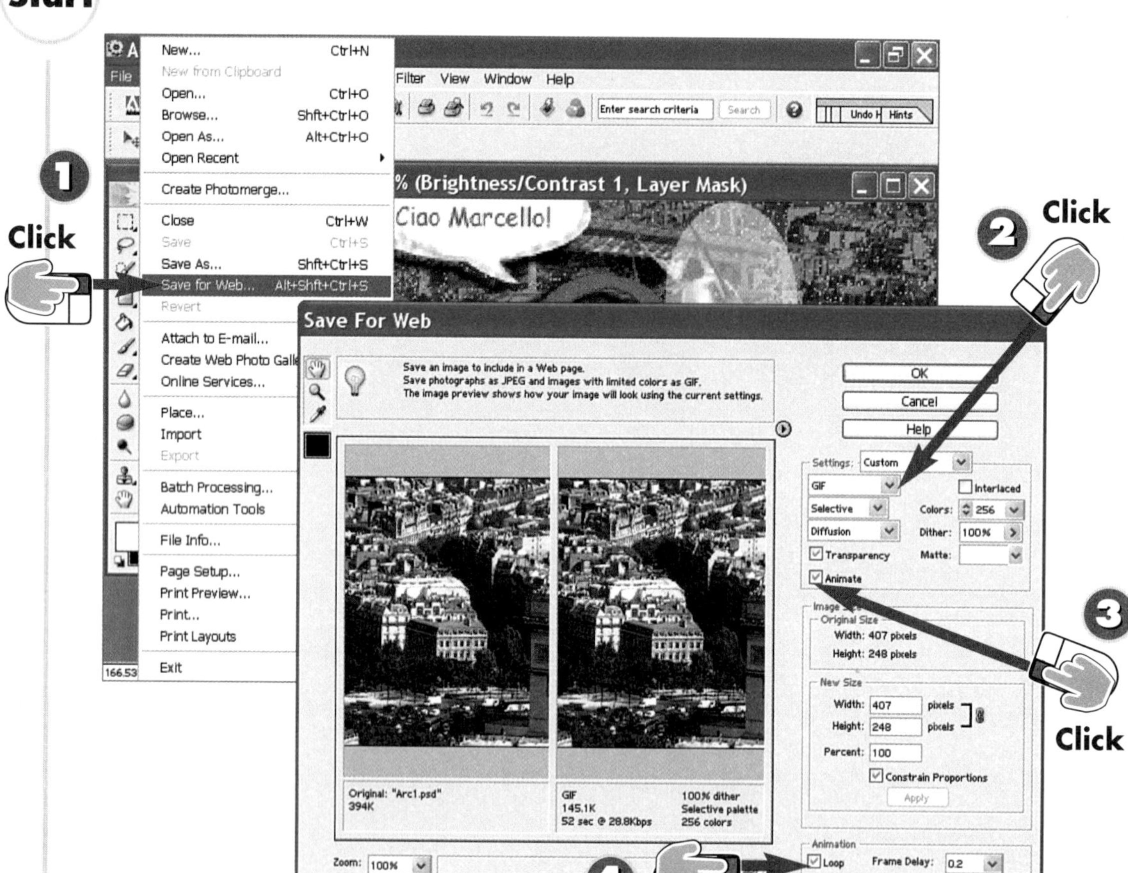

1. With a multilayered image in the active image area, choose **File**, **Save for Web**.
2. In the Settings section, select **GIF** as the picture type.
3. Check the **Animate** box.
4. In the Animation section, check the **Loop** box (for continuous playback).

INTRODUCTION

These conversion steps take any layered file and convert it to a series of GIF frames (animated .gif file). Displayed on a Web page in rapid succession, a simple but effective animation sequence can be created. For example, text on successive layers appears to pop onto a background image.

TIP

Easy Animation

You can control the animated sequence by reordering the layers of your image in the Layers palette before you convert to GIF.

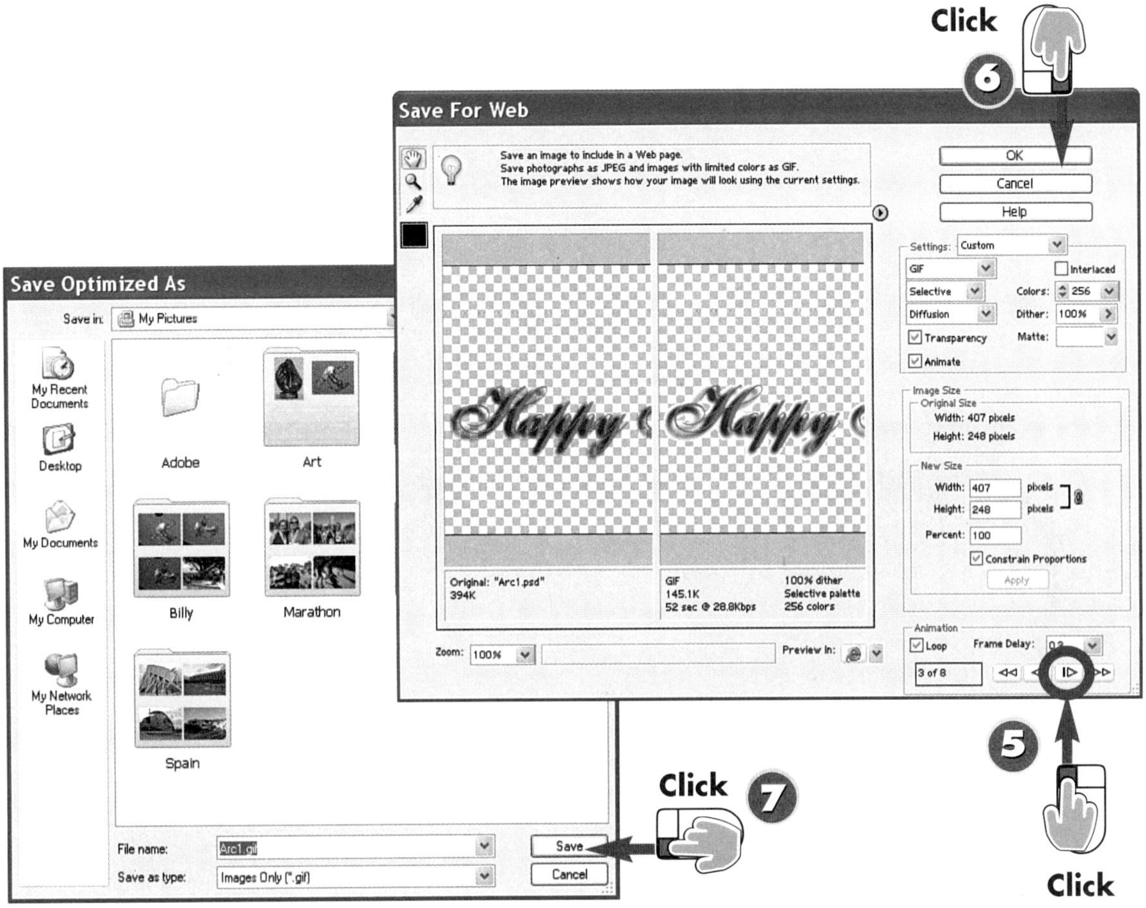

5. Step through to preview the animation by clicking the **Next Frame** button.

6. Click **OK**.

7. Click **Save**.

Frame Delay

HINT

This option in the Animation section of the Save for Web window lets you vary the delay between frames (layers) from 0–10 seconds. If you don't check Loop, the sequence plays once and stops.

Layered Imagery

HINT

Native Photoshop (.psd) files make excellent source material for this type of animation. For example, text can appear to pop onto a background. Creating different text layers can cause a message to be built up in steps.

Downloading and Installing the JPEG 2000 Plug-In

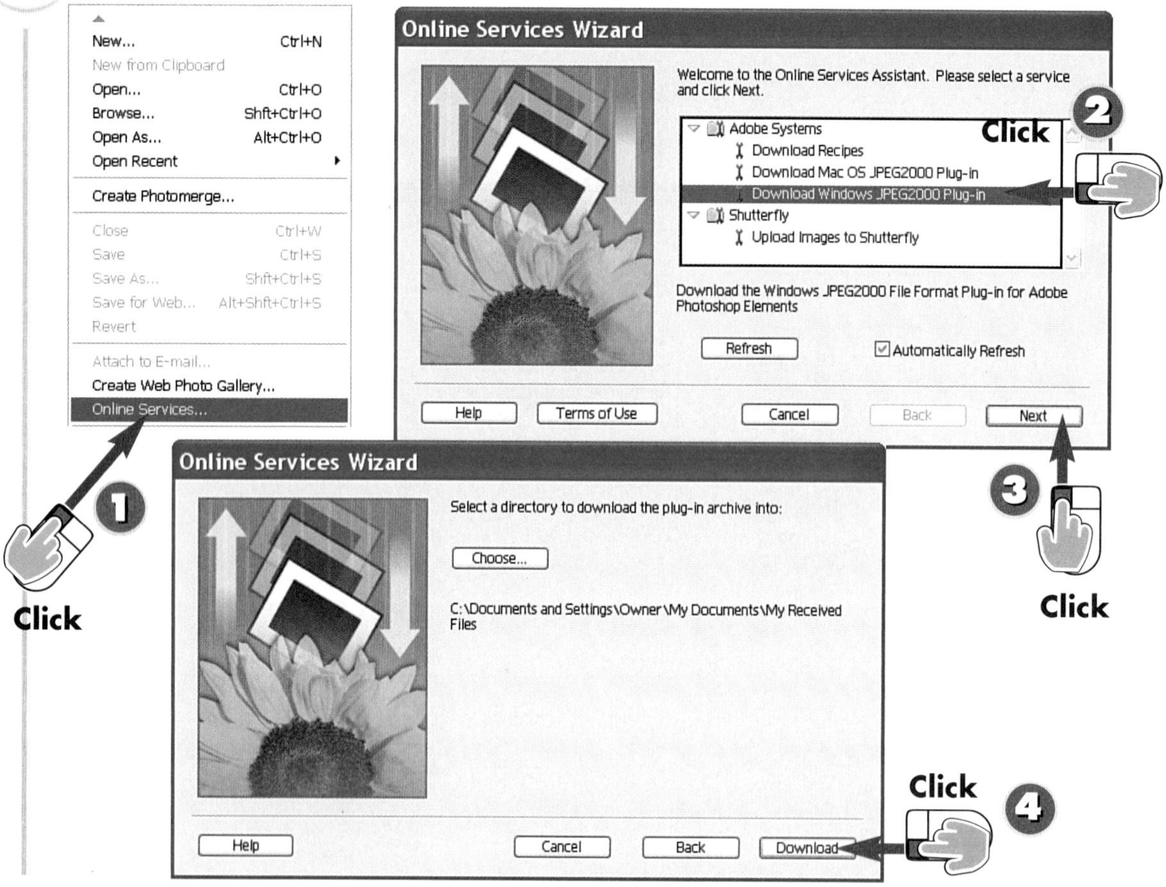

1. Start with no image files open. Choose **File**, **Online Services**.
2. Select **Download Windows JPEG2000 Plug-in**.
3. Click **Next**.
4. Click **Download**.

INTRODUCTION

Download *plug-in* support for JPEG 2000 files to stay current with emerging Web photo standards. You'll need it if you become involved in creating and editing Web sites. When installed, the new JPX and JP2 file types will be available as options when you choose File, Save As or File, Open As.

HINT

Read Up on It
For more information on JPEG 2000 installation, see the file JPEG2000_Readme.pdf, which is included in the downloaded zip package.

HINT

Other Formats
In addition to opening and saving JPX and JP2 files, you'll also be able to open (but not save) JPC and J2K files and then save them as any other supported format.

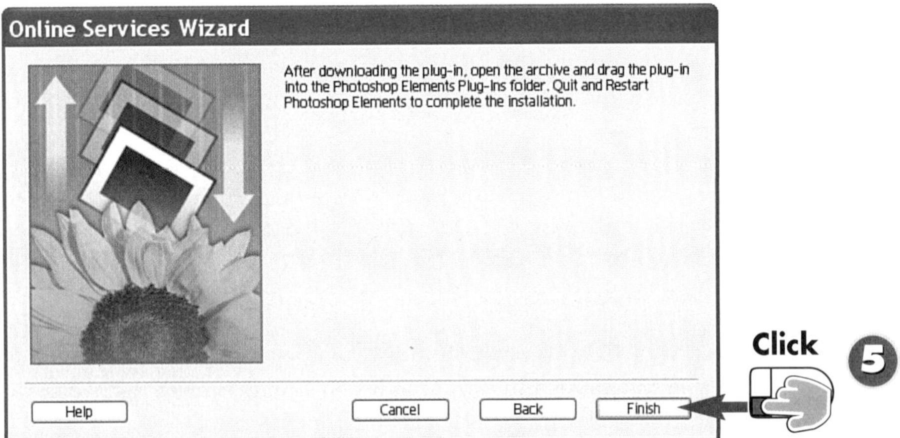

5 Click **Finish**. Close Photoshop Elements and install the plug-in; then restart the application.

TIP

After You Choose Finish

In Windows Explorer, unzip JPEG2000.zip and extract the downloaded file JPEG2000.8BI. Copy the file to C:\Program Files\Adobe\Photoshop Elements 2\Plug-Ins\File Formats.

HINT

Got Zip?

Unzipping requires a utility program such as WinZip, PKZip, PowerZip, or PicoZip. You can download shareware utilities from **www.tucows.com**.

PART 11

Choosing Output File Types

As long as you're working for Me-Myself-and-I Productions—taking pictures, manipulating them, and printing them—stick with the Adobe Photoshop format, and you'll live happily ever after.

But the minute you want to share your stuff with the rest of the world, you face a bundle of challenges. For example, as some of the tasks in Part 10 show, if you want to post your pictures on the Web or send them via email, you need to convert the files to a *compressed* format such as JPEG.

For other purposes, such as creating artwork for publication, the choices can make your head swim. In those situations, tasks in this part can help you cut through the techno-babble and pick the right horse to run the course.

Many of these choices have to do with file *compression*. Here's what you need to know about that: The smaller (more compressed) the file, the faster it will be to send or receive on the Net, but the more likely the compression will be *lossy*, or sacrificing picture quality. Some compression schemes, such as *LZW* and *ZIP* for TIFF files, are *lossless*, or nearly so, but they produce bigger files.

As every racing fan knows, there are horses for courses.

Different File Types for Different Purposes

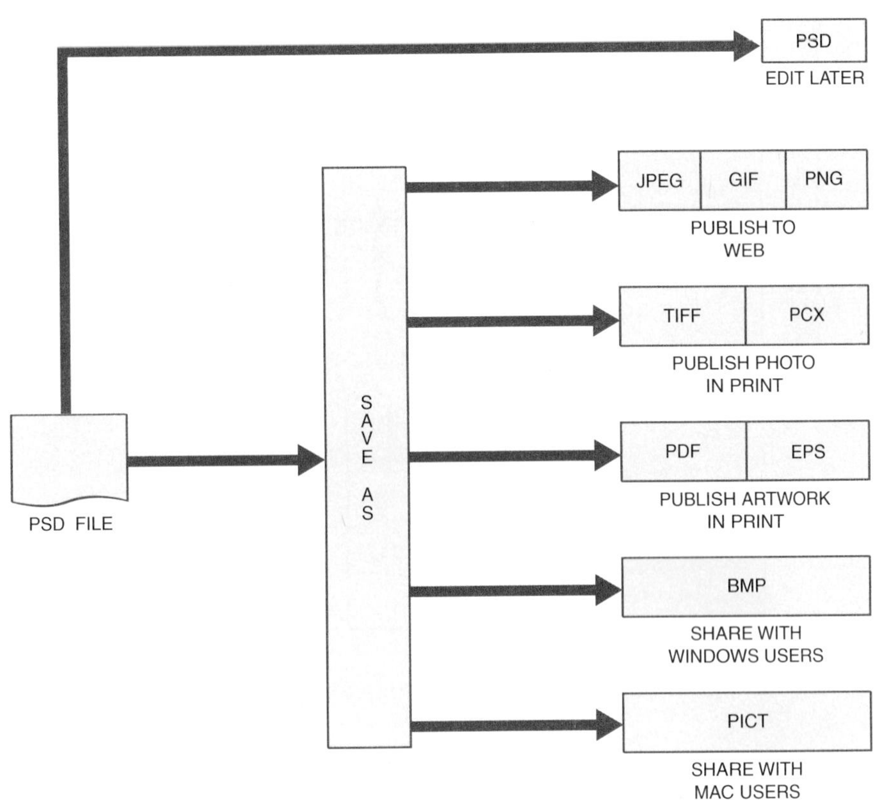

Saving Best-Quality Photos for Printing

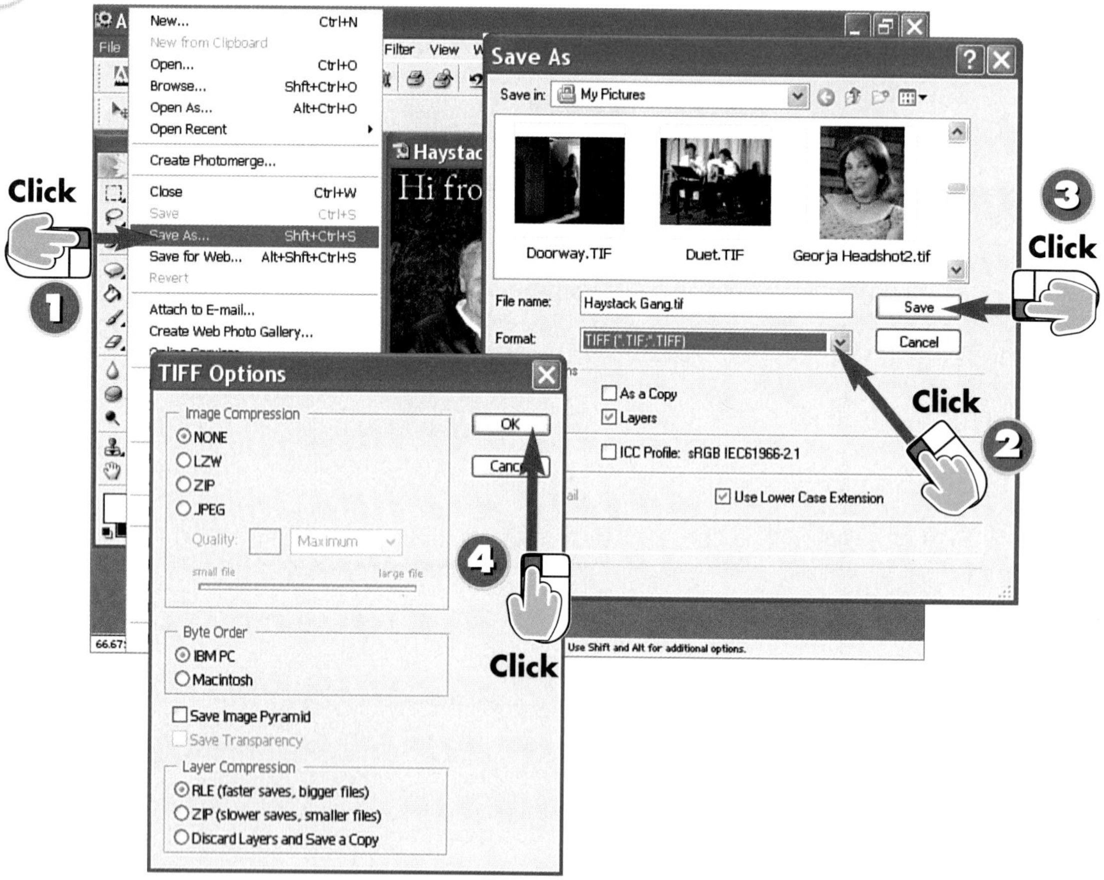

1. With an image open in the active image area, choose **File**, **Save As**, or press **Shift+Ctrl+S**.
2. In the Format drop-down menu, select **TIFF**.
3. Click **Save**.
4. Click **OK**.

INTRODUCTION

Of all the file formats, Tagged Image File Format (TIFF) is probably the best for saving a high-quality photograph that you intend to submit to a printer or publisher. The result is a file with a .tif extension.

TIP

Compression Options

Image Compression: LZW or ZIP are preferable to JPEG. LZW is the safest choice. ZIP can create smaller files, but some users won't be able to open them. Layer Compression: Select **Discard Layers and Save a Copy** unless the recipient needs to edit them.

File Formats for Desktop Publishing

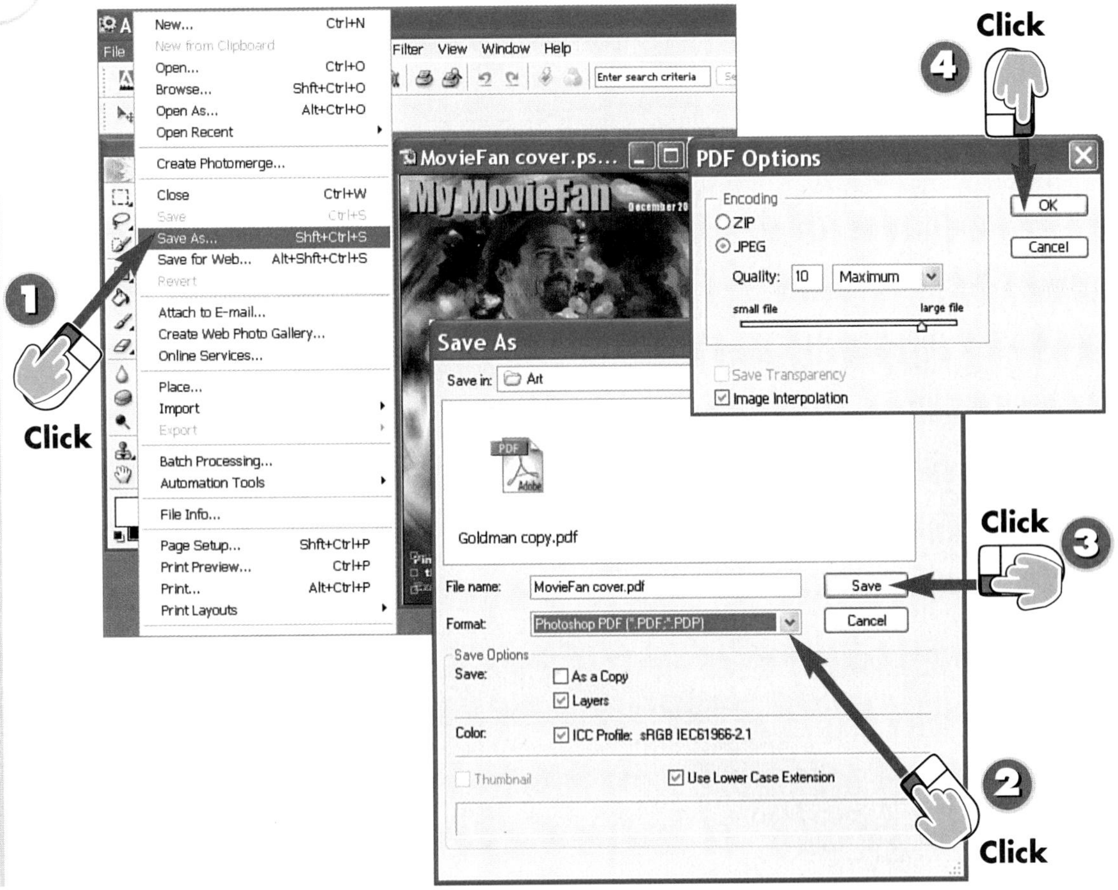

1. With an image open in the active image area, choose **File**, **Save As**, or press **Shift+Ctrl+S**.
2. In the **Format** drop-down menu, select **Photoshop PDF**.
3. Click **Save**.
4. Click **OK**.

INTRODUCTION

Adobe's Portable Document Format, or PDF, is the best choice for sharing finished-quality images and artwork with anyone anywhere, regardless of the computer make or model they happen to be using. When in doubt about which type of file your recipient can handle, this one is a safe bet.

HINT

Encoding Option

In the PDF Options window, even though JPEG is the default value, you'll get better picture quality (but a larger file) by selecting **ZIP** instead.

HINT

PSD and Prepress PDF

Although you can convert from other files types when saving, starting with a Photoshop file usually gives the best results. To save as Prepress PDF, which contains print job information as well as image data, upgrade to Photoshop CS.

Renaming a Batch of Files

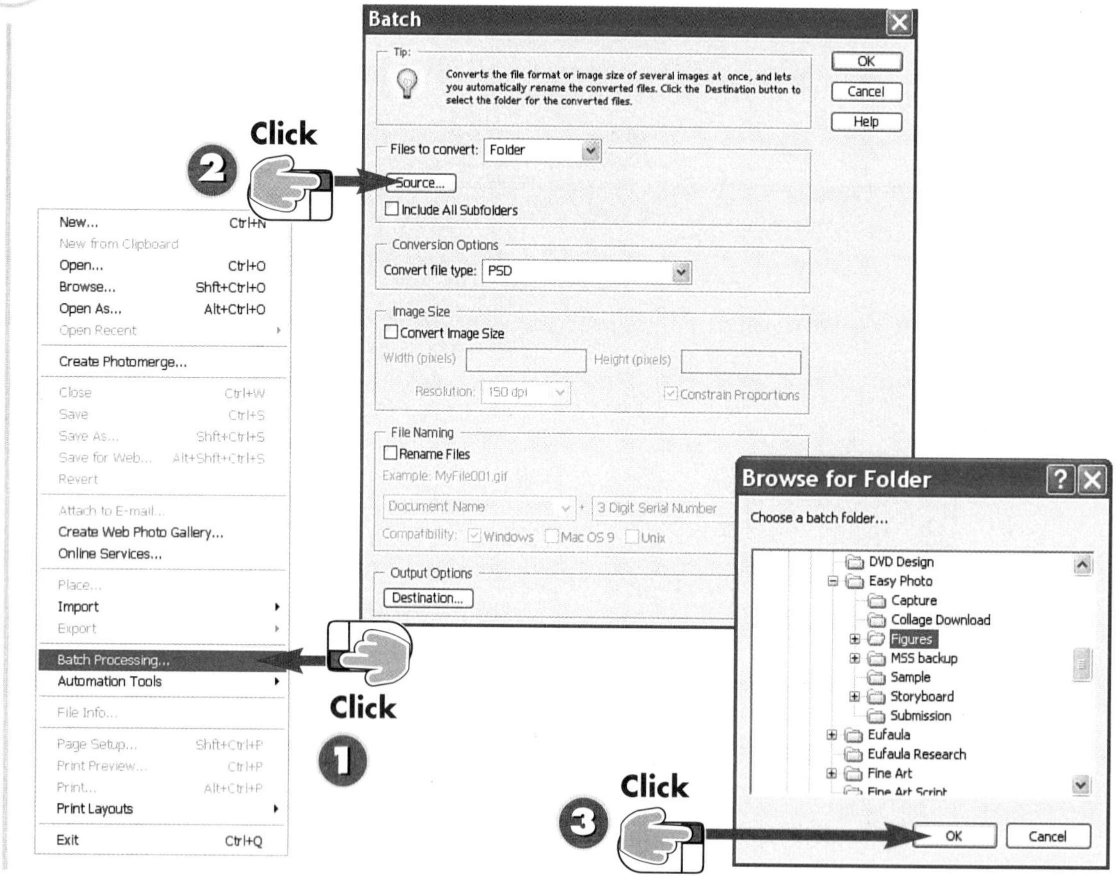

1 With all files closed, choose **File**, **Batch Processing**.

2 Click **Source**.

3 Navigate to select the folder that contains the files, and click **OK**.

INTRODUCTION

The names digital cameras assign to your shots look like so much alphabet soup. Here's a handy way to rename all files in a given folder—using a common prefix you type, or combination of date, serial numbers, and/or serial letters.

CAUTION

Extension Caution

This renaming procedure won't change file extensions—and that's something you shouldn't be doing anyway. Changing an extension indicates to the computer a different file type. To convert a batch of files to the same type, see the next task.

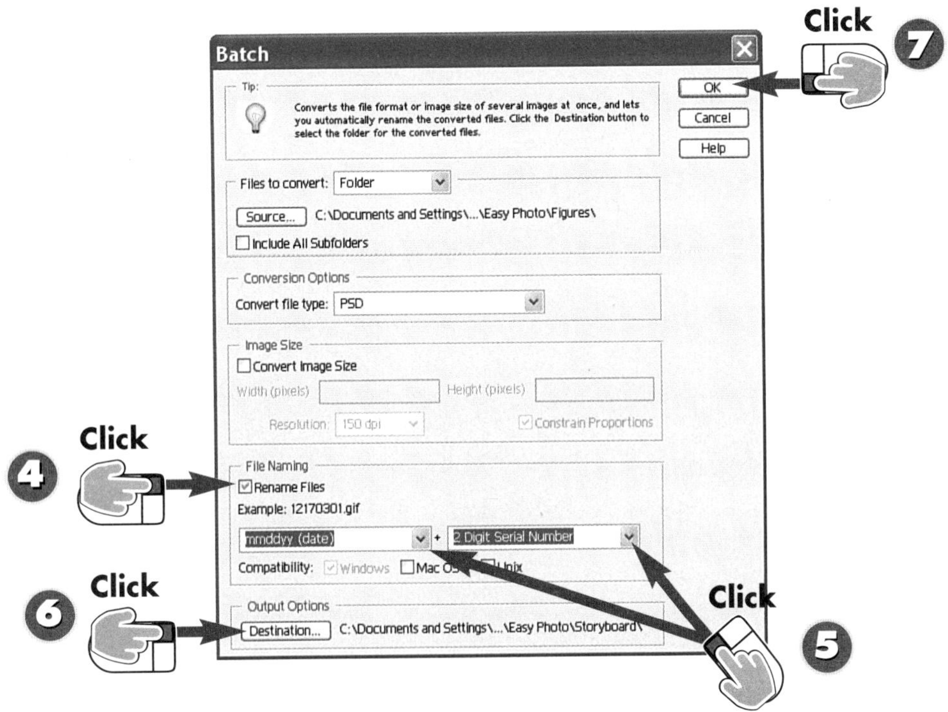

4 Check **Rename Files**.

5 Make selections in the **Naming Rules** drop-down menus.

6 Click **Destination**, navigate to select a folder to hold the new files, and click **OK**. The path to your selected folder appears in the Batch dialog box.

7 Click **OK**.

TIP

Naming Rule Option

If you select **None**, you can type an explicit name in the text field. Then specify some increment, such as a serial number to append in the second text field.

HINT

Compatibility Options

Check one or both of these boxes to create filename extensions compatible with Mac OS 9 or Unix computers. (Mac OS X can recognize Windows filenames.) Note that many Web-host servers run Unix.

Converting Files in a Batch

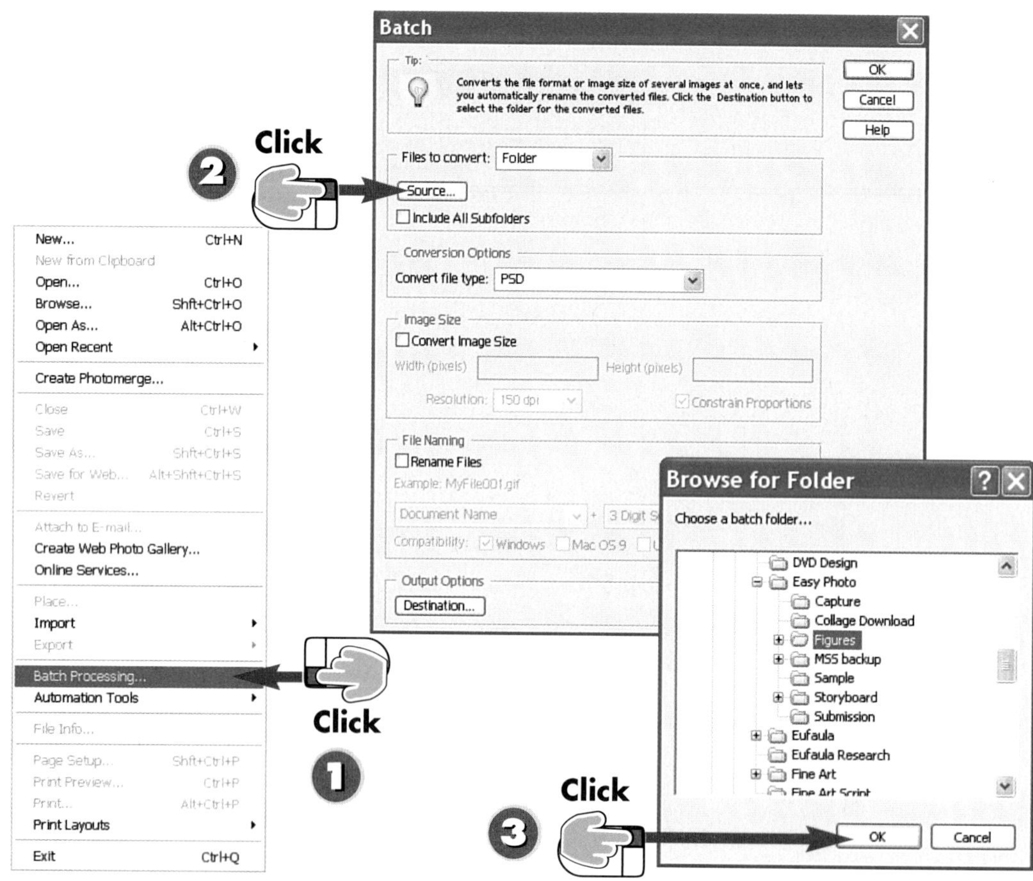

1. With all files closed, choose **File**, **Batch Processing**.

2. Click **Source**.

3. Navigate to select the folder that contains the files to be converted, and click **OK**.

INTRODUCTION

There are many ways to use this feature, but one you'll probably use a lot is converting a set of full-resolution photos into smaller JPEG thumbnails for posting on a Web site or sending via email.

HINT

All Created Equal
Regardless of the source file types, which can be different, all the output files are converted to the same file type—the one you specify in step 4.

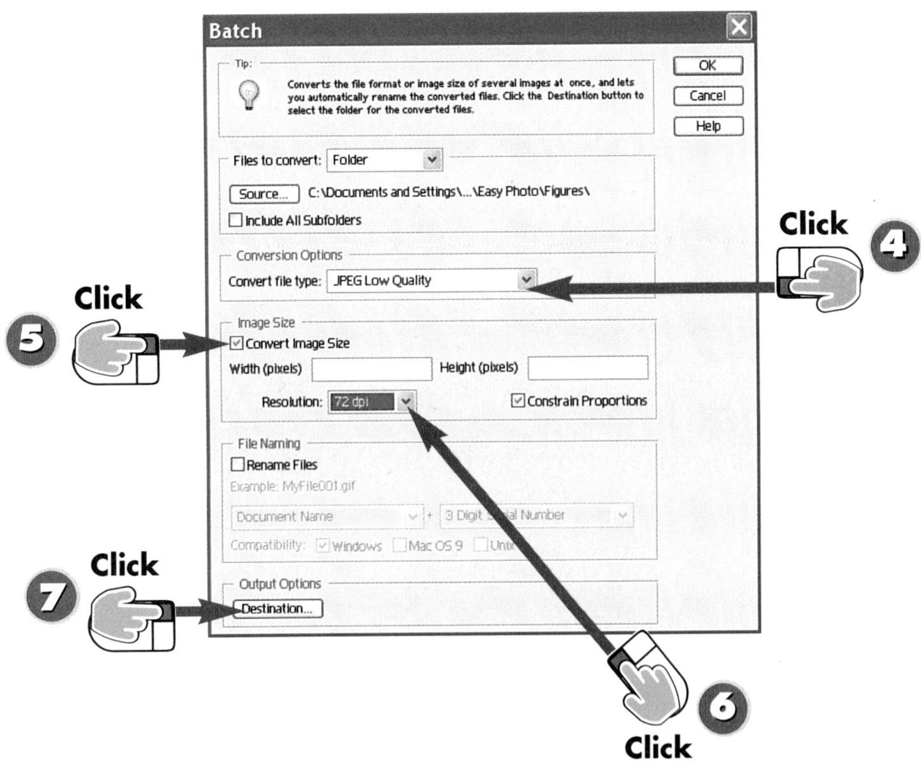

4. Set **Convert file type** to the type of file you want as output, such as **JPEG Low Quality** for Web pictures and thumbnails.

5. Optionally, check **Convert Image Size** (handy for making thumbnails).

6. Set the Resolution, such as **72 dpi** (for images that will be viewed on computer or TV screens).

7. Click **Destination**.

See next page

TIP

Need Thumbnails?
To make postage-stamp–sized images, type in a **Width** and **Height** (in pixels) in the Image Size section. At 72 dpi, a width of 2.5 inches is 72×2.5, or 180 pixels.

CAUTION

Constrain Yourself!
Don't uncheck the **Constrain Proportions** option in the Image Size section unless you deliberately want to distort the images.

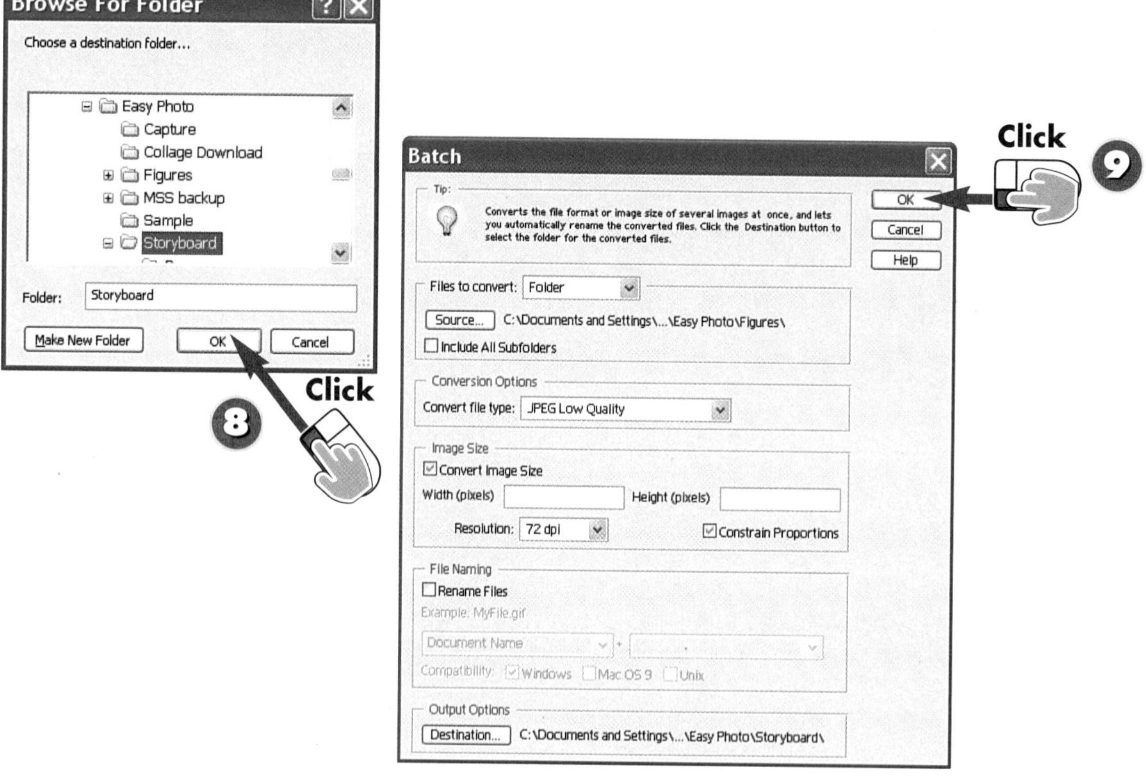

8 Navigate to select a folder to hold the output files, and click **OK**.

9 Click **OK** in the Batch dialog box.

HINT

Convert Down, Not Up
These steps work well for converting images from higher to lower resolutions. Going the other way—say, from JPEG thumbnails to PSD files—results in disappointing picture quality.

Applying a Copyright Notice

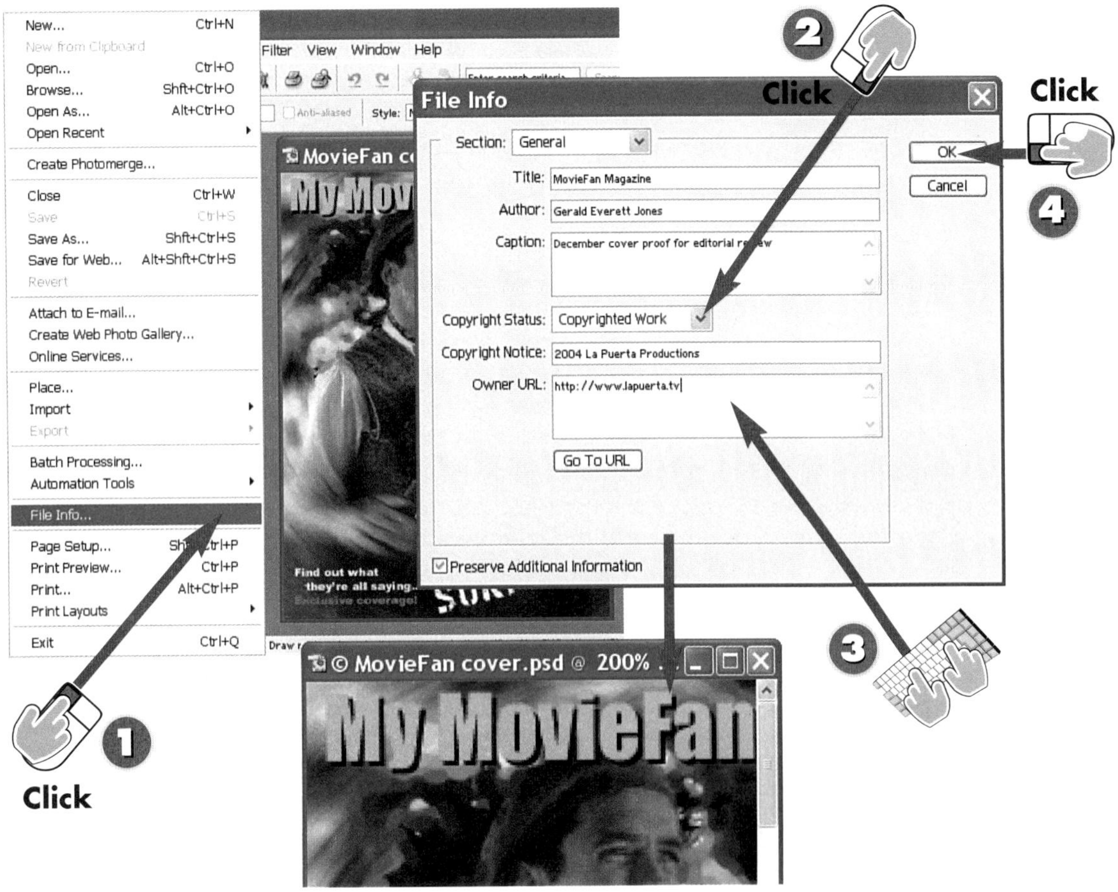

1. With the picture in the active image area, choose **File**, **File Info**.
2. Choose **Copyrighted Work** in the Copyright Status drop-down.
3. Type information in **Title**, **Author**, **Caption**, **Copyright Notice**, and **Owner URL** fields.
4. Click **OK**. A copyright notice is included in the file information, and the © symbol appears in the image title bar.

INTRODUCTION

For copyright purposes, a photographer is considered the author of the image and can hold *intellectual property rights (IPR)* to it—including licensing its use by others. This task shows you how to append a copyright notice to your images in the form of text data attached to the file.

HINT

Getting Permission
If a file you downloaded is marked as copyrighted, the Go to URL button in the File Info dialog box takes you to the author's Web site, where you should find licensing and contact information.

HINT

Proprietary Watermarks
Copyrighted images you download from the Web may also contain ownership information as *digital watermarks* in the image itself. To inspect a file for a watermark, choose **Filter**, **Digimarc**, **Read Watermark**.

PART 12

Just for Fun

It's only after you've mastered a set of tools that you can begin to take real joy in using them. Then, you can let the logical, step-by-step calculating part of your brain take a back seat and let your imagination do the driving.

If you've worked through most, if not all, of the preceding tasks, you're ready—and you've earned the right—to have some fun. Tasks in this part are all about fooling around, experimenting, and exploring ways of manipulating electronic images like collage artists use paper cutouts and a set of paints.

There isn't space in this little book to take you through all the things you can do with Photoshop Elements. (If, with so many possible choices and combinations, it's even possible.) But with the basic skills you've picked up here, the more your work with this incredibly rich and flexible computer application will seem like play. As you continue to explore, you'll sweat the technical details less and less, and you'll find a marvelous new outlet for your personal expression.

And if, perchance, some of your fantasies seem, er, just a bit bizarre—add a talk bubble or a clever caption and turn them into personalized greeting cards!

Not Quite the Story of My Life

Do I deserve this?

Must be something I did a long time ago....

Placing Artwork in an Image

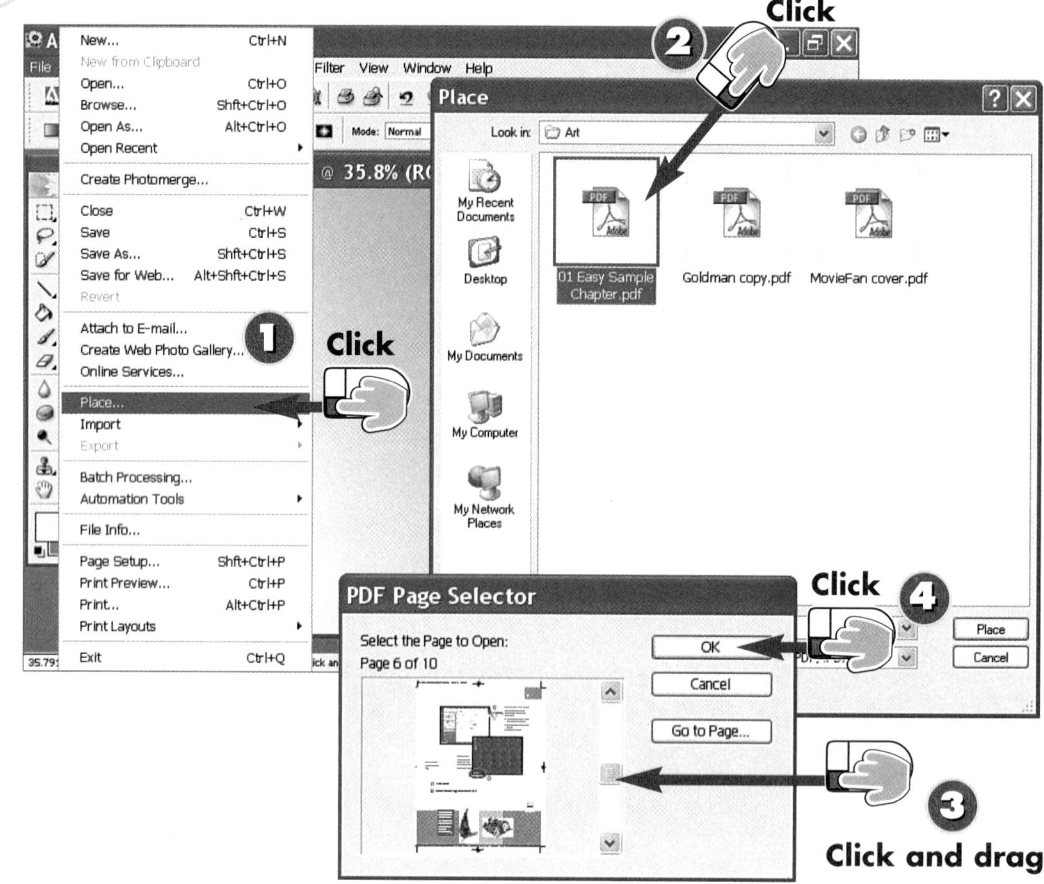

1. With a background or background image in the active image area, choose **File**, **Place**.
2. Locate and double-click the file that contains the artwork (or select it and click **Place**).
3. If the file contains multiple pages, select the page you want to insert.
4. Click **OK**. The artwork or page is inserted into a new layer in the active image.

INTRODUCTION

Commands you may already have used for combining imagery are File, New From Clipboard; File, Import; and the pair Edit, Copy and Edit, Paste. Here's a handy alternative, a quicker way to insert artwork from an external file that's in one of the other Adobe formats (.ai, .eps, .pdf, or .pdp extensions).

TIP

Missing Fonts
If you see this warning window after step 3, choose **Continue**, and some other fonts that are available in your computer will be substituted.

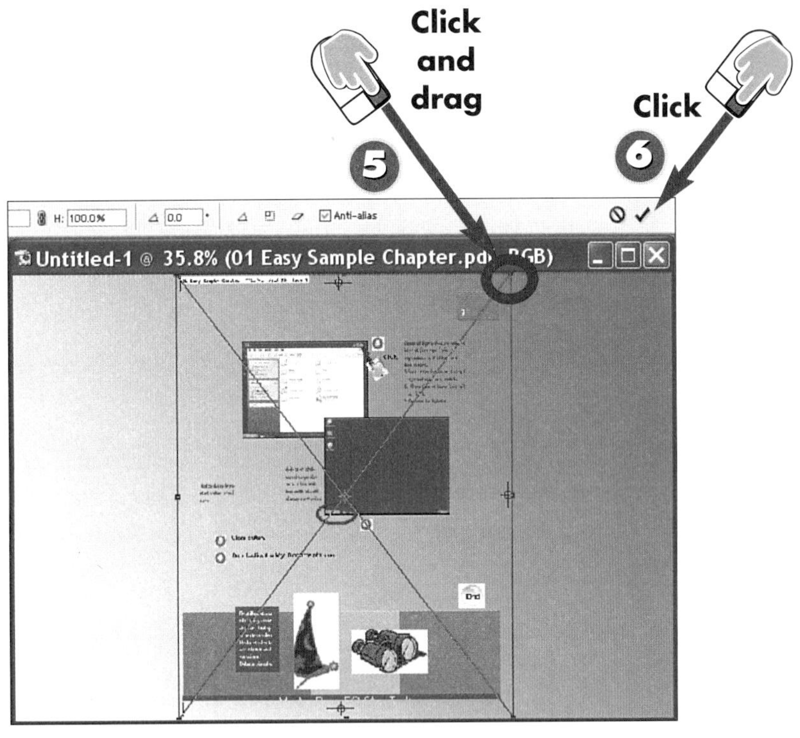

5. Optionally, drag a handle to move or resize the artwork to fit your canvas.

6. Click the **Commit** button, or press **Enter**.

HINT

PDF Pages and Images
The **File**, **Place** command inserts entire pages from a PDF as new layers. Use **File**, **Import**, **PDF Image** instead to get its images separately. White or background areas in the original become transparent.

HINT

Vectors Get Rasterized
Vector graphics in the source file get simplified, or *rasterized* (converted to pixels), when you choose Commit. The objects take on the same resolution as the target image.

Creating Panoramic Views

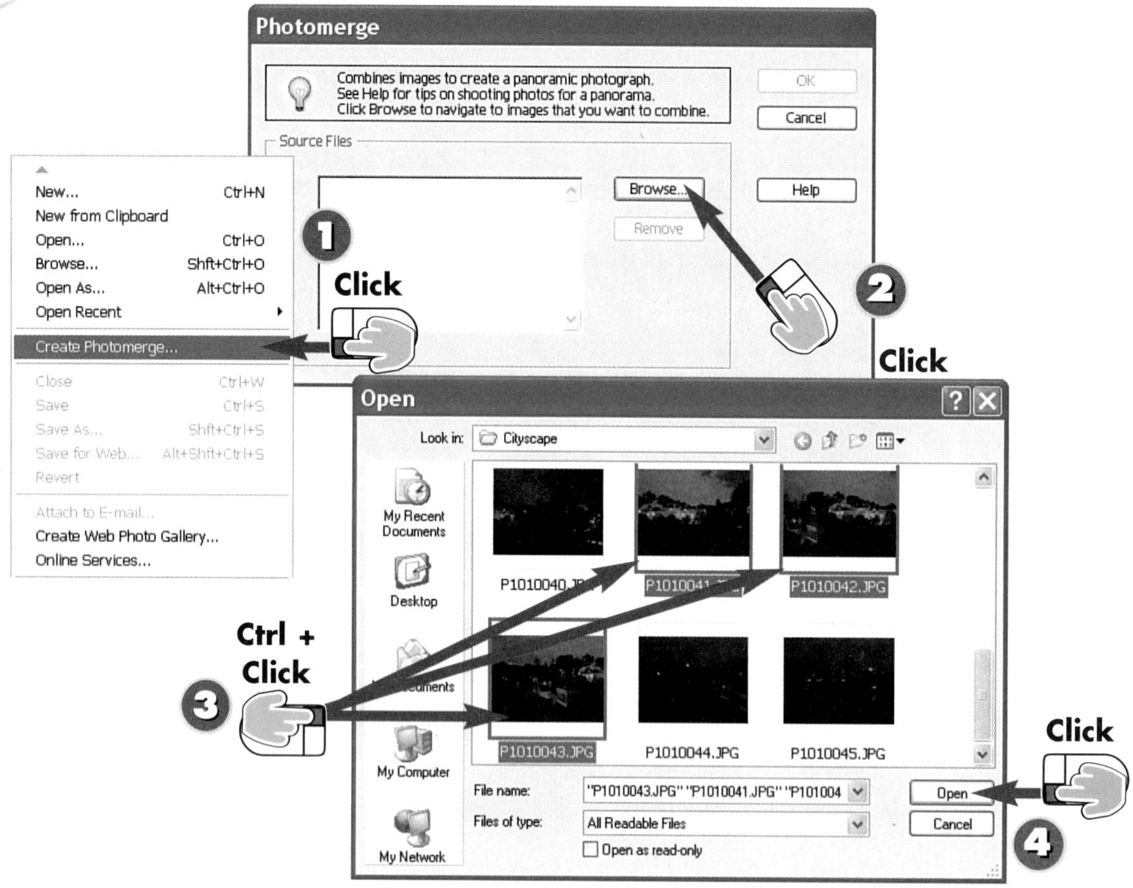

1. With all files closed, choose **File**, **Create Photomerge**.
2. Click **Browse**.
3. Ctrl+click two or more images to combine.
4. Click **Open**.

INTRODUCTION

It's truly amazing how sensitive digital cameras are, even in near darkness. These photos were taken in a moonless night, lit only by the glow of city lights. Photoshop Elements has the smarts to blend the edges of several scenic photos seamlessly into one gorgeous panorama.

HINT

Pan Your Snaps
Shots must be adjacent so their edges align: Mount the camera on a tripod. Take your source photos all at the same vertical angle, *panning* from left to right, so that the edges overlap the scene.

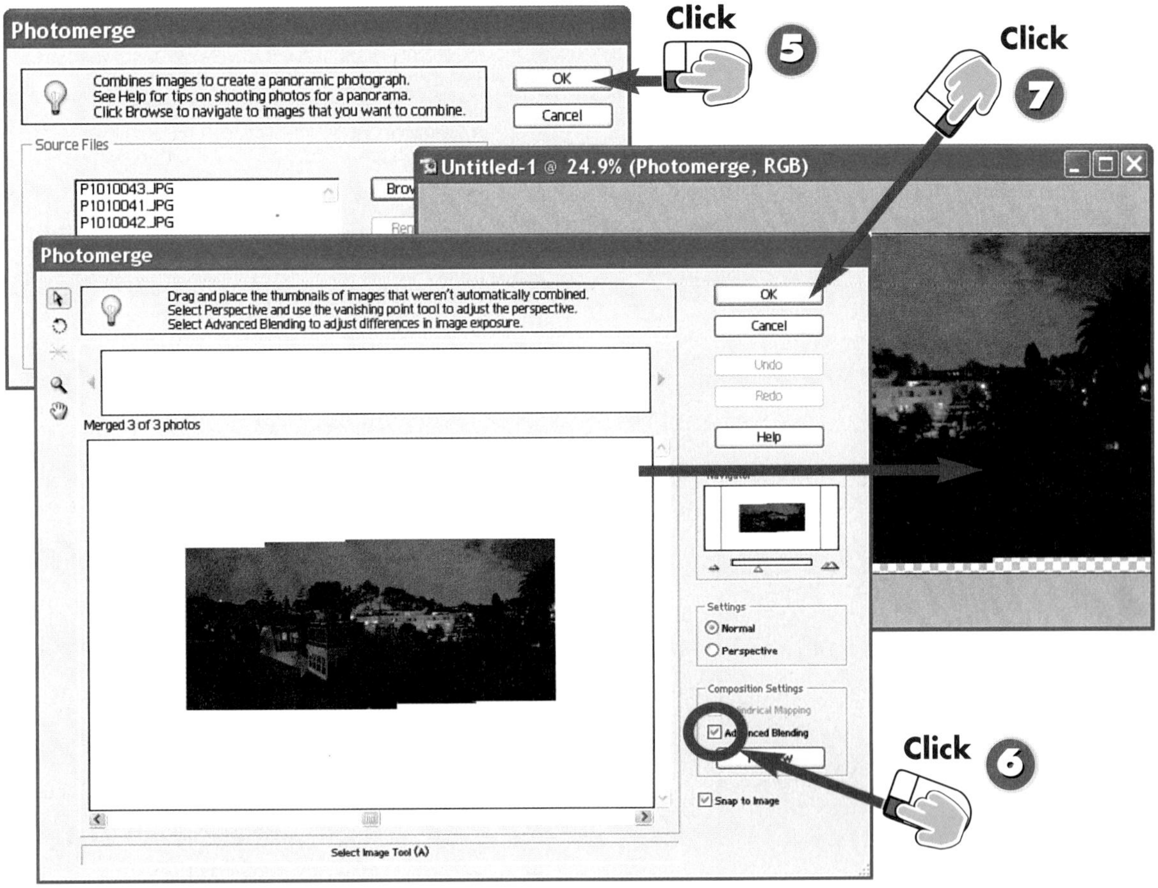

5. Click **OK**.

6. Optionally, check **Advanced Blending** to create seamless edges.

7. Click **OK**. The composite picture appears in the active image window.

TIP

Photomerge Options
Perspective can heighten the panoramic effect. Available in combination with this option, Cylindrical Mapping emphasizes curvature. Advanced Blending (recommended) not only aligns edges but also makes exposures match.

HINT

Crop to Finish
Finish off by cropping the image, because no matter how careful you are, the horizontal edge of the composite image probably won't be smooth.

Achieving a 3D Effect

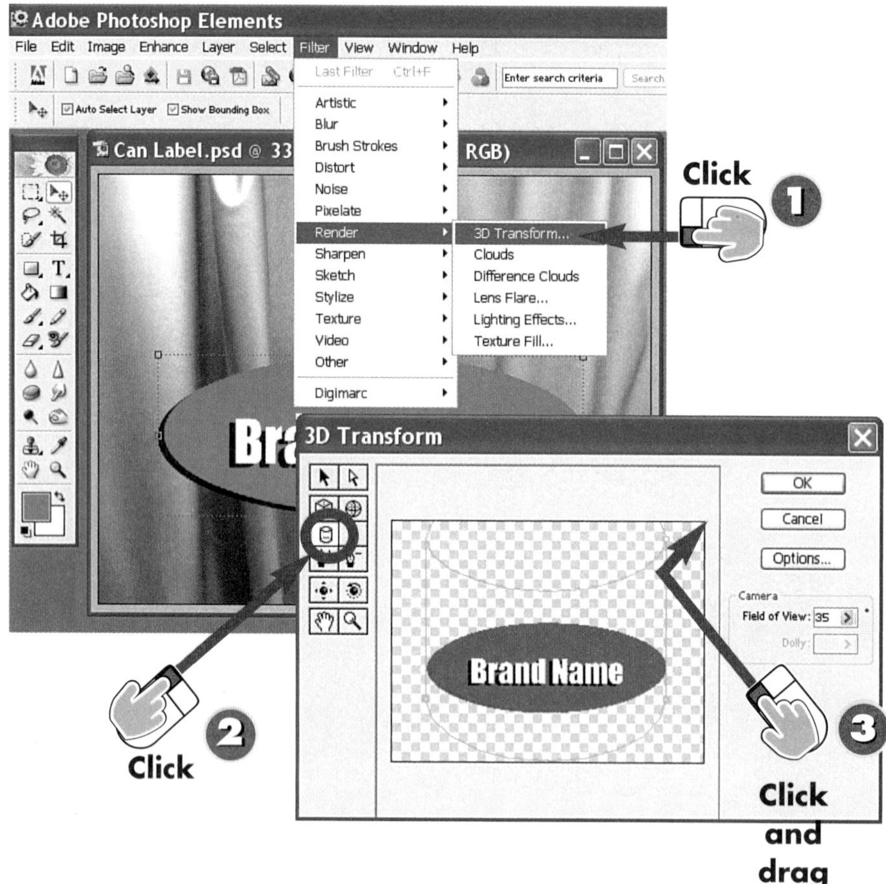

1. With the object you want to transform selected, choose **Filter**, **Render**, **3D Transform**.
2. Select a transformation shape, such as **Cylinder** (or press **C**).
3. Click and drag to size the shape in the 3D Transform preview window.

INTRODUCTION

Three-dimensional transformation opens up all kinds of creative possibilities. Think of the image you start with as being printed on a rubber sheet that you can wrap around a cube, a sphere, or a cylinder.

HINT

Repositioning Vertices
Choose a selection tool; then click and drag any *vertex* (movable point on the shape) to change the outline of the cylinder—to make it look like a vase, for example.

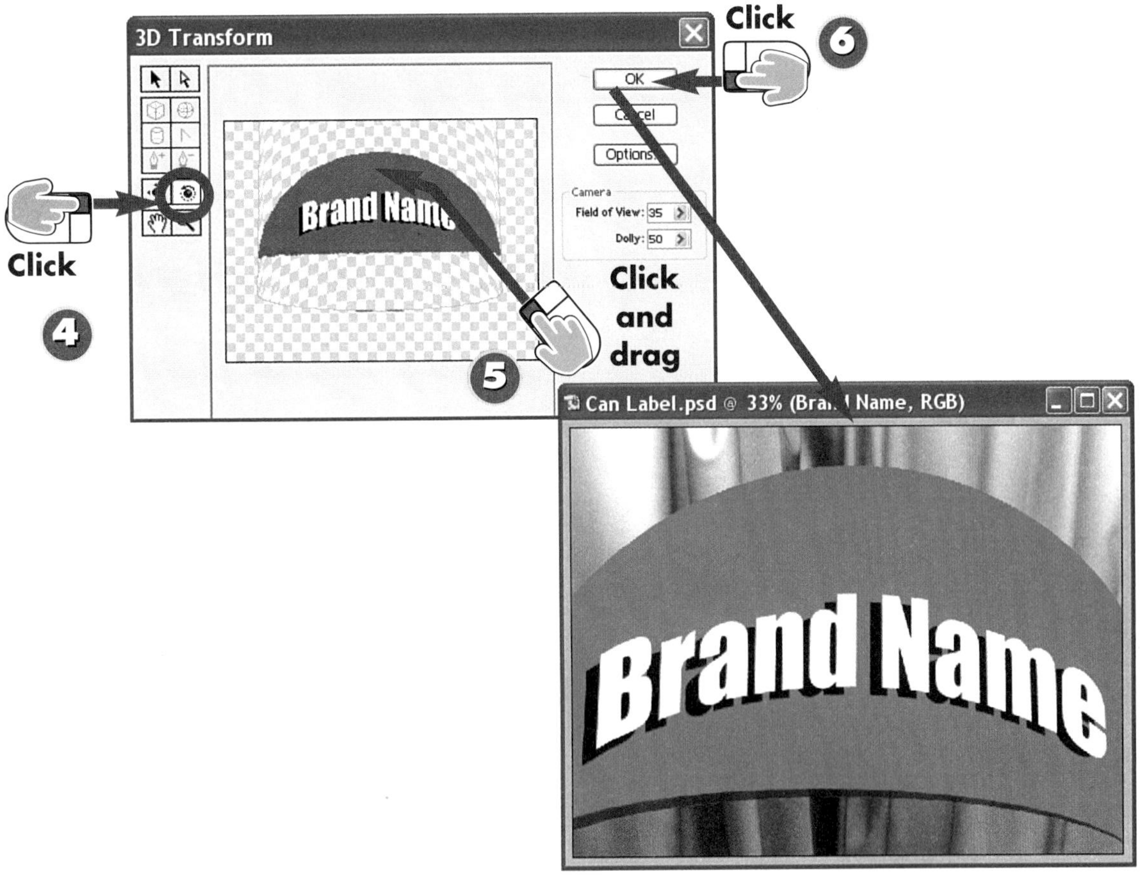

4. Click the **Trackball** tool (or press **R**). (You can also use the Pan Camera tool, or press E.)

5. Click and drag to adjust the effect in the preview window.

6. Click **OK**. The transformed object appears in the active image window.

TIP

Anchor Points

The *anchor point* is a vertex on the shape to which the image can attach. For the Cylinder shape only, the Convert Anchor Point, Add Anchor Point, and Delete Anchor Point tools become available.

Try Some "Trick" Photography

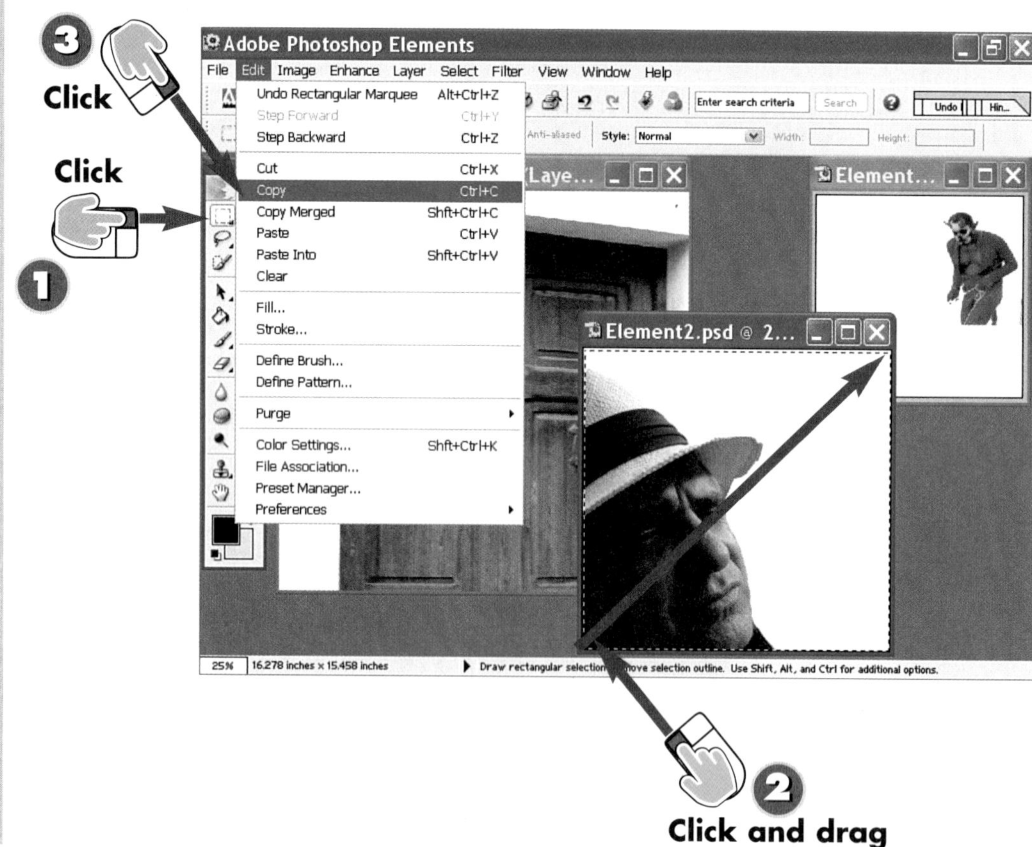

1. Start with three images open—a background and two other images. Click a selection tool, such as **Rectangular Marquee**, or press **M**.
2. Select an object in the first image.
3. Choose **Edit**, **Copy**, or press **Ctrl+C**.

INTRODUCTION

Trick photography takes many forms, but most involve combining and reworking real images to create an unrealistic or improbable scene. This example creates a collage from three separate pictures and then adds some artwork to finish the job.

TIP

Managing the Elements

As you combine images, Photoshop Elements inserts them as separate layers. To keep track of layers and control their stacking order, choose **Window**, **Layers** to open the Layers palette.

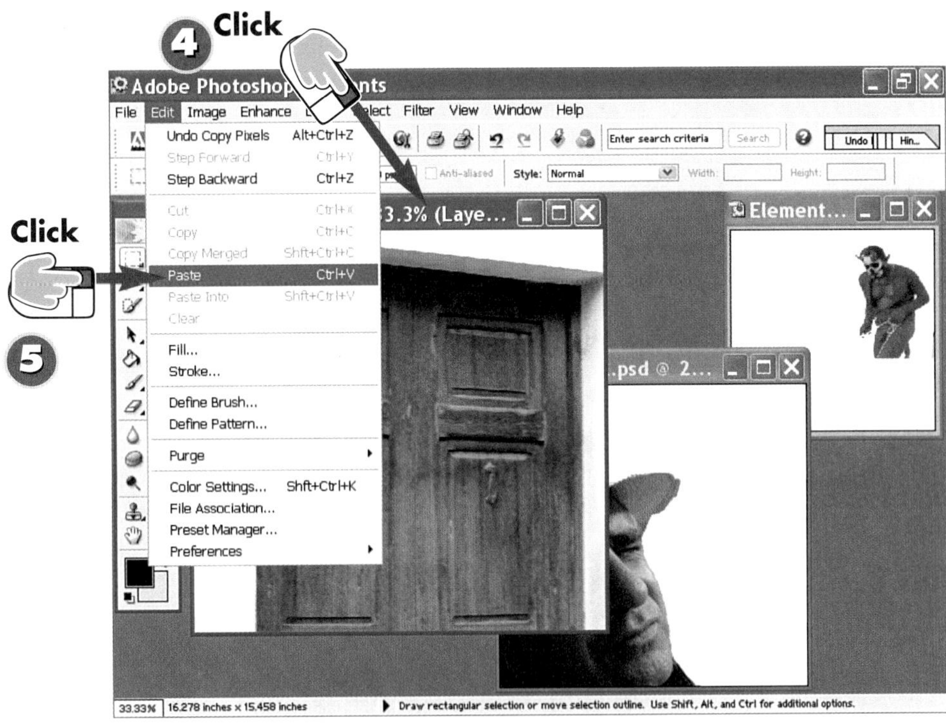

4. Select the background image by clicking its title bar.

5. Choose **Edit**, **Paste**, or press **Ctrl+V**. Repeat steps 2–5 to add more objects or images.

See next page

TIP

Merry Merging

After choosing **Edit**, **Copy**, a quick way to combine imagery, as shown in some previous tasks, is to use the **Edit**, **Paste Into** command. But remember, when you do this, the insertion does not create a separate layer.

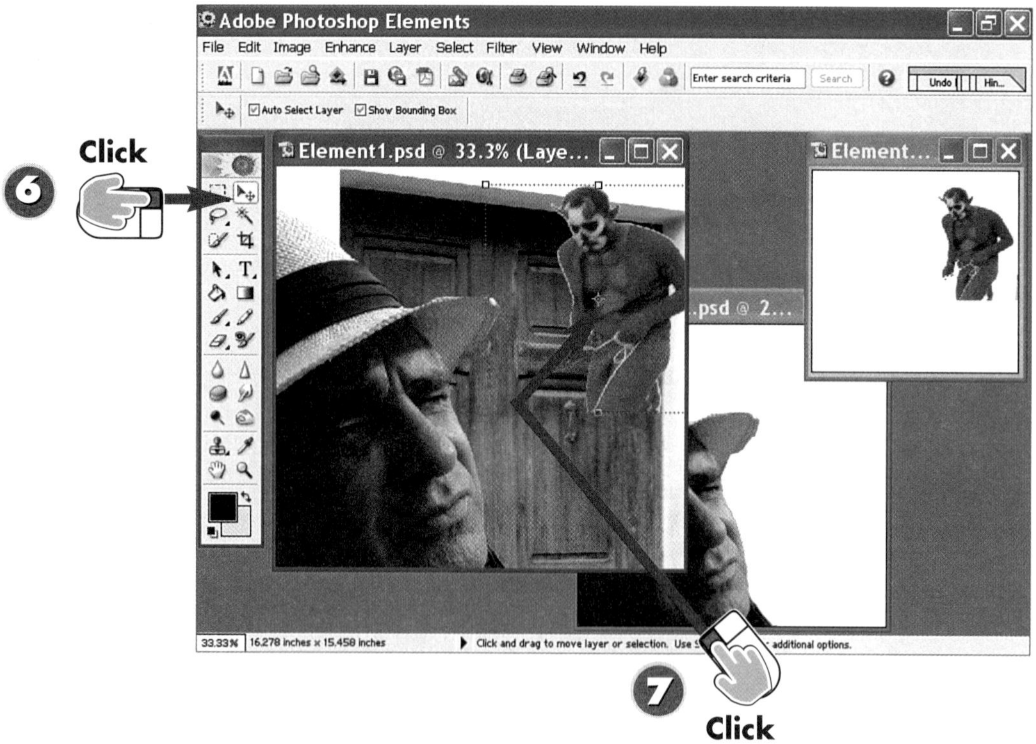

6. Select the **Move** tool, or press **V**.

7. Click and drag object handles to move or resize the objects and compose the picture.

INTRODUCTION

The ability to combine images in improbable ways apparently brings out the humor in some people. If you use email at all, you've no doubt received pictures of pets doing superhuman feats, celebrities and politicians in compromising positions, or ordinary people with extraordinary physical characteristics!

TIP

Shape Selection

In step 6, if the inserted picture contains multiple shapes, you can use the Shape Selection tool to select and manipulate them individually, as long as you haven't yet simplified or merged the layer.

8. Select a **Brush** tool (or a shape tool).
9. Click and drag to draw on the image. Repeat steps 8 and 9 to add more lines and shapes to your drawing.

TIP

Special Effects
After you've created a collage of images, you can go wild transforming them with any of the commands from the **Image**, **Transform**, or **Filter** menus.

Getting an Antique Look

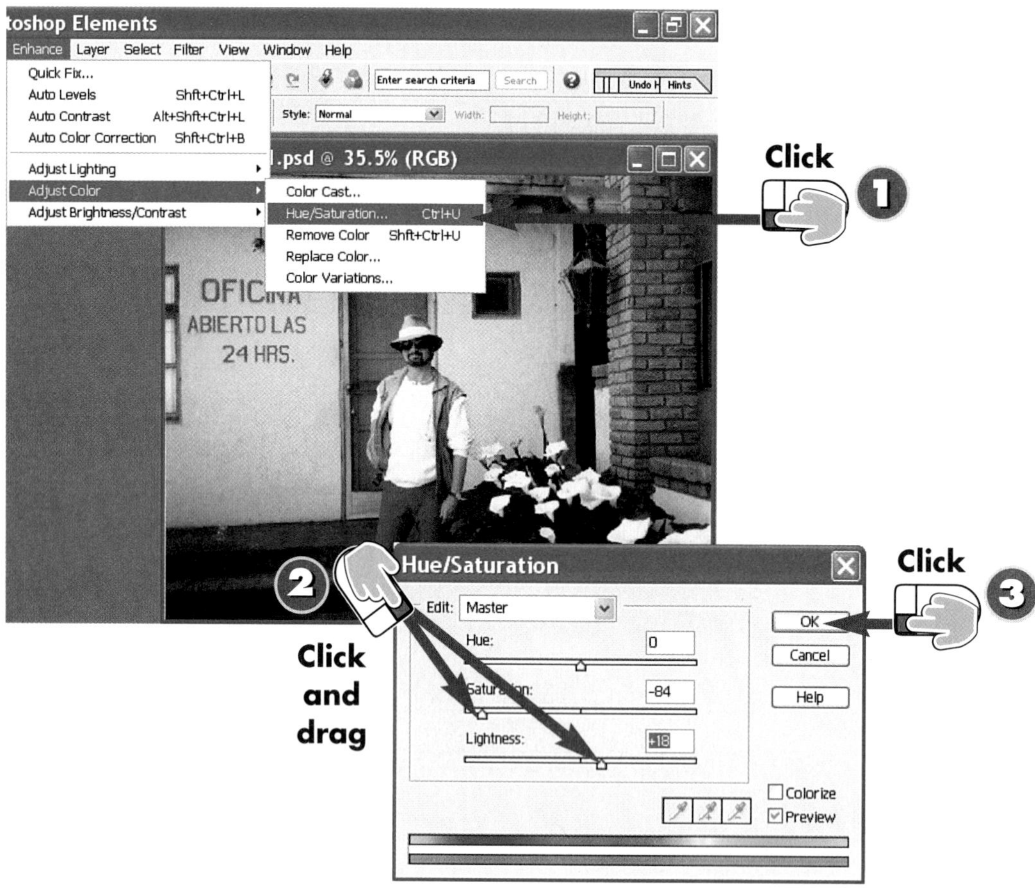

1. With a photo in the active image window, choose **Enhance**, **Adjust Color**, **Hue/Saturation**.
2. Decrease the **Saturation** and increase the **Lightness** sliders.
3. Click **OK**.

INTRODUCTION

Of course, "antique" is relative to your age—or the ages of the relatives you want to transform. In this case, decreasing the saturation setting creates a look of old, faded Kodachrome. Adding Film Grain enhances the realism, and the Feather effect on the border adds to the impression of a faded snapshot.

TIP

Fading and Sepia
Decreasing Saturation can create a monochrome picture, but one that still contains color information. You can then apply Color Variations to get a *sepia* effect. By contrast, choosing **Image**, **Mode**, **Grayscale** discards all color.

TIP

Remove Color Command
An alternative conversion to grayscale that still preserves color information is the command **Enhance**, **Adjust Color**, **Remove Color**, which makes red, green, and blue values equal and reduces Saturation to zero.

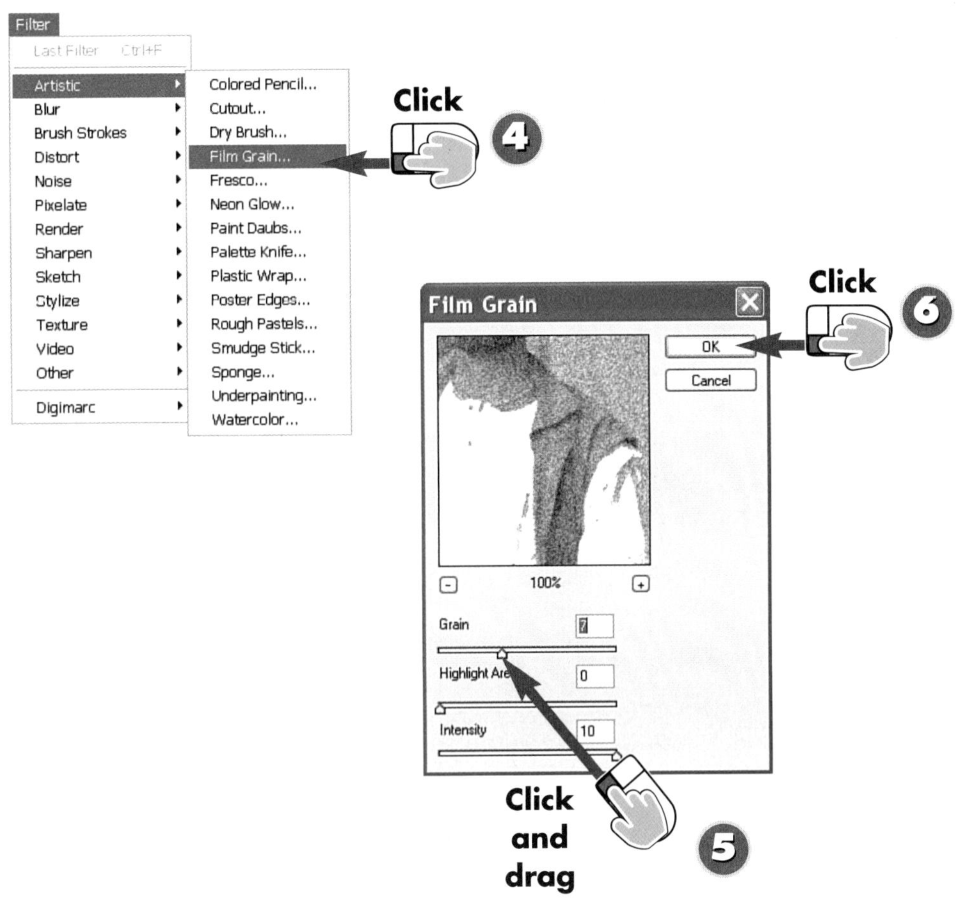

4. Choose **Filter**, **Artistic**, **Film Grain**.

5. Adjust the sliders for effect, such as increasing the **Grain** size.

6. Click **OK**.

Film Grain

HINT

This same type of filter can be applied in the Adobe After Effects application to make your DV movies look like film.

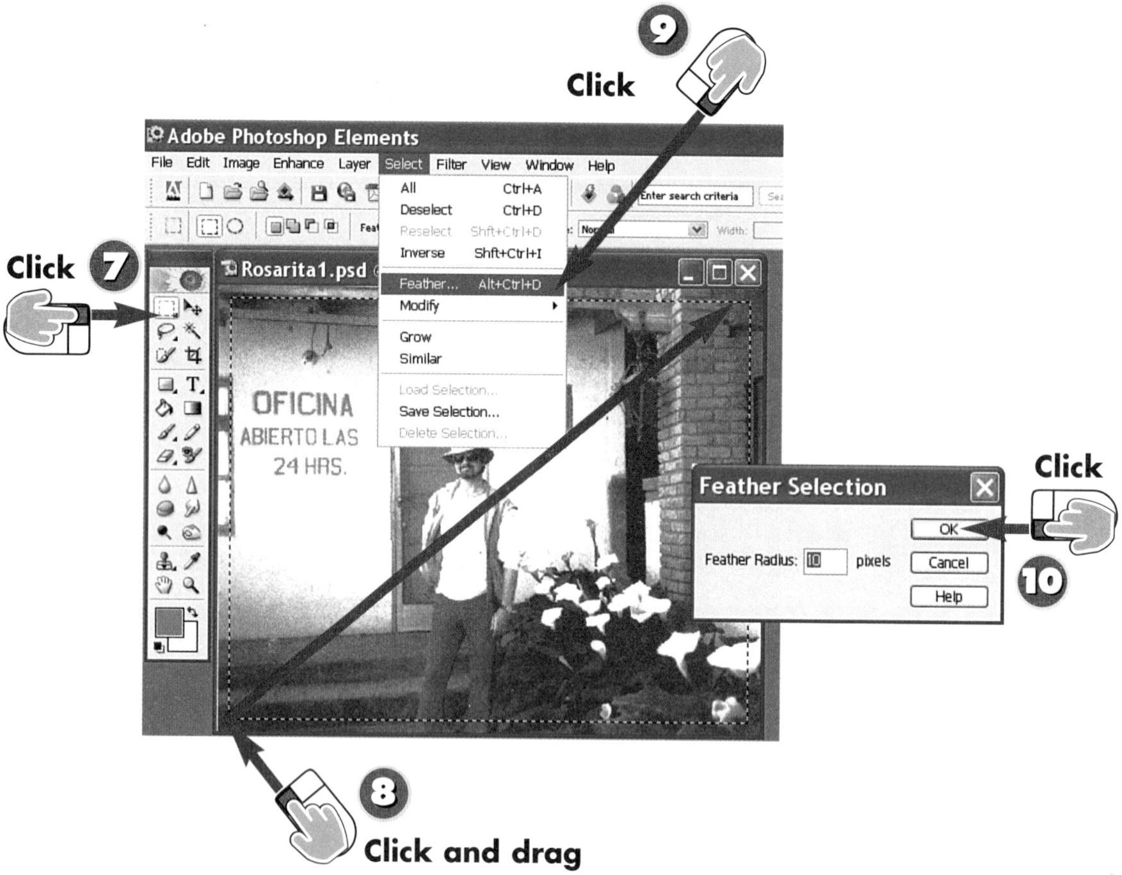

Click 9

Click 7

Click 10

Click and drag 8

7 Select the **Rectangular Marquee** tool, or press **M**.

8 Click and drag to size a border around the picture.

9 Choose **Select**, **Feather**.

10 Click **OK**.

INTRODUCTION

Digital technology has evolved to the point where people are beginning to think its results are too clean and pure to be aesthetically pleasing. For example, it's becoming common practice in music studios to add low levels of audio noise to digital recordings to make them more natural-sounding. As you can see, Photoshop Elements has many ways to make your digital photos funkier and crummier!

TIP

Feather Radius

In step 10, remember that the size of the Feather effect is proportional to Image Size in pixels. For example, you may have to increase the Radius value to make the effect more obvious.

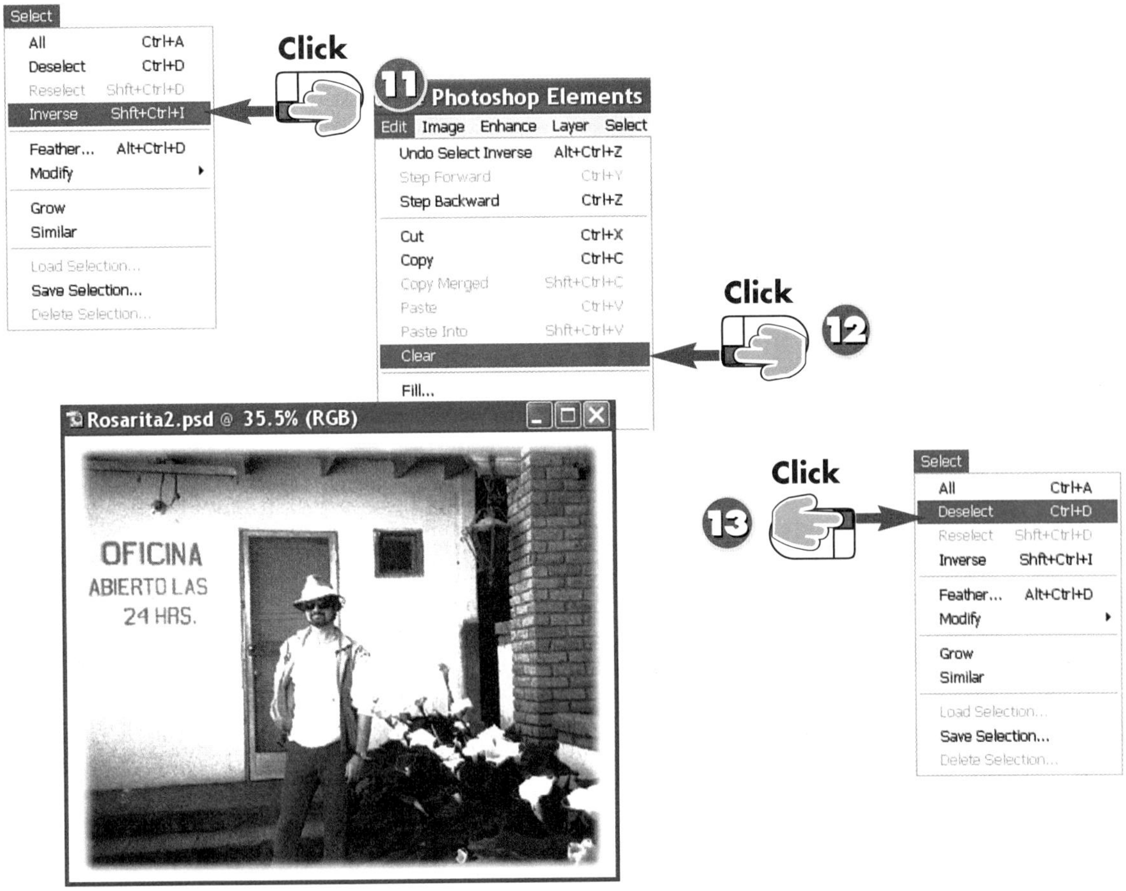

11 Choose **Select**, **Inverse**, or press **Shift+Ctrl+I**.

12 Choose **Edit**, **Clear**, or press **Delete**.

13 Choose **Select**, **Deselect**, or press **Ctrl+D**.

HINT

Experiment!
This kind of experimentation with Photoshop Elements can bring into play any and all of the techniques you've learned in this book. Have fun!

Glossary

A

active image area Application window that displays the image contained in the currently open file.

active layer Virtual drawing plane, or cel, currently selected in an open image.

adjustment layer In a multilayered image, a layer inserted to affect the overall appearance of all layers beneath it; in effect, a digital photographic filter.

anchor point Point to which a graphic object will be attached.

auto select Procedure whereby selecting a shape or text object automatically causes its layer to be selected, as well.

autofocus Automatic focusing capability of digital cameras.

automatic white balance Digital camera function that sets color rendition on the assumption that the lightest area in the frame is pure white.

B

backlight Photographic light source emanating from behind the subject.

base layer When layers are grouped, the bottommost layer that sets the boundaries of the upper ones, determined by the boundaries of a shape on that layer.

bitmap Digital image composed of pixels; raster image; pixel array; in Photoshop, a black-and-white image.

blending mode In a multilayered image, a layer option that determines how colors on different layers combine; an option for various tools and filters. Examples: Normal, Dissolve, Hard, Soft.

blow out To totally overexpose an area of an image so that it is pure white and contains no picture detail.

brush dynamics Options for the size, shape, and behavior of the Brush tool that control the quality of its brush stroke.

brush tip Size and shape of the tip of the Brush tool, set in the Options bar after the tool is selected.

burn In traditional darkroom technique, to underexpose masked areas of a film negative prior to making a print.

C

canvas size Paper or media size associated with an image file.

caption Printable text that describes the content of a picture.

capture To upload image data from a camera, camcorder, or scanner into a computer.

catalog In Adobe Photoshop Album, a collection of image files from which a presentation can be created.

cel Movie animation artist's transparent sheet of celluloid, analogous to a Photoshop layer.

Clipboard Scratchpad memory area in Windows through which data, including graphics and images, can be exchanged between open applications.

Close box X button in the top-right corner of any Windows window by which it may be closed, or turned off.

collage Art term for a composition made from cut-out images pasted onto a board.

color cast Overall tint of a photograph, particularly noticeable and in need of correction when it creates unflattering flesh tones in the subjects.

color components Separate channels, or primary colors, within a color model; Red, Green, and Blue in the RGB color model; Hue, Saturation, and Lightness in the HSL model.

color management Coordination of color reproduction devices, such as cameras, computer screens, and printers, so that colors rendered on all of them appear to match.

color matching Fine-tuning the output of two or more color reproduction devices, such as a screen and a printer, so that colors appear the same on both.

color space The range of all colors available in a color model.

composite Combination or merging of two or more images.

composition Artistic arrangement of subjects within the picture frame.

compression Mathematical transformation of a digital file so as to describe its contents in fewer bits, thereby creating a smaller file, and degrading its quality or accuracy as little as possible.

constrain To limit the repositioning or resizing of a shape or text to perpendicular angles; to prevent distortion; to maintain proportions (aspect ratio).

contact sheet Film photographer's reference print created in the darkroom by exposing filmstrips in direct contact with a sheet of print paper.

contrast Range of brightness between the highlights and shadows in a photograph.

crop To reframe an image, moving its edges to exclude unwanted areas.

crushed blacks Underexposed areas of a picture that are totally black and contain no picture detail.

D

default Preselected program option settings.

digital watermark Invisible copyright or proprietary notice within the image area of a photograph that can be read by Photoshop Elements or special reader software; Digimarc.

digitize To convert a film print or analog video clip to a stream of pixel values; to scan a photo.

discard layers To merge and simplify all layers in an image at once, rendering text and artwork uneditable as objects; see also ***flatten***.

dither To render a subtle color by juxtaposing dots of two or more primary colors.

dock To close a palette to the palette well.

dodge In traditional darkroom technique, to overexpose unmasked areas of a film negative prior to making a print.

dpi Unit of resolution of a digital printer; dots per inch; equivalent to pixels/inch.

duotone Two-color image.

DV Abbreviation of the Digital Video recording standard.

DVD Abbreviation for Digital Versatile Disc, optical recording medium for videos and movies.

DVD menu Onscreen selections of DVD chapters, each indicated by a user-selection button.

E

exposure Length of time light is permitted to strike a camera's film or sensors (called *CCD chips* in a digital camera).

extension In a computer filename, characters to the right of the rightmost period, indicating the file type. Examples: .psd, .jpg, .doc, .mpeg.

eyelight Small photographic light source aimed directly into subject's eyes to make them sparkle.

F

feather Blurred edges of a shape; vignette.

file type Indicated by the extension in the filename, a description content data type (such as native Photoshop file) and the associated application required to open it.

fill Solid area or pattern within a shape, text, or image area.

fill flash Bright photographic light source used to supplement key light and fill in the area surrounding the subject. In Photoshop Elements, the ability to lighten the darkest (usually foreground) areas of a photo, leaving the bright (usually background) areas unchanged.

filter In Photoshop Elements, a prebuilt artistic effect that can be applied to an image; in conventional photography, a glass covering for a lens that changes the quality of light.

FireWire Apple trademark for the connection between a camcorder or other device and a computer, designated IEEE 1394; equivalent to Sony's iLINK.

flatten To merge and simplify all layers in an image at once; see also ***discard layers***.

flip To create a mirror image of a shape, text, or image.

focus In Photoshop Elements, to sharpen or blur the edges of a selection; in conventional photography, to adjust the camera lens to achieve the same effect.

folder In a computer file system, a named directory that contains files.

font In typography, a typeface in a particular point size; in computer applications, a typeface.

f-stop Camera setting that controls how much light is admitted during an exposure.

FTP Abbreviation of File Transfer Protocol, a method of uploading files to the Internet.

G

Gaussian blur Named for mathematician Carl Friedrich Gauss, a filter that enables finer control over how an image is blurred than does Blur or Blur More.

gradient Blended color used to fill a shape or background.

grain Noise filter applied to a digital image to simulate the grain of photographic film.

grayed out Referring to menu commands or dialog box options that are unavailable based on current settings; dimmed.

grayscale Monochrome picture that contains shades of black and white.

group Combination of palettes or graphic objects so they can be manipulated as a single palette or object.

H

halation effect Artifact of early film that created a beatific glow around closeups of movie stars.

halftone screen Dot pattern used in commercial printing to render shaded images using tiny, solid dots of black (B&W) or four primary colors (CMYK).

handle Corner on a selection that can be dragged to resize or reposition the object.

hard Quality of light that produces sharp edges and dark shadows.

hidden tool Any tool in the toolbar that can be selected by right-clicking a related tool.

HSL Color model and mixing scheme based on components Hue (primary color), Saturation (tint), and Lightness (light-dark value).

I-J

ICC Abbreviation of International Color Consortium, which promotes color standards for the printing industry.

Impressionist brush Tool used to lay down blurred brush strokes, after the technique of painters who rebelled against doing pictures in painstaking detail.

indexed color Restricted color tables for specific uses, such as Web or Windows system display.

ink-and-paint Conventional movie animator's technique of drawing a cartoon character's outline in ink on a clear sheet of celluloid and then filling in solid shapes with acrylic paint.

intellectual property rights (IPR) Copyrights, patents, and trademarks; copyright applies to photographs, to which the photographer is author and rights holder.

K

key light Main photographic light source aimed to highlight the subject.

keystoning Photographic distortion produced by aiming the camera at a steep angle, high or low, in relation to the subject.

L

landscape Rectangular image or printer orientation with the long dimension horizontal.

layer Separate drawing, painting, text, or image plane among multiple planes, or layers, in a Photoshop image; analogous to movie animator's cel.

layer style Options, such as bevels or drop shadows, that affect all objects on a given layer.

level Value of Red, Green, or Blue, or Black input or output channel to produce brightness and contrast.

linking layers Marking and associating layers so that they can be manipulated together.

lossless File compression that results in no perceptible loss of quality or accuracy.

lossy File compression that *does* result in a loss of quality or accuracy.

LZW File compression scheme based on a transformation named for mathematicians Lempel, Ziv, and Welch.

M

mapping Transformation that bends and spreads an image or texture over the surface of an object.

menu bar Main pull-down program selections in an application such as Photoshop Elements, near the top of the program window, beginning with the File menu on the left and proceeding to the Help menu on the right.

merge To both simplify and combine layers in a single operation.

midtone Pixel values in the middle range between highlights and shadows.

mixed media Art term for works that may combine assemblage, collage, and painting or drawing.

mode Image rendering as either grayscale or color.

monochrome Single-color image, but not necessarily black and white.

multisession Describing a CD or DVD to which files can be written, or appended, at different times.

N–O

navigate Procedure for finding files and folders by exploring the file system, based on a hierarchy of files within folders (possibly within folders) on a device (such as a disk).

negative Reverse image from processing camera film, resulting in shadow areas rendered as highlights, highlights as shadows, and color primaries as their opposites (red as green, blue as orange, and so on).

nudge To move a selection by small increments with the Arrow keys.

opacity Degree to which light is blocked by an object or layer; inverse of transparency.

options bar Settings for a tool, such as Brush, that become available beneath the menu bar after the tool has been selected.

orientation Rotation angle of an image or printout; portrait or landscape.

P–Q

palette Floating window containing effects, commands, and help grouped by category.

palette tab Handle by which a palette can be selected, docked, or undocked from the palette well.

palette well Storage location in the work area for frequently used palettes.

pan Rotating a camera, typically mounted on a tripod, from left to right or from right to left in the same horizontal plane.

panorama Scenic, wide-angle landscape; Photomerge output.

picture package Commercial photographer's offered assortment of prints in various sizes, from wallet-sized to larger sizes suitable for framing.

pixel Picture element; colored dot in a bitmap image.

pixels/inch Resolution of a bitmap image; equivalent to printer dots per inch (dpi).

place To insert artwork from an external file into an open image.

plug-in Add-on software module that extends the capability of an application; example: JPEG 2000 filter for Photoshop Elements.

point size Size of type in a selected font.

Pointillize filter Limiting brush strokes to tiny dots of primary color; technique pioneered by Impressionist painter Georges Seurat.

port Input/output channel and connection in a computer.

portrait Rectangular image or printer orientation with the long dimension vertical; headshot.

posterization Garish color effect produced by the command Image, Adjustments, Posterize.

preferences User option settings that override default values.

printable area Rectangular area of a printout that excludes margins by which the printer grips the paper, and therefore where it can't print an image.

profile Stored color table used for color management.

progressive mode JPEG file setting that causes a downloaded image to be built up in visible stages, intended to improve the viewing experience over slow connections.

publish Upload files to the World Wide Web.

R

rasterize To convert a vector shape or type object to pixels; to simplify.

recipe Sequential instructions delivered by the Help system for performing a specific task.

red eye Undesirable reflection in a subject's eyes caused by flash photography.

redo Reverse the previous Undo command.

related topics Help selections that appear in the Hints palette after doing a search.

render To apply changes to a digital image and display or print it.

resample To change the resolution (pixels/inch) of an image.

reset To return to previous option settings.

resolution Measure of picture quality or degree of detail; pixels/inch; dpi.

retouch To use artistic techniques to improve the appearance of photographic subjects or scenes; in portrait work, to soften wrinkles, remove blemishes, and so on.

revert To cancel pending edits without saving and return to the original version of a file; see also ***undo***.

RGB Color model and mixing scheme used in Photoshop Elements, based on components Red, Green, and Blue.

S

search field Text box in the top-right center of the Photoshop Elements work area into which a text description of a problem or task can be typed to trigger searching of Help files.

selection Active object or area within the image area to which the next command or operation will be applied.

sepia Tinted monochrome image; typical of antique photographs.

shape Geometric object in Photoshop Elements; examples: Rectangle, Ellipse.

sharpen To increase pixel contrast at object boundaries; to bring into focus.

shortcuts bar Row of buttons with icons just beneath the menu bar, representing single-click activation of commonly used commands.

simplify To convert vector shape or type to pixels; to rasterize.

skew To apply a spatial transformation to a selected object that causes its sides to be slanted.

slider Program control in some dialog windows that can be adjusted by clicking and dragging.

soft Blurred; out of focus.

stacking order Priority of layers in a multilayered image that determines visibility of objects; objects on upper layers will obscure overlapping objects beneath.

still Single-frame photographic image (as opposed to moving image created by a sequence of frames in a movie or video).

streaming video Video clip, usually low resolution, optimized for downloading over the Web.

superimpose To overlay one graphic object on another.

swatch A single, saved color; one of a table of color selections coordinated for a specific purpose, such as Web-safe colors.

system colors Set of swatches containing only colors displayable without dithering on Windows computers.

T

texture Variegated surface or area; pattern.

thumbnail Small, low-resolution image used to preview file selections without incurring the delay of opening the full-resolution file.

title bar Top band on any Windows window showing the name of its selections (or filename of the image or document it contains, and by which the window may be moved by clicking and dragging.

tool Selection, drawing, and retouching tools found in the Photoshop Elements toolbar, located by default on the left edge of the work area.

ToolTip Name or function of a tool or button, as well as its shortcut key (if any), which pops up when you hover the pointer over it prior to making a selection.

toolbox Collection of Photoshop Elements tools, located by default on the left edge of the work area.

transparency Degree to which objects and colors on underlying layers are visible; the inverse of opacity.

tutorial Online training lesson available through the Help menu.

type mask Type-shaped selection area, typically used to create hollow text to let the background or lower layer show through.

U–V

undo To reverse or cancel the most recently executed command or change; see also ***redo***.

undock To open a palette from the palette well; see also ***dock***.

ungroup To make a previously grouped set of palettes accessible individually; see also ***group***.

upload To transfer a digital file from a device, such as a camera, camcorder, or scanner, to a computer; to capture.

USB Abbreviation for Universal Serial Bus; a type of computer port that supports digital cameras and printers.

vector Mathematical description of a geometric object; a resolution-independent object description.

vertex Point on the edge of a geometric object.

vignette Portrait with feathered edges.

W–Z

Web site index page Home page on the World Wide Web.

WIA Abbreviation of Windows Image Acquisition, a standard for connecting scanners and cameras to computers.

work area The Photoshop Elements desktop display.

ZIP Lossless file compression scheme.

zoom To magnify the view of an image; an alternative for Blur effect besides Radial.

Index

A

D

J-K-L

S

T

How can we make this index more useful? Email us at indexes@quepublishing.com

U-V-W

X-Y-Z